# HANDBOOK OF ENVIRONMENTAL ACCOUNTING

# Handbook of
# Environmental Accounting

*Edited by*

Thomas Aronsson

*Professor of Economics, Umeå University, Sweden*

Karl-Gustaf Löfgren

*Professor of Economics, Umeå University, Sweden*

**Edward Elgar**
Cheltenham, UK • Northampton, MA, USA

Published by
Edward Elgar Publishing Limited
The Lypiatts
15 Lansdown Road
Cheltenham
Glos GL50 2JA
UK

Edward Elgar Publishing, Inc.
William Pratt House
9 Dewey Court
Northampton
Massachusetts 01060
USA

A catalogue record for this book
is available from the British Library

Library of Congress Control Number: 2009941011

MIX
Paper from
responsible sources
FSC
www.fsc.org    FSC® C018575

ISBN 978 1 84720 384 7 (cased)

Typeset by Servis Filmsetting Ltd, Stockport, Cheshire

Printed and bound by MPG Books Group, UK

# Contents

# Figures and tables

## FIGURES

# TABLES

# Contributors

**Thomas Aronsson**, Department of Economics, Umeå University, Sweden.

**Geir B. Asheim**, Department of Economics, University of Oslo, Norway.

**Kenneth Backlund**, Department of Economics, Umeå University, Sweden.

**Kirk Hamilton**, Policy and Economics, Environment Department, The World Bank.

**John M. Hartwick**, Economics Department, Queen's University, Kingston, Canada.

**Chuan-Zhong Li**, Department of Economics, Uppsala University, Sweden.

**Karl-Gustaf Löfgren**, Department of Economics, Umeå University, Sweden.

**Ram Ranjan**, Graduate School of the Environment, Department of Environment & Geography, Macquarie University, Sydney, Australia.

**Eva Samakovlis**, National Institute of Economic Research, Stockholm, Sweden.

**Jason F. Shogren**, Department of Economics and Finance, University of Wyoming Laramie, WY, USA.

**Tomas Sjögren**, Department of Economics, Umeå University, Sweden.

**Martin L. Weitzman**, Department of Economics, Harvard University, Cambridge, MA, USA.

# 1 An introduction to the theory of social accounting

*Thomas Aronsson and Karl-Gustaf Löfgren*

## 1 BACKGROUND

At least since the 1970s, much research effort has been devoted to the use and design of national accounts. One of the basic ideas behind this work has been to provide a coherent framework for measuring national and/or global welfare in a dynamic economy as well as understanding how the current system of national accounts ought to be modified with this particular objective in mind. A suitable name for this research area is 'social accounting': according to *The New Palgrave Dictionary of Economics*, this refers to 'the body of data that portrays a nation's economic activity in terms of output produced and incomes created, the stocks of capital goods and other inputs required, and the financial pathways and instruments used'. Herein lies also the task of measuring the social value of this economic activity, which is where the welfare-economic perspective comes in. More specifically, measuring the social value of economic activity – whether this activity refers to a nation or a supranational community – requires a welfare economic theory of social accounting, and such a theory has gradually evolved (and is still evolving). The purpose of this introductory chapter is to briefly discuss some of the main insights that we believe that this theory has produced.[1] We will do so by focusing on three interrelated issues: (i) principles for measuring welfare in a community at a given point in time, (ii) cost–benefit rules for measuring welfare change and (iii) principles for measuring sustainability, which are the three main topics addressed by this Handbook. Our purpose here is to present a starting point for the analyses carried out in later chapters.

The outline of the present chapter is as follows. In Section 2, we discuss the problem of measuring welfare at a given point in time in a dynamic economy and, in particular, the relationship between welfare and the Hamiltonian. Section 3 deals with cost–benefit analysis – again in the context of a dynamic economy – whereas Section 4 deals with sustainability. We end the chapter by presenting an outline of the Handbook as well as briefly discussing each of the remaining chapters.

## 2   WELFARE MEASUREMENT AND THE HAMILTONIAN

What does a 'national welfare measure' look like in a dynamic economy, and can we use entities from national accounts to calculate a static equivalent to this welfare measure? Most of the early welfare measures were wealth-like concepts such as the present value of future utility or consumption; see for example Samuelson (1961). However, although such a measure is accurate – as long as the future utility for society is measured correctly – it is not very practical. This is so for an obvious reason: it is forward looking and would, therefore, necessitate predictions of all welfare-relevant entities far into the future. Much would be gained if it were possible to construct a static equivalent to future utility. The comprehensive net national product, to be referred to as 'comprehensive NNP' for short, serves this purpose. The comprehensive NNP is an extension of the conventional NNP concept, where the extension captures *all* aspects of consumption and capital formation that are relevant for society. A comprehensive concept of consumption should reflect consumer preferences and not be restricted to conventional goods and services; it is also likely to include other 'utilities' such as leisure and environmental quality (entities which are not part of the conventional NNP). Similarly, a comprehensive measure of net investment should include all capital formation undertaken by society and not merely changes in the stock of physical capital. Other stocks of importance for production and/or utility are natural resource stocks, stocks that represent (or influence) environmental quality, and the stock of human capital. The net changes in these stocks, measured over a period of time, also qualify as capital formation. Depending on focus, the comprehensive NNP is sometimes also referred to as the 'green NNP', at least if applied to economies where consumption and/or capital aspects of the natural environment are important parts of the economic system. We shall here use the concepts of comprehensive and green NNP synonymously.

Weitzman (1976) was first to show that comprehensive NNP, if measured in terms of utility, constitutes an exact welfare measure in a dynamic economy. In technical terms, the result derived by Weitzman implies that the current value Hamiltonian of the underlying optimal growth problem is proportional to the present value of future utility facing the representative consumer. This Hamiltonian-based welfare measure is, therefore, a static equivalent – or annuity equivalent – to future utility, which explains why it is so frequently referred to in the literature. The current value Hamiltonian is, in turn, often interpreted as the comprehensive NNP, measured in units of utility, as it represents the utility value of current consumption (broadly defined to capture all goods and services that give rise to instantaneous utility) plus the utility value of all current investments (which include changes in all capital stocks of relevance for society). Although Weitzman himself did not use the term 'comprehensive NNP' in his 1976 paper, the NNP concept should be interpreted in a broader sense than the conventional NNP: Weitzman wrote that, in addition to physical, man-made capital, 'pools of exhaustible natural resources ought to qualify as capital, and so should stocks of knowledge resulting from learning or research activities'. This view of NNP has inspired much of the subsequent research on welfare measurement, where different aspects of capital formation have been addressed.[2]

As we will argue later, however, the welfare interpretation of the current value Hamiltonian relies on a set of assumptions, which appears to be somewhat restrictive. To be more specific, the Hamiltonian-based welfare measure assumes a stationary technology and an optimal resource allocation. The first assumption rules out disembodied technological change, whereas the second rules out typical market failures such as uninternalized externalities or involuntary unemployment. If either of these two assumptions is relaxed, the welfare measure will contain forward-looking terms (in addition to the current value Hamiltonian), which cannot be estimated solely by using information that is part of the current value Hamiltonian, that is, the Hamiltonian-based indicator is no longer an exact welfare measure. This suggests that market imperfections may undermine the welfare economic foundation for comprehensive NNP (if based on the Hamiltonian concept). For obvious reasons, it also means that practical applications of social accounting are difficult to carry out, at least if the welfare economic foundation is to be taken seriously.

### 2.1   A Dynamic Model with Stock Pollution

In this subsection, we present a model developed by Brock (1977), where production releases emissions, and where the stock of pollution – accumulated via emissions – gives rise to a consumption externality. We have chosen this particular model primarily for two reasons. First, the model is particularly suited for studying environmental aspects of social accounting, allowing us to connect with a major theme in earlier literature, namely, the welfare-economic foundations for 'green national accounts'. Second, by introducing a market failure, we are also able to distinguish between a first-best welfare measure and a welfare measure applicable in an imperfect market economy. The analyses carried out in subsections 2.2 and 2.3 below are largely based on Aronsson and Löfgren (1999a). To shorten the presentation as much as possible, we only consider utility-based welfare measures here; as our purpose is to address principles (not the step from theory to application), this implies no loss of generality by comparison with money-metrics based welfare measures.

We consider an economy where the consumers are identical and have infinite planning horizons.[3] We also follow the convention in much of the earlier literature on social accounting of disregarding population growth and normalizing the population to equal one. The instantaneous utility function at time $t$ is written as

$$u(t) = u(c(t), x(t))$$
(1)

where $c$ is private consumption and $x$ the stock of pollution. The consumer is assumed to supply one unit of labor inelastically at each instant. This simplification is justified here because endogenous labor supply behavior adds nothing essential to the analysis carried out below. We assume that the function $u(\cdot)$ is increasing in $c$, decreasing in $x$ and strictly concave.

Turning to production, we assume that identical competitive firms, whose number is normalized to one, produce a homogeneous good by using labor (normalized to one and suppressed), physical capital and energy. The technology is stationary, and the production function is given by

$$y(t) = f(k(t), g(t)).$$
(2)

In equation (2), $y$ denotes net output, meaning that depreciation has been accounted for, $k$ the stock of physical capital and $g$ energy input. We assume that the function $f(\cdot)$ is increasing in each argument and strictly concave.

The accumulation of pollution is governed by the following differential equation:

$$\dot{x}(t) = g(t) - \gamma x(t)$$
(3)

where $\gamma \in (0, 1)$ reflects the assimilative capacity of the environment. To connect emissions to energy input in a simple way, we assume (with little loss of generality) that the emissions equal the input of energy.

Finally, the accumulation of physical capital obeys the resource constraint

$$\dot{k}(t) = f(k(t), g(t)) - c(t).$$
(4)

Equation (4) means that net output is used for private consumption and net investment.

## 2.2   First-Best Social Optimum and the Hamiltonian-Based Welfare Measure

To derive the first-best social optimum, it is convenient to assume that the resource allocation is decided upon by a social planner, whose objective coincides with the utility function facing the representative consumer. The decision-problem facing the social planner can be written as

$$\underset{c(t),\, g(t)}{Max} \int_0^\infty u(c(t), x(t)) e^{-\theta t} dt \tag{5}$$

subject to

$$\dot{k}(t) = f(k(t), g(t)) - c(t) \tag{6}$$

$$\dot{x}(t) = g(t) - \gamma x(t) \tag{7}$$

as well as subject to the initial conditions $k(0) = k_0 > 0$ and $x(0) = x_0 > 0$, and the terminal conditions $\lim_{t \to \infty} k(t) \geq 0$ and $\lim_{t \to \infty} x(t) \geq 0$. Therefore, the decision-problem facing the social planner is here represented by a standard optimal control problem with two control variables, $c$ and $g$, and two state variables, $k$ and $x$. The parameter $\theta$ is the utility discount rate.

The present value Hamiltonian corresponding to the social planner's decision-problem becomes

$$H(t) = u(c(t), x(t)) e^{-\theta t} + \lambda(t)\dot{k}(t) + \mu(t)\dot{x}(t). \tag{8}$$

In equation (8), $\lambda$ and $\mu$ are costate variables associated with the physical capital stock and stock of pollution, respectively. In addition to equations (6) and (7), and in addition to the initial and terminal conditions, the necessary conditions for an interior social optimum include (where the time indicator has been suppressed for notational convenience)

$$\frac{\partial H}{\partial c} = u_c(c, x) e^{-\theta t} - \lambda = 0 \tag{9}$$

$$\frac{\partial H}{\partial g} = \lambda f_g(k, g) + \mu = 0 \tag{10}$$

$$\dot{\lambda} = -\frac{\partial H}{\partial k} = -\lambda f_k(k, g) \tag{11}$$

$$\dot{\mu} = -\frac{\partial H}{\partial x} = -u_x(c, x)e^{-\theta t} + \mu\gamma \qquad (12)$$

where a subscript attached to the utility or production function denotes a partial derivative. Equations (9) and (10) are standard efficiency conditions for the control variables, $c$ and $g$, whereas equations (11) and (12) are the equations of motion for the costate variables, that is, they show how the (utility-based) shadow prices of physical capital and pollution evolve over time along the optimal path. Note also that the costate variable $\mu(t)$ is the appropriate measure of social marginal cost of releasing emissions at time $t$ (measured in units of utility), which the social planner weighs against the marginal benefit of higher output due to increased release of emissions, $\lambda(t)f_g(k(t), g(t))$. Let $\{c^*(t), g^*(t), k^*(t), x^*(t), \lambda^*(t), \mu^*(t)\}_0^\infty$ denote the resource allocation that obeys the optimality conditions presented above, where the superindex * denotes 'first-best optimum'; it represents the best possible outcome given the preferences and constraints described above.

For this economy, one can show that the Hamiltonian constitutes an exact welfare measure. By totally differentiating the present value Hamiltonian with respect to time (assuming differentiability) and using the necessary conditions given by equations (9)–(12), we have (suppressing the time indicator once again)

$$\frac{dH^*}{dt} = -\theta u(c^*, x^*)e^{-\theta t} + \frac{\partial H^*}{\partial c}\frac{dc^*}{dt} + \frac{\partial H^*}{\partial g}\frac{dg^*}{dt} + \frac{\partial H^*}{\partial k}\frac{dk^*}{dt} + \frac{\partial H^*}{\partial x}\frac{dx^*}{dt}$$

$$+ \frac{\partial H^*}{\partial \lambda}\frac{d\lambda^*}{dt} + \frac{\partial H^*}{\partial \mu}\frac{d\mu^*}{dt} = -\theta u(c^*, x^*)e^{-\theta t}. \qquad (13)$$

In equation (13), $H^*$ denotes the present value Hamiltonian evaluated in the first-best optimum. The expression after the second equality in equation (13) is a direct consequence of the dynamic envelope theorem: all indirect effects of time via control, state and costate variables vanish as a consequence of optimization.[4] Therefore, only the direct effect of time, $-\theta u(c^*, x^*)\exp(-\theta t) \equiv \partial H^*/\partial t$, remains in equation (13), which is due to the explicit time dependence of the utility discount factor. By solving equation (13) subject to the transversality condition $\lim_{T\to\infty}H^*(T) = 0$,[5] and transforming the solution to current value, that is, multiplying by $e^{\theta t}$, we obtain (where the superindex $c$ stands for 'current value')

$$\theta V^*(t) = H^{c*}(t) \qquad (14)$$

in which

$$V^*(t) = \int_t^\infty u(c^*(s), x^*(s))e^{-\theta(s-t)}ds \qquad (15)$$

is the optimal value function at time $t$ (that is, the present value of future utility facing the representative consumer at time $t$ under the optimal resource allocation), and $H^c(t) = H(t)e^{\theta t}$ is the current value Hamiltonian at time $t$.

Equation (14) is Weitzman's (1976) welfare measure applied to the model discussed here. It means that the present value of future utility at time $t$ is proportional to the current value Hamiltonian at time $t$, where the utility discount rate constitutes the factor of proportionality. An important implication of equation (14) is that welfare at time $t$ can be measured solely by using information referring to time $t$, although the welfare concept itself is fundamentally intertemporal. In other words, the Hamiltonian constitutes a static equivalent to future utility. The intuition is that, in a first-best resource allocation, the costate variables accurately reflect the future welfare consequences of the actions taken today. This will be described more thoroughly below. Furthermore, possible welfare contributions of technological change are ruled out by the stationary technology assumption made above.[6] Therefore, all sources of welfare are contained in – and accurately measured by – the current value Hamiltonian.

The current value Hamiltonian on the right-hand side of equation (14) can be written as

$$H^{c*}(t) = u(c^*(t), x^*(t)) + \lambda^{c*}(t)\dot{k}^*(t) + \mu^{c*}(t)\dot{x}^*(t) \qquad (16)$$

where $\lambda^c(t) = \lambda(t)e^{\theta t}$ and $\mu^c(t) = \mu(t)e^{\theta t}$ are the costate variables at time $t$ measured in current value. It has become common in earlier literature to interpret the current value Hamiltonian as a measure of comprehensive NNP in utility terms. The intuition is obvious from equation (16): the current value Hamiltonian reflects the instantaneous utility associated with the current consumption (the first term on the right-hand side) plus the utility value of the current net investments (the second and third terms). For the simple economy discussed here, the consumption concept contains two parts – goods and services, $c$, and pollution, $x$ – whereas the net investments refer to the changes in the physical capital stock, $\dot{k}$, and the additions to the stock of pollution, $\dot{x}$.

To take the NNP interpretation one step further, let us first linearize the instantaneous utility function and then use equation (9) to rewrite the instantaneous utility function as follows:

$$u(c, x) = \lambda^c[c + \rho x] + s$$

where $s = u(c, x) - \lambda^c c - u_x(c, x)x$ is the consumer surplus and $\rho = u_x(c, x)/u_c(c, x)$ the marginal rate of substitution between pollution and private consumption. We can now rewrite equation (14) as

$$\theta V^*(t) = \lambda^{c*}(t)[c^*(t) + \dot{k}^*(t) + \rho^*(t)x^*(t) - \tau^*(t)\dot{x}^*(t)] + s^*(t).$$
$$(17)$$

In equation (17), $-\tau^*(t) = \mu^{c*}(t)/\lambda^{c*}(t) < 0$ is the real shadow price of additions to the stock of pollution at time $t$ in the social optimum. As we will show below, $\tau^*(t)$ is also the (intertemporal analogue to the) Pigouvian emission tax that internalizes the consumption externality of pollution. Equation (17) shows that welfare – as represented by the present value of future utility facing the representative consumer – is proportional to the sum of two terms: the linearized current value Hamiltonian and the consumer surplus. The former is, in turn, defined as the real comprehensive NNP times the marginal utility value of capital. For the economy set out here, real comprehensive NNP contains four parts. The first two terms represent the conventional NNP, the third term measures the stock of pollution times the marginal value of this stock at time $t$ (that is, the 'exchange-value' of the public bad at this particular time),[7] and the fourth term represents the marginal value of additions to the stock of pollution (the net investment aspect of the environment). Therefore, the third and fourth terms represent, in a sense, the additional information we would need in order to 'green' the national accounts. In general, therefore, the real comprehensive NNP does not constitute an exact real welfare measure due to the appearance of the consumer surplus in equation (17).[8] Note also that in the special – yet highly unrealistic – case where the instantaneous utility function is linear homogeneous, we have $s = 0$, meaning that the linearized current value Hamiltonian is proportional to the present value of future utility. The Cobb-Douglas utility function $u(c, x) = c^\alpha x^{1-\alpha}$, where $\alpha \in (0, 1)$, exemplifies such a utility function.

We mentioned above that, in the first-best optimum, the costate variables accurately measure the future welfare effects of current actions, that is, intertemporal social opportunity costs. To see this more clearly, let us solve the differential (12) for $\mu(t)$, subject to the transversality condition $\lim_{T\to\infty}\mu(T) = 0$. We have

$$\mu^*(t) = \int_t^\infty u_x(c^*(s), x^*(s))e^{-\theta s}e^{-\gamma(s-t)}ds < 0,$$
$$(18a)$$

or, equivalently, in current value terms through multiplying by $e^{\theta t}$

$$\mu^{c*}(t) = \int_t^\infty u_x(c^*(s), x^*(s))e^{-(\theta+\gamma)(s-t)}ds < 0. \tag{18b}$$

Recall from equation (10) that the shadow price of pollution at time $t$ constitutes the social marginal cost of releasing emissions at time $t$. In equations (18a) and (18b), we can see that this shadow price is forward looking: it measures the present utility value of the future increases in the stock of pollution that the release of emissions at time $t$ gives rise to. Note also that $\gamma$, the rate of depreciation of pollution, appears as an extra discount factor. The intuition is, of course, that the higher the rate of depreciation, *ceteris paribus*, the less will be the effective increase in the future stock. If we were to measure the shadow price of pollution in real terms, instead of in units of utility as in equations (18a) and (18b), we would arrive at the (negative of the) Pigouvian tax mentioned above, that is, the tax that in a market economy would induce the firm to release the socially optimal level of emissions. Therefore, the Pigouvian tax,

$$\tau^*(t) = -\frac{\int_t^\infty u_x(c^*(s), x^*(s))e^{-\theta s}e^{-\gamma(s-t)}ds}{\lambda^*(t)} > 0, \tag{18c}$$

is interpretable in the same general way as the utility-based shadow price. We will return to the Pigouvian tax below, where we consider the welfare measurement problem in the context of a market economy (instead of an economy where the resource allocation is decided upon by a social planner).

### Extension: Welfare measurement in a stochastic environment

The analysis carried out above assumes perfect certainty. Although convenient from an analytical point of view, this assumption is hardly realistic. However, the step towards uncertainty need not necessarily be very complicated. The Hamilton-Jacobi-Bellman equation (a stochastic partial differential equation obeyed by the optimal value function) from stochastic control theory can be used to derive a welfare measure which is an analogue to the deterministic welfare measure analysed above. In the special case with perfect certainty – and under the same assumption about the preferences and technology as those set out above – this technique reproduces the welfare measure presented in equation (14).

Aronsson and Löfgren (1995) consider welfare measurement in a stochastic version of the Ramsey model, in which the rate of population growth follows a Brownian motion. They show that welfare – represented by the expected present value of future utility facing the representative consumer – is measured by a generalized current value Hamiltonian, where the generalization means that it also reflects the valuation of the risk associated with a given investment. If the individual is risk-averse (risk-loving), then this extra term contributes to lower (higher) welfare. As the additional term is proportional to the variance of the stochastic variable, it vanishes under perfect certainty, and we are back in the deterministic welfare analysis addressed above. Weitzman (1998) derives an analogous welfare measure for an economy where the rate of time preference (instead of the rate of population growth) follows a Brownian motion.[9]

### 2.3    Welfare Measurement in an Imperfectly Controlled Market Economy

In a decentralized economy, the resource allocation is not necessarily optimal from society's point of view. The model presented in subsection 2.1 contains a consumption externality, since the release of emissions by firms builds up a stock of pollution, which in turn directly affects the utility of the representative consumer. We will here address the implications for welfare measurement that will follow, if this externality has not become fully internalized.

The structure of the model is the same as before; the only difference is that the decisions about consumption, capital formation and production are here made by consumers and firms instead of by a social planner. The utility maximization problem facing the consumer is given by

$$\underset{c(t)}{Max} \int_0^\infty u(c(t), x(t))e^{-\theta t}dt \tag{19}$$

subject to the asset accumulation equation

$$\dot{k}(t) = \pi(t) + r(t)k(t) + w(t) + T(t) - c(t), \tag{20}$$

as well as subject to the initial condition $k(0) = k_0$, and a No-Ponzi Game (NPG) condition meaning that the present value of the asset (physical capital) is non-negative at the terminal point. The consumer supplies one unit of labor inelastically at each instant and earns labor income $w(t)$ as well as renting out capital at the market rate of interest $r(t)$ to the representative firm. The variables $\pi(t) \geq 0$ and $T(t) > 0$ represent possible profit income and a lump-sum transfer (to be defined below), respectively. Note that the representative consumer treats the stock of pollution, the labor income, the interest rate, the profit income and the lump-sum transfer as exogenous.

The representative firm chooses capital, $k(t)$, and emissions, $g(t)$, to maximize profit at each point in time. Its objective function at time $t$ can then be written as

$$\pi(t) = f(k(t), g(t)) - w(t) - r(t)k(t) - \tau(t)g(t). \tag{21}$$

In equation (21), $\tau(t)$ is a tax per unit of emissions paid by the firm at time $t$. Finally, budget balance for the public sector implies that $\tau(t)g(t) = T(t)$ for all $t$.

If we combine the first-order conditions for the consumer and the firm, the following conditions are among those obeyed by the decentralized equilibrium (suppressing the time indicator for notational convenience);

$$u_c(c, x)e^{-\theta t} - \lambda = 0 \tag{22}$$

$$f_g(k, g) - \tau = 0 \tag{23}$$

$$\dot{\lambda} = -\lambda f_k(k, g). \tag{24}$$

There are two principal differences between the necessary conditions characterizing the decentralized economy and the first-best optimal resource allocation. First, the emission tax is not necessarily the Pigouvian tax described in the previous subsection. Second, the stock of pollution is not an endogenous state variable in the decentralized economy; it is, instead, a side effect of the behavior of the firm and treated as exogenous by the consumer.

Let $\tau^0(t)$ for $t \in [0, \infty)$ represent the emission tax path decided upon by the policy maker (to be discussed more thoroughly below), where the superindex 0 denotes 'imperfectly controlled market economy', so as to distinguish it from the first-best optimum analyzed in subsection 2.2. Suppose that this emission tax path gives rise to the resource allocation

$$\{c^0(t), g^0(t), k^0(t), x^0(t), \lambda^0(t)\}_0^\infty.$$

Note that the first-order conditions presented in equations (22)–(24) look as if they are derived from the following present value pseudo-Hamiltonian (where the subindex $p$ stands for 'pseudo'):

$$H_p^0(t) = u(c^0(t), x^0(t))e^{-\theta t} + \lambda^0(t)\dot{k}^0(t) - \lambda^0(t)\tau^0(t)\dot{x}^0(t). \quad (25)$$

In equation (25), we can interpret $-\lambda^0(t)\tau^0(t)$ as an estimate of the shadow price of pollution at time $t$. If the resource allocation were first best, and thus $\tau^0(t) = \tau^*(t) = -\mu^*(t)/\lambda^*(t)$ would be the Pigouvian emission tax at time $t$, then $c^0(t) = c^*(t)$, $g^0(t) = g^*(t)$, $k^0(t) = k^*(t)$ and $x^0(t) = x^*(t)$. In this case, equation (25) would be the present value Hamiltonian, and it would constitute an exact annuity equivalent to future utility for the reasons presented in subsection 2.2.

Although public policy aims at correcting for the environmental externality, the emission tax does not necessarily need to be an accurate estimate of the marginal social value of an increase in the stock of pollution at each instant; after all, this is the essence of the phrase 'imperfectly controlled market economy'. To operationalize this idea, we follow Aronsson and Löfgren (1999a) by assuming that the actual emission tax reflects a biased estimate of the marginal utility of pollution in the following sense:

$$\tau^0(t) = -\frac{\int_t^\infty (u_x(c^0(s), x^0(s)) + \beta(s))e^{-\theta s}e^{-\gamma(s-t)}ds}{\lambda^0(t)} \quad (26)$$

where the time-varying variable $\beta$ represents the instantaneous bias in the estimate of the marginal utility of pollution. Therefore, if $\beta(t) = 0$ for all $t$, then equation (25) takes the same form as the Pigouvian tax. Similarly, if $\beta(t) = -u_x(c(t), x(t))$ for all $t$, the resource allocation represents an uncontrolled market economy where $\tau^0(t) = 0$ for all $t$. In other words, equation (26) is general enough to encompass both the first-best social optimum and the uncontrolled market economy as special cases.

As before, welfare is defined as the present value of future utility facing the representative consumer, that is, the optimal value function. In the decentralized, and possibly imperfect market economy, the optimal value function at time $t$ can be written as follows:

$$V^0(t) = \int_t^\infty u(c^0(s), x^0(s))e^{-\theta(s-t)}ds. \quad (27)$$

What is the relationship between the optimal value function and pseudo-Hamiltonian defined in equation (25)? If we differentiate equation (25) totally with respect to time and use the necessary conditions in equations

(22), (23) and (24), we have (suppressing the time indicator for notational convenience)

$$\frac{dH_p^0}{dt} = -\theta u(c^0, x^0)e^{-\theta t} + [u_x^0 e^{-\theta t} + \lambda^0 \tau^0 (f_k^0 + \gamma) - \lambda^0 \dot{\tau}^0]\dot{x}^0 \quad (28)$$

where we have used the short notations $u_x^0 = u_x(c^0, x^0)$ and $f_k^0 = f_k(k^0, g^0)$. Now, observe that the time derivative of the emission tax in equation (26) can be written as

$$\dot{\tau}^0(t) = \frac{[u_x^0(t) + \beta(t)]e^{-\theta t}}{\lambda^0(t)} + \tau^0(t)(f_k^0(t) + \gamma). \quad (29)$$

Substituting equation (29) into equation (28) gives

$$\frac{dH_p^0(t)}{dt} = -\theta u(c^0(t), x^0(t))e^{-\theta t} - \beta(t)e^{-\theta t}\dot{x}^0(t). \quad (30)$$

Therefore, the non-autonomous time dependence arises from two sources here: the utility discount factor (as before) and the bias component of the emission tax. By solving equation (30) subject to the transversality condition $\lim_{T \to \infty} H_p^0(T) = 0$ and, finally, transforming the solution to current value, we obtain

$$\theta V^0(t) = H_p^0(t) - \int_t^\infty \beta(s)e^{-\theta(s-t)}\dot{x}^0(s)\,ds. \quad (31)$$

The first term on the right-hand side of equation (31) is the pseudo-Hamiltonian measured in current value, with the same interpretation as its counterpart in the first best, whereas the second term is the present value of future biases, that is, the present value of the uninternalized marginal externality. This component arises for one single reason: the actual emission tax is based on a biased estimate of the marginal utility of pollution, meaning that the resource allocation is not optimal from society's point of view. In the first best, where $\beta(t) = 0$ for all $t$, the second term on the right-hand side vanishes, and equation (31) will reproduce the first-best welfare measure in equation (14). The polar case of an 'uncontrolled market economy' corresponds in our model to $\beta(t) = -u_x(c^0(t), x^0(t))$ for all $t$, meaning that the emission tax is equal to zero along the whole general equilibrium path. In the uncontrolled market economy, therefore, equation (31) changes to read

$$\theta V^0(t) \;=\; H_p^{c^0}(t) \;+\; \int_t^\infty u_x(c^0(s), x^0(s)) e^{-\theta(s-t)} \dot{x}^0(s)\,ds.$$

Two things are worth noticing in equation (31). First, if the resource allocation is not optimal, the Hamiltonian at time $t$ no longer contains all the information needed to measure welfare at time $t$. Second, the final term on the right-hand side of equation (31) is forward looking. In other words, we can no longer measure welfare at time $t$ solely by using information referring to time $t$. The intuition is, of course, that the release of emissions in the present gives rise to increased pollution in the entire future, *ceteris paribus*. Therefore, if the future welfare consequences of released emissions at time $t$ are measured incorrectly, we must adjust the welfare measure to reflect this whole path of future biases. This is precisely what happens here, which explains why the Hamiltonian does not constitute an exact welfare measure.

## 3   COST–BENEFIT ANALYSIS

The concept of welfare measurement need not only refer to the welfare level; it may also refer to changes in welfare following, for example, policy projects or other parametric changes in the economic system. This leads naturally to the principles of cost–benefit analysis in dynamic economies. It should be emphasized that although projects may be small or temporary, they are still likely to have intertemporal consequences. Therefore, the study of cost–benefit analysis in dynamic economies generates insights that are not easily gained in static models.[10] We will give two examples here; one refers to the welfare effect of a policy project in a first-best type of economy, where the resource allocation is defined conditional on the policy parameter in question, and the other refers to the welfare effect of increased emission taxation in an imperfectly controlled market economy.

**Example 1: A parameter change in the first best**
Consider once again the first-best resource allocation presented in subsection 2.2, with the modification that the resource constraint is rewritten as follows:

$$\dot{k}(t) = f(k(t), g(t), \alpha) - I(\alpha) - c(t). \tag{32}$$

The parameter $\alpha$ measures the resources spent on a project – for example, R&D or a public infrastructure investment – that leads to increased output.

We also assume that the intensity parameter $\alpha$ is associated with a social cost, represented by the function $I(\alpha)$, which is increasing and convex in $\alpha$. Given that the economy has reached a first-best resource allocation defined conditional on $\alpha$, we would like to measure the welfare effect of a small permanent increase in $\alpha$. The present value Hamiltonian plays a crucial role in this welfare change measure; the direct effect on the Hamiltonian of a change in this policy parameter represents, in a sense, a measure of instantaneous welfare change. The total welfare change is then found by integration of instantaneous welfare changes over the planning period.[11]

To see this, let us write the optimal value function at time zero as follows:

$$V^*(0, \alpha) = \int_0^\infty u(c^*(t, \alpha), x^*(t, \alpha))e^{-\theta t}dt, \tag{33}$$

which emphasizes that the resource allocation is defined conditional on the parameter $\alpha$. We show in the Appendix to this chapter that the welfare effect of a small change in $\alpha$ can be written as

$$\frac{\partial V^*(0, \alpha)}{\partial \alpha} = \int_0^\infty \lambda^*(t, \alpha)[f_\alpha(k^*(t, \alpha), g^*(t, \alpha), \alpha) - I_\alpha(\alpha)]dt$$

$$= \int_0^\infty \frac{\partial H^*(t, \alpha)}{\partial \alpha}dt. \tag{34}$$

Here, $f_\alpha(\cdot)$ represents the direct effect on output of an increase in $\alpha$ with $k$ and $g$ held constant at their initial levels. The expression in square brackets after the first equality in equation (34) contains two components: the instantaneous direct marginal benefit and the instantaneous direct marginal cost of the project measured in utility terms. Note also that each difference between instantaneous marginal benefit and instantaneous marginal cost is discounted to present value via $\lambda$ (the present value costate variable associated with the capital stock), and the instantaneous net benefits are then integrated over the whole planning period. The expression after the second equality emphasizes that all indirect effects of $\alpha$ vanish, as the initial resource allocation is optimal conditional on $\alpha$; this is a consequence of the dynamic envelope theorem. Therefore, the welfare change can be measured by taking the partial derivative of the present value Hamiltonian with respect to $\alpha$ and then integrating over the planning period.

**Example 2: A small increase in the emission tax in the market economy**
Consider once again the resource allocation addressed in subsection 2.3. Suppose now that the emission tax is increased from $\tau^0(t)$ to $\tau^0(t) + \vartheta$ for all $t$, where $\vartheta$ is a small positive constant. The additional tax revenue is redistributed lump-sum to the consumer. This policy is interpretable in terms of a small permanent increase in the emission tax. If the resource allocation obeys equations (22), (23) and (24), the optimal value function may be written as

$$V^0(0, \vartheta) = \int_0^\infty u(c^0(t, \vartheta), x^0(t, \vartheta))e^{-\theta t}dt \qquad (35)$$

where the initial, that is, pre-reform equilibrium analyzed in subsection 2.3 means that $\vartheta = 0$. By applying the same technique as the one we used above, we can derive the cost–benefit rule that we are looking for. By evaluating this rule in the initial equilibrium where $\vartheta = 0$, we have

$$\frac{\partial V^0(0, \vartheta)}{\partial \vartheta} = \int_0^\infty \left[ u_x(c^0(t, \vartheta), x^0(t, \vartheta))e^{-\theta t}\frac{\partial x^0(t, \vartheta)}{\partial \vartheta} \right.$$
$$\left. + \lambda^0(t, \vartheta)\tau^0(t)\frac{\partial g^0(t, \vartheta)}{\partial \vartheta} \right]dt. \qquad (36)$$

The first term within the square bracket on the right-hand side is the instantaneous marginal benefit of a reduction in the stock of pollution. This component contributes to higher welfare because $u_x(c^0, x^0) < 0$ and $\partial x^0(\cdot)/\partial \vartheta < 0$.[12] Similarly, the second term within the square bracket is the cost of higher taxation in terms of lost consumption (the higher emission tax leads to reduced output, *ceteris paribus*). This component is clearly negative since $\tau^0 > 0$ and $\partial g^0(\cdot)/\partial \vartheta < 0$. One can show that the welfare effect measured by equation (36) vanishes if the initial emission tax is Pigouvian, in which case the resource allocation is first best. One can also relate the welfare effect of increased emission taxation to the extent to which the actual pre-reform emission tax is a biased estimate of the Pigouvian emission tax (for further discussion, see Aronsson and Löfgren 1999a).

Finally, in the uncontrolled market economy, where the emission tax is equal to zero, equation (36) reduces to read

$$\frac{\partial V^0(0, \vartheta)}{\partial \vartheta} = \int_0^\infty u_x(c^0(t, \vartheta), x^0(t, \vartheta))e^{-\theta t}\frac{\partial x^0(t, \vartheta)}{\partial \vartheta}dt > 0. \qquad (37)$$

This neat – yet unsurprising – result means that it is always welfare improving to introduce a small emission tax in the uncontrolled market economy. The intuition is that the policy reform contains no first-order welfare cost in this case, while it gives rise to a first-order welfare benefit in terms of reduced pollution.


## 4   SUSTAINABILITY

Many of the basic ideas underlying the study of sustainability are thoroughly examined in later chapters. We will, therefore, limit the presentation here to a brief discussion of two interrelated issues: (i) genuine saving and (ii) conditions for non-declining instantaneous utility.

The World Commission on Environment and Development, often referred to as the Brundtland Commission, suggested in its 1987 report that 'sustainable development' ought to imply 'development that meets the need of the present without compromising the ability of future generations to meet their own needs'. One possible interpretation of this idea is that sustainable development requires that welfare is non-declining. This suggests, in turn, that the genuine saving, which is an exact measure of welfare change over a short time interval, also constitutes a *local* indicator of sustainable development.[13] Genuine saving is meant to imply the value of comprehensive net investments, possibly augmented with the marginal value of externalities and/or technological change depending on the functioning of the economic system. The focus on a short time interval also explains the above emphasis on the word 'local'.

To see that the genuine saving has this particular property, we shall once again use the model set out in subsection 2.1. We begin by differentiating the optimal value function with respect to time. Independently of whether the resource allocation is first best or an imperfectly controlled market economy, that is, independently of whether the calculation is based on equation (15) or equation (27) above, we obtain

$$\dot{V}(t) = -u(c(t), x(t)) + \theta V(t). \tag{38}$$

If the resource allocation is first best, we can use $\theta V^*(t) = H^{c^*}(t)$ from equation (14) and substitute into equation (38). This gives the welfare-change measure

$$\dot{V}^*(t) = \lambda^{c^*}(t)\dot{k}^*(t) + \mu^{c^*}(t)\dot{x}^*(t). \tag{39a}$$

In the imperfectly controlled market economy, an analogous mathematical operation gives

$$\dot{V}^0(t) = \lambda^{c^0}(t)\dot{k}^0(t) + \mu^{c^0}(t)\dot{x}^0(t) - \int_t^\infty \beta(s)e^{-\theta(s-t)}\dot{x}^0(s)ds \quad (39b)$$

where $\mu^{c^0}(t) = -\tau^0(t)\lambda^{c^0}(t)$. The right-hand side of equations (39a) and (39b) represent the genuine saving, measured in units of utility. Note that the final term on the right-hand side of equation (39b) is forward looking. The intuition is the same as that behind the forward-looking term in the welfare measure discussed in subsection 2.3: the incentives facing consumers and firms at time $t$ (which govern the decisions made at that time) do not accurately reflect all social opportunity costs. Note also that, if we were to extend the model by allowing for disembodied technological change, yet another forward-looking term – the present value of marginal technological change – would enter the measure of genuine saving (see Aronsson, Johansson and Löfgren, 1997, p 106).[14]

It is important to emphasize once again that, if the genuine saving is used as an indicator of sustainability, it only constitutes a local indicator. For instance, the genuine saving says nothing of whether the instantaneous utility is increasing or decreasing along the future equilibrium path. This insight becomes particularly interesting if we reinterpret the model in terms of a continuum of generations (instead of in terms of a single individual with infinite time horizons). To see the argument more clearly, let $i^*(t)$ and $i^0(t)$ denote the measure of genuine saving on the right-hand side of equations (39a) and (39b), respectively. Integrating the final term on the right-hand side of equation (38) by parts (recalling the definition of the optimal value function in subsections 2.2 and 2.3), we can rewrite equations (39a) and (39b) as follows:

$$i(t) = \int_t^\infty \frac{du(c(s), x(s))}{ds}e^{-\theta(s-t)}ds = \int_t^\infty [u_c(s)\dot{c}(s) + u_x(s)\dot{x}(s)]e^{-\theta(s-t)}ds. \quad (40)$$

Therefore, independently of whether genuine saving is defined as in equation (39a) or equation (39b), it reflects a weighted average of changes in future instantaneous utilities. In other words, even if the genuine saving is positive, this does not mean that the instantaneous utilities are increasing along the general equilibrium path: only that a weighted average of future changes in instantaneous utilities is positive.[15] To ensure that the instantaneous utilities are non-declining at each instant along the equilibrium path, we would have to impose conditions on the genuine saving at each instant along this path. The reader is here referred to Hartwick (1977) and Dixit et al. (1980).

# 5   PLAN OF THE HANDBOOK

As we mentioned before, the main topics of the Handbook are: principles for measuring welfare in a community at a given point in time; cost–benefit rules for measuring the welfare change caused by policy (and other) projects; and principles for measuring sustainability. Each of the ten forthcoming chapters addresses one or several of these main topics and extends our knowledge in a variety of directions.

Welfare is typically measured in utility units, and the dominating bulk of earlier studies on social accounting have focused on utility-based welfare measures. Although this approach is theoretically convenient, it is less useful in practical applications simply because utility is unobservable. Therefore, it is important to find a way to transform a utility-based welfare measure into a corresponding money-metrics measure; an issue complicated by the fact that the marginal utility of income is not in general constant over time. In Chapter 2, Karl-Gustaf Löfgren develops a framework for money-metrics-based welfare measurement, showing how an ideal (benchmark independent) price index enables us to take the step from a utility-based welfare measure to a corresponding money-metrics-based measure. The results imply, among other things, that the comprehensive NNP augmented with the consumer surplus constitutes an exact money-metrics welfare measure in a first-best resource allocation. The analysis also shows how money-metrics-based welfare measures for imperfectly controlled market economies can be designed. Yet another issue that the chapter addresses is the relationship between welfare change and growth in real comprehensive NNP.

The traditional approach to social accounting in imperfect market economies has been to focus on the consequences of market failures (such as externalities or unemployment). However, modern literature on behavioral economics also recognizes the possibility that individuals may not be fully rational from the perspective of their own long-run interests. This idea is formalized by the concept of hyperbolic discounting: a mechanism of behavioral failure discussed in recent literature on paternalistic motives for public policy. In Chapter 3, written by Kenneth Backlund and Tomas Sjögren, hyperbolic discounting is integrated into the theory of social accounting. If not properly internalized, behavioral failures imply that the actual resource allocation may deviate from the one that a social planner (who acts on the basis of the consumers' long-run interests) would prefer. The results show that hyperbolic discounting leads to additional, and forward-looking terms in welfare measures. In general, therefore, self-control problems give rise to complications reminiscent of those associated with market failures. The chapter also analyzes, by means of numerical simulations, how effective paternalistic policies are for improving welfare.

Human beings typically face a variety of health risks, such as those associated with being in a particular environment. As these risks directly affect the expected utility, they are also relevant for welfare measurement. At the same time, when faced by risk, individuals are free to choose whether to invest resources to change the likelihood of future good and bad states of nature. Therefore, an important question is how such investments ought to be treated in social accounting. To answer this question, one must first understand the incentives underlying the investment behavior. In Chapter 4, Ram Ranjan and Jason F. Shogren develop a model economy where the representative consumer faces multiple risks of health breakdown, and where he/she can spend resources on self-protection and self-insurance. Among the results, the authors show that self-protection and self-insurance against a particular risk, when considered under multiple risks, can be either higher or lower than that arising under a single risk. In addition, the presence of multiple risks leads to discounting of those health risks that cause lower damage. From the perspective of practical application, measuring the marginal social value of accumulated risk becomes a major challenge for social accounting.

In all developed economies, the public sector plays a crucial role in resource allocation by providing public services and by income redistribution among individuals and groups. In fact, it is not uncommon that government outlays are in the neighborhood of 35–40 per cent of GDP. Furthermore, as the public revenue is raised by distortionary taxes, there is an additional cost of public funds that ought to be considered when measuring welfare. Chapter 5, written by Thomas Aronsson, concerns the treatment of distortionary taxation, public goods and income redistribution in the context of welfare measurement. The analysis is based on a second-best framework, in which the government raises revenue by using either a linear or non-linear income tax. Among other things, the chapter presents a second-best analogue to comprehensive NNP based on the Hamiltonian concept, and the results also show how the marginal cost of public funds affects the accounting price of a public good. In general, and in contrast to first-best welfare measures, a second-best analogue to real comprehensive NNP is not interpretable as an index comprising only aggregate variables; instead, it also reflects the distribution of private consumption and leisure among the consumers.

Alongside the development of a theory of social accounting, a large empirical literature has also evolved. In addition, due to the increased awareness among policy makers that economic growth and environmental concerns ought to be considered simultaneously (instead of as two separate aspects of public policy), attempts have also been made to augment the conventional system for national accounts with important aspects of the natural environment, for example, the value of consumption of 'environmental goods or bads' and investments in different forms of natural capital. Chapter 6, written by Eva Samakovlis, addresses green accounting from a practical perspective, that is, how such accounts are produced in practice. As a number of countries have agreed to introduce green national accounts, a natural starting point here is the guidance provided by the *Handbook for integrated environmental and economic accounting* published by the United Nations et al. (2003), as well as how the environmental accounting programs of different countries relate to these guidelines. The chapter also overviews country-specific experiences in calculating comprehensive NNP (or parts thereof) as well as measurement of genuine saving. There is also discussion about some of the difficulties involved when attempting to construct welfare measures based on green national accounts.

Cost–benefit analysis is a tool for evaluating whether or not a public project is desirable. While the early literature often focused on capital investment projects, the focus has gradually shifted towards policy reform projects or projects relating to the natural environment. As such, part of the modern theory of cost–benefit analysis in dynamic economies has evolved parallel with theories referring to green national accounting and indicators of sustainability. In fact, one may argue that all these developments are to some extent different sides of the same underlying welfare economic theory. In Chapter 7, Chuan-Zhong Li reviews recent advances in the theory of dynamic cost–benefit analysis. The chapter presents and discusses a number of equivalent cost–benefit rules relating to small projects. It also explains the role of comprehensive NNP in cost–benefit analysis, which exemplifies the close connection between cost–benefit rules in dynamic economies and green accounting. The chapter ends with a discussion of the cost–benefit analysis of larger projects that involve price changes. By the result that the Hamiltonian (under ideal conditions) is an exact measure of future utility, the results show that the welfare change measure can be written in the same general way as in the corresponding static theory of cost–benefit analysis.

To estimate the costs of carbon dioxide emissions, we must be able to assess how the global surface temperature responds to the release of carbon dioxide into the atmosphere. Equilibrium climate sensitivity is a key stochastic parameter that converts relative changes in the concentration of atmospheric carbon dioxide into temperature change. It is defined as the global average surface warming following a doubling of carbon dioxide concentration. In Chapter 8, Martin Weitzman addresses the dynamics of climate sensitivity and, in particular, the fat upper tail of its distribution. He shows that the relevant posterior-predictive probability density function of a high-impact low-probability event has a built-in tendency to be fat tailed: the intuition is the difficulty of extrapolating extreme-impact tail behavior from finite data. The analysis also shows that the previous two-period result that fat-tailed climate sensitivity can have strong economic implications survives in a more complete dynamic specification. Therefore, fat tails in the distribution of climate sensitivity in combination with the possibly catastrophic effects of climate change might be of considerable importance for cost–benefit analysis and may even outweigh the influence of discounting.

Since the 1970s, the concept of sustainability has become increasingly important in economic analyses. A key question here is how to maintain a given flow of valuable products when its presence is threatened by various aspects of capital depletion. For instance, non-renewable capital stocks such as oil are inevitably depleted when used as inputs in production. A solution to this problem is given by the Hartwick rule: with some degree of substitutability between different types of capital, non-declining consumption can be maintained by keeping the combined capital in the economy intact over time, that is, the value of net investment – measured over all relevant capital stocks – must be non-negative at each point in time. In Chapter 9, John Hartwick surveys recent literature on sustainable per capita consumption programs. He focuses particular attention on two issues (or 'twists' as he calls them). The first is population growth, that is, how such growth affects the policies necessary to achieve non-declining consumption into the indefinite future, while the second is global warming, where current oil use causes temperature increase via the release of carbon dioxide emissions. The chapter also examines economies with a possibility of boundary-hitting collapse, as well as addressing the formal welfare economics of the notion of sustainability.

As we indicated above, there has been a parallel evolution of theories of social accounting – where a basic purpose has been to construct national (and global) welfare measures in dynamic economies – and theories underlying indicators of sustainability. This is not a coincidence, as concerns for intergenerational well-being are, in a sense, natural aspects of welfare in dynamic economies where future generations are affected by the actions taken today. An interesting question is whether or not measures of welfare improvement can also be used as indicators of sustainability.

This is the starting point of Chapter 10, written by Geir Asheim. The welfare concept used here is total utilitarianism, where instantaneous well-being is given by the product of the population size and the instantaneous utility of per capita consumption, whereas concern for sustainability is based on non-declining utility of per capita consumption. This framework is then used to analyze whether a non-negative value of net investment (that is, genuine saving) implies sustainable development, and whether sustainable development implies a non-negative value of the net investment. Among the results, the author shows that welfare improvement – as measured by a positive value of net investment adjusted for population growth – is not a sufficient condition for non-declining utility of per capita consumption.

The insight that genuine saving under certain conditions is an exact measure of welfare change in a dynamic economy has inspired much recent discussion, and the World Bank now publishes numbers for genuine saving. However, as we mentioned above, genuine saving only constitutes a local indicator of sustainability (by measuring welfare improvement over a short time interval); a non-negative number for genuine saving does not imply that the consumption or utility is sustainable over a longer period. Chapter 11, written by Kirk Hamilton, discusses genuine saving in detail. In addition to a theoretical review, the chapter also contains information on genuine savings in different parts of the world as well as discussing results from empirical research on the relationship between genuine saving and future social welfare. A basic message is the central role that genuine saving can play for countries that aim at accelerating development, as it is both an indicator of welfare change and an indicator of unsustainable development (as a negative number for genuine saving implies that utility must eventually decline). As a consequence, genuine saving is likely to remain as a source of information of importance for public policy.

## APPENDIX

To derive equation (34), we apply the approach to the dynamic envelope theorem suggested by Léonard (1987). Define the present value Hamiltonian

$$\overline{H}(t, \alpha) = u(c^*(t, \alpha), x^*(t, \alpha))e^{-\theta t} + \lambda(t)\dot{k}^*(t, \alpha) + \mu(t)\dot{x}^*(t, \alpha)$$

(A1)

for arbitrary and differentiable functions $\lambda(t)$ and $\mu(t)$. In equation (A1), the equations of motion for physical capital and pollution are given by

$$\dot{k}(t, \alpha) = f(k(t, \alpha), g(t, \alpha), \alpha) - I(\alpha) - c(t, \alpha)$$

and

$$\dot{x}(t, \alpha) = g(t, \alpha) - \gamma x(t, \alpha)$$

in equilibrium. With the exception that the functions $\lambda(t)$ and $\mu(t)$ are arbitrary and do not depend on the parameter $\alpha$, equation (A1) is equivalent to the maximized present value Hamiltonian evaluated in the first-best social optimum. Since $u(c^*, x^*)e^{-\theta t} = \overline{H} - \lambda \dot{k}^* - \mu \dot{x}^*$, and by applying the rules of partial integration, the optimal value function can be written as

$$V^*(0, \alpha) = \int_0^\infty [\overline{H}(t, \alpha) + \dot{\lambda}(t)k^*(t, \alpha) + \dot{\mu}(t)x^*(t, \alpha)]dt$$

$$- \lambda(t)k^*(t, \alpha)|_0^\infty - \mu(t)x^*(t, \alpha)|_0^\infty. \tag{A2}$$

The cost–benefit rule we are looking for is derived by differentiating equation (A2) with respect to $\alpha$ and evaluating the resulting derivative in the first-best social optimum, where $\lambda(t) = \lambda^*(t, \alpha)$ and $\mu(t) = \mu^*(t, \alpha)$. Since $k(0)$ and $x(0)$ are fixed, and if we assume that the transversality conditions $\lim_{t \to \infty} \lambda(t) = 0$ and $\lim_{t \to \infty} \mu(t) = 0$ are fulfilled, we can write the cost–benefit rule as

$$\frac{\partial V^*(0, \alpha)}{\partial \alpha} = \int_0^\infty \left[ \frac{\partial \overline{H}^*(t, \alpha)}{\partial \alpha} + \dot{\lambda}^*(t, \alpha)\frac{\partial k^*(t, \alpha)}{\partial \alpha} + \dot{\mu}^*(t, \alpha)\frac{\partial x^*(t, \alpha)}{\partial \alpha} \right] dt. \tag{A3}$$

By using the first-order conditions for $c$ and $g$ given by equations (9) and (10), the first term within the square bracket of equation (A3) can be written as (where the time indicator and the parameter $\alpha$ have been suppressed for notational convenience)

$$\frac{\partial \overline{H}^*}{\partial \alpha} = [u_x^* e^{-\theta t} - \mu^* \gamma]\frac{\partial x^*}{\partial \alpha} + \lambda^*\left[ f_k^*\frac{\partial k^*}{\partial \alpha} + f_\alpha^* - I_\alpha(\alpha) \right] \tag{A4}$$

where $u_x^* = u_x(c^*, x^*)$, $f_k^* = f_k(k^*, g^*, \alpha)$ and $f_\alpha^* = f_\alpha(k^*, g^*, \alpha)$. Finally substitution of the equations of motion for $\lambda^*(t, \alpha)$ and $\mu^*(t, \alpha)$, given by equations (11) and (12), into equation (A3) gives equation (34).

# NOTES

1.  Readers interested in more thorough literature reviews are referred to Aronsson, Johansson and Löfgren (1997), Weitzman (2003) and Aronsson, Löfgren and Backlund (2004).
2.  Other early theoretical contributions to the study of social accounting are, for example, Hartwick (1990) and Mäler (1991), who analysed Weitzman's welfare measure in the context of economies where environmental and/or natural resources are important components of the economic system. See also Aronsson and Löfgren (1996), who consider welfare measurement in an economy with human capital externalities.
3.  Welfare measurement problems in economies with heterogeneous consumers are addressed by, for example, Aronsson and Löfgren (1999b) and Aronsson (2008).
4.  This is seen by observing that $\partial H/\partial c = 0$, $\partial H/\partial g = 0$, $d\lambda/dt = -\partial H/\partial k$ and $d\mu/dt = -\partial H/\partial x$ from the necessary conditions set out above, while $\partial H/\partial \lambda = dk/dt$ and $\partial H/\partial \mu = dx/dt$.
5.  See Michel (1982).
6.  If the technology is not stationary, then equation (14) may no longer apply. Löfgren (1992) and Aronsson and Löfgren (1993) consider a technology where the production function can be written as $f(k(t), g(t), t)$, where the direct effect of time is interpretable in terms of disembodied technological change. With this seemingly innocent modification, they show that the welfare measure in equation (14) changes to read

    $$\theta V^*(t) = H^{c^*}(t) + \int_t^\infty \lambda^{c^*}(s) f_s(k^*(s), g^*(s), s) e^{-\theta(s-t)} ds$$

    where the second term on the right-hand side measures the present value of marginal technological change. In this case, it follows that (i) the current value Hamiltonian no longer constitutes an exact welfare measure, and (ii) information referring to time $t$ no longer suffices to measure welfare at time $t$. See also Kemp and Long (1982).
7.  The marginal value is measured as the marginal rate of substitution between pollution and private consumption at time $t$, that is, the marginal willingness to pay – in terms of lost private consumption – for a reduction in the stock of pollution at that particular time, *ceteris paribus*. For an early attempt to apply the willingness to pay technique in the context of social accounting, see Peskin and Peskin (1978).
8.  Weitzman (2001) and Li and Löfgren (2002) explain the role of the consumer surplus in social accounting in greater detail. See also Aronsson, Löfgren and Backlund (2004).
9.  In Weitzman's study, the extra term vanishes, as he uses Stratonovich integrals instead of Ito integrals.
10. For further study of cost–benefit analysis in dynamic general equilibrium models, see, for example, Aronsson, Johansson and Löfgren (1997), Dasgupta and Mäler (2000), Arrow, Dasgupta and Mäler (2003) and Li and Löfgren (2008).
11. Seierstad (1981), Léonard (1987), Caputo (1990) and LaFrance and Barney (1991) have all given important contributions by eliciting formal cost–benefit rules for parametric changes in optimal control models. See also Seierstad and Sydsaeter (1987).
12. By solving equation (3) for $x^0(t, \vartheta)$ defined above, we obtain

    $$x^0(t, \vartheta) = x(0)e^{-\gamma t} + \int_0^t g^0(s, \vartheta) e^{-\gamma(t-s)} ds,$$

    which means that

$$\frac{\partial x^0(t, \vartheta)}{\partial \vartheta} = \int_0^t \frac{\partial g^0(s, \vartheta)}{\partial \vartheta} e^{-\gamma(t-s)} ds < 0$$

since $\partial g^0(t, \vartheta)/\partial \vartheta < 0$ for all $t$.

13.  Although Weitzman (1976) did not attempt to examine genuine saving, it is, nevertheless, implicit in his study, as we need Weitzman's welfare measure (or an analogue thereof in the imperfect market economy) to relate the change in welfare over a short time interval to the genuine saving. Standard references for genuine saving are Pearce and Atkinson (1993) and Hamilton (1994, 1996).

14.  Both uninternalized externalities and disembodied technological change contribute to make the economic system non-autonomously time-dependent, which means that both of them give rise to forward-looking terms in the welfare and genuine saving measures, simply because time itself has a direct effect on welfare that does not vanish from the optimal choices made by consumers and firms.

15.  In fact, Asheim (1994) and Pezzey (1993) show that even if the genuine saving is non-negative at a particular point in time, the instantaneous consumption (or instantaneous utility more generally) may actually be declining.

# REFERENCES

Aronsson, T. (2008) Social Accounting and the Public Sector. *International Economics Review* **49**, 349–375.

Aronsson, T., Johansson, P.-O. and Löfgren, K.-G. (1997) *Welfare Measurement, Sustainability and Green National Accounting: A Growth Theoretical Approach.* Cheltenham: Edward Elgar Publishing Limited.

Aronsson, T. and Löfgren, K.-G. (1993) Welfare Consequences of Technological and Environmental Externalities in the Ramsey Growth Model. *Natural Resource Modeling* **7**, 1–14.

Aronsson, T. and Löfgren, K.-G. (1995) National Product Related Welfare Measures in the Presence of Technological Change, Externalities and Uncertainty. *Environmental and Resource Economics* **5**, 321–332.

Aronsson, T. and Löfgren, K.-G. (1996) Social Accounting and Welfare Measurement in a Growth Model with Human Capital. *Scandinavian Journal of Economics* **98**, 185–201.

Aronsson, T. and Löfgren, K.-G. (1999a) Pollution Tax Design and Green National Accounting. *European Economic Review* **43**, 1457–1474.

Aronsson, T. and Löfgren, K.-G. (1999b) Welfare Equivalent NNP under Distributional Objectives. *Economics Letters* **63**, 239–243.

Aronsson, T., Löfgren, K.-G. and Backlund, K. (2004) *Welfare Measurement in Imperfect Markets: A Growth Theoretical Approach.* Cheltenham: Edward Elgar Publishing Limited.

Arrow, K., Dasgupta, P. and Mäler, K.-G. (2003) Evaluating Projects and Assessing Sustainable Development in Imperfect Economies. *Environmental and Resource Economics* **26**, 647–685.

Asheim, G.B. (1994) Net National Product as an Indicator of Sustainability. *Scandinavian Journal of Economics* **96**, 257–265.

Asheim, G.B. (2007) Can NNP be Used for Welfare Comparisons? *Environment and Development Economics* **12**, 11–31.

Brock, W.A. (1977) A Polluted Golden Age. In Smith, V.L. (ed.) *Economics of Natural and Environmental Resources*, New York: Gordon and Breach.

Caputo, M.R. (1990) How to do Comparative Dynamics on the Back of an Envelope in Optimal Control Theory. *Journal of Economic Dynamics and Control* **14**, 655–683.

Dasgupta, P. and Mäler, K.-G. (2000) Net National Product, Wealth and Social Well-being. *Environment and Development Economics* **5**, 69–93.

Dixit, A., Hammond, P. and Hoel, M. (1980) On Hartwick's Rule for Regular Maximin Paths of Capital Accumulation. *Review of Economic Studies* **47**, 551–556.

Hamilton, K. (1994) Green Adjustments to GDP. *Resources Policy* **20**, 155–168.

Hamilton, K. (1996) Pollution and Pollution Abatement in the National Accounts. *Review of Income and Wealth* 42(1), 13–33.

Hartwick, J. (1977) Intergenerational Equity and the Investing of Rents from Exhaustible Resources. *American Economic Review* **66**, 972–974.

Hartwick, J. (1990) Natural Resources, National Accounting and Economic Depreciation. *Journal of Public Economics* **43**, 291–304.

Kemp, M.C. and Long, N.V. (1982) On the Evolution of Social Income in a Dynamic Economy: Variations on a Samuelsonian Theme. In Feiwell, G.R. (ed.) *Samuelson and Neoclassical Economics*, Boston, MA: Kluwer-Nijhoff.

LaFrance, J.T. and Barney, L.D. (1991), The Envelope Theorem in Dynamic Optimization. *Journal of Economic Dynamics Control* **15**, 355–385.

Léonard, D. (1987) Costate Variables Correctly Value Stocks at Each Instant. *Journal of Economic Dynamics and Control* **11**, 117–122.

Li, C.-Z. and Löfgren, K.-G. (2002) *On the Choice of Metrics in Dynamic Welfare Analysis: Utility versus Money Measures*. Umeå Economic Studies no. 590, Umeå: University of Umeå.

Li, C.-Z. and Löfgren, K.-G. (2008) Evaluating Projects in a Dynamic Economy: Some New Envelope Results. *German Economic Review* **9**, 1–16.

Löfgren, K.-G. (1992) Comments on C.R. Hulten, Accounting for the Wealth of Nations: The Net Gross Output Controversy and its Ramifications, *Scandinavian Journal of Economics*, 94 (suppl.), 25–28.

Mäler, K.-G. (1991) National Accounts and Environmental Resources. *Environmental and Resource Economics* **1**, 1–15.

Michel, P. (1982) On the Transversality Conditions in Infinite Horizon Optimal Control Problems. *Econometrica* **50**, 975–985.

Pearce, D.W. and Atkinson, G. (1993) Capital Theory and the Measurement of Sustainable Development: An Indicator of Weak Sustainability. *Ecological Economics* **8**, 103–108.

Peskin, H.M. and Peskin, J. (1978) The Valuation of Nonmarket Goods in Income Accounting. *The Review of Income and Wealth* **24**, 71–91.

Pezzey, J. (1993) *The Optimal Sustainable Depletion of Nonrenewable Resources*. London: University College, London.

Samuelson, P.A. (1961) The Evaluation of Social Income: Capital Formation and Wealth. In Lutz, F.A. and Hague, D. (eds) *The Theory of Capital*, New York: St. Martin's Press.

Seierstad, A. (1981) Derivatives and Subderivatives of the Optimal Value Function in Control Theory. Memorandum from Institute of Economics, University of Oslo.

Seierstad, A. and Sydsaeter, K. (1987) *Optimal Control Theory with Economic Applications*. Amsterdam: North-Holland.

United Nations, Commission of the European Communities, International Monetary Fund, Organisation for Economic Cooperation and Development and World Bank (2003), *Handbook for Integrated Environmental and Economic Accounting* New York: UN. Draft available at http://unstats.un.org/unsd/envaccounting/seea2003.pdf, accessed 16 May 2010.

Weitzman, M.L. (1976) On the Welfare Significance of National Product in a Dynamic Economy. *Quarterly Journal of Economics* **90**, 156–162.

Weitzman, M.L. (1998) *Comprehensive NDP and the Sustainability Equivalence Principle*. Cambridge, MA: Harvard University Press.

Weitzman, M.L. (2001) A Contribution to the Theory of Welfare Accounting. *Scandinavian Journal of Economics* **103**, 1–24.

Weitzman, M.L. (2003) *Income, Capital, and the Maximum Principle*. Cambridge, MA: Harvard University Press.

World Commission on Environment and Development (1987) *Our Common Future*. Oxford: Oxford University Press.

# 2 The money metrics problem in dynamic welfare analysis
## Karl-Gustaf Löfgren

## 1 INTRODUCTION

It has long been known that traditional GDP (Gross Domestic Product), or for that matter traditional NNP (Net National Product), are not exact money metrics welfare indicators. The textbook arguments behind this view contain some obvious reasons. One is related to the definition of net investments: the only information about net investments in the conventional NNP refers to physical, 'man made' capital. This means that changes in other important stocks, such as natural resource stocks, environmental stocks and the stock of human capital are not included. Another – although related – flaw in NNP is that external effects are not handled in an appropriate manner. When present, the market data on which NNP is based are flawed because prices do not reflect the true underlying scarcities. A third example is that traditional NNP, because it is an aggregate number, does not reveal how consumption opportunities are distributed between individuals or generations.[1]

However, all three of the above reasons can be assumed away by moving to an ideal situation, where it is assumed that all types of capital stocks are correctly priced and included in NNP. We can also assume that all consumption services produced by capital goods are included in the consumption vector, and that the corresponding correct rental prices are available. Moreover, we can exclude externalities, and duck distributional issues by assuming that an intertemporal welfare function supports the efficient market solution. Now, in what sense will an augmented NNP concept, comprehensive $NNP$ ($NNP^c$), which does not include the above listed flaws, be a welfare indicator? More specifically, will a higher $NNP^c$ indicate a welfare improvement? And will $NNP^c$ growth indicate a (local) welfare improvement? And, if not, what are the underlying reasons? Or even more important, what would a correct welfare indicator look like?

# 2 SOME OLD KEY RESULTS – THE VALUE PARADOX

To answer the array of questions posed above, we will start by moving to a classical and simple framework. The idea is to convey the intuition behind the answers to the reader in a simple manner. The discussion shows that the classical economists had important insights into matters that even today still cause some confusion.

At the end of the fourth chapter of book one in Adam Smith's celebrated volume *The Wealth of Nations* (1776), he brings up a valuation problem that is usually referred to as the value paradox.[2] He writes

> The word VALUE, it is to be observed, has two different meanings, and sometimes expresses the utility of some particular object, and sometimes the power of purchasing other goods which the possession of that object conveys. The one may be called 'value in use'; the other, 'value in exchange'. The things which have the greatest value in use have frequently little or no value in exchange; and, on the contrary, those which have the greatest value in exchange have frequently little or no value in use. Nothing is more useful than water: but it will purchase scarce anything; scarce anything can be had in exchange for it. A diamond on the contrary, has scarce any value in use; but a very great quantity of other goods may frequently be had in exchange for it.[3]

He is unable to credibly resolve the paradox – although he uses three chapters to convince the reader that it can be resolved by the components of the natural price, that is, essentially the notion that the long-run price is determined by the production costs. Some of the reasons behind the 'failure' are not far-fetched. Adam Smith was aware of supply and demand without being able to produce anything fresh about the fundamental ideas upon which these concepts rest. He was not aware of the idea of modelling the total utility value of consumption in terms of a utility function, and the related idea of assuming that the utility function exhibits a declining marginal utility. To the late scholastic tradition represented by, for example, Ferdinando Galiani (1750/1977) the water and diamond paradox would not have represented any serious difficulty.[4] The scholastics were used to discussing the relationship between utility, scarcity and relative value. Galiani may have claimed that the high total value of water is counteracted by its lack of scarcity, while the reverse is true for diamonds. In other words, the high relative price of diamonds in relation to the price of water can be explained by an extremely high scarcity of diamonds and an extremely low scarcity of water. Although his formal analysis does not make sense in all respects, it is clear that he came close to discovering a decreasing marginal utility. He writes:[5] 'there is nothing more useless than bread for one who is sated'.

Adam Smith wrote his treatise 60–80 years ahead of Cournot (1838), Dupuit (1844) and Gossen (1854), who founded the modern utilitarian framework in economics. His distinction between value-in-use and value-in-exchange nevertheless contain a non-trivial insight, which is fundamental for the answer to the questions under consideration. In fact, he touched upon the answer to most of the questions by pointing out that the value-in-use of a good – its contribution to total welfare – is not the same thing as its value-in-exchange.

In this survey we will try to consider what a perfect welfare indicator looks like in a multi-sector dynamic growth model, and under what conditions $NNP^c$ will be related to this concept in a meaningful way; that is, under what conditions $NNP^c$ will work as well. More specifically we will try to answer the following questions:

1. What does the correct welfare dynamic welfare indicator look like?
2. Under what circumstances can intertemporal welfare be measured and ranked in a money metric?
3. Under what conditions will an increase in $NNP^c$ indicate a welfare improvement?
4. Under what conditions will $NNP^c$ growth indicate a local welfare improvement?
5. If the conditions we are looking for in (3) and (4) do not exist, what are the underlying reasons, and what does a local welfare indicator look like?

## 3   THE SMITH AND DUPUIT ANSWERS

We will start by using the insights provided by, among others, Adam Smith and later by Jules Dupuit to give intuitive but essentially correct solutions to the above questions. Let us start from an extended 'dynamic' version of the standard supply and demand diagram. In Figure 2.1, the first quadrant contains the standard demand curve. For simplicity, and to highlight the particular structure of the problem, we have assumed that the volumes consumed and invested are given as well as the prices for consumer and investment goods.

We can interpret the demand curve as either measured in utility (marginal utility) or in a money metrics, that is, we assume that the marginal utility is equal to the marginal utility of money times the nominal prices of goods. Although Adam Smith did not use any diagrams, it is reasonable to connect the rectangular area $PC$ with the term value-in-exchange, and the rectangular area plus the triangular area CS with the term value-in-

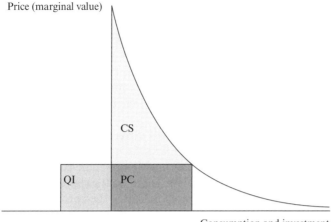

*Figure 2.1    A dynamic version of the value-in-exchange and value-in-use*

use. This is the interpretation made by Dupuit (1844), who wrote: 'Doctor Smith, who recognizes two values in an object – *its value-in-use*, which is its utility as we understand, the value to him who has a need to consume the product; and its *value-in-exchange,* which is the value of the same product to him who has a need to sell it.'[6]

The value-in-exchange is also what the consumer has to pay in terms of utility in order to consume the good. To interpret the diagram as *NNP^c*, we have added net investment in the second quadrant. As the reader can see from the diagram, the price (the marginal value) of the investment good coincides with the price of the consumption good. This will be the case in a one-good dynamic economy along an optimal path, where the consumption good can also be used for investment purposes. In a dynamic context, the current value of investment represents what net investment will yield in utility in terms of future consumption goods. In particular, along an efficient path, consumption and future consumption (investment) should be allocated so that the marginal utilities of future and present consumption coincide. In Figure 2.1, this insight has been used to illustrate a dynamic version of the concept value-in-use, which consequently contains the value of net investment.

Hence, if we use the intuition conveyed by the Smith-Dupuit framework to guess how welfare should be measured in a first-best market economy, an increase in *NNP^c* will, in general, not indicate a welfare improvement. The value-in-exchange does not measure total utility. It measures the value of total consumption and total net investment evaluated at the marginal value of consumption.

Although Smith did not recognize marginal utility or the consumer surplus, his idea – inspired by the value paradox – about the distinction between value-in-exchange and value-in-use can, together with Dupuit's insights (even diagrams) on marginal utility and the consumer surplus, help us to give a non-formal answer to most questions listed earlier. In particular, neither $NNP^c$, nor its growth, seem to be perfect welfare indicators.[7] The reason is that $NNP^c$ is only one component of value-in use; consumer surplus is the other.

From Figure 2.1, which formally only covers a one-good economy, it is clear that comprehensive (utility) NNP = $PC+QI$ is linear in consumption and net investment and, in general, unable to handle consumer surpluses – the triangle $CS$. An informed guess, based on the classical ideas, is therefore that $NNP^c$ and additional terms reflecting the consumer surpluses in all markets will be the basis for both a global and a local welfare indicator in a dynamic economy. It is, however, important to note that total value in a utility metrics cannot be compared at two different times, since utility cannot be measured. Moreover, even if we can write the value-in-use as a product between the marginal utility of income and a money-metrics measure of value-in-use, it cannot be ranked in the money metrics at two different times, since the marginal utility of income is not necessarily constant over time. This is the money-metrics problem in dynamic welfare analysis.

## 4    THE MODERN KEY RESULTS – WEITZMAN'S THEOREM

There is a classical result in Weitzman (1976) on the welfare significance of the Net National Product in a dynamic economy. It tells us that in a Ramsey growth model with a utility function that coincides with an aggregate consumption good and a comprehensive set of capital goods, $NNP^c$ is proportional to future utility along the first-best growth path. The factor of proportionality is the utility interest rate (the rate of time preference). This may sound like good news for $NNP^c$ as a welfare indicator, but Weitzman uses a 'trick' by choosing a linear homogeneous utility function that creates no consumer surplus.[8] This way of presenting the result is strongly suggestive, but Weitzman is, of course, aware of the fact that it does not hold in a more general context. To see this, it is enough to introduce a more general utility function.

Weitzman's result can be expressed in a utility metrics by saying that the current value Hamiltonian of the optimal control problem, that is, the current value of the instantaneous utility function plus the current utility value of the net investment vector, measured along an optimal path, is directly proportional to the discounted sum of future utility. The intuition is that at each instant in time, consumption is allocated such that the marginal utility of consumption equals what a unit of investment would yield in terms of utility from future consumption. Moreover, due to a non-arbitrage condition (the Euler condition) on the value of future investment, it is not profitable to move investment from one point in time to another. Given a constant utility discount rate, integrating the differential equation for the development of the Hamiltonian along an optimal path, given some regularity conditions, yields the result.

This general version of Weitzman's theorem is not practical, since we cannot observe utility. Later researchers in the comprehensive NNP and green accounting tradition, such as Hartwick (1990) and Mäler (1991), and many others, including the author of this paper, have partly circumvented this problem by linearizing the Hamiltonian (the utility function) and dividing by the marginal utility of the consumption good,[9] thereby generating NNP-like linear money metric indexes which have been referred to as Green NNP. This is, of course, an approximation of the true money value of the total utility, and, under a strictly concave utility function, it may be a bad approximation. More importantly, even if one gets rid of the consumer surplus term, the money metrics index cannot be used to compare comprehensive money metrics NNP at two different points in time, since the marginal utility of income changes over time.

The first conclusion from the modern approach is that $NNP^c$ is not a welfare indicator in the sense that we can conclude that an increase (decrease) in comprehensive NNP will mean an increase (decrease) in welfare. It is not quite clear what can be said about $NNP^c$ growth as a local welfare indicator, but the first conclusion sounds like bad news.

## 5 AN EXACT MONEY METRICS WELFARE INDICATOR

Translated into a Ramsey model with $n$ consumption goods and $m$ capital goods, Weitzman's result tells us that

$$H^*(t) = u(\mathbf{c}^*(t)) + \lambda^*(t)\mathbf{i}^*(t) = \theta \int_t^\infty u(\mathbf{c}^*(s))e^{-\theta(s-t)}ds = \theta W^*(t, \mathbf{k}_t)) \quad (1)$$

In other words, the current value Hamiltonian at time $t$ is proportional to the sum of future utility measured along the first-best path of the economy (here denoted by the top index *) or the optimal value function $W^*$. The consumption vector $\mathbf{c}(t) = [c_1(t), \ldots, c_n(t)]$ and the net investment vector $\mathbf{i}(t) = [i_1(t), \ldots, i_m(t)] = \dot{\mathbf{k}}(t)$ are comprehensive in the sense that they contain all consumer and investment goods that are relevant for the consumptive and productive capacity of the economy. $\mathbf{k}(t) = [k_1(t), k_2(t), \ldots, k_m(t)]$ is the vector of capital stocks. $\mathbf{k}_t$ denotes the initial endowment of capital at time $t$. The factor of proportionality, $\theta$, is the utility discount rate, $u(\mathbf{c}^*(t))$ is the instantaneous utility function, and $\lambda^*(t)\mathbf{i}^*(\mathbf{t})$ denotes the vector product of the future utility value of investments, $\lambda^*(t)$, and the vector of net investments, $\mathbf{i}^*(\mathbf{t})$. This means that all the entities in equation (1) are measured in utility. In other words, the Hamiltionian or Utility $NNP^c$, is a perfect welfare indicator in a utility metrics. Moreover, growth in Utility $NNP^c$ is the corresponding perfect local welfare indicator.[10]

Since a lot of the literature after Weitzman (1976) has stayed in a non-measurable utility metrics or as a linear approximation of the Hamiltonian (the utility function), one may wonder what the problems are of moving into a money metrics. To see this we rewrite the instantaneous utility function in the following manner:

$$u(\mathbf{c}^*(t)) = \int_0^{\mathbf{c}^*(t)} u_c(\mathbf{c})d\mathbf{c} = \lambda^m(t)\left[\mathbf{p}^*(t)\mathbf{c}^*(\mathbf{p}^*(t)) + \int_{p^*(t)}^{\bar{p}} \mathbf{c}^*(\mathbf{p})d\mathbf{p}\right] \quad (2)$$

The first equality in equation (2) follows immediately from Figure 2.1 by interpreting the demand curve in a utility metrics as the marginal utility of consumption, $u_c(\mathbf{c})$. The vector integral denotes the sum of the vector of marginal utilities from zero to the optimal consumption vector, that is, it corresponds to the value-in-use. In the last component of the equation, $\lambda^m(t)$ is the marginal utility of money at time $t$, $\mathbf{p}^*(t)$ denotes the price vector that supports the optimal path, and $\mathbf{c}^*(\mathbf{p}^*(t))$ is the demand vector at time $t$. The latter does not contain any income arguments that typically generate 'integrability problems', that is, the value of the (total) consumer surplus will not depend on the integration (price) path. The reason is that the utility function in the Ramsey growth model is additively separable over time. Hence, there are no income effects, and the consumer surplus is well defined.

The second equality is obtained after some technicalities, changing integration variables by setting $d\mathbf{c} = \frac{d\mathbf{c}}{d\mathbf{p}}d\mathbf{p}$ and partially integrating the resulting expression. This means, among other things, that $\bar{p}$ is the choke of price vector, that is, $\mathbf{c}(\bar{\mathbf{p}}) = \mathbf{0}$. The first term on the right-hand side of (2) corresponds to the utility cost of consumption and the second one to the utility value of the consumer surpluses in the economy. However, since the marginal utility of money is not necessarily constant over time, equation (2) cannot be used to transform the right-hand side of equation (1) into a money metrics. The marginal utility of money cannot be moved outside the integral in equation (1), that is, it would remain in a utility metrics. Since the right-hand side can only be ranked in a utility metrics, this will of course also hold for the left-hand side of the equation. A way out would be to assume that the marginal utility of income is constant over time. This is, however, typically not true. By using the Euler equations for the optimization problem, one can show that that the marginal utility of money follows the differential equation[11]

$$\lambda^m(t) = \lambda^m(t_0) e^{(\theta(t - t_0) - \int_{t_0}^t R(\tau)d\tau)}$$

(3)

Here $R(\tau)$ is the nominal interest rate. The key to a money metrics transformation of equation (1) was provided by Weitzman (2001), who introduced the following price index formula:

$$\pi(t) = \frac{\mathbf{p}(t; \mathbf{c})\mathbf{c}}{\mathbf{p}(t_0; \mathbf{c})\mathbf{c}}$$

(4)

On the left-hand side, $\pi$ depends only on time, and indicates that the index is independent of the market basket[12] – 'benchmark independent'. Formally, this means that

$$\lambda^m(t_0) = \pi(t)\lambda^m(t)$$

(5)

The interpretation of the price vectors is that $\mathbf{p}(t, \mathbf{c})$ *and* $\mathbf{p}(t_0, \mathbf{c})$ denote the 'imputed' market clearing prices that would be observed at the two points in time if the market basket of goods being consumed along an optimal path in the economy are $\mathbf{c}$; the vector $\mathbf{p}(t_0, \mathbf{c})$ is also the actual price vector at $t_0$. The name 'ideal measure' is chosen by Weitzman (2001) to denote the direction toward which the formulators of a CPI- or PPP-type index strive when statisticians try to select a representative market basket straddling two economies at a given point in time, or the same economy at two different points in time. Equations (3) and (5) mean that the index can be written

$$\pi(t) = \lambda^m(t_0)/\lambda^m(t) = e^{\int_{t_0}^t R(\tau)d\tau - \theta(t - t_0)}$$

(6)

In other words, since a series of nominal interest rates are typically observable, the index is identified if one can come up with a measure of the utility discount factor $\theta$. The latter is not an easy task, but shows that observability is 'around the corner'. We can now rescale the left-hand side of equation (1) to read

$$H_r^*(t) = \lambda^m(t)\pi(t)\left[\frac{y^*(t) + cs^*(t)}{\pi(t)}\right] = \lambda^m(t_0)[y_r^*(t) + cs_r^*(t)] \qquad (7)$$

where $y_r^*(t) = y^*(t)/\pi(t) = \mathbf{p}_r^*(t)\mathbf{c}^*(t) + \mathbf{q}_r^*(t)\mathbf{i}^*(t)$ is the real comprehensive NNP and $cs_r^*(t) = cs^*(t)/\pi(t)$ the consumer surplus, both expressed in real terms (in the prices of period $t_0$). The real prices for consumer and investment goods are $p_r^*(t) = p^*(t)/\pi(t)$ and $q_r^*(t) = q^*(t)/\pi(t)$, respectively. The expression in (7) has been called the Generalized Comprehensive NNP (GCNNP).[13] A similar operation can now be executed on the right hand side of equation (1), and one ends up with the following money metrics results after putting the constant marginal utility of money at the base year equal to one:

**Theorem 1 (Weitzman (2001) and Li and Löfgren (2002)):** *The Generalized Comprehensive (Green) Net National Product (GCNNP) in (7) is a stationary equivalent of the future value of consumption plus the consumer surplus in real terms such that*

$$\int_t^\infty H_r^*(t)\exp(-\theta(s - t))\,ds$$

$$= \int_t^\infty \left\{\mathbf{p}_r^*(s)\mathbf{c}^*(s) + \int_{\mathbf{p}_r^*(s)}^{\bar{\mathbf{p}}_r}\mathbf{d}_0(p_r)\,d\mathbf{p}_r\right\}\exp(-\theta(s - t))\,ds$$

*or equivalently*

$$H_r^*(t) = \theta M_r^*(t),$$

*where*

$$M_r^*(t) = \int_t^\infty \left[\mathbf{p}_r^*(s)\mathbf{c}^*(s) + \int_{\mathbf{p}_r^*(s)}^{\bar{\mathbf{p}}_r}\mathbf{d}_0(p_r)\,d\mathbf{p}_r\right]\exp(-\theta(s - t))\,ds$$

*is interpreted as generalized welfare (wealth) in real terms.*

*Remark: The theorem is fundamentally due to Weitzman. He used his index idea to compare two economies at a given point in time, while Li and Löfgren used his invention to compare the same economy at two points in time.*

Again returning to Smith and Dupuit, $M_r^*(t)$ can also be interpreted as the total current value-in-use in real money terms. In the same spirit, we may call GCNNP the instantaneous value-in-use in real money terms. The theorem tells us that there is a direct proportionality between the two money metrics value-in-use concepts, and that both are correct welfare indicators under first-best conditions. It also tells us that $NNP^c$ can only be a welfare indicator under special circumstances. One special case emerges if the utility function is linearly homogeneous, that is, when doubling consumption doubles utility. A special 'special' case is when the utility function is linear homogeneous, as in Weitzman's original paper.

# 6 GROWTH AND WELFARE[14]

Given the theorem, it should be obvious that growth in $NNP^c$ cannot indicate a local welfare improvement. To see exactly why it fails to do so, we differentiate equation (7) ($\lambda^m(t_0) = 1$) with respect to time to get

$$\dot{H}_r^*(t) = \dot{y}_r^*(t) + c\dot{s}_r^*(t) = \dot{y}_r^*(t) - \dot{\mathbf{p}}_r^* \mathbf{c}^*(t), \tag{8}$$

where the first term on the right-hand side represents growth in real Green NNP. The second term represents the growth in consumer surplus at time $t$. Obviously, as long as the latter term is not zero, we cannot conclude that $NNP^c$ growth, $\dot{y}_r^*(t) > 0$, indicates a local welfare improvement. The reason for its appearance is that changes in relative prices will take place along the endogenously determined growth path of the economy, and change the value of the consumer surplus.

An idea of how to make comprehensive NNP growth a welfare indicator is to condition growth on some other aspect of the economy at the time of measurement. In a seminal paper, Asheim and Weitzman (2001) show that if $NNP^c$ is deflated by a Divisa consumer price index, which means that the last term in equation (8) becomes zero through the properties of this consumer price index, then growth in Green NNP can serve as a welfare indicator provided that the real interest rate is positive.[15] Li and Löfgren (2006a) show that growth in comprehensive NNP at constant prices (measured at time $t$) indicates a welfare improvement provided that the 'overall marginal rate of return of investment' is positive. The latter concept corresponds to the weighted average of the own-rates of return to capital goods using the corresponding net investment values as weights. The result holds independently of the price index, and the sign of the overall rate of return is observable.[16]

The key to these results is that there exists a simple local welfare criterion that always works, namely genuine saving.[17] To see this, we introduce the optimal value function for the optimal control problem, which can be written

$$W(t, \mathbf{k}_t) = \int_t^\infty u(\mathbf{c}^*(s)) e^{-\theta(s-t)} ds$$

(9)

$$k(t) = k_t.$$

Differentiating with respect to time (the lower integration limit) and using equation (1) yields

$$\dot{W}(t) = -u(\mathbf{c}^*(t)) + \theta W(t, \mathbf{k}(t)) = -u(\mathbf{c}^*(t)) + H^*(t) = \lambda(t)\mathbf{i}^*(t)$$

$$= \lambda^m(t)[\mathbf{q}^*(t)\mathbf{i}^*(t)],$$

(10)

that is, genuine saving coincides with the sum of comprehensive net investment multiplied by the marginal utility of money. Note that in terms of Figure 2.1, we have taken value-in-use in consumption away from total value (the area under the marginal utility curve), and we are left with net investment in the second quadrant. Positive net investment along an optimal path is by definition productive, and hence welfare increases locally.

The overall rate return on investment is defined as

$$\rho(t) = R(t) - \dot{\mathbf{q}}^*(t)\mathbf{i}(t)/\mathbf{q}^*(t)\mathbf{i}^*(t) = \dot{y}^*(t)[\mathbf{q}^*(t)\mathbf{i}^*(t)]^{-1}$$

(11)

Here $\dot{y}(t)$ is growth in NNP measured in constant consumption and investment prices at time $t$. Clearly, $\rho(t) > 0$, and $\dot{y}(t) > 0$ implies that genuine saving is positive, indicating a local welfare improvement.

There is, however, a situation where comprehensive NNP growth breaks down as a welfare indicator, independently of any (non-trivial) conditioning. Say that we are dealing with a spaceship economy[18] in which the resource stock dynamics is given by the differential equation $\dot{x}(t) = -c(t)$, with the limited food supply, $x(0) = x_0$, at time zero. The maximized current value Hamiltonian can be written

$$H^*(t) = u(c^*(t)) - \lambda^{c*}(t)c^*(t)$$

(12)

Linearizing by taking the first differential of the utility function and using the first-order conditions for an optimal path, $u_c(c^*(t)) = \lambda^c(t)$, means that we can approximate the Hamiltonian and, hence, future welfare along the optimal path by the expression

$$H^{c*}(t) \approx u_c(c^*(t))c^*(t) - \lambda^{c*}c^*(t) = \lambda^{m*}(t)p^*(t)[c^*(t) - c^*(t)] \equiv 0 \tag{13}$$

In other words, NNP defined as the value of consumption plus net investment, is identically zero for the spaceship economy, independently of the size of the packed lunch, $x_0$. This means that the rate of return concept defined in equation (11) breaks down as a welfare indicator, since $NNP^c$ growth is identically zero, and hence $\rho \equiv 0$.

Genuine saving tells us that local welfare is decreasing over time. The results in equation (7) and the theorem are of course still valid, and it is straightforward to show that the size of packed lunch matters for welfare, that is, the value of the consumer surplus is positive, but it decreases over time.[19]

## 7 PROPERLY INDEXED $NNP^c$ IS A PERFECT WELFARE INDICATOR[20]

There is, however, an additional possibility for deriving a comprehensive NNP measure that is a perfect welfare indicator. The idea emerges from the classical compensatory index theory that was developed by Konüs (1924), and it uses Weitzman's benchmark independent index that was introduced above to make the Hamiltonian stationary over time. Conditional on the market prices along the first-best path of the economy, one can represent consumer choice at time t as the solution to the following optimization problem

$$\max_{[\mathbf{c}(t), \kappa(t)]} H(t) = u(\mathbf{c}(t)) + \lambda^m(t)\kappa(t) \tag{14}$$

subject to

$$\mathbf{p}(t)\mathbf{c}(t) + \kappa(t) = y(t) \tag{15}$$

where $\kappa(t) = \mathbf{q}(t)\mathbf{i}(t)$ is the total aggregate money value of net investments in the $m$ capital stocks. The marginal utility of money (income) is treated as a constant during the period, as is $NNP^c$, $y(t)$. Since the objective function in (14) is quasi-linear, the solution for current consumption is $\mathbf{c}(t) = \mathbf{d}(\mathbf{p}(t), \lambda^m(t))$, and $\mathbf{d}(\cdot)$ is the $m$-dimensional vector of demand functions. The corresponding net investment value is $\kappa(t) = y(t) - \mathbf{p}(t)\mathbf{c}(t)$. We now define an expenditure function

$$E(\mathbf{p}(t), \lambda^m(t), H(t)) = \min_{\mathbf{c}(t), \kappa(t)} [\mathbf{p}(t)\mathbf{c}(t) + \kappa(t)]. \tag{16}$$

The current value Hamiltonian measures current utility that is obtained from current consumption plus future utility that is obtained from net investment today, and we know from Weitzman's theorem that, except for a constant, it is an exact measure of future utility along the first-best path. Hence, it can in principle be used as a local welfare indicator. There is, however, a remaining problem with the utility function in equation (14), since the preference map will change with changes in the marginal utility of income. With the help of Weitzman's price index above, the static-like problem in (14) and (15) can be rewritten as

$$\max_{[\mathbf{c}(t),\, \overline{\kappa}(t)]} H(t) = u(\mathbf{c}(t)) + \lambda^m(t_0)\overline{\kappa}(t) \tag{17}$$

subject to

$$\overline{\mathbf{p}}(t)\mathbf{c}(t) + \overline{\kappa}(t) = \overline{y}(t) \tag{18}$$

where $\overline{\kappa}(t) = \kappa(t)/\pi^0(t)$ denotes the normalized value of investment, $\overline{\mathbf{p}}(t) = \mathbf{p}(t)/\pi^0(t)$ the normalized consumption prices, and $\overline{y}(t)$ the normalized income (comprehensive NNP) at time $t$. With such a normalization, the price of investment $\overline{\kappa}(t)$ is made constant at the reference level $\lambda(t_0)$, and thus the current-value Hamiltonian functional form (17) becomes a stationary 'generalized utility function' over time. It now becomes possible to define an intertemporal indifference map over the $n+1$-dimensional space $(\mathbf{c}(t), \overline{\kappa}(t))$ by $H(\mathbf{c}(t), \overline{\kappa}(t)) = H^0$.

First, let us consider the base-year problem at time $t_0$, that is, maximizing the current-value Hamiltonian $H(t_0) = u(\mathbf{c}(t_0)) + \lambda^m(t_0)\overline{\kappa}(t_0)$ under the static-like budget constraint $\overline{\mathbf{p}}(t_0)\mathbf{c}(t_0) + \overline{\kappa}(t_0) = \overline{y}_0$. Let $(\mathbf{c}^0, \overline{\kappa}^0)$ denote the optimal solution, then the maximized current-value Hamiltonian can be expressed by $\hat{H}^0 = u(\mathbf{c}^0) + \lambda^m(t_0)\overline{\kappa}^0$ and the expenditure by $\overline{y}_0 = \overline{\mathbf{p}}(t_0)\mathbf{c}^0 + \overline{\kappa}^0$. Now, our question is this: given a price vector $(\overline{\mathbf{p}}(t), \lambda^m(t_0))$ for consumption and normalized investment at any time $t$, what is the minimum expenditure $\overline{y}_t$, which can support a current-value Hamiltonian at the same level as $\hat{H}^0$? Following Konüs (1924), we can express the necessary expenditure level by

$$\overline{y}_t = E(\overline{\mathbf{p}}(t), \lambda^m(t_0), \hat{H}^0) \tag{19}$$

where $\mathbf{c}^c$ and $\overline{\kappa}^c$ denote the compensating demand for consumption and investment such that $H(\mathbf{c}^c, \overline{\kappa}^c) = \hat{H}^0$. With these devices, we can now define the Hamilton-Konüs-dynamic price index by

$$\pi(t) = \frac{\overline{y}_t}{\overline{y}_0} = \frac{\overline{\mathbf{p}}(t)\mathbf{c}^c + \overline{\kappa}^c}{\overline{\mathbf{p}}(t_0)\mathbf{c}^0 + \overline{\kappa}^0}, \tag{20}$$

which can be written as

$$\pi(t) = \alpha\pi_c(t) + (1 - \alpha)\pi_i(t) \qquad (20a)$$

where

$$\alpha = \frac{\bar{\mathbf{p}}(t_0)\mathbf{c}^0}{\bar{\mathbf{p}}(t_0)\mathbf{c}^0 + \bar{\kappa}^0}$$

and

$$1 - \alpha = \frac{\bar{\kappa}^0}{\bar{\mathbf{p}}(t_0)\mathbf{c}^0 + \bar{\kappa}^0}$$

are the weights attached to the consumer price index

$$\pi_c = \frac{\bar{\mathbf{p}}(t)\mathbf{c}^c}{\bar{\mathbf{p}}(t_0)\mathbf{c}^0}$$

and the investment price index

$$\pi_i = \frac{\bar{\kappa}^c}{\bar{\kappa}^0} = \frac{\bar{\mathbf{q}}(t)\mathbf{i}^c}{\bar{\mathbf{q}}(t_0)\mathbf{i}^0}.$$

Thus, the dynamic price index is a weighted average of two static-like indexes, one for current consumption and the other for investment related to the value of future consumption.[21]

The dynamic price index defined in (20) will prove valuable for welfare comparisons over time. Consider the following two situations, one with (normalized) prices $\bar{\mathbf{p}}(t_0)$, $\bar{\mathbf{q}}(t_0)$ and national income (or comprehensive NNP) $\bar{y}_0$ at time $t_0$, and the other with (normalized) prices $\bar{\mathbf{p}}(t)$, $\bar{\mathbf{q}}(t)$ and national income (or comprehensive NNP) $\bar{y}(t)$ at any other time $t$. To compare the intertemporal welfare between the two situations, we can now make use of the dynamic price index defined in (20) to arrive at a double-indexed real $NNP^c$ measure. Let $\bar{y}_r(t) = \bar{y}(t)/\pi(t)$ be the deflated real income at time $t$, then the following claim is true:

**Proposition 1:** *When deflated by the composite dynamic price index $\Pi(t) = \pi^0(t)\pi(t)$, the real comprehensive NNP, $\bar{y}_r(t) = y(t)/\Pi(t) = \bar{y}(t)/\pi(t)$ is a perfect welfare indicator. If $\bar{y}_r(t) > \bar{y}_r(t_0)$, intertemporal welfare at time t is higher than at time $t_0$; and if $\bar{y}_r(t) < \bar{y}_r(t_0)$, the intertemporal welfare at time t is lower than at time $t_0$.*

The reason is straightforward: $\bar{y}_r(t) > \bar{y}_r(t_0)$ implies that $\bar{y}(t) > \pi(t)\bar{y}_0 = \bar{y}_t$, that is, the normalized income at time $t$ is greater than the minimum expenditure required to reach the reference welfare level $\hat{H}^0$. Since marginal utility of income is given by $\lambda^m(t_0) > 0$, the excess income $\bar{y}(t) - \bar{y}_t > 0$ also implies a higher welfare level at time $t$ than at time $t_0$.

## 8    THE IMPERFECT MARKET CASE[22]

What do imperfect markets do to Weitzman's theorem, and how can money metrics measures be designed under market imperfections? The answers to these questions are important, since under first-best, green accounting is, in a narrow sense, rather meaningless. If we live in the best of all worlds, why should we care to measure aggregate income and welfare?

The first to handle the imperfect market topic (a non-autonomous time dependence) in a Ramsey type of problem were Kemp and Long (1982). They showed that market imperfections introduce a fundamental time dependence that introduces extra terms in equation (1) above.[23]

The area is surveyed by Aronsson and Löfgren (1998), and revisited by Dasgupta (2001) and Arrow, Dasgupta and Mäler (2003). Working exclusively in a utility metrics, Aronsson et al. (2004) measure the relative welfare losses (in comparison to first best) resulting from different market imperfections, which in the model turn out to be modest.

Clearly, imperfect market values must also be transferred into a money metrics to obtain consistent rankings over time. There are at least three complications. Firstly, market imperfections add a non-autonomous time dependence that makes the utility from a given consumption vector a function of the magnitude of the imperfections. Secondly, the marginal utility of income will also change over time, implying that the relationship between monetary and utility measures will change over time through a changed yardstick. This makes exact money metrics comparisons over time difficult. Finally, imperfections are not priced or incorrectly priced.

The first two problems should be taken care of simultaneously. We will assume that the instantaneous utility function is separable into a component that contains arguments generating externalities,[24] and a component consisting of 'standard' consumption goods. We will in addition use Weitzman's ideal index formula to normalize prices. The third problem will be solved by assuming that the required marginal values can be elicited by empirical methods (for example willingness to pay studies), that is, the problem is essentially assumed away.

### 8.1    A Multi-Sector Growth Model with Externalities

The model used here is a hybrid of the Weitzman (1976, 2001) multi-sector growth model and the Brock (1977) growth model with externalities. Both models have the standard Ramsey growth theory as the core, but with extensions along different directions. While Weitzman generalized the basic model to accommodate for heterogeneous goods and services in a first-best setting, Brock developed it with an environmental externality in terms of a pollution stock. The first model set-up was used above, while the combined model with stock externalities added to the instantaneous utility function will be used here. The instantaneous utility function is written

$$u(\mathbf{c}(t), \mathbf{x}(t)) = \tilde{u}(\mathbf{c}(t)) + v(\mathbf{x}(t)) \tag{21}$$

where $x(t) = (x_1(t), \ldots, x_k(t))$ is a $k$-dimensional vector of stock externalities. The instantaneous utility function satisfies the usual regularity conditions, that is, it is concave, increasing in $\mathbf{c}(t)$, and in stocks generating positive externalities. It is decreasing in stocks yielding negative externalities. The net investment vector of capital good is denoted $\mathbf{i_k}(t) = \dot{\mathbf{k}}(t)$, and the corresponding net investment vector for stock externalities $\mathbf{i_x}(t) = \dot{\mathbf{x}}(t)$, and $\mathbf{i}(t) = (\mathbf{i_k}(t), \mathbf{i_x}(t))$. The optimal value function of the first-best problem can be written

$$W^*(t, \mathbf{k}_t, \mathbf{x}_t)) = \underset{\mathbf{c}(t), \mathbf{i_k}(t), \mathbf{i_x}(t)}{Max} \int_t^\infty u(\mathbf{c}(s), \mathbf{x}(s)) \exp[(-\theta(s - t)] ds \tag{22}$$

subject to $\mathbf{c}(t), \mathbf{i}(t), \mathbf{k}(t), \mathbf{x}(t) \in A$, where $A$ is a convex production possibility set, and $\mathbf{k}(t) = \mathbf{k}_\tau$ and $\mathbf{x}(t) = \mathbf{x}_\tau$ are the initial conditions for the stocks. This problem is identical to the first-best problem that was investigated above, except for the new stocks that have been added. Here we are interested in a problem where the externalities remain uninternalized. The objective is to maximize the intertemporal welfare subject to the initial conditions $\mathbf{k}(t) = \mathbf{k}_t$, $\mathbf{x}(t) = \mathbf{x}_t$, the stock dynamics $\dot{\mathbf{k}}(t) = \mathbf{i_k}(t)$, and the above feasibility constraint, but with no regard to the dynamics of stock externalities $\dot{\mathbf{x}}(t) = \mathbf{i_x}(t)$. Obviously the resulting sequence $\{\mathbf{c}^0(s), \mathbf{i_k^0}(s), \mathbf{k}^0(s)\}_t^\infty$ will be suboptimal, since the externality sequence $\mathbf{i_x^0}(t), \mathbf{x}^0(t)$ is imposed rather than optimized. The underlying (pseudo) current value Hamiltonian can still be expressed in a similar form

$$H^0(t) = u(\mathbf{c}^0(t), \mathbf{x}^0(t)) + \lambda_k^0(t) \mathbf{i_k^0}(t). \tag{23}$$

Where $\lambda_k^0(t)$ satisfies the Euler equations

$$\dot{\lambda}_k^0(t) - \theta\lambda_k^0(t) = -\frac{\partial H^0}{\partial \mathbf{k}(t)}. \tag{24}$$

But the proportionality relationship between $H^0(t)$, and the optimal value function $W^0(t, \mathbf{k}_t, \mathbf{x}_t)$ will no longer hold. Consider equation (25) below:[25]

$$\widetilde{H}^0(t) = H^0(t) + \int_t^\infty \mathbf{v}_x(s)\dot{\mathbf{x}}(s)e^{-\theta(s-t)}ds = \theta W^0(t, \mathbf{k}(t), \mathbf{x}(t)) \quad (25)$$

A close examination reveals that the integral 1 in equation (25) measures the current value of the externality along the optimal path. The shadow value of an extra unit of emission at time $t$ is given by the partial derivative of the imperfect value function with respect to the initial endowment at time $t$

$$\lambda_x^0(t) = \frac{\partial W^0(\mathbf{k}_t, \mathbf{x}_t, t)}{\partial \mathbf{x}_t} \quad (26)$$

with respect to the initial endowment at time $t$. Arrow et al. (2003), have shown that for a special 'non-optimal autonomous problem' generated by a forward-looking rule determined by a time-autonomous path (an alpha rule) for consumption in a standard Ramsey problem, shadow prices can be backed out to produce an expression $\lambda_{kx}^a(t)\dot{\mathbf{k}}_{kx}^a(t) = \lambda_k^a(t)\mathbf{i}_k(t) + \lambda_x^a(t)\mathbf{i}_x(t)$, which generalizes Weitzman's theorem. They also produce Euler-like equations for the time derivative of the vector of accounting prices, that is, an equation for $\dot{\lambda}_x^a(t)$ along the market solution path $\{\mathbf{c}^a(s,\alpha), \mathbf{k}^a(s,\alpha)\}_t^\infty$. [26] However, in their framework there are no externalities that create non-autonomous terms. The non-optimality follows from the alpha rule not being optimally chosen.

Since we have no proof of a similar result under externalities and other non-autonomous imperfections like monopolistic competition, distortionary taxation and unemployment, we will work from equation (25). The message is that the Weitzman dynamic welfare theorem carries over to imperfect market economies provided that the externalities are also correctly priced along the imperfect market path. However, in the present green accounting practice, only a subset of externalities like stocks are included; to this category belong oil, forests and carbon sequestration. However, the pricing problem is complicated. As pointed out by Dasgupta (2001), estimating relevant accounting prices for certain categories of resources may simply be impossible.

One may wonder how much one overestimates welfare by not being able to measure the accounting prices of negative externalities. Attempts to obtain estimates from, among others, computable general equilibrium models, are available in Weitzman and Löfgren (1997), Backlund (2000) and Aronsson et al. (2004). The verdict, so far, is that the errors are not that huge. It is worth noting that all kinds of market imperfections, that is, not only externalities, result in modified welfare expressions of the same shape as in equation (25), so the jury is still out.

## 8.2   The Money Metrics Version of GCNNP Under Market Imperfections

After having developed a money metrics theory under the first-best setting, it is fairly straightforward to produce the imperfect analogue provided that we assume that the shadow values are known. Li and Löfgren (2006b) show that a money metrics version of equation (25) can be written

$$\tilde{H}_r^0(t) = \lambda^{m_0}(t_0) \left\{ \mathbf{p}_r^0(t)\mathbf{c}^0(t) + \int_{\mathbf{p}_r^0(t)}^{\bar{\mathbf{p}}_r} \mathbf{d}^0(p_r)dp_r + \mathbf{q}_{k_r}^0(t)\mathbf{i}_k^0(t) \right.$$

$$\left. + \mathbf{p}_{x_r}^0(t)\mathbf{x}^0(t) + \int_{\mathbf{p}_{x_r}^0(t)}^{\bar{\mathbf{p}}_x} \mathbf{d}_x^0(p_{x_r})dp_{x_r} + \int_t^{\infty} \mathbf{p}_{s_x}(s)\dot{\mathbf{x}}^0(s)e^{-\theta(s-t)}ds \right\} \quad (27)$$

Here $\mathbf{p}_{x_r}^0(t) = \mathbf{p}_x^0(t)/\pi(t) = v_{x_r}(x(t))$ represents the shadow prices in real terms (normalized prices) of consumption externalities at time $t$ with $t_0$ as base year. When an element of the price vector $\mathbf{p}_{x_r}^0(t)$ is positive, it may be interpreted as the annual willingness-to-pay for year $t$, in year zero's prices, for enjoying the 'amenity' from a marginal externality unit. A negative element would be interpreted as the willingness to pay to avoid a marginal stock externality. The first integral represents the standard consumer surplus in real terms, while the second represents the positive or negative consumer surpluses from externalities. The last integral is the normalized version of the current value of the marginal externality along the imperfect market path.

While the first three terms within brackets in (27) correspond to the conventionally measured GCNNP, the other three terms represent the corresponding green adjustment. The contents of the integrals among these terms deserve some further explanation. The integrand represents a system of demand functions that are the solution to the equation $v_x(\mathbf{d}) = \lambda^{m_0}(t_0)\mathbf{p}_{x_r}^0(t)$ and corresponds to a kind of net surplus value. To fix ideas, assume that all elements of $\mathbf{x}(t)$ represent negative externalities. Then $\mathbf{x} = \mathbf{d}_x^0(\mathbf{p}_{x_r})$ can be interpreted as the demand functions for externality stock reductions at time $t$. The lower integration bound is the marginal willingness to pay for reducing the first unit of the externality at time $t$. The upper integration bound is the marginal value of reducing the last unit. Since the integration bounds meet the requirement that the value at the upper bound is not higher than at the lower, by the properties of the objective function $v(x)$, the net surplus value will be negative. For positive externalities, the integral is positive. In reality, with mixed externalities, the sign of the vector integral is a priori indeterminate. Since $\lambda^{m_0}(t_0)$ is positive, the expressions inside the brackets in (27) will remain in the same relationship with each other over time up to a positive constant. To sum up: In the presence of market imperfections, the adjusted GCNNP in real prices as expressed inside the brackets in equation (27) is a correct measure of dynamic welfare, the growth of which over a short time interval also indicates a local welfare improvement.

## 9   CONCLUSION

The money metrics problem in dynamic welfare analysis has (yet) no empirically feasible solution. The obstacles are many. One of the most important is that the consumer surpluses in all relevant markets have to be measured. Consumer theory can contribute to the specification of such demand systems, but such specifications should be taken with a grain of salt. A difficult problem to handle is that preferences vary significantly from agent to agent. Consumer theory at the micro level tells us that individual demand behavior must obey certain demand restrictions – the Slutsky equations, symmetry, and homogeneity of degree zero in prices and income. These properties are not all carried over to aggregate excess demand functions. As Debreu (1974) has shown, any excess demand system including $l$ goods that satisfies Walras's law can always be generated by $l$ utility maximizing consumers. Loosely speaking, this means that the aggregate excess demand vector tells us nothing about the underlying consumer preferences. It would help a little if preferences were distributed closely around an average representative utility function, but how could we know?

To the consumer surplus estimation problem, one has to add the non-trivial problem of producing an ideal, benchmark independent consumer price index, which involves the estimation of nominal interest rates over time and society's rate of time preference. Both problems can be circumvented by assuming that the marginal utility of income is constant over time, and by moving to a dynamic version of a Konüs's compensation price index that not only contains consumption goods but also an index of net investments, based on the Hamiltonian as the instantaneous utility function. Moreover, the constancy of the marginal utility of money has, so far, implicitly been assumed in all 'static' CPI indexes that have been constructed for compensation purposes so far. The empirical problem that then remains to be solved is that the net investment vector will not contain the net additions to all relevant capital stocks.

# NOTES

1. For a recent study of distributional objectives and redistribution in the context of social accounting, see Aronsson and Löfgren (1999a).
2. First mentioned by John Law (1705).
3. Smith (1776), reprinted as Penguin Classics 1986) pages 131–132.
4. Davanzati (1588) was able to say wise things about the paradox before it had surfaced, by pointing out that the value of water was determined by its scarcity; on the degree of thirst.
5. Galiani (1750/1977) page 26.
6. Dupuit (1844/1952), an English translation. Italics in the original.
7. Note that Figure 2.1 describes the simplest setting and the value-in-exchange still does not work.
8. For a linear utility function $u(\mathbf{c}(t))$, where $\mathbf{c}(t)$ is a vector of consumption goods we find that $u(\mathbf{c}) = u_c(\mathbf{c})\mathbf{c} = \lambda^m \mathbf{pc}$, where $u_c$ is a vector of marginal utilities, $\mathbf{p}$ is a vector of market prices, and $\lambda^m$ is the marginal utility of income (money).
9. The utility functions depend on aggregate consumption.
10. The result in equation (1) is a direct consequence of the Hamilton-Jacobi-Bellman equation in stochastic optimization. Letting the variance go to zero produces the result directly. Weitzman (1976) has an independent proof, and there are other alternatives in the literature. See for example, Aronsson et al. (2004), Chapter 2.
11. See Weitzman (2001) for an intuitive derivation, or Li and Löfgren (2006b) for a formal derivation.
12. To show that the index is independent of the market basket $\mathbf{c}$, that is, benchmark independent, and why this is important, we note that since the utility function is stationary over time, it follows from the first-order conditions for an optimal path that

$$u_c(\mathbf{c}) = \lambda^m(t_0)\mathbf{p}(t_0; \mathbf{c}) = \lambda^m(t)\mathbf{p}(t, \mathbf{c})$$

Multiplying through by the market basket $\mathbf{c}$, and solving for the marginal utility of money at time $t_0$ yields

$$\lambda^m(t_0) = \pi(t)\lambda^m(t),$$

which is a constant.
13. See Li and Löfgren (2002) or Aronsson et al. (2004). Li and Löfgren (2002) contains a formal proof of the theorem, and Weitzman (2001) contains a proof of an analogous result that compares two economies at the same point in time.
14. A recent comprehensive survey is provided by Asheim (2007).
15. Note that the Divisa consumer price index cannot be used to transfer Weitzman's (1976) result into an exact money metrics welfare index. Hence, even if the last term of (8) disappears, the claim must be conditional on a positive real interest rate.
16. The problem of indicating a welfare improvement by means of growth in NNP is also discussed by Dasgupta and Mäler (2000) and Dasgupta (2001). A comprehensive survey of the current state of the art is provided by Asheim (2007).
17. Who first derived this result is not quite clear to us, but our best guess is Weitzman (1976). In his proof of his main theorem, genuine saving appears in equation (14) on page 161, but he does nothing with it other than noting that integration yields the theorem. The measure has been popularized by Pearce and Atkinson (1993) and Hamilton (1994), and used in practice by among others, Hamilton and Lutz (1996), Hamilton and Clemens (1999), and Hamilton (2000). The relevance of genuine saving for sustainability was first developed by Asheim (1994) and Pezzey (1995).
18. The term originates from Boulding (1966). He conducts an insightful verbal discussion of planet earth's sustainability problem. An economy with a similar problem in defining comprehensive NNP would be Kuwait, which is extremely dependent upon its oil resources.

19.  A similar problem occurs with the Asheim-Weitzman welfare indicator, since growth in NNP at changing prices will be zero. To see this, we note that their welfare indicator has the following shape:

$$R(t)q_d^*(t)i^*(t) = p_d^*(t)\dot{c}^*(t) + q_d^*(t)i^*(t) + \dot{q}_d^*i^*(t)$$

In the cake eating model $p_d(t) = q_d(t)$, and $\dot{y}(t) = 0$, that is, NNP at fixed prices equals zero. This means that $\dot{c}^*(t) = -i^*(t)$ for all $t$. From this and the properties of the Divisa index, we can conclude that $\dot{q}_d^*i^*(t) = -\dot{p}_d^*(t)c^*(t) = 0$, implying that NNP at varying prices also equals zero.

20.  For a more full-fledged exposition see Li and Löfgren (2004).
21.  At a disaggregated level, the net financial position of the consumer, assets minus mortgages, would enter a dynamic true cost-of-living index, but aggregated over consumers, this yields the value of net investments. See also Klevmarken (2004).
22.  The exposition below follows Li and Löfgren (2006b).
23.  See also Löfgren (1992).
24.  It seems difficult to handle the externality problem when the instantaneous utility function is not separable.
25.  The result is already hinted at in Weitzman (1976). Kemp and Long (1982) produced the complete non-autonomous version of Weitzman's theorem. See also Löfgren (1992).
26.  Arrow et al. (2003) do not present any proof of the Euler equation – equation (7) in their paper – but the formula is correct.

# REFERENCES

Aronsson, T. and Löfgren, K.-G. (1998) Green Accounting: What do we know and what do we have to know? In H. Folmer and T. Tietenberg (eds) *International Yearbook of Environmental Economics 1998/99*, Cheltenham: Edward Elgar.

Aronsson, T. and Löfgren K.-G. (1999) Welfare Equivalent NNP under Distributional Objectives, *Economic Letters* 63, 239–43.

Aronsson, T., Löfgren, K.-G. and Backlund, K. (2004) *Green Accounting in Imperfect Markets: Growth Theoretical Approach*, Cheltenham: Edward Elgar.

Arrow, K., Dasgupta, P.S. and Mäler, K.-G. (2003) Evaluating Projects and Assessing Sustainable Development in Imperfect Economies, *Economic Theory* 21, 217–25.

Asheim, G.B. (1994) Net National Product as an Indicator of Sustainability, *Scandinavian Journal of Economics* 96, 257–65.

Asheim, G.B. and Weitzman, M.L. (2001) Does NNP Growth Indicate Welfare Improvement?, *Economic Letters* 73, 233–39.

Backlund, K. (2000) *Welfare Measurement, Externalities and Pigouvian Taxation in Dynamic Economies*, Umeå Economic Studies 527, PhD thesis, Umeå: University of Umeå.

Boulding, K. (1966) The Economics of the Coming Spaceship Earth, In H. Jarrelt (ed.) *Environmental Quality in a Growing Economy*, Baltimore, MD: Johns Hopkins Press for Resources for the Future.

Brock, W.A. (1977) A Polluted Golden Age, in V.L. Smith (ed.), *Economics of Natural and Environmental Resources*, New York: Gordon and Breach.

Cournot, A. (1838) *Recherches sur les Principes Mathematiques de la Theorie des Richesses*, Paris: Hachette.

Dasgupta, P. (2001) Valuing Objects and Evaluating Policies in Imperfect Economies, *Economic Journal* 111, C1–C29.

Dasgupta, P. and Mäler, K.-G. (2000) Net National Product, Wealth and Social Well Being, *Environment and Development Economics* 5, 69–93.

Davanzati, B. (1588/1804) *Lezione delle Monete,* In P. Custodi (ed.) *Scrittorio Classici Italiani di Economica Politica*, parte antica, vol 2. Reprinted Rome: Bizarri, 1965.

Debreu, G. (1974) Excess Demand Functions, *Journal of Mathematical Economics* 1, 15–21.

Dupuit, J. (1844/1952) *De la Mesure de l'Utilité des Travaux Publiques*, reprinted as On the Measurement of the Utility of Public Works, *International Economic Papers* 1952(2), 83–110.

Galiani, F. (1750/1977) *On Money (Della Moneta)*, translated by P.R. Toscano, Ann Arbor, MI: Ann Arbor Microfilms International.

Gossen, H. (1854/1889) *Entwicklung der Gesetze des menschlichen Verkehrs, und der daraus fliessenden Regeln für menschliches Handeln*, Second ed. Berlin: Prager.

Hamilton, K. (1994) Green Adjustment to GDP, *Resource Policy* 20, 155–68.

Hamilton, K. (2000) *Genuine Saving as a Sustainability Indicator*, Environmental Economic Series 77, Washington, DC: The World Bank.

Hamilton, K. and Clemens, M. (1999) Genuine Saving in Developing Countries, *World Bank Economic Review* 13, 333–56.

Hamilton, K. and Lutz, F. (1996) *Green National Accounts: Policy Uses and Empirical Experience*, Environmental Economic Series 39, Washington, DC: The World Bank.

Hartwick, J. (1990) Natural Resources, National Accounting and Economic Depreciation, *Journal of Public Economics* 43, 291–304.

Kemp, M.C. and Long, N.V. (1982) On the Evolution of Social Income in a Dynamic Economy: Variations on a Samuelsonian theme, In G.R. Feiwel (ed.), *Samuelson and Neoclassical Economics*, Boston, NJ: Kluwer-Nijhoff.

Klevmarken, A. (2004) *Towards an Applicable True Cost of Living Index that Incorporates Housing*, Uppsala: Department of Economics, Uppsala University.

Konüs, A. (1924/1939) The Problem of the True Index of the Cost of Living, *The Economic Bulletin of the Institute of Economic Conjuncture*, Moscow, No 9–10, 64–71. Reprinted in *Econometrica*, 7, January, 10–29.

Law, J. (1705/1750) *Money and Trade Considered, with a Proposal for Supplying the Nation with Money*, New ed. Glasgow: Foulis.

Li, C.Z. and Löfgren, K.-G. (2002) *On the Choice of Metrics in Dynamic Welfare Analysis: Utility versus Money Measures*, Umeå Economic Studies No. 590, Umeå: University of Umeå.

Li, C.Z. and Löfgren, K.-G. (2004) *The Role of the Hamiltonian in Dynamic Index Theory*, Umeå Economic Studies, No 626, Umeå: University of Umeå.

Li, C.Z., and Löfgren, K.-G. (2006a) Comprehensive NNP, Social Welfare, and The Rate of Return on Investment, *Economic Letters* 90, 254–259.

Li, C.Z. and Löfgren, K.-G. (2006b) *Money Metrics Welfare Measures in Imperfect Markets under Growth*, Umeå Economic Studies, No 694, Umeå: University of Umeå.

Löfgren, K.-G. (1992) Comments on C.R. Hulten, Accounting for the Wealth of Nations: The Net Gross Output Controversy and its Ramifications, *Scandinavian Journal of Economics*, 94 (suppl.), 25–28.

Mäler, K.-G. (1991) National Accounting and Environmental Resources, *Environmental and Resource Economics* 1, 1–15.

Pearce, D. and Atkinson, G. (1993) Capital Theory and the Measurement of Sustainable Development: An Indicator of Weak Sustainability, *Ecological Economics* 8, 103–108.

Pezzey, J. (1995) *Non-declining Wealth is not Equivalent to Sustainability*, London: Deptartment of Economics, University College, London (mimeographed).

Smith, A. (1776/1986) *The Wealth of Nations, Books I–III*, Harmondsworth: Penguin.

Weitzman, M.L. (1976) On the Welfare Significance of National Product in a Dynamic Economy, *Quarterly Journal of Economics* 90, 156–162.

Weitzman, M.L. (2001) A Contribution to the Theory of Welfare Accounting, *Scandinavian Journal of Economics* 103, 1–24.

Weitzman, M.L. and Löfgren, K.-G. (1997), On the Welfare Significance of Green Accounting as Taught by Parable, *Journal of Environmental Economics and Management* 32, 139–153.

# 3 Welfare measurement, hyperbolic discounting and paternalism

*Kenneth Backlund and Tomas Sjögren*

## 1 INTRODUCTION

Today, there exists a literature which emphasizes that individuals may suffer from bounded rationality.[1] Common examples are the tendencies among some individuals to overconsume alcohol or to undersave. If these decisions are regretted later in life, this behavior is not consistent with the assumption that individuals make rational choices, and as such, there is a potential role for government intervention. This has spurred a literature concerning paternalistic, or non-welfarist motives for public policy.[2]

One type of bounded rationality which has received particular interest is when individuals use a hyperbolic discount function to evaluate the future. Hyperbolic discounting captures the empirically observed tendency among individuals to apply higher discount rates to near-term returns than to returns in the distant future, meaning that the discount rate effectively becomes time dependent.[3] For the discussion below, let us refer to the 'low' discount rate used by individuals to evaluate two points in a distant future as the *pure* rate of time preference, whereas the 'high' discount rate used to evaluate two points in the near future will be referred to as the *effective* rate of time preference.

A time-dependent discount rate has the potential to cause a conflict between an individual's long-run intentions and his/her short-run needs. As such, this may give rise to time-inconsistent behavior, whereby a young self can be viewed as imposing an intrapersonal externality on his/her future selve(s).[4] Several papers have analyzed how paternalistic public policies can be used to improve welfare in this situation.[5] A common assumption in this literature is that the paternalistic government uses the pure rate of time preference as the basis for discounting the future when it determines policy. The policy chosen in this case will be referred to as the standard paternalistic policy (SPP). Since the pure rate of time preference is lower than the effective rate, a paternalistic government will have a higher valuation of the future than individuals. This difference will provide a rationale for policy intervention in the market economy by implementing a policy which induces individuals to behave as if they effectively attach a higher weight to the future than they actually do. One example is subsidies on savings which induce individuals to accumulate capital at the rate preferred by the paternalistic government.

One question raised in this chapter is how effective the SPP is in terms of improving individual welfare. This question is relevant because the SPP is determined by maximizing the policy maker's objective function. By implementing this policy, the social planner induces the individual consumer to replicate the consumption/saving choices the consumer would make if the hyperbolic part of his/her discount function were redundant. However, the consumer will still apply hyperbolic discounting when he/she evaluates the welfare effects of a given policy. As such, since the social planner and the individual consumer have different intertemporal objective functions, the welfare effects of the SPP will differ depending on which objective function is used to evaluate the policy. Evaluating the SPP from the individual consumer's perspective has, to our knowledge, not been done before. In addition, we will also incorporate a 'traditional' externality (environmental damage) into the framework of hyperbolic discounting. There are two reasons for doing this. One is that it adds more realism to the model and the second is to study whether this added complexity will influence the effectiveness of using SPP to improve individual welfare. We will use numerical simulations to evaluate these effects.

Closely related to this issue is another question, namely how to measure welfare in the presence of hyperbolic discounting. In the literature on welfare measurement,[6] the objective is to relate the present value of future utility to variables observed (or at least estimable) today. In fact, the concept of 'comprehensive net national product' has been developed with this particular purpose in mind. However, when individuals apply hyperbolic discounting, the question arises whether it is the policy maker's objective function, or that of the individual, that ought to constitute the basis for measuring welfare. Since the present value calculations may differ significantly depending on which objective function is used to evaluate the future effects of a given policy, this will clearly have implications for welfare measurement. In the seminal work of Weitzman (1976), it is shown that under perfect foresight, and in the absence of externalities and other distortions, the net current value Hamiltonian is a static equivalent of future welfare. The current value Hamiltonian is, in turn, interpretable as measuring the comprehensive net national product in utility terms. Underlying this result are two fundamental requirements: (i) the economy must be on the optimal growth path and (ii) the dynamic optimization problem must not be fundamentally time dependent. The latter requirement means that neither the objective function nor the equation(s) for the state variable(s) contain any explicit time dependency except via the discount factor.[7] However, under hyperbolic discounting, neither condition (i) nor condition (ii) need to be satisfied along the equilibrium path. As such, the basic result in Weitzman (1976) needs to be augmented to take the effects of hyperbolic discounting into account. In this chapter, we will address theoretically some of the implications for welfare measurement.

Let us now turn to the earlier literature in the fields of hyperbolic discounting, paternalistic policy and welfare measurment. Since the works of Strotz (1956), Phelps and Pollak (1968), Pollak (1968) and Goldman (1980), it has been known that a non-constant rate of time preference may create a time consistency problem. The idea of hyperbolic discounting has been motivated by empirical evidence in the cognitive psychology literature which contradicts the predictions of utility functions with stationary fixed discount rates. One example is discussed by Thaler (1981), where people tend to prefer 'one apple today' to 'two apples tomorrow' but at the same time they tend to prefer 'two apples in one year plus one day' to 'one apple in one year'. This and other experiments have led psychologists to suggest that discount functions are generalized hyperbolas, meaning that the instantaneous discount rate falls over time. This observation was used by Laibson (1997), when he argued that agents are highly impatient about consumption between today and tomorrow but much more patient about choices advanced further into the future. This impatience argument implies that a higher discount rate is used to value trade-offs in the near future than trade-offs in the more distant future. Whether hyperbolic discounting leads to time inconsistency depends on whether or not the agents recognize that they have hyperbolic discount functions. Barro (1999) has analyzed the behavior of sophisticated agents (that is, agents who solve the dynamic optimization problem so as to obtain a time consistent solution) in continuous time and he shows that when the individuals have a logarithmic instantaneous utility function, the equilibrium will feature a constant effective rate of time preference which is larger than the pure rate of time preference, but which is observationally equivalent to the standard neoclassical growth model.

Let us now briefly discuss the literature on paternalistic public policy.[8] In the context of hyperbolic discounting, O'Donoghue and Rabin (2003, 2006) use a model where the self-control problem among the consumers manifests itself in terms of high consumption today of a good which is detrimental to health in the long run. They show that the self-control problem can be alleviated by taxing unhealthy goods harder, and other goods less hard, than in the absence of the underlying self-control problem. Gruber and Köszegi (2001, 2004), in turn, focus on smoking and they show that taxes on cigarettes ought to be higher when smokers suffer from a self-control problem than under rational addiction. Aronsson and Thunström (2008) include health as a capital concept and show that a subsidy directed at the stock of health capital should be included in the policy package aimed at alleviating the self-control problem. Another study is Aronsson and Sjögren (2009), which examines a dynamic model with endogenous labor supply, saving and health capital to study paternalistic policy in the context of hyperbolic discounting. By allowing for heterogeneity in ability, they derive the SPP policy within the context of a mixed tax framework where labor and capital taxes, as well as commodity taxes, are used as instruments to achieve both redistribution and externality correction. Among the results, the study shows how (non-linear) income taxes ought to be used as indirect instruments for influencing commodity demand behavior at the individual level since linear commodity taxes are not flexible enough to provide proper incentives for investments in health capital.[9]

This chapter is also related to the literature on welfare measurement in dynamic economies. Since Weitzman (1976), much of the subsequent work has focused on how to augment the basic result in Weitzman's article when the requirements mentioned above do not hold. For example, Aronsson and Löfgren (1993, 1995, 1996) discuss how the welfare measure must be augmented in order to take account of uninternalized external effects as well non-attributable technological change and human capital formation. These mechanisms influence the measurement of welfare because they introduce additional channels by which time explicitly enters the dynamic optimization problem, for example, via an exogenous time path of a stock of natural resources or by exogenous technological change.

The outline of the chapter is as follows. In section 2, we present the basic model and in section 3 we derive the optimal policy chosen by a paternalistic policy maker. In section 4, we discuss some implications of hyperbolic discounting for welfare measurement. This section also contains the numerical analysis. The chapter is concluded in section 5.

## 2   THE BASIC MODEL

Consider an economy with no population growth where the number of consumers is normalized to one. The consumer supplies one unit of labor inelastically and the instantaneous utility function is written $u(c, z)$, where $c$ is consumption and $z$ an indicator of environmental quality. The instantaneous utility function is assumed to be increasing and strictly concave in both arguments, and we also assume that $u_{cz} = 0$. The latter assumption means that $c$ and $z$ will be additively separable in the instantaneous utility function. At each point in time, the indicator of environmental quality is given by $z = z(x)$, where $x$ is a stock of pollution and $z_x < 0$.

Turning to the production side of the economy, the production function is written $f(k,g)$, where $k$ is capital and $g$ energy. We omit the notation of the fixed amount of labor used in the production process. The production function satisfies $f_k, f_g > 0$ and $f_{kk}, f_{gg} < 0$. It is also assumed that $f_{kg} > 0$, meaning that capital and energy are complements in production. Assuming, for notational convenience, that the depreciation rate of capital is zero, the accumulation of capital is given by

$$\dot{k}(t) = f(k(t), g(t)) - I(g(t)) - c(t) \tag{1}$$

where $I(g)$ reflects the cost of using energy in the production. This cost function is increasing and convex in $g$. The use of energy is assumed to add to a stock of pollution, $x$, which develops over time according to

$$\dot{x}(t) = h(g(t)) - \eta \cdot x(t) \tag{2}$$

where $h(g)$ is an emission function which is increasing in $g$, and where $\eta$ is the rate of decay of the stock of pollution.

## 2.1   The Social Planner

Let us follow the convention in the literature and start by characterizing the resource allocation that would be chosen by a social planner. The social planner's intertemporal objective function takes the form

$$U(\tau) = \int_{\tau}^{\infty} u[c(t), z(x(t))] \cdot e^{-\theta \cdot (t - \tau)} dt \tag{3}$$

where $\theta$ is the constant rate of time preference used by the social planner to discount the future and $\tau$ is the current date. The social planner's objective is to maximize equation (3) subject to equations (1), (2) and the initial conditions $x_\tau = x(\tau)$ and $k_\tau = k(\tau)$, as well as subject to the terminal conditions

$$\lim_{t \to \infty} k(t) \geq 0, \; \lim_{t \to \infty} x(t) \geq 0 \tag{4}$$

The present value Hamiltonian corresponding to this problem is written

$$H = u[c, z(x)] \cdot e^{-\theta \cdot (t - \tau)} + \lambda \cdot [f(k, g) - I(g) - c] + \mu \cdot [h(g) - \eta \cdot x] \tag{5}$$

where $\lambda$ and $\mu$ are the present-value shadow prices of the stock of capital and pollution, respectively. Together with equations (1) and (2), the necessary conditions are written

$$0 = u_c(c) \cdot e^{-\theta \cdot (t - \tau)} - \lambda \tag{6}$$

$$0 = \lambda \cdot [f_g(k, g) - I_g(g)] + \mu \cdot h_g(g) \tag{7}$$

$$\dot{\lambda} = -\lambda \cdot f_k(k, g) \tag{8}$$

$$\dot{\mu} = \mu \cdot \eta - u_z(z) \cdot z_x(x) \cdot e^{-\theta \cdot (t - \tau)} \tag{9}$$

and the transversality conditions read

$$\lim_{t \to \infty} [\lambda(t) \cdot k(t)] = 0, \ \lim_{t \to \infty} [\mu(t) \cdot x(t)] = 0 \tag{10}$$

Equations (1), (2), (4) and (6)–(10) implicitly define the optimal time paths for $c$, $g$, $k$ and $x$ from the point of view of the social planner.

For the analysis below, it is convenient to derive an Euler equation for the growth rate of consumption. Differentiating equation (6) with respect to time, and substituting for $\dot{\lambda}$ from equation (8), we obtain the following differential equation for the time path of consumption preferred by the social planner

$$\dot{c}(t) = -\frac{u_c(c(t))}{u_{cc}(c(t))} \cdot [r(t) - \theta] \tag{11}$$

where $r = f_k(k, g)$ is the interest rate. This is a standard condition for optimal consumption growth.

## 3   THE DECENTRALIZED MARKET ECONOMY

Let us now turn to the decentralized economy. There are two important differences between the planned economy and the decentralized market economy. First, in the production side of the economy, which is made up of identical firms, the number of which is normalized to one, the evolution of the stock of pollution is treated as exogenous. This means that the firm will not take equation (2) into account when it maximizes its profit, $\pi$. As such, at each point in time the firm maximizes (here we omit the time indicator for notational convenience)

$$\pi = f(k, g) - w - r \cdot k - I(g) - q \cdot g \tag{12}$$

where $w$ is the wage rate, $r$ the interest rate and $q$ a unit tax on the use of energy. The first-order conditions are written

$$f_k(k, g) - r = 0 \tag{13}$$

$$f_g(k, g) - I_g(g) - q = 0 \tag{14}$$

A comparison of equation (14) with equation (7) shows that since the firm does not recognize how its choice of $g$ affects the evolution of $x$, the use of energy will, for a given time path of the stock of capital, be higher in the unregulated market economy ($q = 0$) than what is preferred by the social planner.

## 3.1   The Consumer

The second difference between the planned economy and the decentralized market economy is that the consumer uses a hyperbolic discount function to calculate the present value of future utility. To incorporate hyperbolic discounting into a framework with continuous time, we follow Barro (1999) by assuming that the consumer's preferences take the following form:

$$\tilde{U}(\tau) = \int_\tau^\infty u[c(t), z(x(t))] \cdot e^{-[\rho \cdot (t - \tau) + \phi(t - \tau)]} dt \tag{15}$$

where '~' refers to a variable associated with welfare from the individual consumer's perspective and where $\phi(t - \tau) \geq 0$ is a continuous twice differentiable function which reflects impatience in the form of hyperbolic discounting. Define $v = t - \tau$ to be the time distance between today, $\tau$, and a future point in time, $t$. Following Barro (1999), we assume $\phi'(v) \geq 0$, $\phi''(v) \leq 0$, $\phi(0) = 0$ and $\lim_{v \to \infty} \phi'(v) = 0$. These conditions imply that the hyperbolic discount function will satisfy the criteria laid out in Laibson (1997). By defining $\rho + \phi'(t - \tau)$ to be the instantaneous rate of time preference, the properties of $\phi(v)$ imply that this rate is high between points in times in the near future but roughly equal to $\rho$ for points in times far off into the future. Hence, $\rho$ corresponds to the consumer's pure rate of time preference mentioned in the introduction to the chapter. Note also that we allow for the possibility that the social planner's constant rate of time preference, $\theta$, may differ from the consumer's pure rate of time preference, $\rho$.

The consumer's budget constraint is written

$$\dot{k} = \pi + (r + s) \cdot k + w - T - c \qquad (16)$$

where $\pi$ is non-labor (profit) income, $s$ a unit subsidy on saving and $T$ a lump-sum tax. The solution to the consumer's decision problem depends on whether he recognizes that he has a self-control problem or not. In this context, the key question is whether the consumer at time $\tau$ can commit his future selves to a consumption plan. A consumer who can do this will be referred to as committed, whereas a consumer who at time $\tau + \Delta t$ refuses to respect the choices made at time $\tau$, and therefore at $\tau + \Delta t$ makes a new consumption plan while retaining the erroneous belief that things will be different from now onwards, will be referred to as naive. Finally, a consumer who recognizes that he cannot commit himself and therefore chooses a consumption plan which is time consistent will be referred to as sophisticated. We will discuss each case in turn.

### 3.1.1  The committed consumer

Under commitment, the time paths for consumption and capital chosen at a given point in time $\tau$ will not be altered at future dates. In this scenario, the consumer at time $\tau$ maximizes the objective function in equation (15) subject to equation (16), and subject to the initial condition $k_\tau = k(\tau)$ as well as subject to the terminal condition $\lim_{t \to \infty} k(t) \geq 0$. Solving this problem, it is straightforward to derive the following differential equation for the growth of consumption along the equilibrium path:

$$\dot{c}(t) = -\frac{u_c(c(t))}{u_{cc}(c(t))} \cdot [r(t) + s(t) - \rho - \phi'(t - \tau)] \qquad (17)$$

Compared with the time path of consumption preferred by the social planner (equation 11), two new elements appear on the right-hand side (RHS) of equation (17). First, $\phi'(t - \tau)$ reflects that the instantaneous discount rate is now fundamentally time dependent and given by $\rho + \phi'(t - \tau)$. Conditional on the properties of the function $\phi(\cdot)$ laid out above, the instantaneous discount rate is high in the near future but approaches $\rho$ as $t$ goes to infinity. As such, the steady state rate of time preference will equal $\rho$. Second, if $\theta = \rho$, a comparison between equations (11) and (17) indicates that without government intervention $(s(t) = 0)$, and for a given time path of the interest rate, the growth rate of consumption will be lower in the unregulated market economy compared with the growth rate preferred by the policy maker. This reflects that in the uncontrolled market economy, the consumer saves less, and therefore consumes a larger proportion of his wealth at each point in time before the steady state is reached, compared with the outcome in the command optimum. However, in the long run,

$\phi'(t - \tau) \to 0$, which means that in the steady state, equation (11) will be equal to equation (17). This implies that the steady-state consumption and capital stock will be equal to that preferred by the social planner (provided that the environmental externality is redundant or internalized).

A problem with the committed consumer's solution is that the point at which the commitment is made, $\tau$, is arbitrary. As such, it is difficult for the policy maker to know from when the consumer will commit himself. Furthermore, if commitments on consumption were possible at all points in time, then these commitments would probably have existed in the past, perhaps in the infinite past, in which case $\phi'(v)$ would already be zero today. Then, the rate of time preference would equal $\rho$ and the standard Ramsey model applies. Another, and possibly more fundamental problem is why a consumer at a future point $\tau + \Delta t$ should stick to a consumption and savings plan determined at time $\tau$. Let us therefore proceed and characterize the outcome when the consumption plan is adjusted.

### 3.1.2   The naive consumer

When the consumer is naive, he at any time $\tau$ believes that he can commit his future selves to a consumption plan. However, in the near future, $\tau + \Delta t$, the naive consumer refuses to respect his preferences at time $\tau$ and instead consumes more than planned. Nevertheless, the consumer at time $\tau + \Delta t$ retains the erroneous belief that he will be able to commit himself. This procedure will be repeated continuously. Recall that the instantaneous discount rate between a given point in time, $\tau$, and the near future, $\tau + \Delta t$, is given by $\rho + \phi'(\Delta t)$. As such, when the consumption plan is updated continuously, that is, when $\Delta t \to 0$, then the consumption decision at all points in times will effectively be based on the effective discount rate $\rho + \phi'(0)$. As such, the actual growth rate of consumption for a naive consumer will be determined by

$$\dot{c}(t) = -\frac{u_c(c(t))}{u_{cc}(c(t))} \cdot [r(t) + s(t) - \rho - \phi'(0)] \qquad (18)$$

Since $\phi'(0) \geq \phi'(t - \tau)$, a comparison between equations (17) and (18) indicates that consumption will grow at a slower pace when the consumer acts naively compared with when he is committed. This reflects that the naive consumer accumulates less capital and therefore has a smaller consumption space in the future than the committed consumer.

However, it is difficult to conceive of a consumer being completely naive in the sense described here. Rather, he is likely to recognize that he has a self-control problem and therefore works out a strategy to deal with it. Let us, therefore, turn to the sophisticated consumer.

### 3.1.3 The sophisticated consumer

A sophisticated consumer recognizes that he has a self-control problem and therefore wants to figure out how to devise a time-consistent consumption plan. This problem was solved by Barro (1999) in continuous time when the consumer has a logarithmic instantaneous utility function. Barro showed that the solution to this problem is observationally equivalent to maximizing the following objective function:

$$\tilde{U}(\tau) = \int_{\tau}^{\infty} \ln(c(t)) \cdot e^{-\varphi \cdot (t-\tau)} dt \tag{19}$$

where the discount function is a standard exponential function, and where the constant instantaneous rate of time preference, $\varphi$, is given by

$$\varphi = \frac{1}{\displaystyle\int_{0}^{\infty} e^{-[\rho \cdot v + \phi(v)]} dv}. \tag{20}$$

It can be shown that $\varphi \in [\rho, \rho + \phi'(0)]$, which means that the solution to the sophisticated consumer's problem is observationally equivalent to the standard Ramsey model but with a higher rate of time preference. As such, Barro's result implies that when the consumer has a logarithmic utility function, the observed time path of consumption will be given by

$$\dot{c}(t) = c(t) \cdot [r(t) + s(t) - \varphi] \tag{21}$$

where we have used the result that the effective instantaneous discount rate is given by $\varphi$ and that $u(c) = \ln(c)$ implies $-u_c/u_{cc} = c$.

## 3.2 The Paternalistic Government

Let us now characterize the paternalistic government which aims to implement the policy defined in section 2.1. If the government uses the consumer's pure rate of time preference to discount the future ($\theta = \rho$), then the solution to the government's problem defines the standard paternalistic policy (SPP) discussed in the introduction to this chapter.

The government has access to three types of policy instruments: the unit tax on emissions, $q$, the unit subsidy on saving, $s$, and the lump-sum tax, $T$. The government's budget balances at each point in time, meaning that the budget constraint reads

$$T + q \cdot g - s \cdot k = 0 \tag{22}$$

The objective of the paternalistic government is to implement a policy which induces the agent to replicate the consumption and savings decision preferred by the social planner. Let us begin by characterizing the optimal choice of *s*.

### 3.2.1   The subsidy on saving

The subsidy on saving is used by the social planner to correct the intrapersonal externality imposed by the consumer on his future selves. As such, the paternalistic government's problem is to choose the time path of $s(t)$ so that the decentralized solution will coincide with the command optimum. Since the saving behavior of the consumer depends on whether he is committed, naive or sophisticated, we have to consider each case in turn.

When the consumer is committed, his time path of consumption is determined by equation (17). Comparing this with equation (11), it follows that the growth of consumption in the market economy will coincide with that in the command optimum if the capital subsidy is set according to

$$s(t) = \rho - \theta + \phi'(t - \tau) \text{ for all } t. \tag{23}$$

To implement the policy in equation (23), the paternalistic government at time $\tau$ announces the time path of the capital subsidy. This provides the consumer with an incentive to increase saving at each point in time which exactly offsets his tendency to undersave. Note that under SPP ($\theta = \rho$), the optimal subsidy reduces to $s(t) = \phi'(t - \tau)$.

Turning to the situation when the consumer is naive, a comparison between equations (11) and (18) implies that the naive consumer will replicate the growth rate of consumption preferred by social planner if the subsidy is set equal to

$$s(t) = \rho - \theta + \phi'(0) \text{ for all } t. \tag{24}$$

Since $\phi''(v) \leq 0$, the subsidy given by equation (24) will be larger than that faced by the committed consumer.

When the consumer is sophisticated and has a logarithmic utility function, the subsidy will be given by

$$s(t) = \varphi - \theta \text{ for all } t, \tag{25}$$

which means that the subsidy will be a constant at all points in time.

### 3.2.2 The environmental tax

Let us now characterize how the environmental tax is set when the government's rate of time preference coincides with the pure rate of time preference, that is, when $\theta = \rho$. In this situation, equations (7) and (14) indicate that for a given time path of the stock of capital, the use of energy will be higher in the uncontrolled market economy ($q(t) = 0$) than what is preferred by the social planner. Combining equations (7) and (14), we can derive an expression for the environmental tax which, if implemented, will induce the firm to replicate the time path of emissions preferred by the social planner. This tax is given by

$$q(t) = -\frac{\mu^c(t)}{\lambda^c(t)} \cdot h_g(g(t)) \text{ for all } t \tag{26}$$

where $\mu^c(t)$ and $\lambda^c(t)$ are the paternalistic government's shadow prices of the stock of pollution and the stock of capital, respectively, evaluated at the social planner's optimum. The superindex $c$ refers to current value. By implementing the Pigouvian tax in equation (26), the firm is forced to take into account the cost of using the environmentally dirty input in production. At an arbitrary point in time $\tau$, the social planner's shadow price will be given by[10]

$$\mu^c(\tau) = \int_\tau^\infty u_z(t) \cdot z_x(t) \cdot e^{-(\theta+\eta)(t-\tau)} dt. \tag{27}$$

Since $u_z \cdot z_x$ can be interpreted as the marginal cost, in utility terms, of an increase in the stock of pollution at a given point in time, the shadow price of the stock of pollution evaluated at time $\tau$ can be interpreted as the present value of all future marginal costs of pollution.

If, on the other hand, the government were to respect the preferences of the representative consumer at time $\tau$, the objective function would be given by equation (15), in which case it is straightforward to derive that the shadow price of the stock of pollution would be given by

$$\tilde{\mu}^c(\tau) = \int_\tau^\infty \frac{du[z(x(t))]}{dz} \cdot \frac{dz(x(t))}{dx} \cdot e^{-[(\rho+\eta)(t-\tau)+\phi(t-\tau)]} dt. \tag{28}$$

Since equation (28) contains the hyperbolic discount function, it follows that $|\tilde{\mu}^c(\tau)| < |\mu^c(\tau)|$ for a given time path of the stock of pollution when $\theta = \rho$. As such, the paternalistic government will attach a higher value to the shadow price of pollution than the representative consumer at any point in time $\tau$.

## 4   WELFARE MEASUREMENT AND SIMULATIONS

Since the social planner and the individual consumer use different discount functions to evaluate the future, welfare can be measured either
from the point of view of the social planner or from that of the individual
consumer. We will consider both perspectives. We start by discussing
welfare measurement in the decentralized market economy where neither
the intrapersonal nor the environmental externality is internalized by the
government. Then we proceed to discuss welfare measurement along the
equilibrium path when the government has internalized both types of
externalities.

### 4.1   The Decentralized Market Economy

Let the superindex ° denote entities along the equilibrium path in the
decentralized market economy. From the perspective of the social planner,
the present value Hamiltonian, where time zero constitutes the basis for
the present value calculations, can be written as

$$H° = u[c°, z(x°)] \cdot e^{-\theta t}$$

$$+ \lambda° \cdot [f(k°, g°) - I(g°) - c°] + \mu° \cdot [h(g°) - \eta \cdot x°]. \quad (29)$$

Differentiating equation (29) with respect to time produces the following
differential equation:

$$\frac{dH°}{dt} = -\theta \cdot u[c°(t), z(x°(t))] \cdot e^{-\theta t}$$

$$+ \Omega°(t) \cdot \dot{c}°(t) + \Phi°(t) \cdot \dot{g}°(t)$$

$$+ \Psi°(t) \cdot \dot{k}°(t) + \mathcal{F}°(t) \cdot \dot{x}°(t) \quad (30)$$

where

$$\Omega°(t) = u°(t) \cdot e^{-\theta t} - \lambda°(t) \quad (31)$$

$$\Phi°(t) = \lambda°(t) \cdot [f_g(k°(t), g°(t)) - I_g(g°(t))] + \mu°(t) \cdot h_g(g°(t)) \quad (32)$$

$$\Psi°(t) = \frac{d\lambda°(t)}{dt} + \lambda°(t) \cdot f_k(k°(t), g°(t)) \quad (33)$$

$$\mathcal{F}°(t) = \frac{d\mu°(t)}{dt} + u_z°(t) \cdot z_x°(t) \cdot e^{-\theta t} - \eta \cdot \mu°(t) \quad (34)$$

The terms appearing on the second and third rows of equation (30) reflect that the time paths of $c°(t)$, $g°(t)$, $k°(t)$ and $x°(t)$ (made by the private agents) are not optimal from the point of view of the social planner. Since equations (31)–(34) correspond to the necessary conditions presented in equations (6)–(9), the terms $\Omega°(t)$, $\Phi°(t)$, $\Psi°(t)$ and $°(t)$ would be zero if the the time paths of $c°(t)$, $g°(t)$, $k°(t)$ and $x°(t)$ had been determined by the social planner. As such, if $\Omega°(t) > 0(<0)$ at time $t$, the social planner has a higher (lower) valuation of consumption than the individual consumer along the equilibrium path. The terms $\Phi°(t)$, $\Psi°(t)$ and $\mathcal{F}°(t)$ can be interpreted in a similar way for $g(t)$, $k(t)$ and $x(t)$ respectively.

To see the consequences for welfare measurement, let us integrate equation (30) over the time interval $(\tau, T)$ while using the result that $\lim_{T \to \infty} H°(T) = 0$ and transforming the resulting expressions into current value terms. This produces

$$H^{c°}(\tau) = \int_{\tau}^{\infty} \theta \cdot u°(t) \cdot e^{-\theta \cdot (t - \tau)} dt$$

$$- \int_{\tau}^{\infty} \Omega^{c°}(t) \cdot \dot{c}°(t) dt - \int_{\tau}^{\infty} \Phi^{c°}(t) \cdot \dot{g}°(t) dt$$

$$- \int_{\tau}^{\infty} \Psi^{c°}(t) \cdot \dot{k}°(t) dt - \int_{\tau}^{\infty} \mathcal{F}^{c°}(t) \cdot \dot{x}°(t) dt. \tag{35}$$

To interpret equation (35), recall first that if the social planner had determined the time paths of $c(t)$, $g(t)$, $k(t)$ and $x(t)$, then $\Omega°(t) = \Phi°(t) = \Psi°(t) = \mathcal{F}°(t) = 0$, in which case equation (35) would reduce to

$$\theta \cdot \int_{\tau}^{\infty} u°(t) \cdot e^{-\theta \cdot (t - \tau)} dt = H^{c°}(\tau). \tag{36}$$

Equation (36) replicates the standard result in the literature on welfare measurement: when all variables have been chosen optimally and all externalities are internalized, the social planner's Hamiltonian will be a static equivalent to welfare in the sense that $H^{c°}(t)$ is proportional to the present value of future utility.

Let us now return to equation (35) and focus on the additional terms that appear on the RHS. We begin with the first term on the second row and observe that if, for example, $\Omega^{c°}(t) > 0$ and $\dot{c}°(t) > 0$, then the first term on the second row (including the minus sign) is negative. This reflects that since consumption has not been chosen optimally from the point of view of the social planner, the Hamiltonian does not fully capture the positive welfare effect of higher consumption in the future. As such, $H^{c\circ}(\tau)$ will underestimate the weighted sum of the present value of all future utilities. By subtracting the first term on the second row from the weighted sum of the present value of all future utilities, this 'error' in the valuation of consumption is adjusted for. The opposite argument applies if, for example, $\Omega^{c\circ}(t) < 0$ and $\dot{c}^{\circ}(t) > 0$. The three remaining terms on the RHS of equation (35) correspond to $g^{c\circ}(t)$, $k^{c\circ}(t)$ and $x^{c\circ}(t)$ respectively, and can be interpreted along similar lines. Note that these types of additional terms bear a resemblance to terms that appear when measuring welfare under market imperfections and/or in the presence of distortionary taxes.[11]

## 4.2   The Paternalistic Economy

Let the superindex * denote entities along the equilibrium path following from the paternalistic policy defined in section 2.1. From the perspective of the social planner, all variables are now chosen optimally, in which case the standard result presented in equation (36) applies. Things will, however, be different if welfare is instead evaluated from the perspective of the individual consumer.

Since the intertemporal objective function of the individual consumer (equation 15) differs from that of the social planner (equation 3), the perceived welfare effect will also differ between them. There are two basic reasons: (i) at each point in time the individual consumer uses a different discount function from the social planner and (ii) the point of reference, $\tau$, changes with time in the function $\phi(t - \tau)$. Observe that the situation in (i) corresponds to the outcome when the individual consumer is committed in the way described in section 3.1.1. We will therefore begin by analysing welfare measurement when the consumer is committed. After that we will briefly discuss welfare measurement when the point of reference, $\tau$, changes with time in the function $\phi(t - \tau)$. This corresponds to the situations described in sections 3.1.2 (naive consumer) and 3.1.3 (sophisticated consumer).

Under commitment, the point of reference in the function $\phi(t - \tau)$ is a fixed point in time. Without loss of generality, this point in time can be normalized to zero, in which case the consumer's objective function at time $\tau$ will be given by

$$\tilde{U}(\tau) = \int_{\tau}^{\infty} u[c(t), z(x(t))] \cdot e^{-\rho \cdot (t-\tau) - [\phi(t) - \phi(\tau)]} dt. \tag{37}$$

By substituting the individual consumer's discount function, as well as his shadow prices, into equation (29), we can define the present value Hamiltonian from the consumer's point of view as

$$\tilde{H}^\circ = u[c^*, z(x^*)] \cdot e^{-\rho \cdot t - \phi(t)}$$

$$+ \tilde{\lambda}^* \cdot [f(k^*, g^*) - I(g^*) - c^*] + \tilde{\mu}^* \cdot [h(g^*) - \eta \cdot x^*] \quad (38)$$

where we have retained the assumption that time zero constitutes the basis for the present value calculations. As long as the consumer discounts the future harder than the social planner, $\tilde{\lambda}^*$ and $\tilde{\mu}^*$ will be smaller than the corresponding shadow prices for the social planner: $\lambda^*$ and $\mu^*$. Differentiating equation (38) with respect to time produces the following differential equation:

$$\frac{d\tilde{H}^\circ}{dt} = -[\rho + \phi'(t)] \cdot u^*(t) \cdot e^{-\rho \cdot t - \phi(t)}$$

$$+ \tilde{\Omega}^*(t) \cdot \dot{c}^*(t) + \tilde{\Phi}^*(t) \cdot \dot{g}^*(t)$$

$$+ \tilde{\Psi}^*(t) \cdot \dot{k}^*(t) + \mathcal{F}^*(t) \cdot \dot{x}^*(t) \quad (39)$$

where

$$\tilde{\Omega}^*(t) = u_c^*(t) \cdot e^{-\rho \cdot t - \phi(t)} - \tilde{\lambda}^*(t) \quad (40)$$

$$\tilde{\Phi}^*(t) = \tilde{\lambda}^*(t) \cdot [f_g(k^*(t), g^*(t)) - I_g(g^*(t))] + \tilde{\mu}^*(t) \cdot h_g(g^*(t)) \quad (41)$$

$$\tilde{\Psi}^*(t) = \frac{d\tilde{\lambda}^*(t)}{dt} + \tilde{\lambda}^*(t) \cdot f_k(k^*(t), g^*(t)) \quad (42)$$

$$\mathcal{F}^*(t) = \frac{d\tilde{\mu}^*(t)}{dt} + u_z^*(t) \cdot z_x^*(t) \cdot e^{-\rho \cdot t - \phi(t)} - \eta \cdot \tilde{\mu}^*(t). \quad (43)$$

Observe the similarity of these equations and the equations presented in (30)–(34). This implies that all terms in equation system (39)–(43) can be interpreted in a similar way to the corresponding terms in equation system (30)–(34). As such, the terms appearing on the second and third rows of equation (39) reflect that the time paths of $c^*(t)$, $g^*(t)$, $k^*(t)$ and $x^*(t)$ (decided upon by the social planner) are not optimal from the point of view of the consumer, and the terms $\Omega^*(t), \Phi^*(t), \Psi^*(t)$ and $\mathcal{F}^*(t)$ reflect whether the consumer at time $t$ has a higher/lower valuation of $c^*(t)$, $g^*(t)$, $k^*(t)$ and $x^*(t)$, respectively, than the social planner. Integrating equation (39) over the time interval $(\tau, T)$ while using the result that $\lim_{T \to \infty} \tilde{H}^*(T) = 0$ and transforming the resulting expressions into current value terms produces

$$\int_{\tau}^{\infty} u*(t) \cdot \Delta(t)dt = \tilde{H}^{c*}(\tau) + \int_{\tau}^{\infty} \Omega^{c*} \cdot \dot{c}*dt + \int_{\tau}^{\infty} \Phi^{c*} \cdot \dot{g}*dt$$

$$+ \int_{\tau}^{\infty} \Psi^{c*} \cdot \dot{k}*dt + \int_{\tau}^{\infty} \mathcal{F}^{c*} \cdot \dot{x}*dt \qquad (44)$$

where $\Delta(t) = [\rho + \phi'(t)] \cdot e^{-\rho \cdot (t-\tau) - [\phi(t) - \phi(\tau)]}$.

To interpret equation (44), observe first that the LHS is a weighted sum of the present value (in terms of time $\tau$) of all future utilities, with the time-dependent discount rate $\rho + \phi'(t)$ being the weight attached to each point in time. This can be related to the standard result presented in equation (36). Putting $\theta$ under the integral, the LHS of equation (36) can be reinterpreted to be a weighted sum of the present value of all future utilities, with $\theta$ being the weight. Since the discount rate is constant, each present value term will be given the same weight in that calculation. The LHS of equation (44) can be given a similar interpretation where the difference is that the discount rate $\rho + \phi'(t)$ in the present value calculation in this equation is time dependent. Since $\phi'(t)$ is a concave function, higher weight will be attached to the near future than to the far-off future. As for the remaining terms in equation (44), they can be interpreted in a similar way to the corresponding terms in equation (35).

The result derived in equation (44) concerns welfare measurement when the consumer can commit himself to a given consumption plan. If we instead assume that the consumer is naive or sophisticated in the sense defined in sections 3.1.2 and 3.1.3 respectively, welfare measurement becomes more complex because then $\tau$, in the function $\phi(t - \tau)$, will change continuously with time. There are two main reasons for this added complexity. First, as the consumer gets older, the hyperbolic part of the discount function, $\phi(t - \tau)$, will change continuously with $\tau$, as will the the discount rate $\rho + \phi'(t - \tau)$. Second, the continuous change in $\phi(t - \tau)$ that results from the continuous change in $\tau$ will also imply that the shadow prices $\tilde{\lambda}*$ and $\tilde{\mu}*$ need to be updated continuously. Both these effects need to be taken into account, and will modify the welfare measures discussed above. However, in this chapter, we will not derive these measures. Instead, let us now turn to the question of how effective the paternalistic policy is in improvng the welfare of the individual consumer. As such, we now turn to the simulations part of the chapter.

## 4.3 Functional Forms

In the simulations, the intertemporal objective function of the paternalistic government is a discrete version of equation (3) while the individual's intertemporal objective function is a discrete version of equation (15). The dynasty of individuals lives for 150 periods (an approximation for $t \to \infty$) and the instantaneous utility function takes the following logarithmic form

$$u[c(t), z(x(t))] = \alpha_1 \cdot \ln[c(t)] + \alpha_2 \cdot \ln[z(t)] \tag{45}$$

where $\alpha_1 = 1$ and $\alpha_2 = 10$. As for the function $\phi(v)$, we follow Barro (1999) and choose the following functional form

$$\phi(v) = \frac{\eta_1}{\eta_2} \cdot (1 - e^{-\eta_2 \cdot v}) \tag{46}$$

with $\eta_1 = 0.25$ and $\eta_2 = 0.5$. Turning to $\varphi$, we use the definition in equation (20), and by setting $\rho = 0.02$, a discrete approximation of that equation gives $\varphi = 0.034$.

The indicator of environmental quality, $z(t)$, is a function of the stock of emissions

$$z(t) = \beta_1 - \beta_2 \cdot x(t)^{\beta_3} \tag{47}$$

where a linear relationship ($\beta_3 = 1$) constitutes the reference case, and where $\beta_1 = 100$ and $\beta_2 = 0.05$. The evolution of the stock of pollution is given by

$$\frac{dx(t)}{dt} = \beta_4 \cdot g(t) - \eta \cdot x(t) \tag{48}$$

where $\beta_4 = \eta = 0.01$ and where $x(0) = 0$. The production function is of Cobb-Douglas type

$$f[l(t), k(t), g(t)] = l(t)^{\gamma_1} \cdot k(t)^{\gamma_2} \cdot g(t)^{\gamma_3} \tag{49}$$

where $\gamma_1 = 0.4$, $\gamma_2 = 0.3$ and $\gamma_3 = 0.3$. In the following, we use the normalization $l(t) = 1$. The initial value of the stock of capital is $k(0) = 100$ and the acccumulation of capital is given by

$$\frac{dk(t)}{dt} = l(t)^{\gamma_1} \cdot k(t)^{\gamma_2} \cdot g(t)^{\gamma_3} - c(t) - \zeta_1 \cdot g(t)^{\zeta_2} - \zeta_3 \cdot k(t) \tag{50}$$

where $\zeta_1 = 0.01$ and $\zeta_2 = 1.1$. Finally, $\zeta_3 = 0.01$ is the depreciation rate of capital.

## 4.4   Simulations Results

As a point of reference, we will begin by considering a simplified model which only features the intrapersonal externality and where the environmental externality is made redundant by setting $x = 0$ at all points in time. Then we reintroduce the environmental externality into the model. In both scenarios, we simulate outcomes in both the unregulated and the regulated market economy.

### 4.4.1   Reference case: no environmental externality
Let us first consider the outcome in the unregulated market economy. To characterize the consumer's behavior in this economy, we follow Barro (1999) and assume that the consumer recognizes that he has a self-control problem and therefore works out a time-consistent consumption plan. As such, consumption in the unregulated market economy (UME) is determined by equation (21) for $s(t) = 0$. The time paths of consumption and capital in the unregulated market economy are given by the dotted curves in Figures 3.1 and 3.2.

These figures also depict the time paths of consumption and capital decided upon by a social planner under SPP[12] (solid curves). As can be

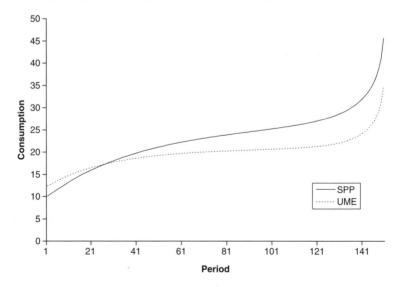

*Figure 3.1   The time path of consumption*

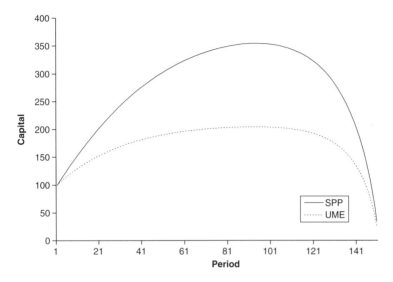

*Figure 3.2   The time path of capital*

seen, under SPP the stock of capital will be larger than in the unregulated market economy whereas the level of consumption under SPP will be larger in later periods of life.

Let us now evaluate individual welfare in the unregulated market economy and then compare it with the welfare that can be attained if the paternalistic government implements the SPP. To do this, we use the individual consumer's intertemporal objective function, given by equation (15), to calculate the discounted value of future utilities in the unregulated market economy and under SPP, respectively. Denote the individual's discounted value of future utility at time $\tau$ along the SPP time path by $\tilde{U}^{SPP}(\tau)$. We evaluate $\tilde{U}^{SPP}(\tau)$ at each point in time, meaning that we calculate $\tilde{U}^{SPP}(\tau)$ for $\tau = 0, 1, 2, \ldots, 150$. By doing this, we end up with a time path of $\tilde{U}^{SPP}(\tau)$ for $\tau \in [0, 150]$. We then compare the time path for $\tilde{U}^{SPP}(\tau)$ with the corresponding time path of welfare, $\tilde{U}^{UME}(\tau)$, in the unregulated market economy. This is illustrated in Figure 3.3, where we use the normalization

$$\alpha = \frac{\tilde{U}(\tau)}{\tilde{U}^{SPP}(\tau)} \text{ for } \tau = 0, 1, 2, \ldots, 150 \tag{51}$$

to compare the welfare in a given regime with the welfare under SPP. As such, $\alpha(SPP) = \tilde{U}^{SPP}(\tau)/\tilde{U}^{SPP}(\tau)$ will be equal to 1 for the SPP policy at all times. This is the solid line in Figure 3.3.

As can be seen, the ratio $\alpha(UME) = \tilde{U}^{UME}(\tau)/\tilde{U}^{SPP}(\tau)$ is less than

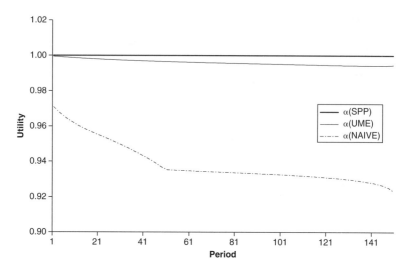

*Figure 3.3    Welfare comparison*

unity at all points in time, indicating that $\widetilde{U}^{SPP}(\tau) > \widetilde{U}^{UME}(\tau)$ for all $\tau$. This illustrates that when the individual consumer applies hyperbolic discounting, the welfare of the consumer can be improved by implementing the SPP. In Figure 3.3, we also depict the outcome in the unregulated market economy when the consumer acts naively in the sense described in section 3.1.2 (corresponds to $\alpha$(NAIVE)). As can be seen, the difference in welfare between acting naively or being sophisticated increases over time.

Let us now compare the SPP with other policy alternatives, where the latter are obtained by allowing the social planner's discount rate, $\theta$, to differ from $\rho = 0.02$. We will consider four policy alternatives based on using $\theta = 0.01$, $\theta = 0.015$, $\theta = 0.03$ and $\theta = 0.04$ respectively, in the social planner's problem. By plugging the time path of consumption corresponding to each of these paternalistic policies into equation (15), we can calculate the time path of $\widetilde{U}(\tau)$ for each policy alternative as well as the ratio defined in equation (51). The ratio corresponding to the policy alternative based on $\theta = 0.01$ will be denoted $\alpha(\theta = 0.01)$ and so on. This is illustrated in Figure 3.4.

To interpret these time paths, recall first that the behavior of a sophisticated consumer who has a pure rate of time preference of $\rho = 0.02$ is observationally equivalent to that of a consumer who uses exponential discounting with a rate of time preference equal to $\varphi = 0.034$. Now, consider the paternalistic policy based on $\theta = 0.04$. As illustrated in Figure 3.4 (the curve $\alpha(\theta = 0.04)$), implementing this policy will not improve

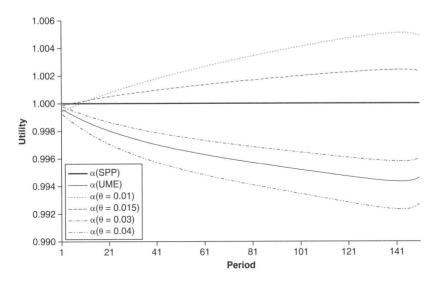

*Figure 3.4    Welfare comparison of different policies*

the welfare of the individual consumer compared with the outcome in the unregulated market economy. However, implementing a policy based on a discount rate that is below $\varphi = 0.034$ will raise the welfare of the individual in later periods of life compared with the outcome in the unregulated market economy. The ranking is monotonic; the lower the discount rate underlying the paternalistic policy, the larger will be the future welfare of the consumer. The explanation is that the lower the paternalistic discount rate, the more capital will be accumulated when following this policy and the larger will be consumption in later time periods. However, this means that the consumer will forego consumption when young. As illustrated in Figure 3.4, this means that the welfare of the consumer when young need not be improved compared with the level attained in the unregulated market economy. As such, it is not possible to say that any of the suggested alternative policies can unambiguously beat the SPP in terms of improving the overall welfare of the consumer. Rather, the simulations show that the different paternalistic policies imply a trade-off. It is possible to produce higher welfare for the individual in the long run by implementing a paternalistic policy based on a discount rate less than the pure rate $\theta = 0.02$, but the cost is that this implies reduced welfare when young compared to SPP. However, the simulations indicate that the improvement in welfare in later periods is potentially larger than the reduction of welfare when young (follows by comparing $\alpha(\rho = 0.01)$ and $\alpha(\rho = 0.015)$ with $\alpha(\rho = 0.02)$).

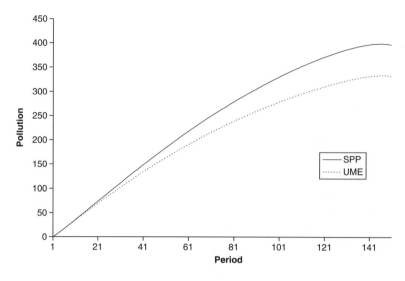

*Figure 3.5  The stock of pollution in an unregulated market economy*

### 4.4.2  General case: two externalities

Let us now turn to the general case where both the environmental and the intrapersonal externality are present. Beginning with the time paths of consumption and capital, they will have similar shapes as the time paths depicted in Figures 3.1 and 3.2. The new feature regards the evolution of the stock of pollution. Figure 3.5 depicts two time paths of pollution in the unregulated market economy (UME). The dotted curve is the time path generated in the UME by a sophisticated consumer whereas the solid curve depicts the pollution in the UME generated by a consumer who applies standard exponential discounting (that is, $\phi(v) = 0$ for all $v$). Both consumers use $\rho = 0.02$. Note that even though the consumer discounts the future harder under hyperbolic discounting, the accumulation of the stock of pollution will be smaller in this setting. The explanation is that since the stock of physical capital will be smaller when the consumer applies hyperbolic discounting, so will the amount of goods produced. This means that less energy will be used in production, which implies that emissions, and hence the growth of the stock of pollution, will be smaller in an economy where the consumer applies hyperbolic discounting. As such, this indicates that the environmental problem may be smaller in an unregulated market economy made up of consumers who apply hyperbolic discounting.

Recall from the discussion in section 3.2 that a social planner whose discount rate is given by $\theta = \rho$ will attach a higher value to the shadow price of pollution than the consumer. Let us therefore illustrate this difference

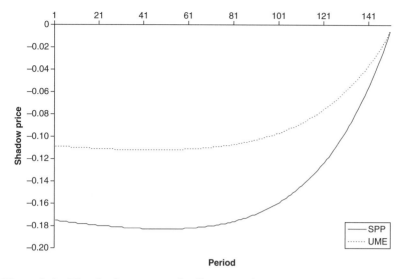

*Figure 3.6*   *The shadow prices of pollution in the unregulated market
economy by the social planner and the individual consumer*

in shadow prices between the social planner and the individual consumer
for the stock of pollution generated in the unregulated market economy
by a sophisticated consumer (Figure 3.6). At the outset, the paternalistic
government's valuation of environmental damage is about 60 per cent
larger, in absolute value, than that of the consumer. Although the difference in valuation diminishes over time, it remains relatively large up to the
time horizon.

Let us now turn to the welfare effects of paternalistic policy. Here also,
we allow the paternalistic government to have a discount rate that differs
from that of the individual consumer, and as in the previous section, we
consider paternalistic policies based on $\theta = 0.01$, $\theta = 0.015$, $\theta = 0.02$
(SPP), $\theta = 0.03$ and $\theta = 0.04$ respectively. Figure 3.7 shows that the
welfare comparison is qualitatively similar to that depicted in Figure 3.4.
As such, the interpretation in that section also applies here.

Finally, let us also consider the outcome if the pollution is transboundary and the consumer resides in small country. Here 'small' means that the
government does not perceive that the emission of the individual country
can affect the level of aggregate emissions. In the absence of cooperation
between countries, the paternalistic government will set the emission tax
to zero, meaning that the government only corrects for the intrapersonal
externality, henceforth referred to as a restricted paternalistic policy.
Normalizing the number of countries to one, let us again compare the

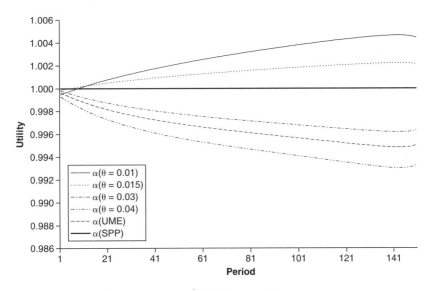

*Figure 3.7   Welfare comparison of different policies*

welfare attained in the unregulated market economy with that experienced under the restricted paternalistic policies based on $\theta = 0.01$, $\theta = 0.015$, $\theta = 0.02$ (SPP), $\theta = 0.03$ and $\theta = 0.04$ (Figure 3.8).

A striking result is that implementing the restricted SPP will reduce the welfare of the consumer compared to the welfare attained in the unregulated market economy. The explanation is that by correcting for the intrapersonal externality, which induces the consumer to save more, the stock of capital and production will increase in the future. This will lead to a corresponding increase in the use of energy, which implies that the acumulation of the stock of pollution increases. Since the paternalistic government does not correct for the environmental externality in this scenario, the negative welfare effect generated by higher pollution dominates the positive welfare effect induced by internalizing the intrapersonal externality. Note also that of the other alternative paternalistic policies, it is only the alternative policy based on $\theta = 0.01$ where the positive effect of higher consumption outweighs the negative effect of a larger stock of pollution.

## 5   CONCLUDING REMARKS

This chapter concerns welfare measurement and the effectiveness of paternalistic policy in terms of improving individual welfare when the

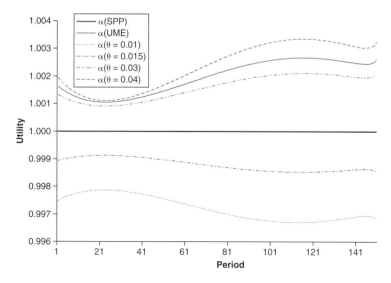

*Figure 3.8  Welfare comparison of different restricted policies*

consumer applies hyperbolic discounting. This issue is analysed within the framework of a Ramsey model in continuous time, and following Barro (1999), we incorporate hyperbolic discounting as an additive non-linear function of time into the traditional exponential discount function with a fixed (pure) rate of time preference.

One main conclusion from the analysis is that hyperbolic discounting will make welfare measurement more complex, basically for two reasons. First, a policy determined at a given point in time need not be optimal from the individual consumer's perspective in subsequent periods. This means that standard dynamic envelope properties do not hold when evaluating the Hamiltonian from the perspective of the individual consumer along the equilibrium path. Second, when the consumer uses a hyperbolic discount function to evaluate the future, this introduces a time dependency into the model which needs to be accounted for. As such, this will affect the relationship between the discounted sum of future utility and the Hamiltonian.

In the chapter, we have also used simulations to analyse the effectiveness of paternalistic policy. We would like to emphasize two results from this part. First, although SPP is the standard approach for deriving paternalistic policies in the presence of hyperbolic discounting, the simulation results indicate that there are other policy alternatives available. The trade-off between SPP and these alternatives basically has to do with the fact that the policy alternatives provide the individual with lower welfare in the near future but with higher welfare in the far-off future compared with the SPP. As such, whether an alternative policy should be favored over SPP is then a 'matter of taste' and depends on whether the positive welfare effect in the future is favored over the negative welfare effect when young. Second, the simulations also indicate that if the paternalistic government is restricted to only internalizing the intrapersonal externality, for example, because of transboundary pollution, implementing a restricted SPP may have a negative effect on welfare.

## ACKNOWLEDGEMENTS

The authors would like to thank Thomas Aronsson and Karl-Gustaf Löfgren for helpful comments and suggestions. Research grants from the Bank of Sweden Tercentenary Foundation, (Stiftelsen Riksbankens Jubileumsfond), the Swedish Council for Working Life and Social Research (FAS) and the National Tax Board (Skatteverket) are also gratefully acknowledged.

## NOTES

1. See Rabin (2002), and Camerer and Loewenstein (2004) for surveys in this field.
2. For a brief literature overview, see below.
3. See Laibson (1997) and Barro (1999).
4. See for example, Phelps and Pollak (1968), Pollak (1968), and Laibson (1996, 1998).
5. See below.
6. For an overview, see Aronsson et al. (1997).
7. The time dependence via the discount factor can be made redundant by solving the problem in current value terms.
8. For a survey, see Camerer and Loewenstein (2004).
9. See also, for example, Blomquist and Micheletto (2006), Tenhunen and Tuomala (2007), and Pirttilä and Tenhunen (2008) for other non-welfarist approaches to optimal taxation.
10. This expression is derived by solving the differential equation in equation (9) subject to the transversality condition $\lim_{t \to \infty} \mu(t) = 0$. Observe that the definition used here means that the shadow price will be negative.
11. See Aronsson (1998).
12. Since the pure discount rate is $\rho = 0.02$, the policy under SPP is obtained by setting $\theta = 0.02$ in the social planner's problem.

## REFERENCES

Aronsson, T. (1998), 'Wefare Measurement, Green Accounting and Distortionary Taxes', *Journal of Public Economics* **70**, 273–295.

Aronsson, T., Johansson, P.-O. and Löfgren K.-G. (1997), *Welfare Measurement, Sustainability and Green National Accounting: A Growth Theoretical Approach.* Cheltenham: Edward Elgar.

Aronsson, T. and Löfgren, K.-G. (1993), 'Welfare Consequences of Technological and Environmental Externalities in the Ramsey Growth Model', *National Resource Modeling* **7 (1)**, 1–14.

Aronsson, T. and Löfgren, K.-G. (1995), 'Natural Product Related Welfare Measures in the Presence of Technological Change: Externalities and Uncertainty', *Environmental and Resource Economics* **5**, 321–332.

Aronsson, T. and Löfgren, K.-G. (1996), 'Social Accounting and Welfare Measurement in a Growth Model with Human Capital', *Scandinavian Journal of Economics* **98 (2)**, 185–201.

Aronsson, T. and Sjögren, T. (2009), 'Quasi-Hyperbolic Discounting and Mixed Taxation', Mimeo, Umeå University.

Aronsson, T. and Thunström, L. (2008), 'A Note on Optimal Paternalism and Health Capital Subsidies', *Economics Letters* **101**, 241–242.

Barro, R. J. (1999), 'Ramsey Meets Laibson in the Neoclassical Growth Model', *Quarterly Journal of Economics* **114 (4)**, 1125–1152.

Blomquist, S. and Micheletto, L. (2006), 'Optimal Redistributive Taxation when Government's and Agents' Preferences Differ', *Journal of Public Economics* **90**, 1215–1233.

Camerer, C. F. and Loewenstein, G. (2004), 'Behavioral Economics: Past, Present, Future', in C. F. Camerer, G. Loewenstein and M. Rabin (eds), *Advances in Behavioral Economics.* Princeton, NJ: Princeton University Press.

Goldman, S. M. (1980), 'Consistent Plans', *Review of Economic Studies* **47**, 533–537.

Gruber, J. and Kőszegi, B. (2001) 'Is Addiction "Rational"? Theory and Evidence', *Quarterly Journal of Economics* **116**, 1261–1305.

Gruber, J. and Kőszegi, B. (2004) 'Tax Incidence when Individuals are Time Inconsistent: The Case of Cigarette Excise Taxes', *Journal of Public Economics* **88**, 1989–2007.

Laibson, D. (1996), *Hyperbolic Discount Functions, Undersaving and Savings Policy*, NBER Working Paper 5635, Cambridge, MA: National Bureau of Economic Research.

Laibson, D. (1997), 'Golden Eggs and Hyperbolic Discounting', *Quarterly Journal of Economics* **62**, 443–477.

O'Donoghue, T. and Rabin, M. (2003), 'Studying Optimal Paternalism, Illustrated by a Model of Sin Taxes', *The American Economic Review*, **93 (2)**, 186–191.

O'Donoghue, T. and Rabin, M. (2006), 'Optimal Sin Taxes', *Journal of Public Economics* **90**, 1825–1849.

Phelps, E. S. and Pollak, R. A. (1968), 'On Second-Best National Saving and Game-Equilibrium Growth', *Review of Economic Studies* **35**, 185–199.

Pirttilä, J. and Tenhunen, S. (2008), 'Pawns and Queens Revisited: Public Provision of Private Goods when Individuals Make Mistakes', *International Tax and Public Finance* **15**, 599–619.

Pollak, R. A. (1968), 'Consistent Planning', *Review of Economic Studies* **35**, 201–208.

Rabin, M. (2002), 'A Perspective on Psychology and Economics', *European Economic Review* **46**, 657–685.

Strotz, R. H. (1956), 'Myopia and Inconsistency in Dynamic Utility Maximization', *Review of Economic Studies* **23**, 165–180.

Tenhunen, S. and Tuomala, M. (2007), *On Optimal Lifetime Redistribution Policy.* Manuscript.

Thaler, R. (1981), 'Some Empirical Evidence on Dynamic Inconsistency', *Economics Letters* **8**, 201–207.

Weitzman, M. L. (1976), 'On the Welfare Significance of National Product in a Dynamic Economy', *Quarterly Journal of Economics* **90**, 156–162.

Weitzman, M. L. (1998), 'Why the Far-Distant Future Should be Discounted at its Lowest Possible Rate', *Journal of Environmental Economics and Management* **36**, 261–271.

# 4 Dynamic endogenous risk and social accounting

*Ram Ranjan and Jason F. Shogren*

## 1 INTRODUCTION

Social accounting aims to better understand the true performance of an economy by including the depreciation of the entire stock of capital, including reproducible capital, human capital and natural capital (see for example, Weitzman, 1976, Peskin and Peskin, 1978, Aronsson et al., 1997). Shadow prices can be used as relative weights to construct an index to measure changes in the capital stock or the entire capital stock. In theory, this index can be used to judge better if unobservable social well-being tracks observable economic progress or regress over time. For the most part, however, social accounting models have focused on temporal issues within deterministic environments. Incorporating risk would add more complications, but in theory at least the cost of risk should be reflected in the shadow prices of the capital stock. That is, if one assumes risk is exogenous and beyond the control of the representative agent (for example, Dasgupta, 2009).

But when faced with risk, private citizens are free to choose whether to invest resources to change our beliefs about good and bad states of nature. We invest in self-protection to reduce the chance of a bad event or self-insurance to reduce the severity of a bad event or both (see for example, Ehrlich and Becker, 1972). Both actions make the risk endogenous to people. Understanding how people decide to go privately for self-protection and self-insurance is crucial for efficient provision of social goods and accurate accounting of social welfare. This holds especially when thinking about how to accommodate risks to human health. While a literature exists on self-protection and self-insurance behavior,[1] the standard endogenous risk model has some limiting properties relative to real-world decision making and the question of social accounting. The model has focused on risk reduction choices within a static expected utility world of one risk. But people make risk management decisions (i) over time (see for example, Blomquist, 2004; Agee and Crocker, 2007),[2] and (ii) over multiple risks.[3] The open question is how dynamics and multiple risks affect the mix of self-protection and self-insurance and the

78

valuation of collective risk reduction activities which would be used in social accounting.

Our analysis extends the welfare measurement and dynamic health risk work of Aronsson et al. (1994) and Johansson and Löfgren (1995) by including both self-protection and self-insurance and multiple risks. Our model reveals four main results. First, self-protection and self-insurance against a particular risk, when considered under multiple risks, might be higher or lower than that arising under a single risk. Second, the presence of multiple risks leads to discounting of those health risks that have lower damage. Third, when health events with lower damage also have higher exogenous risk components, it leads to further lowering in risk reduction efforts relating to such health events. Fourth, when health events with high damage have a larger exogenous risk component, protection is shifted to events with low damage and lower risks. In general, the possibility of optimal allocation of endogenous risk reduction over time implies that when multiple risks are present, higher risk events do not necessarily command a uniformly higher effort throughout as compared to lower risk events. This result may be even more pronounced when the costs and effectiveness of efforts vary for different risks.

## 2   A STATIC BENCHMARK MODEL

Following Shogren and Crocker (1991), consider a person exposed to a health risk from being in a particular environment which he cannot avoid. The hazard poses a risk to health ($h$) which could deteriorate stochastically and suddenly. The person is healthy up to $t$ and then becomes ill. This modeling of health hazard is based upon the dose-response approach, which assumes that as dose increases, health depreciates, and that the critical thresholds for health breakdown are random (Rosen, 1981). The risk and level of poor health can, however, be controlled through self-protection and self-insurance (Ehrlich and Becker 1972; Shogren and Crocker, 1999). When a person invests in self-protection ($s$), he reduces the probability of bad health; by investing in self-insurance ($z$), he reduces the level of bad health if his health breaks down. The probability of health breakdown, $p$, is:

$$p = p(s, r, \gamma), \text{ with } p'_s(s, r, \gamma) < 0 \ \& \ p''_s(s, r, \gamma) > 0 \tag{1}$$

where $r$ parameterizes the exogenous risk beyond his direct control; $\gamma$ is an exogenous parameter that influences the hazard rate in addition to $r$, and $s$ is the level of self-protection used to mitigate the risk of health catastrophe.

The person also takes steps ($z$) to self-insure himself if a health catastrophe is realized, in which case the damage depends on $z$:

$$d = d(z), d'(z) < 0 \tag{2}$$

The costs of self-protection and self-insurance are:

$$c = c(s, z), c'_s(s, z) > 0, c'_z(s, z), c'_{ss}(s, z) > 0, c'_{zz}(s, z) > 0$$
$$\text{and } c'_{zs}(s, z) > 0 \tag{3}$$

In the pre-health event state, a person derives utility from fixed wealth net of the expenditures on self-protection and self-insurance:

$$U_0 = U(w - c(s, z)) \tag{4}$$

In the post-event state, he derives utility from wealth net of the expenditures on self-protection, self-insurance and damage as:

$$U_1 = U(w - c(s, z) - d(z)) \tag{5}$$

Due to the uncertainty related to his health outcome, the person allocates his resources to maximize expected utility $J$:

$$J = U_0(w - c(z, s)) \cdot (1 - p(s, r, \gamma))$$
$$+ U_1(w - c(z, s) - d(z)) \cdot p(s, r, \gamma) \tag{6}$$

Equation (6) is the sum of two terms: pre-event utility and post-event utility. In the pre-event scenario, the person enjoys utility from wages net of self-protection and self-insurance expenditures, whereas in the post-event scenario, he incurs an additional cost of the health event. The first order condition for self-protection is:

$$U'_{0w} \cdot p(s, r, \gamma) \cdot (c'_s(z, s)) - U'_{0w} \cdot (c'_s(z, s)) - U_0 \cdot p'_s(s, r, \gamma)$$
$$= -U'_{1w} \cdot p(s, r, \gamma) \cdot (-c'_s(z, s)) - U_1 \cdot p'_s(s, r, \gamma) \tag{7}$$

Because self-protection influences both the utility function and the probability of the health event, optimization requires changes in pre-event expected utility to equal the changes in post-event expected utility from a marginal self-protection effort.

The first order condition for self-insurance is:

$$U'_{0w} \cdot (-c'_z(z, s)) \cdot (1 - p(s, r, \gamma)) - U'_{1w} \cdot p(s, r, \gamma) \cdot (c'_z(z, s))$$
$$- U'_{1w} \cdot p(s, r, \gamma) \cdot (d'(z)) = 0 \qquad (8)$$

Since self-insurance does not affect the probability of the health outcome, condition (8) requires the expected marginal changes to pre-health utility from a unit of self-insurance to equal the expected marginal changes in the post-event utility from reduced damages.

Finally, we derive the static willingness to pay (WTP) for a marginal reduction in exogenous component of the risk using the implicit function theorem as:

$$-\frac{\dfrac{\partial J}{\partial r}}{\dfrac{\partial J}{\partial w}} = -\frac{p'_r(U_0 - U_1)}{U'_{0w}p + (1 - p)U'_{1w}} \qquad (9)$$

The term in the numerator is the expected difference between the ex ante and ex post utilities from a marginal reduction in risk and the term in the denominator is the expected change in the utility from a change in wealth.

This static model is the baseline against which we now explore how the WTP and the first-order conditions change when risks are dynamic and multiple risks exist. First, for social accounting purposes, dynamic considerations of self-protection and self-insurance are needed to determine shadow prices for the change in the stock of beliefs which would serve as an indicator to guide health-related policy incentives. Dynamic risks allow people to distribute their costs and health risks intertemporally. This allows for a higher utility when people may have a higher preference for current consumption – a phenomenon associated with hyperbolic discounting, which we do not address here. Second, including multiple risks allows us to examine how many risks affect the trade-offs between self-protection and self-insurance for one particular risk. The time path of self-protection and self-insurance over one health event, when decision making spans a multiple risk environment, may be entirely different from the one where multiple risks do not exist. We first explore the influence of intertemporal considerations on decision making.

## 3   A DYNAMIC MODEL

Now suppose the person faces a health risk, $p(t)$ at any time $t$, which causes health breakdown after crossing over a random threshold (see Johansson and Löfgren, 1995).[4] The probability of health breakdown is characterized by a random event with an exponential distribution, the hazard rate of which is given by $\dot{\lambda}(t)$, and is defined as:

$$\dot{\lambda}(t) = p(s(t), r, \gamma) \tag{10}$$

Let the accumulated sum of the hazard rate be defined by the variable $\lambda(t)$ as:

$$\lambda(t) = \int_0^t p(s(x), r, \gamma) dx, \tag{11}$$

The person also takes steps $z(t)$ to insure himself in case of a health catastrophe, following which the level of health damages are determined by the accumulated stock of self-insurance, $k(t)$, defined as:

$$k(t) = \int_0^t (z(x) - \delta) dx, \tag{12}$$

where $\delta$ is the decay rate of the stock of self-insurance.

He derives utility from his wealth net of the expenditures on self-protection and self-insurance measures as:

$$U(t) = U(w - c(s(t), z(t))) \tag{13}$$

His long-term expected utility $J$ is a function of both pre-event and post-event utility. In the post-event scenario, he gets his discounted sum of utility from wages net of health expenses, which is arrived at by integrating the per-period post-event utility as:

$$\int_0^\infty U(w - c(h(k(t)))) \cdot \exp(-\rho \cdot x) dx = \frac{U(w - c(h(k(t))))}{\rho}. \tag{14}$$

In equation (14), once the health damages take place at time $t$, the per-period damages remain constant thereafter. Post-event utility is a function of the level of insurance capital accumulated until the time when the event occurs. We do not model any physical pain and suffering in the post-catastrophe scenario as a part of the person's utility function. His pre-event utility up to any time $t$ is weighted by the probability of surviving the health event up to that time.

Due to the uncertainty related to his long-term health outcome, he allocates his resources inter-temporally to maximize his long-term expected utility, defined as:

$$J = \int_o^\infty p(t) \cdot \exp(-\lambda(t)) \cdot \int_0^t U(w - c(z(x), s(x))) \cdot \exp(-\rho \cdot x) dx dt$$

$$+ \int_0^\infty \frac{U(w - c(h(k(t))))}{\rho} \cdot p(t) \cdot \exp(-\lambda(t)) \cdot \exp(-\rho \cdot t) dt \quad (15)$$

where $c(h(k(t)))$ is the cost of the health event and is a function of the stock of self-insurance measures. In equation (15), the first term is the expected pre-event utility function and the second term is the post-event utility function. Further integrating by parts the first term in equation (15) and combining with the second term, we get:

$$J = \int_o^\infty \left\{ U(w - c(z(t), s(t))) \cdot \exp(-\rho \cdot t) \right.$$

$$\left. + p(t) \cdot \frac{U(w - c(h(k(t))))}{\rho} \cdot \exp(-\rho \cdot t) \right\} \cdot \exp(-\lambda(t)) dt \quad (16)$$

The person maximizes equation (16) subject to the equations of motion for the stocks of insurance capital $k(t)$ and accumulated hazard $\lambda(t)$. The present value Hamiltonian $H(t)$ is:

$$\left\{ U(w - c(z(t), s(t))) + p(s(t), r, \gamma) \cdot \frac{U(w - c(h(k(t))))}{\rho} \right\}$$

$$\cdot \exp(-\lambda(t)) \cdot \exp(-\rho \cdot t) + m_1(t) \cdot p(s(t), r, \gamma)$$

$$+ m_2(t) \cdot (z(t) - \delta) \quad (17)$$

where $m_1(t)$ and $m_2(t)$ are the shadow prices of accumulated risk $\lambda(t)$ and accumulated insurance capital $k(t)$. First-order conditions with respect to self-insurance and self-protection imply:

$$- U'_w \cdot c'_{s(t)} \cdot \exp(-\lambda(t)) \cdot \exp(-\rho \cdot t)$$

$$+ p'_{s(t)}(t) \cdot \frac{U(w - c(h(k(t))))}{\rho} \cdot \exp(-\lambda(t)) \cdot \exp(-\rho \cdot t)$$

$$+ m_1(t) \cdot p'_{s(t)} = 0 \quad (18)$$

$$- U'_w \cdot c'_{z(t)} \cdot \exp(-\lambda(t)) \cdot \exp(-\rho \cdot t) + m_2(t) = 0. \qquad (19)$$

Comparing the first-order conditions to the static case, we see that marginal self-protection and self-insurance are influenced by (i) the rate of time preference $\rho$, and (ii) the shadow prices of $\lambda(t)$ and $k(t)$. These shadow prices reflect the long-term discounted sums of utility changes from an incremental increase in the stocks of $\lambda(t)$ and $k(t)$. For instance, if self-protection is lowered at the margin, the risks of a health event would increase, which would affect the expected damages from the health event.

## 3.1  Dynamic Endogenous Risk and Social Accounting

One key question is how to value accumulated self protection and self-insurance in the context of social accounting (see for example, Aronsson and Löfgren, 1996; Aronsson, 2008). We can derive the WTP measure for risk reduction by reinterpreting the shadow prices in terms of the present value Hamiltonian $H(t)$. The no-arbitrage condition with respect to the shadow price of accumulated risk is given as:

$$\dot{m}_1 = -\frac{\partial H(t)}{\partial \lambda(t)} = (U(w - c(z(t), s(t))) \cdot \exp(-\rho \cdot t)$$

$$+ p(t) \cdot \frac{U(w - c(h(k(t))))}{\rho} \cdot \exp(-\rho \cdot t)) \cdot \exp(-\lambda(t)) \qquad (20)$$

Solving for $m_1(t)$ gives:

$$m_1(t) = \int_0^t (U(w - c(z(t), s(t))) \cdot \exp(-\rho \cdot t)$$

$$+ p(t) \cdot \frac{U(w - c\{h[k(t)]\}}{\rho} \cdot \exp(-\rho \cdot t)) \cdot \exp(-\lambda(t)) dx \qquad (21)$$

Equation (21) sums up the expected value function up to time $t$. This implies that the welfare effect of an increase in the state variable $\lambda(t)$ is the loss in welfare in terms of the change in the total expected value function from that increased risk.

Next, we consider the impact of an exogenous income increase on total welfare. Following the dynamic envelope theorem, we derive the change in the value function $J$ due to an exogenous parameter as (Seierstad and Sydsaeter 1987, p. 216):

$$\frac{\partial J}{\partial w} = \int_0^\infty \frac{\partial H(z^*(t), \lambda^*(t), k^*(t), s^*(t), r, \gamma, m_1(t), m_2(t))}{\partial w} \partial t, \qquad (22)$$

where $\partial H(z^*(t), \lambda^*(t), k^*(t), s^*(t), r, \gamma, m_1(t), m_2(t))$ is the Hamiltonian evaluated at the optimal values of the state and control variables. We can also derive the trade-off between forgone wages for a reduction in the hazard rate, which is:

$$\frac{\partial w}{\partial \lambda} = \frac{\dfrac{\partial J}{\partial \lambda}}{\dfrac{\partial J}{\partial w}}$$

$$= \frac{m_1}{\displaystyle\int_0^t \frac{\partial H(z^*(x), \lambda^*(x), k^*(x), s^*(x), r, \gamma, m_1(x), m_2(x))}{\partial w} \partial x} \qquad (23)$$

Equation (23) presents the shadow price of accumulated risks as a measure of the dynamic willingness to pay. Another way to look at the WTP measure is by the steady state trade-offs in which a person keeps the shadow price of risks constant. Further redefining the shadow prices of accumulated hazard and insurance capital as:

$$m_1(t) \cdot \exp(\lambda(t)) = n_1(t) \text{ and } m_2(t) \cdot \exp(\lambda(t)) = n_2(t), \qquad (24)$$

from (18) and (19), we rewrite the shadow prices of accumulated hazard and the insurance capital as:

$$n_1(t) = \frac{U_w' \cdot c_{s(t)}' - p_{s(t)}' \cdot \dfrac{U(w - c(h(k(t))))}{\rho}}{p_{s(t)}'}, \text{ and} \qquad (25)$$

$$n_2(t) = U_w' \cdot c_{z(t)}' \qquad (26)$$

The shadow price of stock of beliefs as given by (25) is influenced by the rate of time preference. This implies that the higher the time preference, the lower the numerator ($p_s'$ being negative in self-protection effort), thereby decreasing the future costs of a marginal reduction in self-protection. Also, if the costs are non-linear (as assumed), reducing self-protection marginally reduces expenditures at a non-linear rate, thereby lowering the shadow price of risk. The implication of a non-linear cost function in a dynamic environment is to postpone self-protection over time as both damages and costs in the future are discounted.

Next, the no-arbitrage conditions for the two shadow prices are derived as:

$$\dot{n}_1(t) = \left\{ U(w - c(z(t), s(t))) + p(t) \cdot \frac{U(w - c(h(k(t))))}{\rho} \right\}$$
$$+ n_1(t) \cdot (\rho + p(t)) \tag{27}$$

$$\dot{n}_2(t) = \left\{ p(t) \cdot \frac{U'_w \cdot c'_{k(t)}}{\rho} \right\} + n_2(t) \cdot (\rho + p(t)). \tag{28}$$

In steady state, when the person takes self-protection and self-insurance measures so that the shadow prices of hazard stock and insurance capital are constant, equations (27) and (28) are equated to zero. Equation (27) can be further expanded using (25) to get:

$$\dot{n}_1(t) = 0 \Rightarrow \frac{\left\{ U(w - c(z(t), s(t))) + p(t) \cdot \dfrac{U(w - c(h(k(t))))}{\rho} \right\}}{(\rho + p(t))}$$

$$= -\frac{U'_w \cdot c'_{s(t)} - p'_{s(t)} \cdot \dfrac{U(w - c(h(k(t))))}{\rho}}{p'_{s(t)}} \tag{29}$$

The right-hand side of equation (29) is the shadow price $n_1(t)$, which in steady state equals the discounted sum total of per-period expected gains from pre- and post-health events (as given by the left-hand side). The risk of illness adds an additional component to the discount rate. Using the implicit function theorem, the amount of wage increase required to keep the shadow price of accumulated risks constant, when faced with an exogenous risk increase, is given by $\partial \dot{n}_1 / \partial r \cdot \partial w / \partial \dot{n}_1$ as:[5]

$$\frac{\partial w}{\partial r} = -\frac{\dfrac{p'_r \cdot U(w - c(h(k)))}{\rho}}{U'_w + p \cdot \dfrac{U'_w}{\rho} + \dfrac{p + \rho}{p'_s}\left( U''_w \cdot c'_s - \dfrac{p'_s \cdot U'_w}{\rho} \right)}. \tag{30}$$

Equation (30) derives the willingness to pay to avoid a marginal increase in the exogenous environmental risk that would keep the shadow price of the accumulated risks constant. We now develop the model further to consider how multiple risks affect dynamic self-protection and self-insurance and the shadow price of the accumulated risk or the belief stock.

## 4   A DYNAMIC MODEL WITH TWO RISKS

Until now our model has assumed that people face no other risks, or at least if they do, these are not considered in self-protection and self-insurance. In reality, self-protection and self-insurance against one disease may be influenced by the threat of another disease or accident. A person may simultaneously face the risk of cancer through contact with hazardous chemicals at his workplace and the risk of accident while commuting to work. Both kinds of risks present the chance of death. But it is unclear how self-protection and self-insurance for cancer could be influenced by risks of accident. One clue is available through the evaluation of the ex-post scenario for the person when he either gets cancer or has an accident. In either case, he may lose his ability to enjoy life, if not his life itself. We address the question – when the risk of dying or becoming debilitated increases, how do self-protection and self-insurance for cancer change and vice versa?

Suppose the person faces two kinds of risks, $p_1(t)$ and $p_2(t)$, both of which cause health breakdown after a crossing over of the random and unknown threshold. The probability of health breakdown from the first type of risk is characterized by a random event with exponential distribution, the hazard rate of which is defined as $p_1(t)$:

$$p_1(t) = p_1(s_1(t), r_1, \gamma), \tag{31}$$

where the parameter $r_1$ parameterizes the risk posed by the environment which is beyond the persons direct control; $\gamma$ is an exogenous parameter that influences the hazard rate besides $r$; and $s_1(t)$ is the level of self-protection to reduce the risk of health catastrophe. As before, let the accumulated sum of the hazard rate be defined by the parameter $\lambda_1(t)$ as:

$$\lambda_1(t) = \int_0^t p_1(s_1(x), r_1, \gamma) dx, \tag{32}$$

In a similar vein, the accumulated sum of hazard rates for the other kind of risk can be determined as:

$$\lambda_2(t) = \int_0^t p_2(s_2(x), r_2, \gamma) dx. \tag{33}$$

The person optimizes his intertemporal profits by allocating self-protection and self-insurance over time and between risks. The value derived can be broken into three parts: value ($v_0$) before either of the health events takes place; value after health event I takes place ($v_1$); and value after health event II takes place ($v_2$). While it is possible for both health events to take place, for simplicity we assume that once either occurs, the person becomes immune to the other event, or even if it does happen, there is no additional cost (for instance, when both risks are deadly). Following this framework, the value function before either of the events occurs is given by:

$$E[v_0] = \left\{ \int_0^\infty \exp(-\lambda_1(t) - \lambda_2(t)) \cdot (U(w - c(s(t), z(t)))) \right.$$

$$\left. \cdot \exp(-\rho \cdot t) dt \right\}. \tag{34}$$

$E[v_0]$ comprises two components – $E_1[v_0]$ and $E_2[v_0]$. The expected value ($E_1[v_0]$) when health event I happens at time $t$ and before event II, can be given as:

$$E_1[v_0] = \left\{ \int_0^\infty p_1(t) \cdot \exp(-\lambda_1(t)) \cdot \exp(-\lambda_2(t)) \right.$$

$$\left. \cdot \int_0^t (U(w - c(s(x), z(x)))) \cdot \exp(-\rho \cdot x) dx dt \right\}. \tag{35}$$

After integration by parts, this can be further written as:

$$E_1[v_0] = \left\{ \int_0^\infty p_1(t) \cdot \frac{\exp(-\lambda_1(t) - \lambda_2(t))}{p_1(t) + p_2(t)} \right.$$

$$\left. \cdot (U(w - c(s(t), z(t)))) \cdot \exp(-\rho \cdot t) dt \right\}. \tag{36}$$

Similarly, the expected value when health event I happens after event II (which happens at time $t$) is:

$$E_2[v_0] = \left\{ \int_0^\infty p_2(t) \cdot \frac{\exp(-\lambda_1(t) - \lambda_2(t))}{p_1(t) + p_2(t)} \right.$$

$$\cdot (U(w - c(s(t), z(t)))) \cdot \exp(-\rho \cdot t) dt \bigg\}. \tag{37}$$

The expected value before either of the two events occurs is:

$$E[v_0] = E_1[v_0] + E_2[v_0]$$

$$= \bigg\{ \int_0^\infty p_1(t) \cdot \frac{\exp(-\lambda_1(t) - \lambda_2(t))}{p_1(t) + p_2(t)} (U(w - c(s(t), z(t)))) \cdot \exp(-\rho \cdot t) dt \bigg\}$$

$$+ \bigg\{ \int_0^\infty p_2 \cdot \frac{\exp(-\lambda_1(t) - \lambda_2(t))}{p_1(t) + p_2(t)} \cdot (U(w - c(s(t), z(t)))) \cdot \exp(-\rho \cdot t) dt \bigg\}, \tag{38}$$

which when further simplified gives $E[v_0]$ as derived in equation (34). The value function after health event I occurs is given as:

$$E[v_1] = \bigg\{ \int_0^\infty p_1(t) \cdot \exp(-\lambda_1(t)) \cdot \frac{U(w - c(h(k_1(t))))}{\rho} \cdot \exp(-\rho \cdot t) dt \bigg\} \tag{39}$$

and the value function after health event II occurs is given as:

$$E[v_2] = \bigg\{ \int_0^\infty p_2(t) \cdot \exp(-\lambda_2(t)) \frac{U(w - c(h(k_2(t))))}{\rho} \cdot \exp(-\rho \cdot t) dt \bigg\}. \tag{40}$$

Bringing together the three value functions, the objective function is to maximize:

$$E[v_0] + E[v_1] + E[v_2] =$$

$$\bigg\{ \int_0^\infty \exp(-\lambda_1(t) - \lambda_2(t)) \cdot (U(w - c(s(t), z(t)))) \cdot \exp(-\rho \cdot t) dt \bigg\} +$$

$$\bigg\{ \int_0^\infty p_1(t) \cdot \exp(-\lambda_1(t)) \cdot \frac{U(w - c(h(k_1(t))))}{\rho} \cdot \exp(-\rho \cdot t) dt \bigg\} +$$

$$\bigg\{ \int_0^\infty p_2(t) \cdot \exp(-\lambda_2(t)) \cdot \frac{U(w - c(h(k_2(t))))}{\rho} \cdot \exp(-\rho \cdot t) dt \bigg\}. \tag{41}$$

Next, the current value Hamiltonian is specified as:

$$\exp(-\lambda_1(t) - \lambda_2(t)) \cdot (U(w - c(s(t), z(t))))$$

$$+ p_1(s_1(t), r, \gamma) \cdot \exp(-\lambda_1(t)) \frac{U(w - c(h(k_1(t))))}{\rho}$$

$$+ p_2(t) \cdot \exp(-\lambda_2(t)) \cdot \frac{U(w - c(h(k_2(t))))}{\rho}$$

$$+ m_{s1}(t) \cdot p_1(s_1(t), r, \gamma) + m_{z1}(t) \cdot (z_1(t) - \delta)$$

$$+ m_{s2}(t) \cdot p_2(s_2(t), r, \gamma) + m_{z2}(t) \cdot (z_2(t) - \delta). \tag{42}$$

The WTP measure for health event I for the case of multiple risks is:

$$\frac{\partial w}{\partial \lambda} = \frac{\dfrac{\partial J}{\partial \lambda}}{\dfrac{\partial J}{\partial w}}$$

$$= \frac{m_1(t)}{\displaystyle\int_0^t \frac{\partial H(z^*(x), \lambda^*(x), k^*(x), s^*(x), r, \gamma, m_1(x), m_2(x))}{\partial w} dx} \tag{43}$$

where

$$m_1(t) = \exp(-\lambda_1(t) - \lambda_2(t)) \cdot (U(w - c(s(t), z(t))))$$

$$+ p_1(s_1(t), r, \gamma) \cdot \exp(-\lambda_1(t)) \cdot \frac{U(w - c(h(k_1(t))))}{\rho}. \tag{44}$$

Comparing the shadow price of accumulated risks for health event I to the single risk case, we see that the shadow price of any risk within a multiple risk scenario depends on all other risks. The first-order condition for self protection on health risk I is:

$$- U'_w \cdot c'_{s(t)} \cdot \exp(-\lambda_1 - \lambda_2)$$

$$+ p'_{1s(t)} \cdot \frac{U(w - c(h(k(t))))}{\rho} \cdot \exp(-\lambda_1) + m_{1s_1}(t) \cdot p'_{1s(t)} = 0 \tag{45}$$

Next, we derive the no-arbitrage condition for the shadow price of health risk I as:

$$\dot{m}_1 = \exp(-\lambda_1(t) - \lambda_2(t)) \cdot (U(w - c(s(t), z(t))))$$

$$+ p_1(s_1(t), r, \gamma) \cdot \exp(-\lambda_1(t)) \cdot \frac{U(w - c(h(k_1(t))))}{\rho} + \rho \cdot m_1. \quad (46)$$

In steady state:

$$\exp(-\lambda_1(t) - \lambda_2(t)) \cdot (U(w - c(s(t), z(t))))$$

$$+ p_1(s_1(t), r, \gamma) \cdot \exp(-\lambda_1(t)) \frac{U(w - c(h(k_1(t))))}{\rho}$$

$$- \frac{\rho \cdot (-U'_w \cdot c'_{s(t)} \cdot \exp(-\lambda_1(t) - \lambda_2(t)) + p'_{1s(t)} \cdot \frac{U(w - c(h(k(t))))}{\rho} \cdot \exp(-\lambda_1(t)))}{p'_{1s(t)}(t)} = 0 \quad (46)$$

Following the same logic as before, we derive the WTP measure in a steady state:

$$\frac{\partial w}{\partial r} = \frac{\dfrac{p'_{r1} \cdot U(w - c(h(k)))}{\rho} \cdot \exp(-\lambda_1(t))}{D} \quad (48)$$

where $D = U'_w \cdot \exp(-\lambda_1(t) - \lambda_2(t)) + p_1 \cdot \dfrac{U'_w}{\rho} \cdot \exp(-\lambda_1(t))$

$$- \frac{\rho}{p'_{1s}} \cdot (U''_w c'_s) \cdot \exp(-\lambda_1(t)) + \exp(-\lambda_1(t)) \cdot U'_w.$$

Again note that the denominator is influenced by the shadow prices of accumulated risks for both the health events. We now impose some structure on the model to derive further insights related to risk tradeoffs. Assume:

- Wages: $w = h \cdot \tau$, where $\tau$ is factor that converts health into wages
- Utility: $w^\alpha \cdot h^{1-\alpha} = h^\alpha \cdot \tau^\alpha \cdot h^{1-\alpha} = h \cdot \tau^\alpha$
- Cost of self-protection: $s^\beta$, where $\beta$ is the elasticity of cost for self-protection
- Cost of self-insurance: $z^\varepsilon$, where $\varepsilon$ is the elasticity of cost for self-insurance

- Hazard of health event I: $\exp(-s_1)$, where the hazard rate is between 0 and 1
- Hazard of health event II: $\exp(-s_2)$, where the hazard rate is between 0 and 1
- Growth rate of self-insurance parameter: $\dot{k} = z - \delta$, where $\delta$ is the decay rate of the accumulated self-insurance capital
- Health damages from event II reduce the overall individual utility by a factor: $h \cdot d_1/\log(\phi + k_1)$, where $d_1$ is the damage parameter for health event I and $\phi$ is some constant that prevents the damages from going negative
- Health damages from event II reduce the overall individual utility by a factor: $h \cdot d_2/\log(\phi + k_2)$, where $d_2$ is the damage parameter for health event II and $\phi$ is some constant that prevents the damages from going negative.

Substituting these functional forms, the current value Hamiltonian is now:

$$\exp(-\lambda_1(t) - \lambda_2(t)) \cdot (h \cdot \tau^\alpha - z_1^\epsilon - s_1^\beta - z_2^\epsilon - s_2^\beta)$$

$$+ \exp(-s_1) \cdot \exp(-\lambda_1(t)) \cdot \frac{\tau^\alpha \cdot h \cdot \dfrac{d_1}{\log(\phi + k_1)}}{\rho}$$

$$+ \exp(-s_2) \cdot \exp(-\lambda_2(t)) \cdot \frac{h \cdot \tau^\alpha \cdot \dfrac{d_2}{\log(\phi + k_2)}}{\rho}$$

$$+ m_{s_1}(t) \cdot \exp(-s_1) + m_{z_1}(t) \cdot (z_1(t) - \delta) + m_{s_2}(t)$$

$$\cdot \exp(-s_2) + n_{s_2}(t) \cdot (z_2(t) - \delta). \tag{49}$$

We next consider numerical simulations. These are performed using a hypothetical set of parameters as shown in the Appendix to this chapter. We start with two diseases that are identical in terms of their self-protection and self-insurance costs. The damages from health event II ($d_2 = 0.5$) are twice as large as those from health event I. Figure 4.1 shows the survival probability for the two health events. Due to higher damage from health event II, its survival chance (or the chance that the health event will not happen until time $t$) is much larger than that of I. Also, the combined chance that the person will survive both the health events until time $t$ is lower than the individual chances. Further, when only a single health event is considered (health event I), the survival chances for this event are

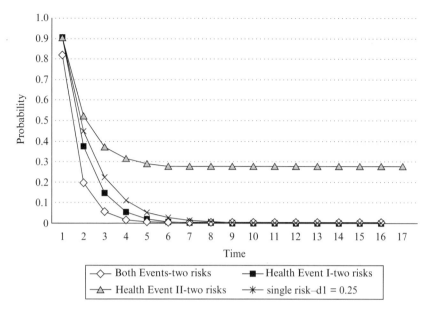

*Figure 4.1   Survival probability of health events: base case*

higher than when both health events are considered. This implies that the presence (or introduction) of another risk affects the survival chances of a pre-existing risk negatively. The total discounted sums of utilities ($v_0$, $v_1$ and $v_2$), are shown in Figure 4.2 as a function of time. $v_2$ is lower than $v_1$, which is lower than $v_0$ as expected. Recall that $v_0$ is the expected value before either of the events takes place, therefore its value is positive. Also, whereas $v_0$ is positive, $v_2$ and $v_1$ are negative as the latter two reflect health damages. Further, $v_0$ declines with time as the probability of either of the health events manifesting in the future increases over time.

Figure 4.3 compares self-protection over health events I and II. Self-protection is higher for event II as it has a higher damage impact. Also, self-protection increases for a single-risk case when damages are doubled. When we interpret the same results by starting with one risk and introducing another, the results demonstrate the influence of one event on protection for another event. If there is currently only one risk in the person's environment (event I with $d_1 = 0.25$) and then another health event with higher damages (event II with $d_2 = 0.5$) manifests, his self-protection against the original risk decreases. Figure 4.4 depicts self-insurance for the two risks. In this case, self-insurance for health event I is higher at the beginning, before being overtaken by that for event II in the later stages. This is prompted by a lower self-protection for health event I, thereby

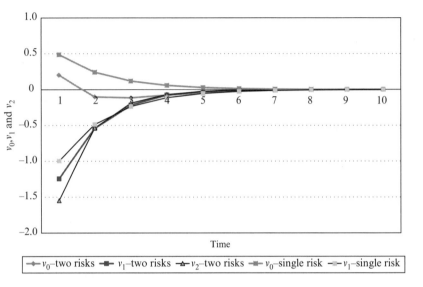

*Figure 4.2    Value functions ($v_0, v_1$ and $v_2$) over time*

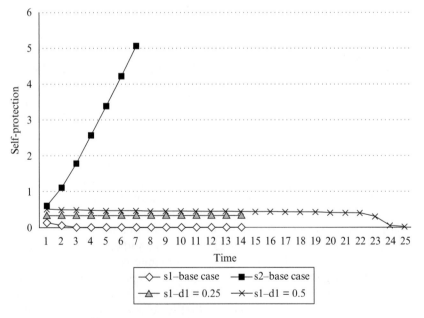

*Figure 4.3    Self-protection over time*

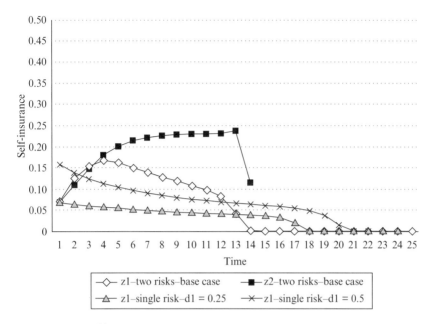

*Figure 4.4    Self-insurance over time*

necessitating higher self-insurance. Higher self-protection for event II allows a lower self-insurance at the beginning as the chances of the event happening in the early stages are reduced. This opportunity for timing of efforts cannot be captured through a static model. Also, we have so far assumed the same cost parameters for the two health events. When the parameters are different, it is possible that a more complex protection strategy may arise.

To illustrate, consider a case in which the initial levels of risks (the exogenous component of the risk given by $\lambda_1(0)$ in Table 4.1 in the Appendix) differ for the two health events, with health event I having a higher starting value of $\lambda_1(0) = 0.5$ as compared to the base case of $\lambda_1(0) = 0.1$. Figure 4.5 compares the base case self-protection for the new scenarios. Self-protection against health event II has increased even though it is event I that has higher starting risks. The intuition behind this change is that as the chances of event I happening have increased substantially, so a marginal expenditure on mitigating event I would produce lower expected rewards than those from health event II. Furthermore, it pays to put more self-insurance into health event II now due to its higher damages, as shown in Figure 4.6. When the exogenous risks of health event II (with higher damages) are raised to 0.4, self-insurance for that event is the lowest of all

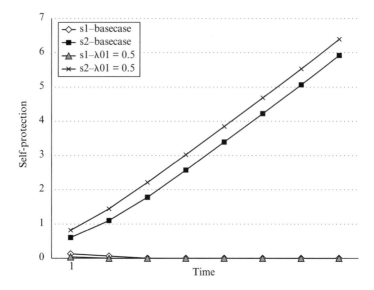

*Figure 4.5    Self-protection under higher accumulated initial risk of health event I ($\lambda_1(0)=.5$)*

cases. This again implies that higher risks lead to a diversion away from such health events.

## 5    CONCLUDING REMARKS

Social accounting aims to better understand the performance of the economy by including the depreciation of capital stock in an economy as valued by shadow prices. This chapter extends the social accounting literature by examining a dynamic endogenous risk model. The dynamic version with single risk demonstrates that time preferences and non-linear cost and damages functions might cause the postponement of self-protection and self-insurance as the present discounted values of both damages and costs are lower in the future. When risks accumulate over time, it is also possible to optimally allocate between self-protection and self-insurance, so initial efforts reduce the need for higher self-insurance in the early stages as the chances of the event are postponed in the future.

Numerical simulations highlight the key results on the role of multiple risks. First, self-protection and self-insurance under multiple dynamic risks can differ substantially from those under a single risk. Multiple risks increase the costs of endogenous risk reduction, which reduces efforts over

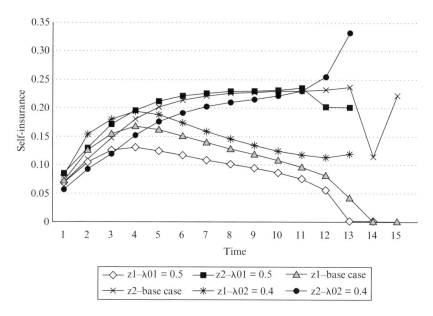

*Figure 4.6 Self-insurance under higher initial accumulated risk of health event I ($\lambda_1(0)=0.5$)*

all health events. Second, multiple dynamic risks cause the agent to discount the health risks with lower damages. This implies less self-protection on such risks relative to a one-risk scenario. Third, if health events with lower damages also have higher exogenous risk components, this further reduces self-protection and self-insurance when another health event with higher damages and lower risk is introduced. Fourth, when health events with higher damages have a higher exogenous risk component, protection is shifted to health events with lower damages and lower risks. In general, optimal allocation of self-protection and self-insurance over time implies that when multiple risks exist, higher risk events do not necessarily command a uniformly higher self-protection and self-insurance. This result can be more pronounced when the costs and effectiveness of self-protection and self-insurance vary for different health risks.

In addition, future research should explore how to incorporate behavioral influences on how people actually react to risk mitigation and adaptation measures. Psychological influences that alter risk perception and introduce risk weighting and risk resilience, could significantly distort self-protection and self-insurance. Ranjan and Shogren (2009) have demonstrated that risk weighting and risk resilience introduce non-linearity in the time paths of self-protection and self-insurance as risks change.

Finally, the step from theory to practical application is relevant for social accounting. Is it possible to find the needed information on shadow prices for the accumulated stock of self-protection or 'belief capital' in practice? This is a challenge. What we are talking about is essentially the shadow price of endogenous optimism. Perhaps this belief is priced in a market with complete contingent claims markets, but if that market existed, we would not need self-protection. As a comparison, the stock of human capital (for example, education) creates more productive workers, which is in a relative sense measurable. We can estimate shadow prices from labor markets to reflect the capital stock. But the stock of self-protection that creates more optimistic beliefs about good states of health being realized will be challenging to measure. While optimism toward health has a shadow price, at this stage we are hesitant to offer advice on how to measure these subjective beliefs produced by self-protection.

# APPENDIX

*Table 4.1    Base case parameters*

| | | |
|---|---|---|
| Cost of self-insurance for health event I | $z_1^{\varepsilon_1}$ | $\varepsilon_1 = 1.75$ |
| Cost of self-insurance for health event II | $z_2^{\varepsilon_2}$ | $\varepsilon_2 = 1.75$ |
| Cost of self-protection for health event I | $s_1^{\beta_1}$ | $\beta_1 = 1.75$ |
| Cost of self-protection for health event II | $s_2^{\beta_2}$ | $\beta_2 = 1.75$ |
| Hazard function for health event I | $\exp(-s_1)$ | |
| Hazard function for health event II | $\exp(-s_2)$ | |
| Effectiveness of self-insurance for health event I | $z_1 - \delta_1$ | $\delta_1 = 0.01$ |
| Effectiveness of self-insurance for health event II | $z_2 - \delta_2$ | $\delta_2 = 0.01$ |
| Starting value of accumulated risk for event I (exogenous risk) | $\lambda_1(0)$ | 0.1 |
| Starting value of accumulated risk for event II (exogenous risk) | $\lambda_2(0)$ | 0.1 |
| Starting value of self-insurance variable for event I | $\kappa_1(0)$ | 0.1 |
| Starting value of self-insurance variable for event I | $\kappa_2(0)$ | 0.1 |
| Discount rate | $\rho$ | 0.1 |
| Health impact parameter | $h$ | 1.0 |
| Health impact parameter | $\tau$ | 0.5 |
| Constant used in damage function | $\phi$ | 3 |
| Damage parameter for health event I | $d_1$ | 0.25 |
| Damage parameter for health event II | $d_2$ | 0.5 |

## ACKNOWLEDGEMENTS

Thanks to the editors for their excellent comments and suggestions.

## NOTES

1. See for example the willingness-to-pay studies for diseases by Shackley and Donaldson (2002) and Protiere et al. (2004), and references therein.
2. For instance, Blomquist (2004) designs a static model to derive the value of statistical life using a willingness-to-pay (WTP) analysis. He notes the limitations of a static model and proposes a life-cycle model as a better approach. The individual entity may span the parent and the child. Using 1991 data from the National Maternal and Infant Health survey for the US, Agee and Crocker (2007) find that mothers valued their child's health at about 55 per cent higher than their own when considered limiting environmental health exposure for their children.
3. Muermann and Kunreuther (2008), for example, consider positive externalities from interdependencies and deduce that in the presence of such effects, people under-invest in self-protection. Income has been found to reduce the perception of risks (Dosman et al. 2001). The explanation for this effect is that wealthier people can buy safer products. Alternatively, lack of income implies lower ability to mitigate risks. Income could also be reduced by the presence of multiple risks, requiring self-protection efforts against several risks. Bhattacharya et al. (2007) find the willingness to pay for risk reduction related to traffic mortality in Delhi, India, is three times larger for a person using a two-wheeler for commuting compared to a pedestrian, even though the risks faced by the latter are much higher.
4. Johansson and Löfgren (1995) develop a model of endogenous health risk in which the probability of death depends on two state variables: stock of health capital and stock of pollution. Their results imply that the economy cannot deliver the first-best health capital unless it subsidizes the stock of health capital. They do not consider explicit forms of self-protection or self-insurance in their model.
5. This assumes that the exogenous risk term is additively separable with the arguments of the hazard function.

## REFERENCES

Agee, M.D. and T.D. Crocker (2007). 'Children's Health Benefits of Reducing Environmental Tobacco Exposure: Evidence from Parents who Smoke', *Empirical Economics* 32, 217–237.

Aronsson, T. (2008).'Social Accounting and the Public Sector', *International Economic Review* 49, 349–375.

Aronsson, T., P.-O. Johansson and K.-G. Löfgren (1994). 'Welfare Measurement and the Health Environment', *Annals of Operations Research* 54, 203–215.

Aronsson, T., P.-O. Johansson and K.-G. Löfgren (1997). *Welfare Measurement, Sustainability and Green National Accounting: A Growth Theoretical Approach*. Cheltenham: Edward Elgar Publishing Limited.

Aronsson, T. and K.-G. Löfgren (1996). 'Social Accounting and Welfare Measurement in a Growth Model with Human Capital', *Scandinavian Journal of Economics* 98, 185–201.

Bhattacharya, S., A. Alberini and M.L. Cropper (2007). 'The Value of Mortality Risk Reductions in Delhi, India', *Journal of Risk and Uncertainty* 34, 21–47.

Blomquist, G. C. (2004). 'Self Protection and Averting Behavior, Values of Statistical Lives, and Benefit Cost Analysis of Environmental Policy', *Review of Economics of the Household*, 2(1), 89–110.

Dasgupta, P. (2009). 'The Welfare Economic Theory of Green National Accounts', *Environmental and Resource Economics* 42, 3–38.

Dosman, D.M., W.L. Adamowicz and S. E. Hrudey (2001). 'Socioeconomic Determinants of Health and Food Safety Related Risk Perceptions', *Risk Analysis* 21(2), 307–317.

Ehrlich, I. and G.S. Becker (1972). 'Market Insurance, SI, and Self Protection', *Journal of Political Economy* 80, 623–648.

Johansson, P.-O. and K.-G. Löfgren (1995). 'Wealth from Optimal Health', *Journal of Health Economics* 14, 65–79.

Muermann, A. and H. Kunreuther (2008). 'Self-protection and Insurance with Interdependencies', *Journal of Risk and Uncertainty* 36, 103–123.

Peskin, H. and J. Peskin (1978). 'The Valuation of Nonmarket Activities in Income Accounting', *Review of Income and Wealth* 24, 71–91.

Protiere, C., C. Donaldson, S. Luchini, J.P. Moatti and P. Shackley (2004). 'The impact of Information on Non-Health Attributes on the Willingness to Pay for Multiple Health Care Programmes', *Social Science and Medicine* 58, 1257–1269.

Ranjan, R. and J. F. Shogren (forthcoming). 'Self Protection and Self Insurance under Multiple Risks: Non-Expected Utility Maximizing and Resilient Agents', *Korean Economic Review*.

Rosen, S (1981). 'Valuing Health Risks', *American Economic Review Papers and Proceedings*, 71, 241–245.

Seierstad, A. and K. Sydsaeter (1987). *Optimal Control Theory with Economic Applications*, Amsterdam: Elsevier Science.

Shackley, P. and C. Donaldson (2002). 'Should We Use Willingness to Pay to Elicit Community Preferences for Health Care? New Evidence from using a "Marginal" Approach', *Journal of Health Economics* 21, 971–991.

Shogren, J. and T. Crocker (1991). 'Risk, Self-protection and ex ante Economic Valuation', *Journal of Environmental Economics and Management* 20, 1–15.

Shogren, J. and T. Crocker (1991). 'Risk and its Consequences', *Journal of Environmental Economics and Management* 37, 44–51.

Weitzman M. (1976). 'On the Welfare Significance of National Product in a Dynamic Economy', *Quarterly Journal of Economics* 90, 156–162.

# 5 Welfare measurement and public goods in a second-best economy

*Thomas Aronsson*

## 1 INTRODUCTION

Earlier chapters of this Handbook have either addressed first-best resource allocations, or resource allocations that – for one reason or another – are suboptimal from society's point of view, in which case society as a whole has not made an optimal choice given its preferences and constraints. A basic message was that the current value Hamiltonian underlying the economic system constitutes an exact welfare measure in utility terms if the resource allocation is first best, whereas it does not in general constitute an exact welfare measure if the resource allocation is suboptimal.[1] One purpose of the present chapter is to address the welfare measurement problem in an economy where the first best is unattainable due to the necessity to raise public revenue by means of distortionary taxes. In such a second-best economy, the government (or social planner) has made an optimal policy choice, although the set of policy instruments might not be flexible enough to implement the first best. Another purpose is to address the treatment of public consumption in the context of social accounting. I will also briefly address redistribution, which is another important aspect of public policy.

Why are taxation, public consumption and redistribution interesting to analyze in the context of welfare measurement and social accounting? First, the public sector plays a crucial role for the allocation of resources in all developed countries by providing public services as well as by redistributing income among individuals and groups. As a consequence, public expenditure is likely to be of considerable importance for well-being, implying that the treatment of such expenditures in social accounting is a relevant issue. Second, if the public revenue is raised via distortionary taxation, there is an additional social cost associated with public expenditures, which ought to be relevant for welfare measurement. On the other hand, if the public revenue were raised via lump-sum taxation, there would be no 'extra' welfare cost of taxation and, therefore, no additional complications for social accounting of raising revenue for purposes of public provision and redistribution.

The chapter begins by analysing the welfare measurement problem implicit in Chamley's (1985) dynamic second-best economy, which is an extension of the Ramsey model in the sense of adding a public sector and assuming that the public revenue is raised by a linear, yet time-varying, labor income tax. The analysis carried out in this part of the chapter relies largely on Aronsson (1998, 2008), who examined how distortionary taxes affect the way in which welfare ought to be measured in a dynamic economy, as well as how public goods ought to be treated in social accounting if the public revenue is raised by distortionary taxes. A change of assumption I make here is that the public good will be assumed to be a state variable (instead of a conventional flow variable), an assumption motivated by the desire to add realism to the description of the economy.[2] Throughout this part of the chapter, I also compare the welfare measurement and valuation procedures of the second-best economy with those that appear in the first best, the latter being a natural special case and, therefore, easy to discuss within the framework of the more general model. The final part of the chapter deals with welfare measurement – and, in particular, measurement of the value of public consumption – in an economy with non-linear taxation. The underlying framework here is the two-type optimal income tax model developed by Stern (1982) and Stiglitz (1982)[3] which is, in turn, a simplification of Mirrlees' (1971) optimal non-linear tax model with a continuum of ability types. Such an extension serves two purposes. First, it adds realism by relaxing the assumption (in the Chamley model) that the use of distortionary taxation is a consequence of restrictions on the set of policy instruments that the government is allowed to use; here, its use is, instead, a consequence of asymmetric information between the private sector and the government. Second, it allows me to provide a closer connection between social accounting and the literature on public good provision, as the policy rule for a public good and, as a consequence, the procedure for measuring its social value, largely depend on the set of tax instruments that the government has at its disposal.

## 2    A DYNAMIC REPRESENTATIVE AGENT MODEL WITH LINEAR TAXATION

The model developed in this section is, to a large extent, based on Chamley (1985), which implies that the consumption side of the economy is characterized by a representative consumer. As a consequence, we disregard any distributional objectives underlying public policy in this section. A multi-consumer economy along with distributional objectives is discussed in Section 3 below.

## 2.1   Consumers

Following the main bulk of literature on social accounting, suppose that the economy is populated by a fixed number of identical consumers. Since this fixed number is of no concern here, it will be normalized to one. The preferences are described by a time-separable utility function. The instantaneous utility function at any time, $t$, takes the form

$$u(t) = u(c(t), z(t), G(t)) \tag{1}$$

where $c$ is consumption of a privately provided good, $z$ leisure and $G$ consumption of a public good. The determination of the public good will be further discussed below. Leisure is defined as a (fixed) time endowment, $\bar{l}$, less the time spent in market work, $l$. The function $u(\cdot)$ is increasing in each argument and strictly concave. The consumer treats the public good as exogenous.

The consumer holds two assets: capital, $k$, and government bonds, $b$. These two assets are assumed to be perfect substitutes and have the same rate of return. If we define the composite asset $a = k + b$, the asset accumulation equation can be written as

$$\dot{a}(t) = r(t)a(t) + w_n(t)l(t) - c(t) \tag{2}$$

with $a(0) = a_0$, where $w_n$ is the net wage rate and $r$ the interest rate. The net wage rate is defined as $w_n(t) = w(t)[1 - \tau(t)]$, where $w$ is the gross wage rate and $\tau$ the tax rate.[4]

The consumer chooses his/her consumption of the private good, $c$, and hours of work, $l$, at each instant to maximize the present value of future utility,

$$U(0) = \int_0^\infty u(c(t), z(t), G(t))e^{-\theta t}dt,$$

subject to equation (2), the initial condition, as well as subject to a so-called No Ponzi Game (NPG) condition, the purpose of which is to ensure that the present value of the asset is non-negative at the terminal point. The parameter $\theta$ is the utility discount rate (that is, the marginal rate of time preference). By using the first order conditions[5]

$$u_c(c(t), z(t), G(t)) - \phi(t) = 0$$

and

$$- u_z(c(t), z(t), G(t)) + \phi(t)w_n(t) = 0,$$

where a subscript attached to the instantaneous utility function denotes partial derivative, and $\phi$ is the marginal utility of wealth in current value terms, one can write the consumption and hours of work as functions of the net wage rate, the marginal utility of wealth and the public good (that is, so called Frisch demand functions)

$$c(t) = c(w_n(t), \phi(t), G(t)) \tag{3}$$

$$l(t) = l(w_n(t), \phi(t), G(t)). \tag{4}$$

The marginal utility of wealth obeys, in turn, the differential equation

$$\dot{\phi}(t) - \theta\phi(t) = -\phi(t)r(t). \tag{5}$$

Finally, by substituting equations (3) and (4) into the instantaneous direct utility function, we obtain the instantaneous indirect utility function, defined conditional on the marginal utility of wealth:

$$v(t) = v(w_n(t), \phi(t), G(t))$$

$$= u(c(w_n(t), \phi(t), G(t)), \bar{l} - l(w_n(t), \phi(t), G(t)), G(t)). \tag{6}$$

Equations (3), (4), (5) and (6) will be used in the public decision-problem to be described below.

## 2.2  Firms

The production side is characterized by identical competitive firms producing a homogeneous good under constant returns to scale. Given these assumptions, the number of firms is, itself, not important for the analysis and will be normalized to one. Output is produced by labor and capital. The production function is given by $f(l(t), k(t))$, and the firm obeys the following first-order conditions at each instant:

$$f_l(l, k) - w = 0 \tag{7}$$

$$f_k(l, k) - r = 0. \tag{8}$$

## 2.3 The Government

As mentioned above, the public good provided by the government is a state variable, and the accumulation of the public good will be described by the differential equation

$$\dot{G}(t) = g(t) - \delta G(t) \tag{9}$$

where $g(t)$ is the contribution to the public good at time $t$ and $\delta$ the rate of depreciation.

Turning to the government's budget constraint, note that the decision variables facing the government are the income tax rate and the contribution to the public good at each instant. The stock of government bonds develops according to

$$\dot{b}(t) = r(t)b(t) + \rho g(t) - [w(t) - w_n(t)]l(t), \tag{10}$$

in which $\rho$ is a fixed unit cost, measured in terms of private consumption, of providing the public good (that is, the marginal rate of transformation between the public good and the private consumption good). Typically, one would normalize this cost to 1; however, I will denote it by $\rho$ here in order to keep track of its role in the welfare measures to be derived below. If we integrate equation (10) subject to an NPG condition, implying that the present value of public wealth (that is, the negative of $b$) is non-negative at the terminal point, we obtain the intertemporal budget constraint of the government.

By combining equations (2), (10) and the zero profit condition, that is, $f(l, k) - wl - rk = 0$, we can derive the resource constraint

$$\dot{k}(t) = f(l(t), k(t)) - c(t) - \rho g(t), \tag{11}$$

meaning that the output is used for private consumption, private net investments and contributions to the public good (that is, public investments). As the present chapter focuses on issues other than depreciation of the physical capital stock, I abstract from such depreciation here. This simplification is not important for the qualitative results presented below.

The decision-problem facing the government will be to choose the tax rate (or net wage rate) and contribution to the public good at each instant in order to maximize the present value of future utility facing the representative consumer, that is,

$$Max_{w_n(t),\, g(t)} \int_0^\infty v(w_n(t),\, \phi(t),\, G(t))e^{-\theta t}dt,$$

subject to the state equations (5), (9), (10) and (11) as well as subject to the static first-order conditions characterizing the private sector, that is, equations (3), (4), (7) and (8). The reason why equation (5) appears as a state-equation constraint in the government's decision-problem is, of course, that the equation of motion for the private marginal utility of wealth is part of the necessary conditions for the consumer and, therefore, a constraint that the optimal tax and expenditure policy must fulfill. The resource allocation must also obey initial conditions for $k$ and $b$ as well as an NPG condition for $b$. As pointed out by Chamley (1985), the government does not face any explicit constraint on the initial marginal utility of wealth, $\phi(0)$.

The present value Hamiltonian associated with the public decision-problem can be written as (neglecting the time indicator for notational convenience)

$$H_p = v(w_n,\, \phi,\, G)e^{-\theta t} + \lambda_p \dot{k} + \mu_p \dot{b} + v_p \dot{\phi} + \psi_p \dot{G}, \tag{12}$$

in which the subindex $p$ attached to the Hamiltonian and the costate variables denotes present value. One may, therefore, interpret $\lambda_p$, $\mu_p$, $v_p$ and $\psi_p$, as the present value shadow price that the government attaches to the relevant state variable (in this case, the stock of physical capital, the stock of government bonds, the private marginal utility of wealth and the public good, respectively). The first-order conditions for the control variables are

$$\frac{\partial H_p(t)}{\partial w_n(t)} = 0 \text{ and } \frac{\partial H_p(t)}{\partial g(t)} = 0 \tag{13}$$

while the equations of motion for the present value costate variables become

$$\dot{\lambda}_p(t) = -\frac{\partial H_p(t)}{\partial k(t)},\, \dot{\mu}_p(t) = -\frac{\partial H_p(t)}{\partial b(t)},\, \dot{v}_p(t) = -\frac{\partial H_p(t)}{\partial \phi(t)} \text{ and}$$

$$\dot{\psi}_p(t) = -\frac{\partial H_p(t)}{\partial G(t)}. \tag{14}$$

We shall return to the interpretation of some of these conditions below, when the model set out here is used for welfare measurement.

**2.4 Welfare Measurement in the Second-Best Economy**

In this subsection, I will derive a welfare measure for the second-best economy set out above and, in particular, analyze the welfare properties of the Hamiltonian underlying this resource allocation. To do this in the simplest way possible, I just assume that a unique solution to the government's decision-problem exists.[6] Therefore, let

$$\{w_n^0(t), g^0(t)\}_0^\infty$$

denote the optimal paths for the government's control variables, where the superindex 0 is used to indicate second-best optimal resource allocation, and let

$$V^0(t) = \int_t^\infty v(w_n^0(s), \phi^0(s), G^0(s)) e^{-\theta(s-t)} ds \tag{15}$$

represent the associated optimal value function for the representative consumer at time $t$. As we are disregarding distributional concerns in this section, equation (15) is also interpretable as a measure of social welfare.

Let me begin by establishing a relationship between the optimal value function in equation (15) and the Hamiltonian underlying the government's decision-problem. By totally differentiating the present value Hamiltonian in equation (12) with respect to time and using the first order conditions summarized by equations (13) and (14) we obtain

$$\frac{dH_p^0(t)}{dt} = -\theta v(w_n^0(t), \phi^0(t), G^0(t)) e^{-\theta t}. \tag{16}$$

The intuition behind equation (16) is that the only non-autonomous time dependence of the optimal control problem facing the government originates from the utility discount factor. In other words, the effects of time via control, state and costate variables vanish as a consequence of optimization, which means that equation (16) follows directly from the dynamic envelope theorem. Therefore, by solving the differential equation (16) subject to the transversality condition[7] $\lim_{t \to \infty} H_p(t) = 0$ and then transforming the solution to current value (that is, multiplying by $e^{\theta t}$), we obtain

$$\theta V^0(t) = H^0(t) \tag{17}$$

where (neglecting the time-indicator)

$$H^0 = v(w_n^0, \phi^0, G^0) + \lambda^0 \dot{k}^0 + \mu^0 \dot{b}^0 + v^0 \dot{\phi}^0 + \psi^0 \dot{G}^0$$

is the current value Hamiltonian evaluated at the second-best optimum. This also means that the costate variables are measured in current value terms, that is, $\lambda(t) = \lambda_p(t) e^{\theta t}$ and similarly for the other costate variables. Equation (17) was originally derived by Aronsson (1998) in a slightly different model from the one used here and establishes a second-best analogue to Weitzman's (1976) first-best welfare measure. In summary, we have established the following result:

**Proposition 1.** *Within the given framework, and if the resource allocation is second best, then the current value Hamiltonian underlying the public decision-problem is proportional to the social welfare function.*

At the same time, although Proposition 1 establishes an analogue to Weitzman's (1976) Hamiltonian-based welfare measure, it is important to observe that the proposition does not mean that the principles for measuring welfare in the first-best and second-best are equivalent. To see this more clearly, note that the costate variable $\mu$ attached to the accumulation of government bonds is a measure of (the negative of) the marginal excess burden of taxation. In a first-best resource allocation, $\mu$ would be equal to zero (as the first-best, in this case, necessitates lump-sum taxation in order to raise the appropriate amount of revenue to finance the contribution to the public good). In addition, as a first-best resource allocation would imply that the private marginal utility of wealth, $\phi$, and the social value of capital, $\lambda$, are identical, one can show[8] that a first-best resource allocation would also imply $v = 0$. Therefore, we have established the following corollary to Proposition 1:

**Corollary 1.** *In the special case where $\mu(t) = v(t) = 0$ and $\phi(t) = \lambda(t)$ for all t, in which the resource allocation is first best, the welfare measure in equation (17) reduces to read*

$$\theta V^*(t) = u(c^*(t), z^*(t), G^*(t)) + \lambda^*(t) \dot{k}^*(t) + \psi^*(t) \dot{G}^*(t)$$

*where the superindex * is used to denote first-best.*

The welfare measure in Corollary 1 is Weitzman's (1976) welfare measure for the model set out here. As such, it can also be derived from a conventional social planner problem, in which the planner chooses private consumption, hours of work and contribution to the public good in order to maximize the consumer's objective function, that is, $U(0)$ above, subject to the equations of motion for $k$ and $G$ (as well as the appropriate initial conditions). Taken together, Proposition 1 and Corollary 1 show how the necessity to collect public revenue by distortionary taxation will affect the welfare measure. This is summarized as follows:

**Corollary 2.** *Within the given framework, the necessity to raise public revenue by means of distortionary taxes affects the welfare measure mainly by (i) adding the marginal excess burden times the change in the stock of government bonds to the conventional Hamiltonian-based welfare measure and (ii) introducing a discrepancy between the private and social marginal value of capital.*

The first part of Corollary 2 is intuitive: as revenue collection is associated with a cost beyond the reduction in private consumption, this additional cost ought to affect the way in which welfare is measured. If $\mu < 0$, as one would normally expect, building up a stock of government bonds gives rise to a welfare cost in the sense that it necessitates more disortionary taxation in the future. To understand the second part of the corollary, note that the public decision-problem is formulated in terms of demand functions and an instantaneous indirect utility function, which are all defined conditional on the private marginal utility of wealth. If evaluated in the first-best, we have $\partial H/\partial \phi = 0$, as the private cost–benefit rule for $c$ and $L$, respectively, would in that case coincide with the corresponding social cost–benefit rule, whereas $\partial H/\partial \phi$ is generally non-zero in the second best due to discrepancies between the private and social cost–benefit rules. As a consequence, changes in $\phi$ influence social welfare via the private decision variables in the second best, which is why the government (acting as a benevolent social planner) attaches a marginal value (positive or negative) to $\phi$.

Let me then turn to the measurement of the value of an addition to the public good, that is, the shadow price (or social value) of the public good in utility terms. To begin with, note from the final part of (14) that the equation of motion for the present value costate variable associated with the public good can be written as (using $v_G(\cdot) = \partial v(\cdot)\partial G$)

$$\dot{\psi}_p^0(t) = -v_G(w_n^0(t), \phi^0(t), G^0(t))e^{-\theta t} - \Delta_p^0(t) + \delta\psi_p^0(t) \qquad (18)$$

in which $\Delta_p^0(t)$ summarizes all indirect effects of $G$ on the present value Hamiltonian that arise because $G$ affects the equations of motion for $k$, $b$ and $\phi$ via the consumption and hours of work, that is, via equations (3) and (4). Solving the differential equation (18) subject to the transversality condition $\lim_{t\to\infty}\psi_p^0(t) = 0$ and then transforming the solution to current value (multiplying by $e^{\theta t}$) gives

$$\psi^0(t) = \int_t^\infty [v_G(w_n^0(s), \phi^0(s), G^0(s)) + \Delta^0(s)] e^{-(\theta+\delta)(s-t)} ds \qquad (19)$$

where $\Delta^0(t) = \Delta_p^0(t) e^{\theta t}$. Note first that $\theta + \delta$ represents the discount rate used to calculate the present value of future marginal benefits of a contribution to the public good at time $t$. The intuition as to why the rate of depreciation of the public good ought to be added to the conventional utility discount rate is, of course, that the greater the depreciation, *ceteris paribus*, the less will be the effective size of past increments. Equation (19) means that the marginal value of an incremental public good at time $t$ is equal to the present value of all future marginal benefits that this increment gives rise to for the consumer plus the present value of the indirect effects via the state equations for $k$, $b$ and $\phi$ mentioned above. An important difference between the way in which the shadow price of the public good is measured in the second-best and in the first-best is that $v_G + \Delta = u_G$ in the first-best equilibrium. The intuition is that the indirect effects of $G$ on the Hamiltonian, which are due to the effects of $G$ on the conditional demand system given by equations (3) and (4), vanish in the first best as a consequence of optimization. In the second best, on the other hand, these indirect effects generally remain.

However, if $G$ is additively separable from the other goods in the utility function in equation (1), meaning that $G$ does not directly influence the conditional demand system given by equations (3) and (4), the second-best principle for measuring the shadow price of an incremental public good coincides with the corresponding principle that applies in the first-best. This means that equation (19) reduces to read[9]

$$\psi^0(t) = \int_t^\infty v_G(G^0(s)) e^{-(\theta+\delta)(s-t)} ds > 0. \qquad (20)$$

To be able to interpret the second-best formula for public provision in a simple way, and since the social shadow price in the simplified case represented by equation (20) is unambiguously positive (as is the shadow price in the first-best), I will throughout this section assume that $\psi^0(t)$ is also unambiguously positive in the general case represented by equation (19). This means that, if the second term on the right-hand side contributes negatively to the shadow price, this effect is not strong enough to dominate the positive direct effect. In this case, therefore, it is straightforward to interpret equation (19) as measuring the benefit side of an incremental public good.

Now, to go further, let me examine the policy rule for public provision of increments to the public good. Since the public decision-problem analyzed here is a second-best problem in which the revenue is raised by distortionary taxation, it is clear that an intertemporal analogue to the standard Samuelson condition[10] – equating the direct marginal benefit facing the consumer derived above with the direct marginal cost – does not in general apply. Part of the intuition behind the failure of the Samuelson condition was outlined elegantly by Pigou (1947),[11] even before the Samuelson condition as we know is was formulated. He wrote:

> Where there is indirect damage, it ought to be added to the direct loss of satisfaction involved in the withdrawal of the marginal unit of resources by taxation, before this is balanced against the satisfaction yielded by the marginal expenditure. It follows that, in general, expenditures ought not to be carried so far as to make the real yield of the last unit of resources expended by the government equal to the real yield of the last unit left in the hand of the representative citizen (1947, page 34).

The first-order condition for the instantaneous contribution to the public good in the present model accords well with this intuition, at least in the special case where the shadow price of the public good is given by equation (20). This is so because with a separable public good, in which case the shadow price of an incremental public good is measured in the same general way as it would have been in the first best, the second-best assumption will only modify the way in which the social cost of raising the additional tax revenue ought to be measured. By using the second part of conditions (13), that is, $\partial H_p(t)/\partial g(t) = 0$, we can derive

$$\psi^0(t) = [\lambda^0(t) - \mu^0(t)]\rho. \tag{21}$$

The left-hand side of equation (21) is the marginal benefit of an incremental public good, which was defined in equation (19) above, whereas the right-hand side represents the marginal cost measured in terms of utility. The latter contains two parts: (i) the direct unit cost of providing the public good, $\rho$ (which is interpretable as the marginal rate of transformation between the public good and the private consumption good), and (ii) the multiplier $\lambda - \mu$, which is interpretable in terms of the marginal cost of public funds. If defined in utility terms, this incorporates both the shadow price of the resource constraint, here represented by $\lambda$, and the marginal excess burden, here represented by $-\mu$. If we follow the convention in the literature in defining the marginal cost of public funds in real terms by dividing the multiplier $\lambda - \mu$ by the marginal utility of consumption, $m(t) = [\lambda(t) - \mu(t)]/\phi(t)$, equation (21) may be rewritten to read

$$\psi^0(t) = \phi^0(t)m^0(t)\rho. \tag{22}$$

Therefore, and in accordance with Sandmo (1998), we may alternatively think of the marginal cost of public funds as the multiplier, $m(t)$, to be applied to the direct resource cost of providing the public good, $\rho$, in order to arrive at the socially relevant shadow price (in real terms) for the public sector. Equations (17) and (22) suggest the following result:

**Proposition 2.** *Within the given framework, and if the resource allocation is second-best, the real accounting price of an addition to the public good at time t can be measured by the direct cost of providing the incremental public good, $\rho$, times the marginal cost of public funds, $m(t)$.*

Proposition 2 closely resembles a result derived by Aronsson (2008); the difference is that he focused on the accounting price of a flow-variable public good, whereas the Proposition above analyzes the accounting price of a state-variable public good. In a second-best economy such as the one addressed here, one would normally expect that $m(t) > 1$, whereas $m(t)$ would be equal to one in the first best. The latter follows because, in the first best, we have $\mu(t) = 0$ and $\lambda(t) = \phi(t)$ for all $t$. One may then immediately infer the following corollary to Proposition 2:

**Corollary 3.** *In the special case where the resource allocation is first best, the appropriate real accounting price of an addition to the public good is given by $\rho$.*

As a consequence, if the first-best accounting price were (erroneously) applied in a second-best economy, and if the marginal cost of public funds is greater then one, we would underestimate the real accounting price of an addition to the public good.

## 3  HETEROGENEITY

The analysis has so far focused on a representative–agent economy. Such a framework is problematic for at least two reasons. First, it completely disregards redistribution, which is arguably one of the most important tasks of the public sector in many real-world economies. As a consequence, it is important to address redistribution also in the context of social accounting. Second, there is no apparent reason why the public sector in the model set out above should use distortionary taxes, other than that we have assumed that it must do so. In fact, as we avoided redistribution and informational asymmetries completely in the previous sections, it ought to have been possible for the government of the model economy to finance public expenditures by a lump-sum tax. I will return to the issue of tax instruments and informational constraints below by analysing welfare measurement in a model where ability is private information.

## 3.1 Briefly on Redistribution and Social Accounting

Very few earlier studies have examined how redistribution ought to be treated in the context of social accounting. Aronsson and Löfgren (1999) analysed redistribution in the context of a first-best economy, in which the government chooses the consumption paths of two individuals (or families) with infinite time horizons in order to maximize a general social welfare function of the type

$$\int_0^\infty \omega(u^1(c^1(t)), u^2(c^2(t))) e^{-\theta t} dt \tag{23}$$

subject to the aggregate resource constraint for the economy as a whole. In equation (23), the individual utility functions, $u^i(\cdot)$, have conventional properties (see above), whereas the aggregator function, $\omega(\cdot)$, is assumed to be increasing in the individual instantaneous utilities and concave. The results presented by Aronsson and Löfgren (1999) show that the current value Hamiltonian associated with this decision-problem, if evaluated in the first-best, constitutes an exact welfare measure (in a way analogous to the representative–agent models used in earlier work). Furthermore, since the first-best resource allocation equalizes the social marginal utility of consumption across agents, the only measure of private consumption that enters the linearized current value Hamiltonian will be aggregate private consumption (although the consumption level, itself, may differ across consumers). Therefore, an approximation of real comprehensive net national product (NNP) derived by linearizing the current value Hamiltonian does not depend on the distribution of consumption in the first best. Relaxing the first-best assumption, Aronsson and Löfgren (1999) also show that if the actual distribution is not the outcome of an optimal policy choice, then the current value Hamiltonian no longer constitutes an exact welfare indicator. In other words, a suboptimal distribution gives rise to additional terms in the welfare measure in a way similar to market failures; see Chapter 1.

Aronsson (2008) extends the analysis to a second-best economy in which the consumers differ with regard to their initial endowments, and where the government raises revenue by means of linear income taxation.

The resulting second-best resource allocation does not, in general, equalize the social marginal utility of consumption among individuals. A linearization of the current value Hamiltonian then suggests that the information about private consumption that ought to be part of real comprehensive NNP not only reflects aggregate private consumption (broadly defined to reflect the instantaneous utility function) as it typically does in the first best; it also depends on the distribution of the relevant aspects of private consumption among individuals. The intuition – which may be understood in terms of equation (23) above – is that if the government is unable to equalize the social marginal utility of consumption among individuals (that is, unable to fully implement its distributional objectives), then this policy failure ought to reflect the way in which the welfare effects of private consumption are measured. This is precisely why information about the distribution of private consumption becomes part of the linearized current value Hamiltonian in that case.

In the next subsection, I shall formally analyse the welfare measurement problem – and in particular the role public goods – in a second-best economy with heterogeneous consumers. I will also discuss the role of redistribution more thoroughly. However, instead of using a model in which the government is restricted to using linear tax instruments, as in the previous section, I will consider a variant of the two-type optimal income tax model originally developed by Stern (1982) and Stiglitz (1982). To my knowledge, this model has not been used before in the context of social accounting. In such a framework, there are no restrictions on the set of policy instruments that necessitate using distortionary taxes for revenue collection and redistribution; instead, the use of distortionary taxes is, in this case, a consequence of optimization from the perspective of the government subject to the available information constraints. By comparison with the analysis carried out in the previous section, this extension also enables me to exemplify how the social value of an incremental public good depends on the tax instruments that the government has at its disposal.

### 3.2   A Model with Two Ability Types and Asymmetric Information

Consider an economy with two types of consumers: a low-ability type (denoted by superindex 1) and a high-ability type (denoted by superindex 2). This distinction refers to productivity, meaning that the high-ability type has a higher before-tax wage rate than the low-ability type. The number of agents of each ability type will be assumed to be fixed. Therefore, without any loss of generality, we normalize the number of agents of each ability type to one at each point in time.

## Consumers and firms

The consumers and firms behave in the same way as in Section 2. Ability type $i$ $(i = 1,2)$ chooses his/her consumption of the private good, $c^i$, and hours of work, $l^i$, at each instant to maximize the present value of future utility,

$$U^i(0) = \int_0^\infty u(c^i(t), z^i(t), G(t))e^{-\theta t}dt,$$

subject to the asset accumulation equation

$$\dot{a}^i(t) = r(t)a^i(t) - \Phi(r(t)a^i(t)) + w^i(t)l^i(t) - T(w^i(t)l^i(t)) - c^i(t)$$

as well as subject to an initial condition and an NPG condition for the asset. In the asset accumulation equation, $T(\cdot)$ refers to the labor income tax and $\Phi(\cdot)$ to the capital income tax: both labor income and capital income are taxed according to non-linear functions. The first-order conditions include (neglecting the time indicator)

$$u_c(c^i, z^i, G) - \phi^i = 0 \tag{24}$$

$$- u_z(c^i, z^i, G) + \phi^i w^i[1 - T'(w^i l^i)] = 0 \tag{25}$$

$$\dot{\phi}^i - \theta\phi^i = -\phi^i r[1 - \Phi'(ra^i)]. \tag{26}$$

Turning to the production sector, I will also here assume identical competitive firms producing a homogeneous good under constant returns to scale, and I will normalize the number of firms to one. The production function is written $f(l^1(t), l^2(t), k(t))$, and the first-order conditions characterizing the firm become (again neglecting the time indicator)

$$f_{l^i}(l^1, l^2, k) - w^i = 0 \text{ for } i = 1, 2, \text{ and } f_k(l^1, l^2, k) - r = 0. \tag{27}$$

## The government

To avoid complications not essential for the results to be derived below, the social objective function will be assumed to be a utilitarian welfare function, that is,

$$U(0) = \sum_i \int_0^\infty u(c^i(t), z^i(t), G(t))e^{-\theta t}dt. \tag{28}$$

As in other literature on the self-selection approach to optimal taxation, I assume that the government can observe income, although ability is private information. In addition, and also by analogy to earlier comparable literature, I assume that the government wants to redistribute from the high-ability to the low-ability type. Therefore, we would like to prevent the high-ability type from mimicking the low-ability type in order to gain from redistribution. This can be accomplished by imposing a self-selection constraint, which means that the high-ability type must (weakly) prefer the allocation intended for him/her over the allocation intended for the low-ability type. To formalize this aspect of the public decision-problem in the simplest possible way, and to avoid that each agent reveals his/her true type at the beginning of the planning period (after which the government would be able to implement non-distortionary lump-sum taxation), I reinterpret each agent type in terms of a continuum of perfectly altruistic consumers and assume that the abilities of the two consumers living at the same time cannot be identified ex ante by the government.[12]

As a consequence, the self-selection constraint that may bind at time $t$ becomes

$$u^2(t) = u(c^2(t), z^2(t), G(t)) \geq u(c^1(t), \bar{l} - \alpha(t)l^1(t), G(t)) = \hat{u}^2(t) \tag{29}$$

where $\alpha = w^1/w^2$ is the wage ratio (relative wage rate), implying that $\alpha l^1$ is the hours of work that the mimicker must supply in order to reach the same income as the low-ability type. By using the first-order conditions for the firm, it follows that the wage ratio can be written as a function of the hours of work by each ability type and the capital stock, that is, $\alpha = \alpha(l^1, l^2, k)$. The expression on the right-hand side of the weak inequality is the utility of the mimicker (that is, a high-ability type pretending to be a low-ability type), which is denoted by the hat. The mimicker enjoys the same consumption as the low-ability type, although the mimicker enjoys more leisure (as the mimicker is more productive than the low-ability type).

The accumulation equation for the public good and the resource constraint take the same forms as in the model discussed in Section 2, that is,

$$\dot{G}(t) = g(t) - \delta G(t) \tag{30}$$

$$\dot{k}(t) = f(l^1(t), l^2(t), k(t)) - \sum_i c^i(t) - \rho g(t). \tag{31}$$

Before proceeding with the public decision-problem, two things are worth noticing. First, and by analogy to other literature on the self-selection approach to optimal labor income taxation, the labor income tax, $T(\cdot)$, can be used to implement any desired combination of work hours and private consumption for each ability type. The reader may, in this case, think about a labor income tax function with ability-type-specific slopes and intercepts. Therefore, it is more convenient to use $l^1$, $c^1$, $l^2$ and $c^2$ as direct decision variables for the government than controlling them indirectly via the parameters of the function $T(\cdot)$. Second, as the government may transfer resources lump-sum over time via the tax system (recall that the general income tax functions have lump-sum components), we only need to consider one from the resource constraint and the government's budget constraint.[13] As I have chosen to use the resource constraint, this means that the costate variable associated with the resource constraint is interpretable in terms of the marginal cost of public funds. Therefore, and by contrast to the analysis carried out in Section 2, the second-best problem is here formulated as a 'command optimum' problem, in which the social planner (or benevolent government) chooses quantities instead of tax rates. By comparing the first-order conditions of this second-best problem with those characterizing the private sector (see above), one can then derive the marginal income tax structure that ought to be used in order to implement the second-best resource allocation.

The second-best resource allocation is derived by choosing $l^1$, $c^1$, $l^2$, $c^2$ and $g$ at each instant to maximize the social welfare function in equation (28) subject to equations (29), (30) and (31), as well as subject to initial and terminal conditions. The present value Hamiltonian is given by (where the time indicator is suppressed)

$$H_p = \sum_i u(c^i, z^i, G)e^{-\theta t} + \lambda_p \dot{k} + \psi_p \dot{G}, \tag{32}$$

and the present value Lagrangean becomes $L_p = H_p + \eta_p[u^2 - \hat{u}^2]$. Notice that although the Lagrangean contains the self-selection constraint, which the second-best resource allocation must obey (according to the assumptions made above), the Hamiltonian takes the same general form as its first-best counterpart. I will return to this discussion below, when the appropriate procedure for measuring welfare is analyzed. The first order conditions include (where the time indicator has been suppressed once again)

$$\frac{\partial L_p}{\partial l^1} = -u_z^1 e^{-\theta t} + \eta_p \hat{u}_z^2 \left[ \alpha + \frac{\partial \alpha}{\partial l^1} l^1 \right] + \lambda_p w^1 = 0 \tag{33}$$

$$\frac{\partial L_p}{\partial c^1} = u_c^1 e^{-\theta t} - \eta_p \hat{u}_c^2 - \lambda_p = 0 \tag{34}$$

$$\frac{\partial L_p}{\partial l^2} = -u_z^2 e^{-\theta t} + \eta_p \left[ -u_z^2 + \hat{u}_z^2 \frac{\partial \alpha}{\partial l^2} l^1 \right] + \lambda_p w^2 = 0 \qquad (35)$$

$$\frac{\partial L_p}{\partial c^2} = u_c^2 e^{-\theta t} + \eta_p u_c^2 - \lambda_p = 0 \qquad (36)$$

$$\frac{\partial L_p}{\partial g} = \psi_p - \lambda_p \rho = 0 \qquad (37)$$

$$\dot{\lambda}_p = -\frac{\partial L_p}{\partial k} = -\lambda_p f_k(l^1, l^2, k) - \eta_p \hat{u}_z^2 \frac{\partial \alpha}{\partial k} l^1 \qquad (38)$$

$$\dot{\psi}_p = -\frac{\partial L_p}{\partial G} = -[u_G^1 + u_G^2] e^{-\theta t} - \eta_p [u_G^2 - \hat{u}_G^2] + \psi_p \delta, \qquad (39)$$

in which $u^i = u(c^i, z^i, G)$, and subindices attached to the instantaneous utility and production functions denote partial derivatives.

### Welfare measurement and public good provision

The implications in terms of optimal marginal income tax rates (in a dynamic model) of a binding self-selection constraint have been discussed by other studies (for example, Pirttilä and Tuomala 2001), and it would be beyond the purpose of this study to address implementation here. I will, instead, analyze the model from the point of view of welfare measurement. As in Section 2, the superindex 0 is used below to indicate the second-best resource allocation.

As the government faces a utilitarian objective function by assumption, the optimal value function – the welfare function we are about to analyze – may be written as

$$V^0(t) = \sum_i V^{i,0}(t) = \int_t^\infty \sum_i u(c^{i,0}(s), z^{i,0}(s), G^0(s)) e^{-\theta(s-t)} ds. \qquad (40)$$

Now, by totally differentiating the Lagrangean with respect to time and using the first-order conditions given by equations (33)–(39), we obtain

$$\frac{dL_p^0(t)}{dt} = -\theta \sum_i u(c^{i,0}(t), z^{i,0}(t), G^0(t)) e^{-\theta t}. \qquad (41)$$

Solving the differential equation (41) subject to the transversality condition $\lim_{t \to \infty} L_p(t) = 0$, using the result that $L_p^0(t) = H_p^0(t)$ at the optimum and, finally, transforming the solution to current value (that is, multiply-ing by $e^{\theta t}$), the welfare measure can be written in the now familiar way

$$\theta V^0(t) = H^0(t). \tag{42}$$

Equation (42) is analogous to equation (17) and may be interpreted as follows:

**Proposition 3.** *In a second-best economy with heterogeneous consumers and a binding self-selection constraint, the current value Hamiltonian underlying the public decision-problem is proportional to the social welfare function.*

It is interesting to compare Proposition 3 with Aronsson and Löfgren (1999), who derived a similar result in the context of a first-best resource allocation: in an economy with heterogeneous consumers, they also found that the present value of social welfare is proportional to the current value Hamiltonian facing the social planner. Therefore, the basic intuition behind equation (42) is, of course, the same as that offered by them: the underlying decision-problem is time-autonomous (except for the direct dependence of time through the utility discount factor). At the same time, it is important to emphasize that equation (42) is *not* a first-best welfare measure. This will become evident below, where equation (42) is used to address how the marginal value of the public good ought to be measured.

To simplify the notations, let $MRS^i_{G,c}(t) = u^i_G(t)/u^i_c(t)$ and $M\hat{R}S^2_{G,c}(t) = \hat{u}^2_G(t)/\hat{u}^2_c(t)$ denote the marginal rate of substitution between the public good and private consumption for ability type $i$ and the mimicker, respec-tively, at time $t$. One can then derive the following result with respect to the public good:[14]

**Proposition 4.** *If the income tax is optimally chosen, the marginal utility value of an incremental public good at time t can be written as*

$$\psi^0(t) = \int_t^\infty \left\{ \lambda^0(s) \sum_i MRS^{i,0}_{G,c}(s) \right.$$

$$\left. + \eta^0(s)\hat{u}^{2,0}_c(s)\left[MRS^{1,0}_{G,c}(s) - M\hat{R}S^{2,0}_{G,c}(s)\right] \right\} e^{-(\theta + \delta)(s-t)}ds.$$

Proof: see the Appendix to this chapter.

By analogy to the corresponding shadow price derived in Section 2, note first that the appropriate rate to discount the future adjusted marginal benefits of an increment to the public good at time $t$ (where the adjustment refers to the effects via the self-selection constraint) is given by the sum of the utility discount rate and the rate of depreciation of the public good. The first term on the right-hand side of the formula in Proposition 4 reflects the sum of marginal rates of substitution between the public good and private consumption, that is, the sum of the marginal willingness to pay by the consumers. Note that this sum is not only measured over consumers living at the same time; it is measured over time as well, since an increment to the public good at time $t$, *ceteris paribus*, will affect all future $G(s)$ for $s \in (t, \infty)$ and, therefore, also the future instantaneous utilities.

The second term on the right-hand side is due to the self-selection constraint: it shows that a binding self-selection constraint at any future time affects the value that the government attaches to an increase in the contribution to the public good at time $t$. The intuition is that the public good constitutes an instrument by which the government can relax the self-selection constraint; this, in turn, allows for more redistribution. How the government ought to modify its use of public provision due to the self-selection constraint depends, in turn, on how the marginal willingness to pay for the public good is related to the leisure choice.[15] If leisure is substitutable for the public good in the sense that the low-ability type is willing to pay more at the margin for the public good than the mimicker, that is, $MRS^1_{G,c} > M\hat{R}S^2_{G,c}$, increased public provision leads to a greater utility gain for the low-ability type than it does for the mimicker. In this case, therefore, the government may relax the self-selection constraint by increasing the contribution to the public good at time $t$, which means that the government attaches a higher marginal value to the public good than it would otherwise have done. If, on the other hand, leisure is complementary to the public good in the sense that the mimicker is willing to pay more at the margin for the public good than the low-ability type, so $MRS^1_{G,c} < M\hat{R}S^2_{G,c}$, the government may, instead, relax the self-selection constraint by lowering its contribution to the public good, in which case it attaches a lower marginal value to the public good than it would otherwise have done. Finally, in the special case where leisure is weakly separable from the other goods in the utility function – which with the formulation set out above means that $MRS^1_{G,c} = M\hat{R}S^2_{G,c}$ for all $t$ – the self-selection constraint would have no direct effect on the marginal value that the government attaches to the public good.[16]

However, although the marginal social value of the public good derived in Proposition 4 is measured in a different way than in the representative agent models analysed in Section 2, the qualitative content of Proposition 2 applies here as well. This is seen from the first-order condition for the contribution to the public good, that is, equation (37), which implies $\psi^0(t) = \lambda^0(t)\rho$ for all $t$. In other words, the marginal social value of the public good reflects the product of the direct marginal cost of providing the public good and the marginal cost of public funds (here measured in utility terms). The difference between the model set out in this section and the model in Section 2 is, instead, that the marginal cost of public funds here reflects that revenue collection affects the self-selection constraint, not the necessity per se to use distortionary taxation as in Section 2. Note also that, in the special case when the self-selection constraint does not bind (in any period), we obtain the first-best resource allocation, where $\phi^1 = \phi^2 = \lambda$, implying that the marginal social value of the public good can be elicited by using an intertemporal analogue to the conventional Samuelson condition, that is,

$$\int_t^\infty \sum_i \phi^0(s)\, MRS^{i,0}_{G,c}(s)\, e^{-(\theta+\delta)(s-t)}\, ds = \phi^0(t)\rho.$$

**Briefly on redistribution and distributional objectives**
The distribution of resources between the consumers is implicit in the welfare measure given by equation (42). Despite the fact that the underlying resource allocation is optimal from the perspective of society, note that the government is not able to fully implement its distributional objectives. With the objective function set out above, the (benevolent) government would have liked to equalize the marginal utility of consumption between the two ability types at each instant; however, concern for the self-selection constraint prevents it from doing so. An interesting question is whether this inability ought to affect the way in which the comprehensive NNP is measured. Following much of the earlier literature on social accounting,[17] I will here define the comprehensive NNP by using the linearized current value Hamiltonian, and then use the result that the current value Hamiltonian can be written as the sum of the linearized current value Hamiltonian and the consumer surplus.

Let $w_n^i = w^i(1 - T'(w^i l^i))$ denote the marginal wage rate of ability type $i$, and denote the exchange value of leisure by $q^i = w_n^i z^i$. In addition, and to simplify the notations even further, let $\phi_m$, $c_m$ and $q_m$ denote the average marginal utility of consumption, average consumption and the average exchange value of leisure respectively. Then, since $E[\phi c] = \phi_m c_m + \text{cov}(\phi, c)$ and $E[\phi q] = \phi_m q_m + \text{cov}(\phi, q)$, where $E[\cdot]$ denotes the mean operator, and if we define the consumer surplus[18] as $s = \Sigma_i[u(c^i, z^i, G) - u_c^i c^i - u_z^i z^i - u_G^i G]$, equation (42) may be rewritten as follows (suppressing the time indicator):

$$\theta V^0 = \phi_m^0[C^0(1 + \zeta_c^0) + Q^0(1 + \zeta_q^0) + \sum_i \alpha^{i,0} MRS^{i,0}_{G,c} G^0$$

$$+ \overline{m}^0 \dot{k}^0 + \overline{m}^0 \rho \dot{G}^0] + s^0, \tag{43}$$

in which I have used the short notations $\alpha^i = \phi^i/\phi_m$ and $\overline{m} = \lambda/\phi_m$, and where $C = \Sigma_i c^i$, $Q = \Sigma_i q^i$, $\zeta_c = \text{cov}(\phi, c)/(\phi_m c_m)$ and $\zeta_q = \text{cov}(\phi, q)/(\phi_m q_m)$. The first five components on the right-hand side of equation (43) together constitute the linearized current value Hamiltonian, which is interpretable as the comprehensive NNP times the average marginal utility of consumption. The variables $\zeta_c$ and $\zeta_q$ are distributional characteristics, and reflect the correlations between, on the one hand, the marginal utility of consumption and, on the other, the private consumption and exchange value of leisure, respectively. These distributional characteristics would be absent in the first best, in which case equation (43) reduces to read (as the first best implies $\phi^1 = \phi^2 = \phi = \lambda$ and $\overline{m} = 1$)

$$\theta V^* = \phi^* \left[ C^* + \sum_i w^{i,*} l^{i,*} + \sum_i MRS_{G,c}^{i,*} G^* + \dot{k}^* + \rho \dot{G}^* \right] + s^*, \quad (44)$$

in which the comprehensive NNP only comprises aggregate variables. The essence is that equation (44) is derived in a situation where the marginal utility of consumption has become equalized across agents (meaning that $\zeta_c = \zeta_q = 0$), whereas equation (43) is based on a second-best resource allocation with a binding self-selection constraint, in which case the government is not able to equalize the marginal utility of consumption.

A comparison between equations (43) and (44) suggests that, if the government is able to fully implement its distributional objectives – and given the form of the social welfare function assumed here – only the aggregate value of each private decision variable (in this case private consumption and leisure) ought to be part of comprehensive NNP. However, if the government is not able to fully implement its distributional objectives, then this policy failure ought to be recognized, which is why the 'accounting prices' for aggregate private consumption and the aggregate exchange value of leisure reflect distributional characteristics in the second-best resource allocation.

## 4   CONCLUSION

This chapter has analyzed some aspects of welfare measurement in a second-best economy, where public revenue is raised by distortionary taxation, and much attention has been paid to the treatment of a state-variable public good. I would like to emphasize two general conclusions from the analysis carried out above. First, a second-best analogue to Weitzman's (1976) Hamiltonian-based welfare measure contains information about the welfare cost of raising revenue. Second, the shadow price associated with an addition to the public good (that is, the marginal benefit of an incremental public good) is, to some extent, model specific, and depends on the exact nature of the social decision-problem. This was exemplified by using two different models, that is, an intertemporal representative agent model with linear taxation (where indirect effects of the public good affect the value attached to it by the government) and an intertemporal variant of the two-type optimal income tax model (in which the desire to relax the self-selection constraint affects the marginal value of the public good). In either case, however, an optimal choice from the perspective of the government implies that this shadow price is equal to the product of the direct cost of providing the public good and the marginal cost of public funds. In a sense, therefore, this product provides a static equivalent to the forward-looking shadow price of a state-variable public good.

It is not difficult to imagine several possible, and very interesting directions for future research. One would be to extend the analysis to a global economy, in which individual countries engage in tax competition for mobile capital. Such an extension appears well motivated due to the increased openness (and capital mobility) that has been observed during the last 20 or 30 years. In addition, since many services typically provided by the public sector in real-world economies have the character of private goods, another extension would be to analyze the role of public provision of private goods. Earlier research shows that such provision might be an important means of redistribution, which makes it relevant to address also in the context of welfare measurement. Finally, issues associated with the measurement of sustainable development have so far primarily been analyzed in an environmental economics context, which typically abstracts from other aspects of public policy. Yet another possible direction for future research is, therefore, to address the measurement of sustainability in an economy where the public finance aspects addressed in this chapter are also considered. I leave these, and other possible extensions for future research.

## APPENDIX

### Proof of Proposition 4

Note first that equation (39) can be written as

$$\psi_p = - MRS^1_{G,c} u^1_c e^{-\theta t} - MRS^2_{G,c} u^2_c [e^{-\theta t} + \eta_p] + \eta_p \hat{u}^2_c M\hat{R}S^2_{G,c} + \psi_p \delta. \tag{A1}$$

By using equations (34) and (36) to obtain $u_c^1 e^{-\theta t} = \eta_p \hat{u}_c^2 + \lambda_p$ and $u_c^2 [e^{-\theta t} + \eta_p] = \lambda_p$, substituting into equation (A1) and rearranging gives

$$\psi_p = -\lambda_p \sum_i MRS_{G,c}^i - \eta_p \hat{u}_c^2 [MRS_{G,c}^1 - M\hat{R}S_{G,c}^2] + \psi_p \delta. \quad (A2)$$

Solving equation (A2) subject to the transversality condition $\lim_{t \to \infty} \psi_p(t) = 0$ and then transforming the solution to current value gives the expression in Proposition 4.

## ACKNOWLEDGEMENTS

The author would like to thank Karl-Gustaf Löfgren and Tomas Sjögren for helpful comments and suggestions. A research grant from FORMAS is also gratefully acknowledged.

## NOTES

1. As we mentioned in Chapter 1, the basic welfare economic foundation for social accounting in a first-best economy originates from Weitzman (1976). For an overview of the literature dealing with social accounting in imperfect market economies, see Aronsson et al. (2004).
2. Typical textbook examples of public goods – or public good-like variables – often include measures of environmental quality, national infrastructure and national defence, all of which struck me as better described as state variables than conventional flow variables.
3. See also Pirttilä and Tuomala (2001) and Aronsson et al. (2009) for extensions of the two-type optimal income tax model to dynamic economies.
4. Note that I abstract from capital income taxes in what follows. Since the model already contains one distortionary tax, adding another will not affect the principal findings below. See Chamley (1986) for a dynamic representative agent model with linear taxes on labor income and capital income.
5. Note that the current value Hamiltonian implied by the consumer's decision-problem can be written as (if the time-indicator is suppressed) $\Im = u(c, z, G) + \phi \dot{a}$.
6. For details regarding properties of the optimal solution, the reader is referred to Chamley (1985).
7. This property of a well-behaved optimal control problem was derived by Michel (1982) for the situation where neither the instantaneous objective nor the instantaneous constraint functions depend explicitly on time (as in our case). See also Seierstad and Sydsaeter (1987) for an extension of this result to a situation where the instantaneous objective and the instantaneous constraint functions may depend explicitly on time.
8. To see this, note that as $\phi(0)$ is free in the public decision-problem, the optimal resource allocation must obey the initial transversality condition $v(0) = 0$. Therefore, since $\mu(t) = 0$ and $\phi(t) = \lambda(t)$ for all $t$ in the first best, we would also have $\partial H(t)/\partial \phi$ $(t) = 0$ for all $t$ in the first best, in which case $v(t) = 0$.
9. Note that if the utility function is additively separable in the public good, then the

marginal utility of the public good measured in terms of the conditional indirect utility function, that is, $v_G(\cdot)$, does not depend on $w_n$ and $\phi$.

10. The Samuelson condition is often formulated such that the marginal rate of substitution between the public good and private consumption should be equal to the marginal rate of transformation between the public good and the private consumption good. In the context of the model used here, an intertemporal analogue to the Samuelson condition can be written as

$$\frac{\int_t^\infty u_G(c^0(s), z^0(s), G^0(s))e^{-(\theta+\delta)(s-t)}ds}{\phi^0(t)} = \rho.$$

11. Major early contributions to a more formalized theory of public good provision under linear taxation date back to the early 1970s; see Diamond and Mirrlees (1971), Stiglitz and Dasgupta (1971) and Atkinson and Stern (1974).

12. This simplification enables me to formulate the public decision-problem in a way similar to earlier literature on the self-selection approach to optimal income taxation in dynamic models; see, for example, Brett (1997), Pirttilä and Tuomala (2001) and Aronsson et al. (2009).

13. See Atkinson and Sandmo (1980) and Pirttilä and Tuomala (2001).

14. Public good provision in economies with non-linear taxation has been addressed by, for example, Christiansen (1981) and Boadway and Keen (1993). See also Pirttilä and Tuomala (2001) for an extension to a dynamic economy, in which the public good is a state variable.

15. Recall that the only difference between the low-ability type and the mimicker is that the mimicker is more productive, and consumes more leisure, than the low-ability type.

16. Note that, even if we were to add the assumption that leisure is weakly separable from the other goods in the utility function, a binding self-selection constraint will, nevertheless, indirectly affect the marginal value the government attaches to the public good, as a binding self-selection constraint means that the marginal utility of consumption differs between the consumers as well as differing from the shadow price of capital.

17. An overview of the literature is given by Aronsson et al. (2004).

18. For a thorough analysis of the role of the consumer surplus in the context of welfare measurement, see Li and Löfgren (2002).

# REFERENCES

Aronsson, T. (1998) Welfare Measurement, Green Accounting and Distortionary Taxes. *Journal of Public Economics* **70**, 273–295.

Aronsson, T. (2008) Social Accounting and the Public Sector. *International Economics Review* **49**, 349–375.

Aronsson, T. and Löfgren, K.-G. (1999) Welfare Equivalent NNP under Distributional Objectives. *Economics Letters*, **63**, 239–243.

Aronsson, T., Löfgren, K.-G. and Backlund, K. (2004) *Welfare Measurement in Imperfect Markets: A Growth Theoretical Approach*. Cheltenham: Edward Elgar Publishing Limited.

Aronsson, T., Sjögren, T. and Dalin, T. (2009) Optimal Taxation and Redistribution in an OLG Model with Unemployment. *International Tax and Public Finance*, **16**(2), 198–218.

Atkinson, A. and Sandmo, A. (1980) Welfare Implications of the Taxation of Savings. *Economic Journal* **90**, 529–548.

Atkinson, A. and Stern, N. (1974) Pigou, Taxation and Public Goods. *Review of Economic Studies*, **41**, 119–128.

Boadway, R. and Keen, M.J. (1993) Public Goods, Self-Selection and Optimal Income Taxation. *International Economic Review*, **34**, 463–478.

Brett, C. (1997) A Note on Nonlinear Taxation in an Overlapping Generations Model. Mimeo.

Chamley, C. (1985) Efficient Taxation in a Stylized Model of Intertemporal General Equilibrium. *International Economic Review*, **26**, 451–468.

Chamley, C. (1986) Optimal Taxation of Capital Income in General Equilibrium with Infinite Lives. *Econometrica*, **54**, 607–622.

Christiansen, V. (1981) Evaluation of Projects under Optimal Taxation. *Review of Economic Studies*, **48**, 447–457.

Diamond, P. and Mirrlees, J. (1971) Optimal Taxation and Public Production: Tax Rules. *American Economic Review*, **61**, 261–278.

Li, C.-Z. and Löfgren, K.-G. (2002) *On the Choice of Metrics in Dynamic Welfare Analysis: Utility versus Money Measures*. Umeå Economic Studies no 590. Umeå University of Umeå.

Michel, P. (1982) On the Transversality Conditions in Infinite Horizon Optimal Control Problems. *Econometrica*, 50, 975–985.

Mirrlees, J.A. (1971) An Exploration into the Theory of Optimum Income Taxation. *Review of Economic Studies*, **38**, 175–208.

Pigou, A.C. (1947) *A Study in Public Finance*. New York: MacMillan.

Pirttilä, J. and Tuomala, M. (2001) On Optimal Non-Linear Taxation and Public Good Provision in an Overlapping Generations Economy. *Journal of Public Economics*, **79**, 485–501.

Sandmo, A. (1998) Redistribution and the Marginal Cost of Public Funds. *Journal of Public Economics*, **70**, 365–382.

Seierstad, A. and Sydsaeter, K. (1987) *Optimal Control Theory with Economic Applications*. Amsterdam: North-Holland.

Stern, N.H. (1982) Optimum Taxation with Errors in Administration. *Journal of Public Economics*, **17**, 181–211.

Stiglitz, J.E. (1982) Self-Selection and Pareto Efficient Taxation. *Journal of Public Economics*, **17**, 213–240.

Stiglitz, J. and Dasgupta, P. (1971) Differential Taxation, Public Goods, and Economic Efficiency. *Review of Economic Studies*, **38**, 151–174.

Weitzman, M.L. (1976) On the Welfare Significance of National Product in a Dynamic Economy. *The Quarterly Journal of Economics*, **90**, 156–162.

# 6 How are green national accounts produced in practice?
*Eva Samakovlis*

## 1 INTRODUCTION

During the last part of the twentieth century, the effect of human activity upon the environment became an important policy issue. There is now a growing concern about how economic activity affects the environment and it has become increasingly recognised that economic growth is dependent upon the provision of environmental services. To be able to combine economic growth with a healthy environment in terms of a sustainable use of natural resources, a better understanding of the relationships between economy and ecology needs to be developed.

The awareness that economic development and environmental aspects cannot be treated separately was the background to the Brundtland Commission, formally the World Commission on Environment and Development set up by the United Nations (UN) in 1983. The commission was created to address the concern about the accelerating deterioration of the environment and its consequences for economic and social development. According to the Brundtland report, sustainable development is largely about the allocation of resources within and between generations (United Nations, 1987). One of the most often cited definitions of sustainability was adopted by the commission, that 'Sustainable development is development that meets the needs of the present without compromising the ability of future generations to meet their own needs'.[1] How to measure sustainable development was, however, never conveyed by the Commission and has proven to be remarkably difficult. The early discussions on sustainable development departed from capital stocks, and gave two views on how certain types of capital can replace each other: weak and strong sustainability. The concept of weak sustainability originates from Hartwick's rule, which shows, under certain assumptions, that the rent derived from resource depletion is exactly the level of capital investment needed to achieve constant consumption over time (Hartwick, 1977).[2] In other words, weak sustainability implies that all forms of capital are more-or-less substitutes for one another. This approach then allows for the depletion and degradation of natural resources, as long as such depletion is offset by increases in the stocks of other forms of capital. Strong sustainability, on the other hand, implies that all forms of capital must be maintained intact independent of each other, implying no substitution between different forms of capital (Daly and Cobb, 1989; Daly, 1990). Several ways of measuring sustainable development have been suggested, involving both theoretical and empirical weaknesses.[3] The welfare measures comprehensive net national product (Weitzman, 1976)[4] and genuine savings (Pearce and Atkinson, 1993), which are firmly founded in neo-classical economic theory and potential indicators of weak sustainability, will be discussed in this chapter.

The Net National Product (NNP) equals the sum of consumption of conventional goods and services and the value of net investment in physical capital. A comprehensive NNP should also include consumption of other utilities, such as leisure and environmental quality, and changes in natural resource and human capital stocks. The genuine savings measure equals comprehensive NNP less consumption. Weitzman (1976) shows that comprehensive NNP is an exact indicator of welfare under the restrictive assumptions of an economy with a stationary technology, no externalities and perfect foresight. If the economy is also closed with a constant population and only one capital good, NNP is an exact indicator of sustainability (Asheim, 1994).[5] The welfare significance of genuine savings was first derived by Pearce and Atkinson (1993).

A well-known shortcoming of the System of National Accounts (SNA) is that it does not consider the impact of environmental pollution and depletion of natural resources on welfare.[6] This has been a growing concern ever since the development of the system in the 1940s (Smith, 2007). At the UN Conference on Environment and Development in Rio de Janeiro in 1992, the full text of Agenda 21 was revealed and 179 governments adopted the programme.[7] It included the establishment of systems for integrated environmental and economic accounting. The basis for action stated that a first step towards the integration of sustainability into economic management is better measurement of the role of the environment. The objectives included the expansion of existing systems of national economic accounts using sound theory and practicability, 'in order to integrate environment and social dimensions in the accounting framework, including at least satellite systems of accounts for natural resources in all member states'. One of the stated activities was for the UN to make a handbook on integrated environmental and economic accounting, involving practical guidelines, available to all member countries (United Nations Statistical Commission, 2007). In 1993, the UN published the first handbook on environmental accounting (UN, 1993). It aimed to supplement existing accounts with environmental and natural resource accounts, employing the same type of accounts, branches and definitions as the SNA. In 2003, a revision of the handbook was released.

Even though the handbook was not published until as late as 1993, the development of applied green accounting dates back to the 1970s. Great efforts were made, from the beginning, by individual countries and practitioners developing their own frameworks and methodologies to represent their environmental priorities. Some of the earliest work was undertaken in Norway (Alfsen et al., 1987; Alfsen and Greaker, 2007), followed by France (Theys, 1989), but by the time of the first handbook, Australia, Canada, Denmark, Finland, Germany, Indonesia, Italy, Japan, the Netherlands, the Philippines, Sweden and the United Kingdom had joined the efforts. These experiences on green accounting range from environmental asset and flow accounts to environmentally adjusted macroeconomic aggregates.

This chapter is structured as follows. Section 2 describes the development of the handbook of integrated environmental and economic accounting, including the four components of environmental accounts and how the environmental accounting programmes of different countries relate to them. Section 3 provides an overview of country experiences of adjusted welfare measures, including comprehensive net domestic product attempts and the genuine savings project carried out by the World Bank. Sections 4 and 5 include case studies of green accounting projects carried out in Norway and Sweden. Norway was one of the pioneers of green accounting and Sweden is one of the few countries with an environmental accounting programme that includes the calculation of environmentally adjusted macroeconomic aggregates. Section 6 discusses the difficulties encountered in pursuing monetary green national accounts, and Section 7 summarises and concludes the chapter.

## 2    INTEGRATED ENVIRONMENTAL AND ECONOMIC ACCOUNTING

### 2.1    The Development of SEEA 1993 and 2003

In 1993, the UN published its *Handbook of National Accounting: Integrated Environmental and Economic Accounting*, or SEEA 1993 (United Nations, 1993). It was the first handbook on environmental accounting, and although it is considered a modest step forward in treating the environment within the national accounts, it was the first time any serious consideration was given to the issue (Smith, 2007). SEEA 1993 was published as a set of international recommendations rather than as an international standard. As a consequence, countries that had already established environmental accounting programmes did not necessarily adjust their efforts to align with it (Smith, 2007). Other countries, including Columbia, Ghana, Indonesia, Korea and the Philippines, started experimenting with the compilation of the new satellite accounting framework (Hamilton and Lutz, 1996). To exchange experiences among countries and to advance methodologies, the London Group on Environmental Accounting was created in 1994. All of the leading national and international agencies working with environmental accounting joined the group, and the UN Statistical Commission (UNSC) formally requested it to collaborate with the UN Statistical Department on the revision of SEEA 1993 (United Nations Statistical Commission, 2007). The revised handbook, SEEA 2003, was published jointly by the UN, the International Monetary Fund, the Organization of Economic Cooperation and Development, the Statistical Office of the European Commission and the World Bank (United Nations et al., 2003). It offers guidance on a complete and integrated set of environmental accounts, both in physical and monetary units. The main purpose of SEEA 2003 is 'to explore how sets of statistical accounts can be compiled which will permit investigation and analysis of the interaction between the economy and the environment' (UN et al., 2003, p. 1). The UN Committee of Experts on Environmental and Economic Accounting has recently decided to make SEEA 2003 an international standard by 2010. This will increase the pressure to conform to its concepts and methods (Smith, 2007).

### 2.2   The Four Components of Environmental Accounts

SEEA 2003 comprises four categories of accounts: flow accounts for pollution, energy and materials; environmental protection and resource management expenditure accounts; natural resource asset accounts; and valuation of non-market flow and environmentally adjusted aggregates.

Pollutant and material flow accounts consider purely physical data relating to flows of pollution, materials and energy. The accounts, which follow the SNA accounting structure, provide industry-level information about the use of energy and materials as inputs to production and the generation of pollutants and waste. The objective of these accounts is to show the interdependence between the economy and the environment. Since the accounts follow the SNA, links can be made to other economic series. Flow data in physical and monetary terms can be combined to produce so-called 'hybrid' flow accounts, which, for example, can be used to analyse 'decoupling', that is, the lessening of correlation or dependency between variables such as economic production and environmental quality. The

National Accounting Matrix with Environmental Accounts (NAMEA) is a well-known type of hybrid account developed by Statistics Netherlands in the 1990s, and shows the link between economic indicators and the environment.

Environmental protection and resource management expenditure accounts identify expenditures incurred by industry, the government and households to protect the environment or to manage natural resources. These accounts are consistent with the SNA but summarise all environment-related transactions separately in satellite accounts. The reason behind establishing these type of accounts is 'to identify and measure society's response to environmental concerns through the supply and demand for environment goods and services, through the adoption of production and consumption behaviour aimed at preventing environmental degradation and by managing environmental resources in a sustainable way' (UN et al., 2003, p. 170).

Natural resource asset accounts comprise accounts for environmental assets such as land, fish, forest, water and minerals. An asset account shows opening and closing balances and the related changes over the course of the accounting period. The accounts are measured both in physical and monetary terms. The physical accounts are easier to construct but cannot be aggregated and are therefore not very useful in studying trade-offs among capital stocks. The monetary accounts, on the other hand, have both practical and conceptual problems related to the limitations and legitimacy of the valuation methods (Smith, 2007). To value natural capital depletion (a quantity reduction in a natural resource), SEEA 2003 recommends the net present value (NPV), which equals the net return on the extracted resources less the interest gained on the remaining capital (Dietz and Neumayer, 2007). Other methods mentioned are the net price method and the El Serafy method (also called the user cost method).[8] Valuing natural capital degradation (a quality damage of a natural resource) is however more controversial than valuing depletion. Hence, methods of valuing degradation are discussed among the last type of accounts, which SEEA 2003 states are more 'hypothetical'. The asset accounts are relevant to the capital-based approaches to sustainable development. SEEA 2003, however, focuses only on natural capital and does not cover human and social capital, which also need to be included when measuring sustainability. There is a debate on the degree of substitutability of natural capital by other forms of capital, and this has led to two forms of capital-based approaches: weak and strong sustainability (see Section 1). Since strong sustainability implies no substitution between different kinds of capital, there is no need for monetary evaluation. In order to see if weak sustainability is obtained (if the whole capital stock is left intact), the separate stocks need to be valued monetarily.

The valuation section in SEEA 2003 focuses on valuation techniques for measuring degradation and their applicability in answering policy questions. Cost-based pricing techniques such as structural adjustment, abatement and restoration costs are described as well as damage- and benefit-based pricing techniques in terms of revealed and stated preference methods. Methodological reservations are made, stating that the valuation techniques are still being developed, and the data requirements to implement them are both extensive and resource intensive and thus generally incomplete. The difficulty involved in using these methods 'at the national scale and under the consistency requirements of the national accounts' is also emphasised. The section on environmentally-adjusted aggregates, which is even more tentative, focuses on 'how the conventional national accounts could be adapted to show the interaction between the economy and the environment in monetary terms' and discusses the calculation and (dis)advantages of macroeconomic aggregates.[9] According to SEEA 2003, 'There is no consensus on how green GDP could be calculated and, in fact, still less consensus on whether it should be attempted at all'. It is clearly stated that the lack of consensus is so large that some of the 'collaborators in the preparation of the handbook would prefer that this chapter were omitted from the book'. Some of these critics are reluctant to incorporate presumed effects of environmental flows into the well-established economic accounts, while others emphasise the data problems involved. To complete the picture of integrated environmental and economic accounting, SEEA 2003 also covers: depletion of natural resources, defensive expenditures (expenditures to combat environmental degradation), and degradation. For each topic there is a discussion of the pros and cons, bringing the issue into the macro aggregate.

## 2.3   Countries with Environmental Accounting Programmes

Several countries are constructing environmental accounts in their statistical offices or in other government departments on an ongoing basis. In addition, there are numerous academic studies. Table 6.1 lists the countries with ongoing programmes and the types of accounts they focus on. Notable is the fact that only six countries have tried to construct environmentally adjusted macroeconomic aggregates. In addition, a closer look at them (see Section 3.2) reveals that these attempts were only made for a certain year or for a short time.

*Table 6.1  Countries with environmental accounting programmes*

| | Natural resource asset accounts | Flow accounts for pollutants and materials | | Environmental protection & resource management expenditures | Environmentally-adjusted macroeconomic aggregates |
| --- | --- | --- | --- | --- | --- |
| | | Physical | Monetary | | |
| *Industrialised countries* | | | | | |
| Australia | X | X | | X | |
| Canada | X | X | | X | |
| Denmark | X | X | | X | |
| Finland | X | X | | X | |
| France | X | X | | X | |
| Germany | X | X | X | X | X |
| Italy | X | X | | X | |
| Japan | X | X | X | X | X |
| Norway | X | X | | | |
| Sweden | X | X | X | X | X |
| UK | X | X | | X | |
| USA | X | | | X | |
| *Developing countries* | | | | | |
| Botswana | X | X | X | | |
| Chile | X | | X | X | |
| Korea | X | X | X | X | X |
| Mexico | X | X | X | X | X |
| Moldova | | X | | | |
| Namibia | X | X | X | | |
| The Philippines | X | X | X | X | X |

*Source:*  Lange (2003).

## 3   COUNTRY EXPERIENCES OF ADJUSTED MACROECONOMIC AGGREGATES

The purpose of most monetary environmental macroeconomic aggregates has been to provide a more relevant welfare measure. One of the most well-known adjusted macroeconomic aggregate is the comprehensive NNP. A related indicator is genuine savings, which measures changes in asset values rather than income. The first section will provide a brief theory of welfare measurements to illustrate how NNP and genuine savings would be optimally constructed empirically if all information were available, and how these measures relate to each other. Contrary to the theorists, the empiricists often use the measure Net Domestic Product (NDP) instead of NNP.[10] The following sections will give an overview of some of the rather few countries that have tried to derive a comprehensive NDP and of the genuine savings project carried out by the World Bank.

### 3.1   A Brief Description of the Theory of Welfare Measurement

The conventional NNP includes consumption of goods and services and net investments limited to physical capital. In order to make it a better welfare measure, it needs to be enlarged to a comprehensive NNP and include all aspects of consumption and capital formation (including environmental quality and natural resource stocks) relevant for society. Most studies of a comprehensive NNP are based on a fundamental theorem by Weitzman (1976), where comprehensive NNP is shown to be an exact indicator of welfare under certain conditions. More precisely, he shows that if an economy with a stationary technology follows the first-best optimal path, then a comprehensive NNP is directly proportional to the present value of future utility.[11] In other words, along the first-best optimal path, the value function is proportional to the current value Hamiltonian (in the social planner's optimisation problem), which can be interpreted as the comprehensive NNP in utility terms. With this definition, the comprehensive NNP measure in utility terms is thus a static equivalent to future welfare.

To derive Weitzman's welfare measure and to illustrate the relation between comprehensive NNP in utility terms and genuine savings, the model from Aronsson et al. (1997, Chapter 4) is applied. A social planner maximises the present value of future utility according to:

$$\underset{c_t,\, m_t}{Max} \int_0^\infty u(c_t,\, x_t)e^{-\theta t}dt \tag{1}$$

subject to

(i) $\dot{k}_t = f(k_t, m_t) - c_t$

(ii) $\dot{x}_t = m_t - \zeta x_t$ (2)

(iii) $k(0) = k_0 > 0$ and $x(0) = x_0 \geq 0$

(iv) $\lim_{t \to \infty} k(t) \geq 0$ and $\lim_{t \to \infty} x(t) \geq 0$.

Consumer utility is assumed to be a function of consumption per unit of labour (per capita) $c_t$, and a stock of pollution per capita $x_t$. The production of the consumption good uses capital, labour and emissions (through the use of energy) as inputs. The labour endowment is fixed and normalised to unity. Then $k_t$ and $m_t$ are, respectively, the capital and energy used per unit of labour. Investments equal production less consumption. The stock of pollution $x_t$ develops through the flow of emissions $m_t$ (which depends on production) and the environment's assimilative capacity ($0 \leq \zeta \leq 1$). The present value Hamiltonian can be written as:

$$H_t = u(c_t, x_t)e^{-\theta t} + \lambda_t \dot{k}_t + \mu_t \dot{x}_t. \quad (3)$$

Let $H_t^c = H_t e^{\theta t}$ be the current value Hamiltonian, which is often used as a measure of comprehensive NNP in utility terms. Then the analogue to Weitzman's welfare measure can be derived as:

$$\theta W(t) = H_t^c = u(c_t, x_t) + \lambda_t^c \dot{k}_t + \mu_t^c \dot{x}_t, \quad (4)$$

where $W(t) = \int_t^\infty u(c_z, x_s)e^{-\theta(s-t)}ds$ is the value function. To transform this measure into what looks like a real NNP concept, the instantaneous utility is approximated with a linear function $u(c, x) \approx \lambda^c c + u_x(c, x)x$.[12] This gives the linearised welfare measure:

$$\theta W(t) \approx \lambda_t^c[c_t + \dot{k}_t + \rho_t x_t - \tau_t \dot{x}_t], \quad (5)$$

which measures the comprehensive NNP in real terms times the marginal utility of consumption at time $t$. The comprehensive NNP consists of the conventional NNP plus two additional terms. The third term measures the value of the stock of pollution at time $t$, where $\rho = u_x/\lambda^c$ is the marginal consumption value of the stock of pollution. The fourth term is the value of additions to the stock of pollution, and $\tau = -\mu/\lambda^c$.

It is also possible to illustrate that genuine savings is a measure of welfare change:

$$\dot{W}(t) = -u(c_t, x_t) + \theta W(t) = \frac{dH_t^c}{dt}$$

$$= H_t^c - u(c_t, x_t) = \lambda_t^c \dot{k}_t + \mu_t^c \dot{x}_t. \tag{6}$$

Thus, genuine savings in utility terms equals NNP less consumption.

### 3.2    Country Experiences of Comprehensive Net Domestic Product

One of the best-known natural resource accounting studies is Repetto et al.'s (1989) calculation of an Indonesian comprehensive NDP carried out in order to make policy makers realise the importance of environmental degradation and depletion of natural capital. They construct resource accounts in physical and monetary terms for oil, forests and soil, and use the net price method (see Section 2.2), where rents are determined by the commodity price less all factor costs for extraction, to value depreciation of oil and forests. For soil erosion, the loss of potential future farm income is used. The results from the resource accounts are then aggregated and deducted from the GDP. This results in an incomplete measure of comprehensive NDP since the depreciation of produced assets is not included. The comprehensive NDP figures calculated for 1971–84 are generally lower than the GDP (−2 per cent to −24 per cent), except for 1971 and 1974, when they are higher due to oil discoveries (Hamilton and Lutz, 1996). A similar exercise was undertaken for Costa Rica (Repetto and Cruz, 1991) focusing on forests, fisheries and soil for 1970–89. There the comprehensive NDP figures are lower than the GDP, ranging from −8 per cent to −13 per cent.

These early attempts were followed by a number of countries. Table 6.2 shows the countries with ongoing environmental accounting programmes that occasionally produce environmentally adjusted macroeconomic aggregates (Costa Rica, Indonesia, Germany, Japan, Korea, Mexico, Sweden and the Philippines). In these projects, the macroeconomic aggregates are affected very differently depending on several factors such as the period studied, type of coverage and valuation method used. This makes it impossible to compare the results among countries. Notable is that the effect on the macroeconomic aggregate for Indonesia and Costa Rica is expressed in percentage of GDP and for the other countries in percentage of NDP.

Some countries, like Germany, Japan and Mexico, have calculated comprehensive NDPs for one specific year, while others, like Costa Rica, Indonesia, Korea and the Philippines, have calculated comprehensive NDPs for an extended period. The type of coverage varies a lot, depending on the natural resource abundance and the environmental problems in each country, as well as on data availability. Germany, for example, made an attempt to calculate a comprehensive NDP in 1990; it amounted to 97 per cent of the conventional NDP aggregate, implying that the economy generated about DM 59 billion in environmental (degradation and depletion) costs that year. This was mostly due to the large cost associated with an assumed 40 per cent carbon dioxide ($CO_2$) emission reduction (note that the cost of reducing $CO_2$ emissions was also included by Japan, while the other countries did not). The agriculture and energy supply sectors incurred the largest environmental costs per value added, accounting for around 34 per cent of total environmental costs (Bartelmus and Vesper, 2000). The narrow focus of the Swedish project on environmental degradation caused by sulphur and nitrogen emissions is motivated by data availability, since the environmental effects from these emissions are quite well documented. This narrow focus, however, explains the small change compared to conventional NDP (for a broader selection of analyses carried out in Sweden, see Section 5).

Large methodological variation can also be seen. Most countries estimated industry-specific abatement costs, while Korea, for example, assumed the same abatement costs in all industries in its project for 1985–1992 (Lange, 2003). The Mexico project of 1985, carried out jointly by the UN Statistical Office, the World Bank and the National Institute of Statistics, Geography and Informatics of Mexico, used two different methods to value depletion of natural resources (oil and timber): the net price method and the user cost, or El Serafy, approach (see Section 2.2). The net price method resulted in a net rent of 1162 pesos/barrel and an average stumpage value of 21.5 pesos/m³, while the corresponding figures for the El Serafy approach were much lower: 160 pesos/barrel and 1.6 pesos/m³ (Heal and Kriström, 2005). The purpose of the Swedish project was to present and evaluate the UN System of Environmental and Economic Accounts in relation to a methodology closer to the theoretically consistent comprehensive NDP. In this project, the issue of double counting (including degradation already included in conventional NDP measures) was taken into account.

### 3.3 Genuine Savings at the World Bank

As illustrated in Section 3.1, there is a clear relationship between the two welfare measures, comprehensive NNP and genuine savings. Comprehensive NNP equals consumption plus the sum of the net changes in all capital stocks valued at their shadow prices, and genuine savings equals comprehensive NNP less consumption. Negative genuine savings

*Table 6.2  Comprehensive NDP*

| Country | Period | Effect on macroeconomic aggregates | Coverage | Valuation method |
|---|---|---|---|---|
| Costa Rica | 1970–89 | GDP reduced 8%–13% | Depletion of forest, fish<br>Degradation of land | Net price method<br>Maintenance cost |
| Indonesia | 1971–84 | GDP reduced 2%–24%[a] | Depletion of oil, forest<br>Degradation of land | Net price method<br>Maintenance cost |
| Germany | 1990 | NDP reduced 3% | Depletion of minerals<br>Degradation of land, air, water, including $CO_2$ | Economic depreciation<br>Maintenance cost |
| Japan | 1990 | NDP reduced 2.4% | Depletion of minerals<br>Degradation of land, air, water, including $CO_2$ and CFCs | Net price method<br>Maintenance cost |
| Korea | 1985–92 | NDP reduced 2.6%–4.1% | Depletion of minerals<br>Degradation of land, air, water | Net price method<br>Maintenance cost |

| | | | | |
|---|---|---|---|---|
| Mexico | 1985 | NDP reduced 11%–15% | Depletion of oil, forest | Net price method and El Serafy's approach |
| | | | Degradation of water, air, soil | Maintenance cost |
| The Philippines | 1988–94 | NDP reduced 2%–13% | Depletion of forests, fish, minerals | Net price method |
| | | | Degradation of soil, air, water | Maintenance cost |
| Sweden | 1993 and 1997 | NDP reduced 1–2% | Depletion of minerals | Economic depreciation |
| | | | Environmental damage due to $SO_x$ and $NO_x$ | Damage cost |
| | | | Environmental protection expenditures | Market cost |

*Notes:* [a] Except for 1971 and 1974, when NDP increased.

*Source:* Own compilation from Lange (2003) and the country-specific studies: Costa Rica (Repetto and Cruz, 1991); Indonesia (Repetto et al., 1989); Germany (Bartelmus and Vesper, 2000); Japan (Oda et al., 1998); Korea (Korea Environment Institute et al., 1998); Mexico (Van Tongeren et al., 1992); the Philippines (Bartelmus, 1999); Sweden (Skånberg, 2000).

rates are usually interpreted as a decline in wealth, and persistently negative rates as unsustainable development. The World Bank has, in a simplified form, operationalised the genuine savings measure and called it 'adjusted net savings'. It has calculated adjusted net savings for around 200 countries since 1970, using the following expression (Hamilton, 2000):

$$G = GNP - C - \delta K - n(R - g) - \sigma(e - d) + m.$$

More specifically, the World Bank adjusted net savings includes four types of adjustments:

1. The capital consumption of fixed assets, $\delta K$, is deducted from gross saving to obtain net saving.
2. The education expenditures, $m$, are added to net domestic savings as a measure of the value of investments in human capital.
3. The depletion of natural resources, $n(R - g)$, is deducted to reflect the decline in asset values associated with extraction and harvest, where $g$ represents resource stock growth, $R$ depletion and $n$ net marginal resource rents. This includes rents on forest, energy (oil, natural gas, hard coal, brown coal) and mineral depletion (bauxite, copper, iron ore, lead, nickel, zinc, phosphate, tin, gold, silver), representing the excess returns to these production factors. The forest rent is calculated as the market value of the resources less the average extraction cost for all harvest above sustainable yield. For non-renewable resources there is no sustainable yield (Hecht, 2007).
4. Pollution damages, $\sigma(e - d)$, are deducted, where $e$ represents pollution emissions, $d$ natural dissipation and $\sigma$ the marginal cost of pollution. This includes only the estimated damage caused by $CO_2$ emissions, which is valued at US$ 20/metric ton based on Fankhauser (1994).

Table 6.3 displays a comparison of gross domestic savings and genuine savings for the countries included in the World Bank project aggregated into different regions and income levels in 2004. According to Section 3.1, a comprehensive measure of genuine savings should include net changes in all the capital stocks valued at their shadow prices. The World Bank estimate includes a limited amount of market-valued natural resources (for example water, fish and soil are excluded) and only one pollutant, and completely excludes non-market-valued resources (biodiversity, nutrient cycling, carbon storage and so on). It could also be questioned whether the US$ 20/metric ton of carbon is sufficient to cover the carbon dioxide damage.

Table 6.3  Adjusted net savings 2004 (per cent of Gross National Income)

| | Gross domestic savings | Consumption of fixed capital | Net domestic savings | Education expenditure | Energy depletion | Mineral depletion | Net forest depletion | Carbon dioxide damage | Genuine domestic saving |
|---|---|---|---|---|---|---|---|---|---|
| *Income* | | | | | | | | | |
| Low income | 22.7 | 9.2 | 13.5 | 3.4 | 6.7 | 0.4 | 0.7 | 1.1 | 8.0 |
| Middle income | 28.3 | 11.1 | 17.2 | 3.6 | 8.4 | 0.5 | 0.0 | 1.0 | 10.7 |
| High income | 19.4 | 13.2 | 6.2 | 4.6 | 1.4 | 0.0 | 0.0 | 0.3 | 9.1 |
| *Region* | | | | | | | | | |
| East Asia & Pacific | 39.1 | 10.5 | 28.6 | 2.3 | 4.1 | 0.4 | 0.0 | 1.2 | 25.1 |
| Europe & Central Asia | 23.4 | 10.7 | 12.7 | 4.1 | 12.0 | 0.3 | 0.0 | 1.4 | 3.0 |
| Latin America & Carib. | 22.7 | 12.1 | 10.6 | 4.4 | 7.2 | 1.1 | 0.0 | 0.5 | 6.3 |
| Middle East & N. Africa | 30.0 | 11.2 | 18.8 | 4.5 | 27.3 | 0.1 | 0.1 | 1.2 | −5.3 |
| South Asia | 23.6 | 9.1 | 14.4 | 3.6 | 2.7 | 0.3 | 0.7 | 1.2 | 13.2 |
| Sub-Saharan Africa | 17.1 | 10.9 | 6.2 | 3.9 | 9.8 | 0.4 | 0.6 | 0.7 | −1.5 |
| World | 20.8 | 12.7 | 8.1 | 4.4 | 2.8 | 0.1 | 0.0 | 0.4 | 9.2 |

*Source:*  Own compilation from World Bank (2007).

The adjusted net savings vary considerably and are less than gross domestic savings for all regions. It is obvious that resource depletion is generally lower in high-income countries. Education expenditure is higher in high-income countries than in middle- and low-income countries. $CO_2$ damage is higher in low- and middle-income countries compared to high-income countries. The East Asia and Pacific region exhibits high gross and genuine savings and low resource depletion. Notable is that adjusted net savings are actually negative for two regions (the Middle East and North Africa, and Sub-Saharan Africa), indicating that these economies are living off their assets rather than creating new wealth. The Middle East and North Africa region depletes an exhaustible resource, violating Hartwick's (1977) rule, which requires the sum of the value of the net changes of stocks to be zero in order for welfare not to decrease. A World Bank report has compared the adjusted net savings rates of different countries in 1970–1993, and concluded that the Sub-Saharan African average genuine savings rates rarely exceeded 5 per cent of GNP during the 1970s and then started a sharp negative trend at the end of that decade, from which the region has never recovered. The Middle East and North Africa region consistently had negative genuine savings rates as a percentage of GNP throughout the period, varying from −5 to −35 percent (World Bank, 1997).

However, the adjusted net savings rate project at the World Bank has been criticised. Neumayer (2000), for example, argues that its conclusions depend on its method of computing user costs from resource exploitation. He takes Saudi Arabia as an example, which according to the World Bank calculations has had negative rates since 1976 (varying from −3 to −48 per cent), leading to the conclusion, which he considers counterfactual, that the country has depleted its capital to an extent that implies that its inhabitants should be severely impoverished. As an alternative, Neumayer employs the El Serafy method (see Section 2.2), which he argues is superior since it does not depend on efficient resource pricing. A calculation of adjusted net savings using the El Serafy method changes the results: Sub-Saharan Africa does not exhibit persistent negative rates and the region of North Africa and the Middle East turns out to be a strong genuine saver. The sensitivity of the results leads the author to warn policy makers not to draw the wrong policy conclusions for the wrong countries based on the World Bank rates (Neumayer, 2000). Dietz and Neumayer (2004) also argue that the adjusted net savings rates are sensitive to the method of calculating rents from resource extraction, and claim that the World Bank estimates are at the high end and probably overestimate the unsustainability of certain resource-dependent regions. Also, Pillarisetti (2005) argues that the measure is empirically imperfect and that policy implications based on this measure are erroneous. For example, investment in human capital measured by education expenses strongly influences the numerical values of genuine savings.[13] Genuine savings (without education expenses) are almost identical to unadjusted net savings for a majority of countries (Pillarisetti, 2005).

# 4 NORWAY – ONE OF THE FIRST CONSTRUCTORS OF GREEN ACCOUNTS

## 4.1 Natural Resource Accounting

One example of an early national effort in constructing natural resource accounts is Norway (Alfsen et al., 1987; Alfsen and Greaker, 2007).[14] The task, which was introduced before the development of the SEEA, was given to Statistics Norway by the Norwegian Ministry of Environment in 1978 with the aim of ensuring better long-term natural resource management.[15] The accounting system was initially very ambitious, covering a large number of natural resources and environmental issues (such as energy, minerals, sand and gravel, forests, fish, land use, freshwater, air pollution and waste). The resource accounts were divided into material and environmental accounts and expressed in physical terms, but were complemented with market prices when available.[16] The material accounts included three parts: (1) reserves accounts (the in- and out-going resource base including adjustments, that is, discoveries, reappraisals, new technology and so on); (2) extraction, conversion and trade accounts by sector; and (3) end use accounts by sector. Almost ten years after implementation, the accounting experience was evaluated (Alfsen et al., 1987). The results were disappointing, indicating that most were under-utilised by policy makers. In fact, the only account that was regularly used was the energy account. This led to a more narrow coverage of natural resource accounting with a stronger focus on energy resources and air pollutants. At present, the macroeconomic models employed by the Ministry of Finance for medium- and long-term economic projections include energy and air pollution variables as well as waste.

## 4.2  National Wealth

Although the idea of constructing a comprehensive NDP in Norway was considered in the early 1990s, it was immediately abandoned. It was not considered correct for the statisticians to take decisions about the value of environmental assets and to incorporate such decisions into apparently

*Table 6.4    Definition of national wealth*

The Sum of:

i)    Present value of future resource rents from renewable natural resources.
ii)   Present value of future resource rents from non-renewable natural resources.
iii)  Present value of future contribution from human capital.
iv)   Current value of fixed capital as given by the national accounts.
v)    Net financial wealth.

*Source:*   Alfsen and Greaker, 2007.

neutral information about the trend in an environment-adjusted GDP (Alfsen and Greaker, 2007). Instead, Statistics Norway has occasionally calculated the changes in national wealth, defined in Table 6.4. As recognised, the national wealth measure also has several shortcomings. First, quite a number of renewable resources are not included, since market prices for their services do not exist. Second, future prices are too uncertain. Third, human capital is calculated residually.[17]

### 4.3   Indicators of Sustainable Wealth

In order to try to solve the problem of how to measure sustainability, an official commission was asked to develop a core set of indicators for sustainable development. The strategy of the commission was 'to choose indicators that best reflect the value, defined as the welfare effects, of the various components of national wealth' (Ministry of Finance of Norway, 2005). This resulted in the 16 indicators shown in Table 6.5.

A central question is how these indicators are interpreted. For example, can a decrease in one wealth component be offset by growth in other wealth components, that is, is there substitutability? The Ministry of Finance argues that since there are different opinions on this point, the question of 'weak' versus 'strong' sustainability needs to be determined by political authorities (Ministry of Finance of Norway, 2005). Strong sustainability does not, however, appear to be practically applicable.

Physical indicators to measure sustainability have also been developed by the UN, the OECD and the EU as well as by individual countries. Most indicators follow the DPSIR model introduced by the OECD in the 1970s and further developed by the EU. The DPSIR abbreviation implies that the indicators should measure: *D*riving forces of environmental change (for example, industrial production); *P*ressures on the environment (for example, emissions of air pollutants); *S*tate of the environment (for example, urban air quality); *I*mpact on the population, economy and

*Table 6.5    Indicators of sustainable wealth*

| Issues to be covered | Indicators |
| --- | --- |
| 1.  Climate change | Emissions of greenhouse gases compared to the Kyoto Protocol target |
| 2.  Acidification | Percentage of land area where the critical load for acidification has been exceeded |
| 3.  Terrestrial ecosystems | Population trends of nesting wild birds |
| 4.  Freshwater ecosystems | Percentage of rivers and lakes with clearly good ecological status |
| 5.  Coastal ecosystems | Percentage of localities (coastal waters) with clearly good ecological status |
| 6.  Efficiency of resource use | Energy use per unit GDP |
| 7.  Management of renewable resources | Recommended quota, total allowable catch actually set and catches of Northeast Arctic cod |
| 8.  Hazardous substances | Household consumption of hazardous substances |
| 9.  Sources of income | Net national income per capita, by sources of income: <br> • Resource rent from renewable natural resources <br> • Resource rent from non-renewable natural resources <br> • Return on produced assets <br> • Return on human and environmental capital <br> • Return on net income from abroad |
| 10.  Sustainable consumption | Petroleum adjusted savings |
| 11.  Level of education | Population by highest level of education completed |
| 12.  Sustainable public finances | Generational accounts: need for tightening of public finances as a share of GDP |
| 13.  Health and welfare | Life expectancy at birth |
| 14.  Exclusion from the labour market | Long-term unemployed persons and disability pensioners as percentage of population |
| 15.  Global poverty reduction | Trade with Africa, by LDC countries and other African countries |
| 16.  Global poverty reduction | Norwegian development assistance as percentage of gross national income |

*Source:*   Ministry of Finance of Norway, 2005

ecosystems; and *R*esponse of the society (pollutant taxes). Although the indicators are useful for following the development within certain areas of importance for sustainability, they cannot provide any guidance as to whether the development is sustainable or not. The indicator approach departs from the view that certain resources are especially important for sustainable development and have to be held intact. This is not unproblematic since it is very difficult to determine which resources are important for future generations. Furthermore, since the indicators are not weighed together, the approach implies that all indicators have to move in the right direction in order for the development to be sustainable, that is, strong sustainability (see Section 1). Generally, it is not realistic to assume that deterioration in one indicator cannot be compensated by an improvement in another. When interpreting the indicators, one therefore needs to be careful not to judge the negative direction of one indicator as meaning that the overall development is not sustainable.

## 5   SWEDEN – ONE OF THE FEW CONSTRUCTORS OF COMPREHENSIVE NDP

The Commission for Environmental Accounting was appointed in 1990 to investigate the possibilities for supplementing Sweden's national accounts with accounts of national resources and the environment. In June 1992, the commission's recommendations resulted in three new government commissions: Statistics Sweden was made responsible for resource accounting in physical terms, the Environmental Protection Agency was made responsible for compiling environmental indices of the state of the environment, and the National Institute of Economic Research (NIER) was made responsible for pursuing monetary green accounting.

The initial work at Statistics Sweden included the linkage between economic statistics and the following types of energy and environmental data: energy accounts in physical and monetary terms; accounts of emissions of sulphur dioxide, carbon dioxide, nitrogen oxide and volatile organic compounds; accounts of nitrogen and phosphorus flows; and environmental protection statistics for the nation, local authorities and industry (NIER and Statistics Sweden, 1998). Since 1992, the green accounting work at Statistics Sweden has developed in several dimensions.[18] One of the most recent projects is the description of the economic structures and environmental pressure in the Swedish river basin districts in 1995–2005 (Statistics Sweden, 2007).

More specifically, the NIER assignment consisted of investigating the possibilities of evaluating the environmental accounts in monetary terms, that is, developing methods for pursuing monetary green accounting. The monetary accounts obtained in this way could then be used as a basis for environmental adjustment of different macroeconomic measures. The task also included the development of environmental economic models for economic impact analysis. The analyses that were carried out had different focuses. Common for the approaches is that they start off in a theoretically consistent framework and that an empirical example is then applied to the framework. A transparent, consistent framework is important in order to identify sectors of the economy that are affected, to separate different types of externalities and to avoid double counting. The remainder of this section will present a selection of the analyses carried out at NIER.

### 5.1 Correcting NDP for Emissions: Implementing Theory in Practice

The empirical work on green accounting is usually separated from the theoretical work. The theorists develop advanced models with interesting theoretical aspects but do not consider what data is available and possible to measure. Empirics, on the other hand, are more focused on data and are not as interested in and knowledgeable about theoretical aspects. The purpose of Ahlroth's (2003) analysis was to combine theoretical and empirical work in order to provide a structure for damage valuation. The approach, which builds on the SEEA, was one of the first attempts to bridge a gap between two traditions in the green accounting literature (Heal and Kriström, 2005). Ahlroth developed an optimal control theory model for adjusting NDP for the effects of sulphur and nitrogen emissions and inserted empirically estimated values into the model. The utility function includes consumption of an aggregate consumption good, a vector of emissions (sulphur dioxide, nitrogen oxide and ammonia) and a vector of the stocks of these pollutants. The production uses labour, capital and flows of natural resources and emissions/energy, and can be used for consumption of market goods, emission abatement and investments. The stock of capital has a constant depreciation rate and an additional depreciation that depends on current emissions (corrosion due to acidification). Pollution affects labour supply through the increase in absences due to sickness and early retirements. Growth in natural resource stocks is affected by the stock of pollution, which in turn is assumed to increase by the emitted amount less the dissipation rate (buffering ability). The derived NDP includes adjustments to labour supply and the natural resource stock, and corrections in terms of consumer disutility from the flow and level of the pollution stock, and environmental degradation. In the empirical part, the damages are mainly stock effects, but some flow effects from emissions are included. Specifically, the depreciation of real capital,

*Table 6.6   Components of adjustment of NDP, 1991 price level*

|  | Million US$ | Valuation method |
| --- | --- | --- |
| Timber | 94 | Dose-response function |
| Fishing, professional | 11 | Dose-response function |
| Labour supply | 49 | Dose-response function |
| Fishing, households | 106 | CV study |
| Recreation, Baltic | 294 | CV study |
| Recreation, Lakes | 882 | CV study |
| Recreation, Forest | 271 | CV study |
| Nitrates in groundwater | 235 | CV study |
| Health | 388 | CV study |
| Total adjustment | 2331 | |

*Source:*   Ahlroth, 2003

natural capital and labour stock (health) is accounted for. Table 6.6 lists the figures which should be included in an adjustment of NDP. The results show that the total effect amounts to US$2331 million, or approximately 1.6 per cent of NDP.

### 5.2   Applying the Contingent Valuation Method in Resource Accounting

Although the Contingent Valuation Method (CVM) is the dominant method for valuation of non-market goods, there is no established agenda for its application in green accounting (see Section 2.2 above). A CVM project intended to extend the existing empirical research on green accounting was started in 2000 at NIER. Until then, the research had been focused primarily on market data (avoidance costs, damage costs, and so on). Boman et al. (2003) developed a model for environmental accounting that can be applied in an empirical contingent valuation experiment. Their work focused particularly on five of the sixteen environmental goals that Sweden had decided upon: reduced climate impact; natural acidification only; clean air; zero eutrophication; and a rich diversity of plant and animal life. It is assumed that these targets can be viewed as a type of quantity index for environmental quality, such that the consumption decision is first made with respect to total environmental quality and then with respect to the specific environmental goals.

Boman et al. (2003) specify a theoretical framework in which the consumer derives utility from consumption and environmental quality (measured as disutility from emissions and concentrations of pollutants, utility from biodiversity preservation, and utility from the remaining natural resource goods and services). The derived NDP should be adjusted positively with respect to the value of increases in environmental and natural resources, and negatively with respect to the value of harmful pollution flows. To adjust the NDP in monetary terms, the CVM is suggested in order to derive marginal willingness to pay for approaching the environmental goals. Boman et al. (2003) outline fifteen survey versions, in which three levels of change for each of the five environmental goals are stipulated. All versions include both a question about willingness-to-pay (WTP) to avoid one level of change for one environmental goal, and a question about WTP to achieve all sixteen environmental goals. The CVM has an advantage in that it typically includes the consumer surplus, but since the approach is not able to capture the preferences of future generations, it does not provide sufficient information for resource accounting (Aronsson et al., 2004).

## 5.3   Monetary Green Accounting and Ecosystem Services

In the theoretical literature, the environment is usually described in terms of flows and stocks of pollutants. The purpose of Gren's (2003) analysis was to derive a monetary green accounting system where the value of changes in natural capital is derived from the capital stocks' production of ecosystem services. She developed a theoretical model in which the economy produces a composite good and non-marketed goods in terms of ecosystem services. Both types of goods use natural capital and emit pollutants, and the marketed goods additionally need man-made capital. The change in the stock of natural capital is determined by its own growth, ecosystem management and pollutant deposition. Utility in society is determined by consumption of marketed and non-marketed goods and services. In addition, pollutants affect utility directly through their impacts on health. Adjustments to the NDP should be made with regard to non-marketed ecosystem services. These adjustments include current utility from pollutants and ecosystem services, and change in future utility from ecosystem services caused by the period's change in the stock of natural capital. Gren (2003) also gives an empirical demonstration of the accounting system that focuses on the natural capital assets (forests, agricultural landscape, wetlands, air quality, and coastal and marine ecosystems) and the ecosystem services (recreation, health impacts and pollutant sink). The correction of NDP implies an increase of between 0.9 and 3.3 per cent, mainly due to the value of recreation, forest carbon sequestration and wetland nitrogen cleaning.[19] The analysis was later extended to the ten-year period from 1991 to 2001 (Gren and Svensson, 2004). Figure 6.1 shows the annual growth in NDP and

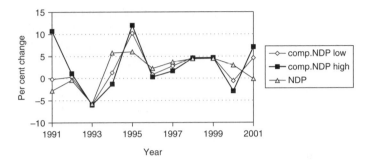

*Source:*   Gren and Svensson, 2004

*Figure 6.1    Annual growth in NDP and comprehensive NDP, 1991–2001*

the comprehensive NDP for two assumptions regarding the values of environmental services (low and high values). The differences in growth between comprehensive NDP and NDP were small in 1992, 1993 and 1996–1999, and large in the other years.

### 5.4    Air Pollution, Ill Health and Welfare

When investigating analytically the measurement of welfare and health effects induced by pollution, health usually enters the utility function as a capital stock (see for example Aronsson et al., 1994 and Johansson and Löfgren, 1995). As the problems of measuring a positive value for 'normal' health status in accounting terms are well-known, the analysis by Huhtala and Samakovlis (2007) opts for valuation methods that are suitable for estimating negative impacts, or damage to health, to show how monetary valuation of the health effects of air pollution can be carried out in practice. They present a theoretical framework for comprehensive national accounting that considers the health effects of air pollution. A production externality is included, which causes both direct disutility and an indirect welfare effect by negatively affecting labour productivity. The usefulness of the framework is demonstrated by applying it to data from a dose-response analysis between respiratory-restricted activity days and nitrogen oxide as an indicator of urban air pollution (Samakovlis et al., 2005) and a contingent valuation study valuing disutility from respiratory ill health episodes (Samakovlis and Svensson, 2004).

In the theoretical framework, a simple dynamic model is used to illustrate how an accounting system that incorporates the health effects of air pollution can be developed. The accounting framework is modelled as a social planner's optimisation problem, where a fixed amount of labour is allocated between production of a composite commodity and a healthcare sector. The healthcare sector corresponds to the defensive expenditures undertaken to improve health. Capital and a polluting input are used in addition to labour to produce the composite commodity. Utility is derived from consumption of the composite commodity, whereas air pollutants cause disutility, which can be alleviated with inputs for healthcare and mitigation. The theoretical framework indicates that the NDP adjusted for health impacts from air pollution involves two extra terms. One is a negative term that reflects the welfare effects of pollution; it captures the direct perceived disutility of symptoms related to air pollutants. The other term is positive and measures the avoidance of disutility by mitigating problems and symptoms associated with pollution-related illnesses through defensive expenditures. However, defensive expenditures should not be subtracted from the NDP. The logic is that while it may be negative from a social point of view that the output of the healthcare sector increases due to pollution, the increase nevertheless contributes to the NDP. Certain social costs, such as defensive expenditures, are thus implicit in the level of NDP. To have NDP indicate the negative effects not captured in market transactions, it should be adjusted only with the disutility from pollution. In total, the negative health effects of nitrogen dioxide emissions amount to 0.6 per cent of the Swedish GDP.

## 5.5 EMEC – An Environmental Medium-term Economic Model

Determination of the overall economic impact of taxes and regulations in the environmental area often involves using a general equilibrium model that reflects relationships both within the economy and between the economy and the environment. As a response to the task provided by the governmental commission, NIER developed the EMEC[20] model based on the physical environmental accounts of Statistics Sweden (Östblom, 1999; Östblom and Berg, 2006). The model has been used in a number of government studies, mostly related to the medium-term survey at the Ministry of Finance or to different formulations of climate policy (SOU 2000:7; SOU 2000:23; SOU 2000:45; SOU 2001:2; NIER 2002 and 2003; SOU 2003:60; SOU 2004:19; SOU 2005:10), and in scientific studies (Nilsson and Huhtala, 2000; Östblom, 2003; Nilsson, 2004; Östblom and Samakovlis, 2007).

The model has 26 business sectors and one general government sector. Firms and households demand a mix of 33 goods and services as manufacturing inputs for investment and for household consumption. The total labour supply is determined exogenously, and capital is offered according to an exogenously determined rate of interest. All production factors are

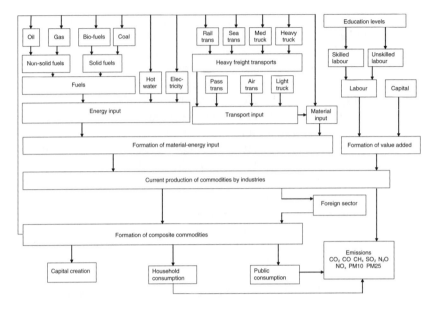

*Note:*    The arrows indicate the direction of flows.

*Source:*    Östblom and Berg, 2006

*Figure 6.2    Flows of commodities, factors and emissions in the EMEC*

freely mobile among sectors. Free competition prevails in all markets, and there are no economies of scale in production. It is assumed in the model that firms and households fully adjust to price changes. Household consumption and the activities of the business sector give rise to environmental pollution. Combustion is the primary source of carbon dioxide, sulphur dioxide and oxides of nitrogen. Energy and environmental taxes are imposed on the use of energy by households and firms. Any existing exceptions in the taxation of manufacturing firms are taken into consideration in the tax rates used. The principal limitations on economic growth are the availability of production factors and the state of technological development. The model is continuously under development and recent extensions include a more detailed representation of transport demand and a disaggregation of the electricity and district heating sector (Östblom and Berg, 2006; Berg, 2007). Currently, the waste sector is being incorporated into the model. Figure 6.2 presents the flows of commodities, factors and emissions in the model.

General equilibrium models can be used to construct macroeconomic indicators for an 'environmentally adjusted economy', or in other words, a greened economy GDP (geGDP).[21] In this approach, the key variables of the conventional national accounts are modelled into the future, showing the economic and environmental consequences of scenarios for a more sustainable economic development. The purpose is to permit quantification of economy–environment policy trade-offs at the macroeconomic level – that is, to estimate output losses or economic opportunity costs associated with environmental standards (O'Connor, 2001). Similar analyses, focusing specifically on $CO_2$ emissions, have been carried out with the EMEC model in order to inform politicians about the likely macroeconomic impacts of achieving different formulations of climate policy.[22]

# 6  DIFFICULTIES ENCOUNTERED IN CONSTRUCTING WELFARE MEASURES

There are several difficulties involved in pursuing green accounting in practice. The most substantial ones relate to the monetary valuation of degradation and to the environmentally adjusted macroeconomic aggregates. This is why the chapters in the SEEA handbook that include these issues have been subject to so much controversy among the collaborators on the handbook. This section discusses some of the theoretical weaknesses and empirical difficulties encountered when constructing welfare measures.

## 6.1  The Theoretical Weaknesses of Welfare Measures

Weitzman (1976) shows that the comprehensive NNP measured in utility terms is proportional to the optimal value function, defined as the maximised objective function in a dynamic economy with stationary technology and perfect competition.[23] This implies that the comprehensive NNP can be interpreted as a static equivalent to future utility (Aronsson et al., 2004). The most severe weakness of this measure is the strong assumptions needed to justify a welfare interpretation. The restrictive assumptions of a stationary technology and perfect competition imply no disembodied technological change and a first-best allocation, both circumstances that do not hold in reality. When these assumptions are relaxed, welfare depends on time itself, meaning that the derived welfare measure will be biased (Aronsson and Löfgren, 1995). In addition, Dasgupta and Mäler (1998) show that a comprehensive NNP is not suitable for making intertemporal and cross-country comparisons of social well-being, unless the analysed economies are in stationary states. Assuming that the economy is on an optimal path corresponds rather poorly to the starting point of the debate on sustainability, namely the concern about the accelerating

deterioration of the environment, which implies that the resource allocation is not optimal (Aaheim and Nyborg, 1995). Asheim (1994) also shows
that with multiple capital stocks, it is generally not possible to construct an
exact indicator of sustainability based solely on comprehensive NNP.

The genuine savings rate constitutes the net changes in all the capital
stocks valued at their shadow prices. As indicated in Section 3.3, negative genuine savings rates are usually interpreted as a decline in wealth
and persistently negative rates as unsustainable development. However,
it has been shown that a positive value for genuine savings is a necessary
but not sufficient condition for achieving sustainability, implying that
non-negative rates cannot rule out unsustainable development (Asheim,
1994; Pezzey and Withagen, 1995). The most significant weaknesses of
the measure are that genuine savings is based on a model of an inter-
temporally efficient economy; that the genuine savings model is vulner-
able to exogenous shocks (technological progress, terms-of-trade effects,
non-constant discount rates), implying that existing prices are no longer
optimal and need to be re-estimated; that the population is assumed to be
constant; and that genuine savings rates are sensitive to the calculation
of natural capital depreciation and to the way environmental pollution is
accounted for (Dietz and Neumayer, 2004).[24]

### 6.2    Lack of Data and Scientific Knowledge

The calculation of a comprehensive NDP requires that we determine in
physical terms how the flow of environmental services is affected and how
the stocks of natural capital have changed during the year. Determining
physical changes in natural capital involves both quantitative and qualitative changes from one year to the next. The genuine savings measure has
essentially the same data needs. The flow of environmental services can
be affected through noise, other health effects or damage to crop har-
vests; this in turn affects the value of private and public consumption.[25]
Almost all other environmental damage can be assigned either entirely
or partly to changes in the natural capital stocks that try to capture the
change in the value of the stock that is passed on from one period to the
next. This includes, for example, all the effects from acidification (except
the health-related ones) and most of the consequences from the emissions
of nutrients. The effects from sulphur dioxide, nitrogen oxide, ammonia,
hydrocarbons and persistent organic compounds give rise to both health
effects and changes in the stocks of natural capital. The emission of nitrogen and phosphorus to water and chlorinated organic compounds and
biochemical oxygen demand mainly affect the stocks of natural capital.
In practice, however, it is very difficult and in certain cases impossible to

separate flow effects from effects on capital assets, since a certain emission (or interference) often gives rise to both.

To be able to make correct deductions from (or additions to) the NDP, one must define what is considered a harmful (or beneficial) environmental effect and how it has changed during the year. If critical loads have been derived, then emissions exceeding these levels can be considered harmful. Another question relates to the curvature of the so-called dose-response or exposure-response functions. Are relationships linear or do we need to determine non-linearities for certain substances (for example in the form of threshold effects) when making assumptions about the marginal effects of different pollutant levels? The lack of scientific knowledge regarding environmental damage is obviously a problem when trying to construct a comprehensive NDP. Additional knowledge will probably lead to the discovery of new problems. The discovery of the Antarctic ozone hole, for example, changed the view of chlorofluorocarbons. Additional knowledge makes it necessary to revise assumptions about relationships and effects. These discoveries imply, in the calculation of a yearly comprehensive NDP, an immediate capital loss even though the change might have been going on for a long time. Methods to measure changes in natural capital stocks can also change, affecting the size of the stock and the comprehensive NDP even if the actual stock has not changed. This obviously renders it more difficult to make meaningful comparisons over time. One difficulty also lies in the fact that it is not always possible to establish the relationship between emission and damage. In some cases the relationships can be incompletely known, and in other cases the damage occurs as a response to the interaction of several factors (that is, most of the individuals who develop lung cancer from radon are smokers).

A prerequisite for making these types of calculations is of course that data regarding physical changes and damages (or improvements) is available. Data on the use of non-renewable resources and the emission of air pollutants such as carbon dioxide, sulphur dioxide and nitrogen oxide are usually well documented, while data on emissions of chemicals and waste are usually weaker and characterised by large uncertainties.

## 6.3   The Valuation of Non-market Goods

Valuations in national accounts are usually based on market prices. Valuation of goods not traded in any market is more problematic, although necessary if we want to adjust the NDP for changes in the state of the environment. Both the changes in the flow of environmental services and the changes in the stock of the natural capital assets need to be valued.

There are two main methods for valuing environmental changes in monetary terms: through damage cost estimations and through individuals' willingness to pay (WTP) to avoid the damage or negative changes. Although some of the actual damage can in principal be valued at market prices (for example, corrosion and damage to crops and fish), it is more difficult to value, for example, health effects and loss of species. As exemplified in Section 5.4, the costs of health effects from air pollution consist not only of medical care and production losses, but also of disutility from the disease. This disutility value cannot be determined by market prices. A more appropriate method is to use the Contingent Valuation (CV) method. The application of CV in a green accounting context is surrounded by several difficulties. Although the number of CV applications has increased immensely over the last decades, not all environmental aspects have been valued. Even if most aspects had been valued, there would have been several problems involved in transferring the results, since each study only determines the willingness to pay for the object in the study.[26] Furthermore, one cannot add the results of several studies to determine the population's total WTP, since the resulting sum can become larger than the individuals' budget constraints. Large-scale multiple goods valuation is required in order to avoid the problem of adding valuation studies. A proposed method to overcome the difficulty with exceeding the budget constraint – asking individuals how much money they would be prepared to spend totally on measures to improve the environment which then could be allocated to the different environmental targets – was discussed in Section 5.2. Another factor is that the WTP studies reflect the preferences of present generations, while we also need to know the preferences of future generations.

The comprehensive NDP measure has been criticised for combining actual market transactions with hypothetical WTP values. The criticism relates to the fact that the use of WTP values does not take into account the economic adjustments that would occur in the economy. Had the WTP values actually been paid, then relative prices throughout the economy would have changed and thereby affected economic behaviour and, ultimately, the NDP. It is, in other words, not enough to find the value of the environmental change in order to adjust the NDP; the traditional NDP measure must also be adjusted, which requires a model of the economy that analyses its interrelationships (Alfsen and Greaker, 2007).

Other critics argue that one should not try to measure non-market goods and services in monetary terms at all. This objection does not consider that some kind of implicit valuation is always made. In practice, the political decisions often serve as an implicit valuation of the environment. It appears, therefore, better that the decision is made based on a more complete analysis where environmental resources have been made more visible. Some critics argue that the methods erroneously use money as a superior value. However, using money to value environmental benefits is practical, since it makes it easier to compare the benefits with the costs, which are measured in monetary terms. Others argue that the comprehensive data demands make valuation impossible. Environmental valuations can in some cases overestimate and in others underestimate the value of the environment. The reason can be that there are uncertainties regarding ecological relationships (see Section 6.2), but there can also be uncertainties regarding substitution possibilities and changing preferences. Even if there are practical problems surrounding the valuation of environmental changes, it is reasonable to use the existing methods (Ministry of Finance of Sweden, 2000).

## 7   CONCLUSIONS

Green accounting in practice comprises natural resource asset accounts, flow accounts for pollutants and materials, and environmental protection expenditures, as well as environmentally adjusted macroeconomic aggregates. In this chapter, we have focused on the last type of accounts and more specifically on the welfare measures comprehensive net national product (NNP) and genuine savings. These measures have both theoretical and empirical weaknesses. Theoretical flaws include the strong assumptions needed for the measures to be exact indicators of welfare or to justify an interpretation of sustainable development. Empirical difficulties include data availability and valuation of non-market goods. The data requirements are gigantic, and there are several uncertainties and often a plain lack of knowledge regarding environmental effects. Valuation of non-market goods has to address the various issues of aggregation, market versus shadow prices, discounting and benefit transfer and so on, associated with the use of the different methods. As the review of country experiences of creating comprehensive NDPs indicates, the attempts are either focused on the most urgent environmental problems or where the data availability is satisfactory in each specific country. Although this might seem wise, it is not enough to base welfare comparisons on. The genuine savings project at the World Bank totally excludes non-market valued resources and only includes a limited amount of market-valued natural resources. Due to these weaknesses and difficulties, there is reason to be sceptical of the derived welfare measures. It is actually useless to partially adjust the NNP or other macroeconomic aggregate with the information that is available. An incomplete or wrongly measured adjusted NNP is generally not a better measure of welfare than the conventional measure, and could in fact be even worse (Aronsson, 1998). Regardless of how interesting it would be (especially from a political point of view) to measure sustainable development, at this date there are no theoretically consistent and empirically feasible measures that are able to indicate whether development is sustainable.

What should be done instead depends on the issue at stake. If we are interested in analysing the effects of environmental policy proposals on the overall economy, then, for example, general equilibrium models are more flexible and better suited than national accounts. These models, which can be run several times, varying different formulations of the policy measures, try to give a consistent and comprehensive picture of economic development, capturing repercussions among different sectors in the economy. A case in point is the greened economy GDP, which estimates national income looking into a hypothetical future in which economic development must meet certain environmental standards. The impact on the economy is estimated by internalising the costs of reducing environmental degradation. The purpose is to provide policy makers with guidance about the likely impacts of alternative development paths and the instruments for achieving them (World Bank, 2006). On the other hand, if we are interested in measuring environmental changes, the environmental accounts are better suited for this purpose.

The environmental statistics derived in the environmental accounts are necessary in the models to evaluate environmental policy. General equilibrium models make extensive use of the input-output tables created by the national and green accounts. Other types of models use other parts of the green accounts. Thus, even though the calculation of environmentally adjusted macroeconomic aggregates cannot be the ultimate goal of compiling environmental accounts, the potential for environmental statistics to increase the understanding of the relation between economy and the environment is unlimited.

## ACKNOWLEDGEMENTS

This paper has benefited substantially from comments by Thomas Aronsson and Karl-Gustaf Löfgren

## NOTES

1.  The definition originates from the discussion on sustainable income by Fisher (1906), Lindahl (1933) and Hicks (1939).

2. These assumptions include a constant population, a closed economy and substitutability between natural resources and produced capital.

3. These measures can be divided into: 1) Welfare measures; 2) Socio-political indicators: the Index of Social and Economic Welfare (Daly and Cobb, 1989; Cobb et al., 1995) and the Genuine Progress Indicator (United Nations Development Programme, 1996); 3) Ecological/environmental indicators: Ecological footprints (Rees and Wackernagel, 1994) and Environmental space (Friends of the Earth, 1995); and 4) Single indicators (such as air and water quality, soil erosion). For an analysis of sustainability measures for Scotland during 1980–93, see Hanley et al. (1999).

4. Comprehensive NNP in utility terms is defined using the current value Hamiltonian of the underlying optimal growth problem.

5. Comprehensive NNP in utility terms can thus be interpreted as the yield from an eternal bond.

6. Another shortcoming includes the treatment of human and social capital.

7. Agenda 21 is a 'comprehensive blueprint of action to be taken globally, nationally and locally by UN organisations, governments and major groups in every area in which humans impact on the environment' (http://en.wikipedia.org/wiki/Agenda_21, accessed 25 May 2010).

8. The net price method, based on the Hotelling model (Hotelling, 1931), assumes that the value of the resource stock can be calculated simply as the current rent per unit of the resource (difference between the price of the resource and the marginal cost of extraction) times the size of the stock. The El Serafy method (El Serafy, 1989) splits the resource rent into an income component that can be consumed and a depletion cost (user cost). The user cost should be reinvested so that its yield will contribute to the generation of income both during extraction and after the resource has been exhausted.

9. SEEA 2003 does not explicitly recommend a specific environmentally adjusted aggregate.

10. The key difference between NNP and NDP is that NNP measures all output produced by the citizens of a country regardless of where that production takes place, and NDP measures all output produced within the national borders, regardless of the citizenry of the producers.

11. If these assumptions are violated, the welfare measure will contain unobservable forward-looking terms because technological progress and/or uninternalised externalities make the economic system non-autonomous (Aronsson et al., 2004).

12. This is a poor approximation if the utility function deviates strongly from linearity. To then make the comprehensive NNP a perfect welfare indicator, the consumer surplus has to be added (Li and Löfgren, 2002).

13. A measure of the value of investments in human capital in terms of education expenditures lacks information about the societal value of education (Aronsson et al., 1997). As a better alternative, Jorgenson and Fraumeni (1992) suggest a method for valuing education where its investment character is recognised: education increases the productivity of an individual, which increases future earnings.

14. Another early effort was made by France (for information on that project see Theys, 1989).

15. The text in this section draws heavily on the article by Alfsen and Greaker (2007).

16. Methods used to value goods not traded in any market were not applied.

17. Return on human capital = net national income − resource rents − net return on fixed capital.

18. For more information about the green accounting projects carried out at Statistics Sweden, see http://www.scb.se/templates/Product____38161.asp

19. The range is due to different assumptions regarding the potential for forest carbon sequestration and wetland nitrogen cleaning.

20. *E*nvironmental *m*edium term *e*conomic model.

21. For applications and a more detailed explanation of geGDP, see O'Connor (2001). Another modelling approach is Hueting's sustainable national income (SNI), which estimates the level of national income that would occur if the economy met certain

environmental standards using available technology (World Bank, 2006). For a survey of simulation models for social accounting, see Chapter 3 in this volume.

22.  One example is the governmental commission on a system and regulatory framework for the flexible mechanisms of the Kyoto Protocol, where the model analysis led to the recommendation that it is the quantity of emission allowances allocated to the Swedish trading sector that should be compared with the national target and not the actual emissions (SOU 2003:60).

23.  Weitzman (1976) also assumed a linearly homogeneous utility function, which implies that the consumer surplus equals zero and that the comprehensive NNP constitutes an exact welfare measure.

24.  Genuine savings can, however, be extended to take into account technological development and market imperfections.

25.  Most of the discussion in this section is based on the report from the Swedish Commission for Environmental Accounting (SOU 1991:37).

26.  Ready et al. (2004) show in a European study which estimated the value of avoiding disutility episodes from respiratory ill health caused by air pollution through national CV surveys for five countries, that transferring results from one country to another on average leads to an over- or under-estimation of 38 per cent.

# REFERENCES

Aaheim, A. and K. Nyborg (1995), 'On the interpretation and applicability of a "Green national product"', *Review of Income and Wealth* 41(2), 57–71.

Ahlroth, S. (2003), 'Correcting NDP for SO2 and NOx Emissions: Implementation of a Theoretical Model in Practice', *Review of Income and Wealth* 49(3), 425–440.

Alfsen, K. H. , T. Bye, and L. Lorentsen (1987), *Natural Resource Accounting and Analysis: The Norwegian Experience 1978–1986*. Sosiale og Økonomiske Studier no. 65. Oslo: Central Bureau of Statistics of Norway, Oslo.

Alfsen, K. and M. Greaker (2007), 'From natural resources and environmental accounting to construction of indicators for sustainable development', *Ecological Economics* 61, 600–610.

Aronsson, T. (1998), 'Bör vi försöka utvidga nettonationalprodukten till en välfärdsindikator', *Ekonomisk Debatt* 4, 255–257.

Aronsson, T., P.-O. Johansson and K.-G. Löfgren (1994), 'Welfare measurement and the health environment', *Annals of Operation Research* 54(1), 203–315.

Aronsson, T., P.-O. Johansson and K.-G. Löfgren (1997), *Welfare Measurement, Sustainability And Green National Accounting*, Cheltenham, UK and Northampton, MA, USA: Edward Elgar.

Aronsson, T. and K.-G. Löfgren (1995), 'National product related welfare measure in the presence of technological change, externalities and uncertainty', *Environmental and Resource Economics* 6, 321–32.

Aronsson, T., K.-G. Löfgren and K. Backlund (2004), *Welfare Measurement in Imperfect Markets: A Growth Theoretical Approach*, Cheltenham, UK and Northampton, MA, USA: Edward Elgar.

Asheim, G. (1994), 'Net national product as an indicator of sustainability', *Scandinavian Journal of Economics* 96, 257–265.

Bartelmus, P. (1999), 'Green accounting for a sustainable economy: Policy use and analysis of environmental accounts in the Philippines', *Ecological Economics* 29, 155–170.

Bartelmus, P. and A. Vesper (2000), *Green Accounting and Material Flow Analysis: Alternatives or Complements?* Wuppertal Papers No. 106, Wuppertal: Wuppertal Institute.

Berg, C. (2007), 'Household transport demand in a CGE-framework', *Environmental and Resource Economics* 37(3), 573–597.

Boman, M., A. Huhtala, C. Nilsson, S. Ahlroth, G. Bostedt, L. Mattsson, and P. Gong

(2003), *Applying the Contingent Valuation Method in Resource Accounting: A Bold Proposal*, Working paper No. 85, Stockholm: National Institute of Economic Research.

Cobb, C., E. Halstead and J. Rowe (1995), *The Genuine Progress Indicator: Summary of Data and Methodology: Redefining Progress,* San Francisco: Redefining Progress.

Daly, H.E. (1990), 'Toward some operational principles of sustainable development', *Ecological Economics* 2 (1), 1–6.

Daly, H.E. and J.B. Cobb (1989), *For the Common Good: Redirecting the Economy toward Community, the Environment, and a Sustainable Future.* Boston, MA: Beacon.

Dasgupta, P. and K.-G. Mäler (1998), *Decentralization Schemes, Cost–Benefit Analysis, and Net National Product as a Measure of Social Well-Being,* Beijer discussion paper Series No. 116, Stockholm: Beijer International Institute of Ecological Economics.

Dietz, S. and E. Neumayer (2004), 'Genuine savings: A critical analysis of its policy-guiding value', *International Journal of Environment and Sustainable Development*, 3(3/4), 276–292.

Dietz, S. and E. Neumayer (2007), 'Weak and strong sustainability in the SEEA: Concepts and measurement', *Ecological Economics* 61, 617–626.

El Serafy, S. (1989), 'The proper calculation of income from depletable natural resource', in Y.J. Ahmad, S. El Serafy and E. Lutz (eds), *Environmental Accounting for Sustainable Development: A UNDP–World Bank Symposium.* Washington DC: The World Bank.

Fankhauser, S. (1994), 'Evaluating the social costs of greenhouse gas emissions', *The Energy Journal* 15(2), 157–184.

Fisher, I. (1906), *The Nature of Capital and Income*, New York: Macmillan.

Friends of the Earth (FoE) Europe (1995), *Towards a Sustainable Europe*, Brussels: FoE.

Gren, I.M. (2003), *Monetary Green Accounting and Ecosystem Services*, Working paper No. 86, Stockholm: National Institute of Economic Research.

Gren, I.M. and L. Svensson (2004), *Ecosystems, Sustainability and Growth for Sweden during 1991–2001*, Occasional Studies No. 4, Stockholm: National Institute for Economic Research.

Hamilton, K. (2000), *Genuine Saving as a Sustainability Indicator*, Environmental Economic Series No. 77, Washington, DC: The World Bank.

Hamilton, K. and E. Lutz (1996), *Green National Accounts: Policy Uses and Empirical Experience*, Environment Department Papers No. 39, Washington, DC: The World Bank.

Hanley, N., I. Moffatt, R. Faichney, and M. Wilson (1999), 'Measuring sustainability: A time series of alternative indicators for Scotland', *Ecological Economics* 28, 55–73.

Hartwick, J.M. (1977), 'Intergenerational equity and the investing of rents from exhaustible resources', *The American Economic Review* 67(5), 972–974.

Heal, G. and B. Kriström (2005), 'National income and the environment', in K.-G. Mäler and J.R. Vincent (eds), *Handbook of Environmental Economics*, Vol. 3, chapter 22, 1147–1217, Amsterdam: Elsevier.

Hecht, J.E. (2007), 'National environmental accounting: a practical introduction', *International Review of Environmental and Resource Economics*, 1, 3–66.

Hicks, J.R. (1939), *Value and Capital* (2nd ed.), Oxford: Clarendon Press.

Hotelling, H. (1931), 'The economics of exhaustible resources', *Journal of Political Economy* 39(2), 137–175.

Huhtala, A. and E. Samakovlis (2007), 'Air pollution, ill health and welfare', *Environmental and Resource Economics* 37, 445–463.

Johansson, P.-O. and K.-G. Löfgren (1995), 'Wealth from optimal health', *Journal of Health Economics* 14, 65–79.

Jorgenson, D.W. and B.M. Fraumeni (1992), 'Investment in education and U.S. economic growth', *The Scandinavian Journal of Economics* 94, supplement, 51–70.

Korea Environment Institute, UNDP and UNSD (1998), 'Pilot compilation of environmental-economic accounts', Seoul: Korea Environmental Institute.

Lange, G.-M. (2003), *Policy Applications of Environmental Accounting*, Environmental Economics Series Paper No. 88, Washington, DC: The World Bank Environment Department.

Li, C.H. and Löfgren, K.-G. (2002), *On the Choice of Money Metrics in Dynamic Welfare*

*Analysis: Utility versus Money Measures*. Umeå Economic Studies No. 590, Umeå, University of Umeå.

Lindahl, E. (1933), 'The concept of income', in G. Bagge (ed.), *Economic Essays in Honor of Gustaf Cassel*, London: George Allen and Unwin.

Ministry of Finance of Norway (2005), *Indicators for Policies to Enhance Sustainable Development*, Oslo: Ministry of Finance of Norway.

Ministry of Finance of Sweden (2000), 'Vad är hållbar utveckling?' Appendix 7 of Langtidsutredningen *1999/2000*.

National Institute of Economic Research (2002), *Economic Effects of Restrictions on Carbon Dioxide Emissions: Scenarios for Sweden to 2010* (in Swedish), Report 2002:1, Environmental accounts.

National Institute of Economic Research (2003), *Economic Effects for Sweden of Limited Carbon Dioxide Emission Trade within EU* (in Swedish), Report 2003:1, Environmental accounts.

National Institute of Economic Research and Statistics Sweden (1998), *SWEEA Swedish Economic and Environmental Accounts*, Environmental Accounts Report 1998:2.

Neumayer, E. (2000), 'Resource accounting in measures of unsustainability', *Environmental and Resource Economics* 15, 257–278.

Nilsson, C. (2004), *Studies in Environmental Economics: Numerical Analysis of Greenhouse Gas Policies*, PhD Dissertation, Stockholm School of Economics, Stockholm.

Nilsson, C. and A. Huhtala (2000), *Is CO2 Trading Always Beneficial? A CGE-Model Analysis on Secondary Environmental Benefits*, Working Paper No. 75, Stockholm: National Institute of Economic Research, Sweden.

O'Connor, M. (2001), *Towards a Typology of Environmentally Adjusted National Sustainability Indicators*, Eurostat Working Papers 2/2001/B/4.

Oda, K., K. Arahara, N. Hirai and H. Kubo (1998), 'Japan: The system of integrated environmental and economic accounting (SEEA) – trial estimates and remaining issues', in K. Uno and P. Bartelmus (eds), *Environmental Accounting in Theory and Practice*, Dordrecht: Kluwer Publishers.

Östblom, G. (1999), *An Environmental Medium Term Economic Model EMEC*, Working Paper No 69, Stockholm: National Institute for Economic Research.

Östblom, G. (2003), 'Vinner Sverige på att delta i utsläppshandel?' *Ekonomisk Debatt* 31(8), 27–34.

Östblom, G. and C. Berg (2006), *The EMEC Model: Version 2.0*, Working Paper No 96, Stockholm: National Institute for Economic Research.

Östblom, G. and E. Samakovlis (2007), 'Costs of climate policy when pollution affects health and labour productivity :A general equilibrium analysis applied to Sweden', *Climate Policy* 7(5), 379–391.

Pearce, D. and G. Atkinson (1993), 'Capital theory and the measurement of sustainable development: An indicator of weak sustainability', *Ecological Economics* 8(2), 103–108.

Pezzey, J. and C. Withagen (1995), 'The rise, fall, and sustainability of capital-resource economies', *Scandinavian Journal of Economics* 100, 513–527.

Pillarisetti, J.R. (2005), 'The World Bank's genuine savings measure and sustainability', *Ecological Economics* 55, 599–609.

Ready, R., S. Navrud, B. Day, R. Dubourg, F. Machado, S. Mourato, F. Spanninks and M.X. Vazquez Rodriquez (2004), 'Benefit transfers in Europe: How reliable are transfers between countires?' *Environmental and Resource Economics* 29, 67–82.

Rees, W. and M. Wackernagel (1994) 'Ecological footprints and appropriated carrying capacity: measuring the natural capital requirements of the human economy', in A.M. Jansson, M. Hammer, C. Folke and R. Costanza (eds), *Investing in Natural Capital: The Ecological Economics Approach to Sustainability*, Washington, DC: Island Press.

Repetto, R. and W. Cruz (1991), *Accounts overdue: Natural Resource Depreciation in Costa Rica*, Washington DC: World Resources Institute.

Repetto, R., W. Magrath, M. Wells, C. Beer and F. Rossini (1989), *Wasting Assets: Natural Resources in the National Accounts*, Washington DC: World Resources Institute.

Samakovlis, E., A. Huhtala, T. Bellander and M. Svartengren (2005), 'Valuing health effects of air pollution: focus on concentration-response functions', *Journal of Urban Economics*, 58(2), 230–249.

Samakovlis, E. and L. Svensson (2004), 'Valuing morbidity effects of air pollution in Sweden' (in Swedish), Environmental accounts, Report 2004: 2, Stockholm: National Institute of Economic Research.

Skånberg, K. (2000), *A Partially Environmentally Adjusted Net Domestic Product for Sweden 1993 and 1997*, Working Paper No 76, Stockholm: National Institute for Economic Research.

Smith, R. (2007), 'Development of the SEEA 2003 and its implementation', *Ecological Economics* 61, 592–599.

SOU 1991:37, *Räkna med miljön! Förslag till natur- och miljöräkenskaper*, Betänkande av miljöräkenskapsutredningen.

SOU 2000:7, *Medium Term Survey*, Ministry of Finance, Sweden.

SOU 2000:23, *Förslag till Svensk Klimatstrategi: Klimatkommitténs betänkande*.

SOU 2000:45, *Handla för att uppnå klimatmål!: Kostnadseffektiva lösningar med flexibla mekanismer inom klimatområdet*.

SOU 2001:2, *Effektiv hushållning med naturresurser*.

SOU 2003:60, *Handla för bättre klimat*.

SOU 2004:19 *Medium Term Survey*, Ministry of Finance, Sweden.

SOU 2005:10 *Handla för bättre klimat: Från införande till utförande*.

Statistics Sweden (2007), *The Economic Structures and Environmental Pressure in the Swedish River Basin Districts 1995–2005* (in Swedish), Environmental Accounts Report 2007:1.

Theys, J. (1989), 'Environmental accounting in development policy: the French experience'. In: Y. Ahmad, Y. S. El Serafy, and E. Lutz (eds), *Environmental Accounting for Sustainable Development*, Washington, DC: The World Bank.

United Nations (1987), *Report of the World Commission on Environment and Development*, General Assembly Resolution 42/187, 11 December 1987.

United Nations (1993), *Handbook of National Accounting: Integrated Environment and Economic Accounting*, Series: F, No. 61, New York: UN.

United Nations (2007), *Agenda 21 Chapter 8*, www.un.org/esa/dsd/agenda21/res_agenda21_08.shtml, accessed 16 May 2010.

United Nations Development Programme (1996), *Human Development Report 1996*, Oxford: Oxford University Press.

United Nations, Commission of the European Communities, International Monetary Fund, Organisation for Economic Cooperation and Development and World Bank (2003), *Handbook for Integrated Environmental and Economic Accounting*, New York: UN. Draft available at http://unstats.un.org/unsd/envaccounting/seea2003.pdf, accessed 16 May 2010.

United Nations Statistical Commission (2007), Environmental-Economic Accounting, http://unstats.un.org/unsd/envaccounting/EnvAcc_Brochure_FINAL1.pdf, accessed 16 May 2010.

Van Tongeren, J., S. Schweinfest, E. Lutz, M. Gomez Luna and G. Martin (1992), 'Integrated Environmental and Economic Accounting: the Case of Mexico', paper presented at *CIDIE Workshop on Environmental Economics and Natural resource Management in Developing Countries*, World Bank, Washington D.C., 22–24 January.

Weitzman, M.L. (1976), 'On the welfare significance of national product in a dynamic economy', *The Quarterly Journal of Economics* 90, 156–162.

World Bank (1997), *Expanding the Measure of Wealth: Indicators of Environmentally Sustainable Development*, Washington DC: World Bank.

World Bank (2006), *Where is the Wealth of Nations?* Washington DC: World Bank.

World Bank (2007), website: http://web.worldbank.org/WBSITE/EXTERNAL/TOPICS/ENVIRONMENT/EXTDATASTA/0,,contentMDK:20502388~menuPK:2935543~pagePK:64168445~piPK;64168309~theSitePK:2875751~isCURL:Y,00.html

# 7 The theory of dynamic cost–benefit analysis: some recent advances
## *Chuan-Zhong Li*

## 1 INTRODUCTION

Cost–benefit analysis is a branch of applied welfare economics which aims to serve as a tool for evaluating the social desirability of public projects. The main body of the theory and method has been developed since the 1950s (see Green Book, 1950; Eckstein, 1958; Maass, 1962; Dasgupta and Pearce, 1972; Little and Mirrlees, 1974; Sugden and Williams, 1978; and Drèze and Stern, 1987, for example). While the interest was mainly on capital investment projects in the earlier years, the focus has gradually shifted to more general projects such as public policy reforms and environmental programs to promote sustainable development.

The change in emphasis of project types and the long-run nature of environmental effects have also led to a paradigm shift in the method of framing cost–benefit rules. One characteristic is the use of forward-looking welfare indices which represent some constancy equivalents of future utilities rather than the stream of project consequences (see Aronsson et al., 1997; Dasgupta and Mäler, 2000; Weitzman, 2001; Arrow et al., 2003; Li and Löfgren, 2008). For such a paradigm shift, accounting prices have played an essential role. A different but related area is the measurement of sustainable development, which since the publication of the Brundtland 1987 report has become a popular phrase. As a matter of fact, these two areas belong to the same theory package but have been labeled somewhat differently as welfare comparisons over 'space' and 'time'. For cost–benefit analysis, the problem is to examine whether a project involving a perturbation of resource uses in 'space' at a given time would improve welfare, whereas the problem for sustainability studies is to infer on whether welfare would increase over time. The latter may be regarded as a special type of cost–benefit analysis where the 'project' is the elapse of time.

The aim of this chapter is to provide an interpretive overview of the recent literature in dynamic cost–benefit analysis with special reference to the welfare significance of comprehensive net national product (NNP) and consumer surplus measures. We shall concentrate on theory, with no attempt to survey empirical issues such as the various non-market valuation techniques. In addition, we abstract from interpersonal welfare comparisons in order to focus more on the intertemporal aspect reflecting the benefit trade-offs over generations.

The chapter is structured as follows. In section 2, we formulate a theory of intertemporal welfare measurement as a basis of dynamic cost–benefit analysis. The theory is presented in such a way that it can accommodate both optimal and non-optimal (conditionally optimal) economies. Section 3 presents the dynamic cost–benefit rules for small projects; it highlights the welfare significance of comprehensive NNP. Section 4 uses the well-known Ramsey-Solow model to illustrate the various cost–benefit rules with the saving rate as a policy parameter. Section 5 extends the analysis to cost–benefit rules for evaluating large projects with considerable price effects, and section 6 sums up.

## 2   A THEORY OF INTERTEMPORAL WELFARE MEASUREMENT

In this section, we present a multisector growth model formalized by Weitzman (1976, 2001) and adapted by Li and Löfgren (2008) for dynamic cost–benefit analysis. As commonly assumed in the literature, social well-being is measured by the Ramsey-Koopman-type intertemporal welfare function

$$W_0 = \int_0^\infty U(\mathbf{C}(t))\exp(-\theta t)\,dt \tag{1}$$

where $\mathbf{C} = (C_1, C_2, \ldots, C_m)$ is an m-dimensional vector of consumption flows at a given time $t$, and $\theta$ is the utility rate of discount. We assume that such a vector exhausts all possible goods and services that are relevant to the standard of living of a representative individual. In addition to the usual market commodities, environmental services such as forest amenities, biodiversity and ecosystem functions, in flow terms, are also considered as elements of the consumption vector. The instantaneous utility $U(\mathbf{C})$ is assumed to be a concave, non-decreasing function with continuous second-order derivatives defined for $\mathbf{C} \geq 0$.

Associated with consumption is a vector of capital $\mathbf{K} = (K_1, K_2, \ldots, K_n)$ which encompasses all types of capital goods in the economy. By definition, the change in capital, that is, $\dot{K}_i = I_i, i = 1, 2, \ldots, n$, is net investment or disinvestment depending on the sign of the change. In vector notation, we have $\mathbf{I} = \dot{\mathbf{K}}$, with $\mathbf{K}(0) = \mathbf{K}_0 > 0$ representing the initial state. At each point in time $t$, consumption $\mathbf{C}(t)$ and investment $\mathbf{I}(t)$ are allocated within the $(m + n)$ -dimensional attainable-possibility set $S(\mathbf{K}(t); \alpha)$, conditional on a collection of parameters (see Drèze and Stern, 1987), $\alpha$, such that

$$(\mathbf{C}(t), \mathbf{I}(t)) \in S(\mathbf{K}(t); \alpha), \tag{2}$$

which is assumed to be strictly convex. The parameters $\alpha$, which were introduced by Li and Löfgren (2008) into the Weitzman model, may represent any premise that modifies the attainable set for consumption and investment allocations. This includes aspects such as a given property right regime or an inherent public infrastructure which are not normally optimized in the economic system.[1] Conditional on the parameters, the decision maker is assumed to maximize the current-value Hamiltonian at each point in time $t$,

$$H(t) = U(\mathbf{C}(t)) + \Psi(t)\mathbf{I}(t) \tag{3}$$

with respect to $\{\mathbf{C}(t), \mathbf{I}(t)\}$ subject to (2), where $\Psi(t)$ is the $n$ -dimensional vector of the utility shadow prices (co-state variables) of capital satisfying the following equation of motion

$$\dot{\Psi} = \theta\Psi - \nabla H_{\mathbf{K}}|_{*(t)} \tag{4}$$

where the expression $|_{*(t)}$ means evaluation along the optimal trajectory at time $t$.

As touched upon above, the attainable possibility set for the optimization problem, $S(\mathbf{K}(t); \alpha)$, contains a collection of governance parameters in addition to the resource constraints, and therefore the optimal trajectory of consumption, investment and capital will also be conditional on the parameters $\alpha$. For simplicity, we assume that there exists a unique *conditional* optimum trajectory $\{\mathbf{C}^*(\alpha, t), \mathbf{I}^*(\alpha, t), \mathbf{K}^*(\alpha, t)\}$ for all $t \geq 0$, with which the following welfare concepts are defined.

**Definition 1** *The intertemporal welfare (wealth) at time t is defined by*

$$W^*(\alpha, t) \equiv \int_t^\infty U(\mathbf{C}^*(\alpha, s))\exp(-\theta(s - t))ds, \tag{5}$$

*which is the conditionally maximized present discounted value of the future utility stream from time t onwards.*[2]

**Definition 2** *The maximized current-value Hamiltonian*[3] *(utility NNP) at time t is defined by*

$$H^*(\alpha, t) \equiv U(\mathbf{C}^*(\alpha, t)) + \Psi^*(\alpha, t)\mathbf{I}^*(\alpha, t), \tag{6}$$

*which is the sum of the utility value of consumption and that of investment at time t.*

**Definition 3** *Money NNP (an affine transformation of utility NNP) at time t is defined by*

$$Y^*(\alpha, t) = \mathbf{P}^*(\alpha, t)\mathbf{C}^*(\alpha, t) + \mathbf{Q}^*(\alpha, t)\mathbf{I}^*(\alpha, t), \tag{7}$$

*which is the money value of consumption plus investment, all evaluated at their respective accounting prices*

$$\mathbf{P}^*(\alpha, t) = \nabla U(\mathbf{C}^*(\alpha, t))/\lambda(t) \ and \ \mathbf{Q}^*(\alpha, t) = \Psi(\alpha, t)/\lambda(t),$$

*with $\lambda(t)$ as the marginal utility of income.*

Due to the assumption of completeness in consumption and investment, all the measures here need be understood in a comprehensive sense, namely *comprehensive wealth, comprehensive utility* and *comprehensive money NNP*. For dynamic welfare analysis, it has long been known that the wealth-like measure in (5) is a correct index of welfare since any increase in its value would increase the overall consumption possibility set for the present and the future. The problem with this measure lies in the heavy informational demand over an infinite future for calculating its value.

Fortunately, Weitzman's (1976) seminal contribution has brought the application of the wealth-like measure a step forward by compressing the infinite utility stream to a forward-looking Hamiltonian measure (6) at a single point in time. More exactly, he found that the Hamiltonian value, which is in principle estimable from statistical data available at time *t*, can be expressed as the annuity associated with the wealth-like measure such that $H^*(\alpha, t) = \theta W^*(\alpha, t)$. Accordingly, the Hamiltonian measure may be used as a perfect surrogate for the wealth-like measure if the utility rate of discount is constant and positive, that is, $\theta > 0$.

In spite of this great progress, the Hamiltonian measure may not be directly operational as it is a non-linear function in consumption and defined in an unobservable utility metric. In the quest for more operational measures of dynamic welfare, economists have attempted to further explore the advantage of the Hamiltonian by taking a linearized version of it, that is, the observable money-metric NNP as in (7). This move is not completely innocuous, however, as much of the welfare significance would not carry over from the utility to money-metric measures. Thus, it has become a challenging field of study to identify the conditions under which the money-metric NNP can serve as a satisfactory dynamic welfare measure. In the next section, we will turn to the welfare significance of money-metric NNP for the evaluation of small projects.

## 3   COST–BENEFIT RULES FOR SMALL PROJECTS

In this section, we provide an interpretive overview of the dynamic cost–benefit rules for evaluating small projects, with emphasis on the role of comprehensive NNP. By a small project, we mean an infinitesimal perturbation in the parameters $\alpha$, $d\alpha$, from a given initial value $\alpha_0$. The choice of small projects here motivates our use of differential techniques. Depending on situations, the concept of a 'small project' may be flexibly operationalized to accommodate projects of various types. For the twin-economy model in Weitzman (2001), for example, the project would represent an instant and costless change in the initial capital configuration with $d\alpha = [dk_1(0), dk_2(0), \ldots, dk_n(0)]$. For a permanent policy reform as in Dasgupta and Mäler (2000), the project may represent a change in their governance parameter set (for example, the saving rate) with $d\alpha$ for $t \in [0, \infty)$. For a capital investment project with a finite project period $t \in [0, T], T > 0$, as shown in Li and Löfgren (2008), the project may be expressed by $d\alpha = \{d\widetilde{\mathbf{C}}(t), d\widetilde{\mathbf{I}}(t)\}|_0^T$ with $d\widetilde{\mathbf{C}}(t)$ and $d\widetilde{\mathbf{I}}(t)$ as the *direct* perturbations in the consumption and investment vectors, respectively.

For any of the project types, the general evaluation criterion is the same, that is, the reform $d\alpha$ is socially profitable if it increases the wealth-like measure in (5), that is, $dW^*(\alpha, 0) = \partial W^*(\alpha, 0)/\partial\alpha \cdot d\alpha > 0$ as evaluated at $\alpha = \alpha_0$ and $t = 0$. As shown in Aronsson et al. (2004), Arrow et al., (2003) and Li and Löfgren (2008), this amounts to the following general dynamic cost–benefit rule:

**Proposition 1** *If the present discounted value of changes in future consumption caused by a small project $d\alpha$, expressed by*

$$dW^*(\alpha, 0)|_{\alpha=\alpha_0} = \lambda(0)\int_0^\infty \mathbf{P}^*(t)\,d\mathbf{C}(t)\exp\left(-\int_0^t r(\tau)\,d\tau\right)dt \qquad (8)$$

*is positive, then the project is socially profitable, where $d\mathbf{C}(t) = \partial\mathbf{C}(t)/\partial\alpha \cdot d\alpha$ denotes the total effect on the consumption vector at time $t \geq 0$, $r(\tau) = \theta + \dot{\lambda}(\tau)/\lambda(\tau)$ for $\tau \in [0, t]$ denotes the money rate of discount, and $\lambda(0) > 0$ is the marginal utility of income at time 0, which can be normalized to unity.*

Although equation (8) represents the theoretically correct criterion for social cost–benefit analysis of small projects, there are practical difficulties in its applications. Firstly, the effect on consumption at each point in time involves all 'general equilibrium' effects on the whole economy; and, secondly, the decision maker has to evaluate the effects over an infinite time horizon. In practice, to predict all such effects over an infinite time horizon would be very difficult, if not impossible.[4] Several attempts have been made recently to resolve the problem. One is to use the forward-looking Hamiltonian measure as a criterion for assessing the present and future consequences of the project under consideration. To start with, let us first examine the permanent project case in Dasgupta and Mäler (2000), with $d\alpha = \alpha_1 - \alpha_0$ in the whole future. Imagine that the decision maker has solved two parallel dynamic optimization problems as in (1) with all other conditions identical except the parameters values $\alpha_0$ and $\alpha_1$. Since the maximized Hamiltonian as defined in (6) is a perfect surrogate for the wealth-like measure in (5) for any $t \in [0, \infty)$, the change in its value caused by $d\alpha$ will completely capture the corresponding change in wealth due to $dH^*(\alpha, 0) = \theta dW^*(\alpha, 0)$. This leads to the following Dasgupta and Mäler (2000) cost–benefit rule:

**Proposition 2** *If the total change in the Hamiltonian value* $H^*(\alpha, 0)$ *caused by a small project* $d\alpha$ *is positive, that is,*

$$\frac{dH^*(\alpha, 0)}{d\alpha}\bigg|_{\alpha = \alpha_0} = \Pi^*(\alpha_0, 0)\frac{dC(\alpha, 0)}{d\alpha} + \frac{d[\Psi^*(\alpha, 0)\mathbf{I}^*(\alpha, 0)]}{d\alpha}$$

$$= \lambda(0)\left\{ \mathbf{P}^*(\alpha_0, 0)\frac{dC(\alpha, 0)}{d\alpha} + \mathbf{Q}^*(\alpha, 0)\frac{d\mathbf{I}^*(\alpha, 0)}{d\alpha} \right\}$$

$$+ \mathbf{I}^*(\alpha_0, 0)\frac{d\Psi^*(\alpha, 0)}{d\alpha} > 0 \qquad (9)$$

*where* $\Pi^*(\alpha_0, 0) = \lambda(0)\mathbf{P}^*(\alpha_0, 0)$, *then the project is socially profitable; otherwise not.*

The first equality in (9) is interpreted to indicate that if the value of changes in consumption plus the change in the value of investments at time $t = 0$ is positive, it is socially worthwhile to undertake the project. Note that 'the change in the value of investments' is meant to be the sum of the value of changes in investments evaluated at their local accounting prices and the change in the value of investment caused by price changes, as expressed in the second equality. By definition, the expression in the braces corresponds to the change in comprehensive money NNP. However, the presence of the last term $I^*(\alpha_0, 0) d\Psi^*(\alpha, 0)/d\alpha$ indicates clearly that the change in comprehensive NNP is not the correct criterion for evaluating the project $d\alpha$ except in the trivial case with no price effect. In other words, only if the accounting prices remain constant with $d\Psi^*(\alpha, 0)/d\alpha = 0$, can one use the change in comprehensive money NNP to infer whether or not the project is profitable. And this is the case for an instant project, as Dasgupta and Mäler (2000) stated in the following proposition:

**Proposition 3** *For the instant small project $d\alpha$ within an infinitesimal period of time $t \in [0,\tau)$ for $\tau \to 0$, the change in comprehensive NNP at time $t = 0$, that is,*

$$\frac{dY^*(\alpha, 0)}{d\alpha}\Big|_{\alpha=\alpha_0} = P^*(\alpha_0,0)\frac{dC(\alpha, 0)}{d\alpha} + Q^*(\alpha, 0)\frac{dI^*(\alpha, 0)}{d\alpha} \qquad (10)$$

*is a correct criterion for evaluating the project. If the change is positive, the project is socially profitable; otherwise not.*

For more general projects, however, it is necessary to take into account the price effects that the project would have given rise to. The intuition behind the above two propositions is that while the instant change in NNP in (10) measures the welfare effect of a concurrent sub-project, one would need the other term $d\Psi^*(\alpha, 0)/d\alpha$ to capture the effect of the part of the reform beyond the period $[0, \tau)$. In other words, even if comprehensive NNP could be a perfect measure of welfare due to a concurrent change, it is too much to ask it to reflect the welfare effect of changes which have taken place outside that period. Then it seems natural to have an extra term as a complement to NNP in order to measure welfare.

The difference between the original Hamiltonian value and money NNP is that the former allows variations in consumption, investment and investment prices, whereas the latter by definition treats investment prices as given constants. By accepting the fact that NNP lacks some degrees of freedom, we will now pursue a more realistic objective by requiring comprehensive NNP at time $t$ to simply capture the intertemporal welfare effect caused by the part of the 'policy reform' $d\alpha$ which takes place at time $t$.

Suppose that the whole project $d\alpha$ can be decomposed into a series of sub-projects $d\alpha = \{d\tilde{\alpha}(t)\}|_0^T$, each with a welfare effect captured by the variation in $Y^*(\alpha, t)$. Then, by aggregating the welfare effects of all sub-projects $d\tilde{\alpha}(t)$ over the project period $[0, T]$, we would be able to assess the total welfare effect over the whole future, which would be recorded by the change in wealth at $W^*(\alpha, 0)$ at time $t = 0$. The idea here is that we use the concurrent changes to calculate the corresponding variation in comprehensive NNP, which in turn measures the welfare effect over the whole future, rather than using the NNP measure to capture the welfare effect of future changes in the policy parameter α.

Loosely speaking, the variation in NNP at time $t$ is a forward-looking measure of future welfare arising from concurrent rather than anticipated future policy changes. Under such a more realistic requirement, we can derive the following two dynamic cost–benefit rules, which may restore the welfare significance of comprehensive NNP. First, we present the dynamic cost–benefit rule using the social profit notion by Dixit et al. (1980). Let the triple $\{d\mathbf{C}(t), d\mathbf{I}(t), d\mathbf{K}(t)\}_0^T$ denote the total input and output effects on consumption, investment and capital at time $t$, arising from past and concurrent sub-projects $d\tilde{\alpha}(s)|_0^t$ up to time $t$. Then, we have the following dynamic cost–benefit rule:

**Proposition 4** *The project* $d\alpha = d\tilde{\alpha}(s)|_0^T$ *is socially profitable if the present discounted value of the resulting social profits is positive, that is,*

$$dW^*(\alpha, 0) = \int_0^T [\mathbf{P}^*(t)d\mathbf{C}(t) + \mathbf{Q}^*(t)d\mathbf{I}(t) + \mathbf{R}^*(t)d\mathbf{K}(t)]e^{-\int_0^t r(\tau)d\tau}dt > 0 \tag{11}$$

*where* $\mathbf{R}^*(t) = [\dot{\Psi}(\alpha_0, t) - \theta\Psi(\alpha_0, t)]/\lambda(t)$ *denotes the capital rental prices, and* $r(\tau)$ *the money rate of discount at time* $\tau, \tau \in [0, T]$.

This is the widely known dynamic cost–benefit rule (see Asheim 2000; Dasgupta and Mäler, 2000; Arrow et al., 2003; Li and Löfgren 2008). Now, what is the relationship between the dynamic cost–benefit rule (11) and the cost–benefit rule in (8)? As formally shown by Li and Löfgren (2008), they are two sides of the same coin. The rationale behind this is that the integral of the sum of the last two terms, together with the discount factor, corresponds to $\lambda(0)\int_T^\infty \mathbf{P}^*(t)d\mathbf{C}(t)\exp(-\int_0^t r(\tau)d\tau)dt$, that is, the change in the post-project period welfare caused by the policy reform. Together with the within-period welfare effects the integral of the first term represents, the total intertemporal welfare effect is captured by (11).

As argued by Sugden and Williams (1978, page 97), any decision (any sub-project) sets in motion a ripple of effects which spreads outwards to affect the whole economy. In a dynamic economy, the ripple will also spread over time over the whole future. This implies that there will be widespread indirect or induced effects both over space and time. As a consequence, to evaluate any given project using the social profit notion, one would have to assess all such economy-wide and dynamic effects in order to arrive at a decision on whether the project is socially profitable. Therefore, Sugden and Williams claim that whenever possible, one should try to use the theory of perfect competition to net out the indirect effects to simplify the cost–benefit rule.

Now, we attempt to do so by separating the direct input effects $d\tilde{\alpha}(t) = (d\tilde{C}(t), d\tilde{I}(t))$ from the resulting indirect effects $(\Delta\tilde{C}(t), \Delta\tilde{I}(t))$, where $\Delta\tilde{C}(t) = \Delta C(t) - d\tilde{C}(t)$ and $\Delta\tilde{I}(t) = \Delta I(t) - d\tilde{I}(t)$. By using the first-order necessary conditions for the within-project period $t \in [0, T]$, $\nabla U_{\tilde{C}}^* + \Psi^*\partial I^*/\partial C = 0$ and $\dot{\Psi}^* - \theta\Psi^* = -\partial H^*/\partial K$, along the conditional optimal trajectory with a given $\alpha = \alpha_0$, Li and Löfgren (2008) have managed to simplify the social profit expression (Dixit et al., 1980) as in (11) to obtain an interesting dynamic envelope result. After having canceled all the indirect effects on consumption, investment and capital stocks, what is left in the integrand of (11) is the variation in the comprehensive net national product. The simplified dynamic cost–benefit rule can then be expressed as:

**Proposition 5** *Consider a small policy reform, $d\alpha$, over the interval $[0, T]$, which would lead to a direct perturbation in consumption and investment with $d\tilde{C}(t)$ and $d\tilde{I}(t)$, respectively. We measure the change in the present discounted value of NNP over the project period by:*

$$dW^*(\alpha, 0) = \int_0^T \{\lambda(t)\mathbf{P}^*(t)d\tilde{C}(t) + \Psi^*(t)d\tilde{I}(t)\}\exp(-\theta t)\,dt$$

$$= \lambda(0)\int_0^T \{\mathbf{P}^*(t)d\tilde{C}(t) + \mathbf{Q}^*(t)d\tilde{I}(t)\}\exp\left(-\int_0^t r(\tau)\,d\tau\right)dt. (12)$$

*If this change is positive, the project is socially profitable;[5] if it is negative, the project is socially unprofitable.*

Note that this rule only requires information about the direct effect of the reform without any need to trace all the general equilibrium effects. In Drèze and Stern's (1987) terms, this dynamic cost–benefit rule is based on an evaluation of the reform parameters or instruments, and does not entail the consequences of the reform or the general equilibrium effects. After having canceled out all indirect effects, what remains in the integrand of the integral in (12) is exactly the variation in (comprehensive) NNP caused by the reform! In addition, the decision maker only needs to evaluate the effects within the project period, since the consumption effects over the post-project period have already been taken into account by the change in the value of investment within the project period. The reason why the capital cost term vanishes in (12) is that the cost of holding capital is exactly offset by the benefits it would have generated.

# 4 AN ILLUSTRATION WITH THE RAMSEY-SOLOW MODEL

This section illustrates the five cost–benefit rules presented in the previous section. We use the well-known Ramsey-Solow model, parameterized in Arrow et al. (2003), for the illustration. It is assumed that there is an all-purpose durable good, which can either be consumed or reinvested for further accumulation. Let the capital stock at time $t$ be $k_t$ with initial value $k_0 > 0$, and assume that the production function is linear-in-capital such that $y_t = \mu k_t$ with $\mu > 0$ as the output–wealth ratio. Let $\alpha$ be the saving ratio with $\alpha \in [0, 1]$, which may not be optimized. Then, we examine whether or not a change in this policy parameter $\alpha$ is welfare improving. Consumption at time $t$ is given by $c_t(k_t, \alpha) = (1 - \alpha)\mu k_t$ and net investment by $\dot{k}_t(k_t, \alpha) = (\alpha\mu - \gamma)k_t$ where $\gamma$ denotes the rate of capital depreciation. If $\alpha\mu > \gamma$, then the economy would grow exponentially at the rate $\alpha\mu - \gamma$. For simplicity, we assume $\gamma = 0$ here, so that we have $k_t(\alpha) = k_0\exp(\alpha\mu t)$. Current utility at time $t$ is considered to be $U(c_t) = -c_t^{1-\eta}$ with $\eta > 1$ as the elasticity of marginal utility of consumption. The maximized intertemporal welfare as defined in (5), conditional on a given saving rate $\alpha$, is derived to be

$$W^*(\alpha, t) \equiv \int_t^\infty -c_s^{1-\eta}\exp(-\theta(s - t))\,ds$$

$$= -\frac{[(1 - \alpha)\mu k_t]^{1-\eta}}{\alpha\mu(\eta - 1) + \theta}. \tag{13}$$

The current accounting price per unit of consumption reads

$$p_t(\alpha) = -\frac{\partial c_t^{1-\eta}}{\partial c_t} = (\eta - 1)[(1 - \alpha)\mu k_t]^{-\eta} \tag{14}$$

and the accounting price per unit of capital good $k_t$, with utility as numeraire, is given by

$$q_t(\alpha) = \frac{\partial W^*(\alpha, t)}{\partial k_t} = \frac{(\eta - 1)[(1 - \alpha)\mu]^{1-\eta}k_t^{-\eta}}{\alpha\mu(\eta - 1) + \theta}, \tag{15}$$

which, as shown in Arrow et al. (2003), follows the following differential equation:

$$\dot{q}_t(\alpha) = \theta q_t(\alpha, t) - p_t(\alpha_0)\frac{\partial c_t}{\partial k_t} - q_t(\alpha)\frac{\partial \dot{k}_t}{\partial k_t}. \tag{16}$$

In general, $p_t(\alpha, t)$ is not equal to $q_t(\alpha, t)$ unless the saving rate is optimally chosen at

$$\alpha^* = \frac{\mu - \theta}{\mu\eta}. \tag{17}$$

In cost–benefit analysis, the decision maker is not assumed to optimize the saving rate but to make a policy reform $d\alpha$ from an initial value $\alpha_0$. The question is thus to evaluate whether or not the reform is welfare improving. Without loss of generality, let the project period be $[0, T]$ with $T$ as a positive constant in the normal case. If $T \to 0$, then we have the case of an instant project with the change $d\alpha$ over an infinitesimal period from $\alpha_0$, and then shifting back to $\alpha_0$. At the other extreme, when $T \to \infty$, then the change from $\alpha_0$ by $d\alpha$ is permanent. In all cases, the effects of the reform would spread over the whole future. Let the total changes in capital, consumption and investment be represented, respectively, by

$$dk_t = \frac{\partial k_t}{\partial \alpha}d\alpha = k_0\mu t \cdot \exp(\alpha\mu t)\,d\alpha \tag{18}$$

$$dc_t = \underbrace{\frac{\partial c_t}{\partial \alpha}d\alpha}_{\substack{\text{Direct} \\ \text{effect}}} + \underbrace{\frac{\partial c_t}{\partial k_t}\frac{\partial k_t}{\partial \alpha}d\alpha}_{\substack{\text{Indirect} \\ \text{effect}}} = [-\mu k_t + (1 - \alpha)\mu dk_t]\,d\alpha \tag{19}$$

$$d\dot{k}_t = \underbrace{\frac{\partial \dot{k}_t(k_t, \alpha)}{\partial \alpha}}_{\substack{\text{Direct} \\ \text{effect}}} + \underbrace{\frac{\partial \dot{k}_t(k_t, \alpha)}{\partial k_t}\frac{\partial k_t}{\partial \alpha}da}_{\substack{\text{Indirect} \\ \text{effect}}} = [\mu k_t(\alpha_0) + \alpha_0 dk_t]\,d\alpha, \tag{20}$$

all evaluated at the status quo saving rate $\alpha_0$. To fix ideas, we take the following numerical values for calculating the welfare effects: $k_0 = 1$, $\mu = 0.25$, $\eta = 2$, $\theta = 0.15$, which implies that $\alpha^* = 0.2$ according to (17). Now, we will illustrate the five cost–benefit rules with this model where each 'case' refers to the corresponding proposition with the same reference number.

**Case 1** *The present value of changes in future consumption caused by a permanent reform $d\alpha$ is according to (8) given by*

$$dW^*(\alpha, 0)|_{\alpha=\alpha_0} = \int_0^\infty p_t(\alpha_0)\,dc_t\exp(-\theta t)\,dt$$

$$= \frac{(1 - \eta)[(1 - \alpha_0)\mu k_0]^{-\eta}\mu k_0}{\alpha_0\mu(\eta - 1) + \theta}$$

$$\left\{1 - \frac{(1 - \alpha_0)\mu}{\alpha_0\mu(\eta - 1) + \theta}\right\}d\alpha. \tag{21}$$

If $\alpha_0 = 0.1$, then we have $dW^*/d\alpha \simeq 8.06 > 0$, indicating that an infinitesimal increase in the saving rate from its initial value, 0.1, is welfare improving, and thus the project $d\alpha$ is worth undertaking. On the other hand, if $\alpha_0 = 0.3$, then $dW^*/d\alpha \simeq -8.06 < 0$, indicating that any increase in the saving rate is welfare deteriorating, and the project is not worth undertaking. These results are very intuitive: when the saving rate is below its optimal level $\alpha^* = 0.2$, it pays to increase it, whereas if it is already too high, any further increase in its value would worsen the situation.

**Case 2** *The change in the Hamiltonian value*

$$H^*(\alpha, 0) = U[c_0(k_0(\alpha), \alpha)] + q_0(\alpha)\dot{k}_0(a)$$

*caused by a small project with a permanent change* $d\alpha$ *is*

$$dH^*(\alpha, 0)|_{\alpha=\alpha_0} = p_0(\alpha_0)\,dc_0 + q_0(\alpha_0)\,d\dot{k}_0 + q_t'(\alpha)|_{\alpha=\alpha_0}d\alpha\dot{k}_0(k_0, \alpha_0) \tag{22}$$

*where*

$$p_0(\alpha_0) = (\eta - 1)[(1 - \alpha_0)\mu k_0]^{-\eta} \tag{23}$$

*and*

$$q_0(\alpha_0) = \frac{(\eta - 1)[(1 - \alpha_0)\mu]^{1-\eta}k_0^{-\eta}}{\alpha_0\mu(\eta - 1) + \theta} \tag{24}$$

*denote consumption and investment prices, respectively, and the derivative*

$$q_t'(\alpha)|_{\alpha=\alpha_0} = \frac{(\eta - 1)^2\mu[(1 - \alpha_0)\mu k_0]^{-\eta}}{\alpha_0\mu(\eta - 1) + \theta}\left[1 - \frac{(1 - \alpha_0)\mu}{\alpha_0\mu(\eta - 1) + \theta}\right] \tag{25}$$

*represents the change in investment price due to the project* $d\alpha$.

Note that the change in consumption $dc_0/d\alpha = \frac{\partial c_0(\kappa_0, \alpha)}{\partial \alpha} = -\mu k_0$ and investment $d\dot{k}_0/d\alpha = \frac{\partial \dot{k}_t(\bar{k}_0, \alpha)}{\partial \alpha} d\alpha = \mu k_0$ at time $t = 0$ only involves the direct effects, since the initial capital $k_0 > 0$ is a fixed constant. The expression $\dot{k}_0(k_0, \alpha_0) = \alpha_0 \mu k_0$ represents the status quo value of investment. For $\alpha_0 = 0.1$, we have $dH^*(\alpha, 0)/d\alpha|_{\alpha = \alpha_0} \simeq 1.21 > 0$, indicating that the reform is socially profitable, whereas for $\alpha_0 = 0.3$, $dH^*(\alpha, 0)/d\alpha|_{\alpha = \alpha_0} \simeq -1.21 < 0$, indicating that the project is not socially profitable. Note that the conclusion on social profitability is exactly the same as in case 1. This is not surprising since the theory indicates that

$$dH^*(\alpha, 0)/d\alpha|_{\alpha = \alpha_0} = \theta dW^*(\alpha, 0)/d\alpha|_{\alpha = \alpha_0} \simeq 0.15 \cdot 8.06 \simeq 1.21.$$

As compared to the application of proposition 1, here we do not need to calculate the value of the integral over an infinite time horizon. To calculate the effect of the project on the initial investment price as in (25), however, may be difficult in practice. As a special case, if the project $d\alpha$ were to prevail only instantly, then things were to be much easier, as shown in the following.

**Case 3** *The change in the initial net national product (NNP) as defined in (7) caused by a small project with an instant change $d\alpha$ is*

$$\begin{aligned} dY^*(\alpha, 0)|_{\alpha = \alpha_0} &= p_0(\alpha_0) dc_0 + q_0(\alpha_0) d\dot{k}_0 \\ &= (\eta - 1)[(1 - \alpha_0)\mu]^{-\eta}(-\mu k_0 d\alpha) \\ &+ \frac{(\eta - 1)[(1 - \alpha_0)\mu]^{1-\eta}}{\alpha_0\mu(\eta - 1) + \theta}\mu k_0 d\alpha, \end{aligned} \qquad (26)$$

*which corresponds to the sum of the first two terms in (22).*

For $\alpha_0 = 0.1$, we have $dY^*(\alpha, 0)/d\alpha|_{\alpha = \alpha_0} \simeq 1.41 > 0$, indicating that the reform is socially profitable, whereas for $\alpha_0 = 0.3$, $dY^*(\alpha, 0)/d\alpha|_{\alpha = \alpha_0} \simeq -1.81 < 0$, indicating that the project is not socially profitable. Note that the cost–benefit results are the same as above with the right algebraic signs. The sizes are different, however. The reason for the difference is that while the change in the initial NNP at $t = 0$ is an instant matter, the change in the Hamiltonian reflects a constancy-equivalent change in NNP over the whole future. Due to the positive discount rate, the change in NNP in the distant future plays a smaller role, and thus the change in Hamiltonian values is smaller than that in the present value NNP.

Now, let us take a look at projects with a finite project period $[0, T]$ with a finite $T > 0$.

**Case 4** *The present discounted value of social profits resulting from a small project $d\alpha$ over $t \in [0, T]$ is given by*

$$
dW^*(\alpha, 0) = \int_0^T [p_t(\alpha_0)dc_t + q_t(\alpha_0)d\dot{k}_t + v_t(\alpha_0)dk_t]\exp(-\theta t)dt
$$

$$
= \int_0^T \left\{ p_t(\alpha_0)\left(\frac{\partial c_t}{\partial \alpha}d\alpha + \frac{\partial c_t}{\partial k_t}\frac{\partial k_t}{\partial \alpha}d\alpha\right) \right.
$$ (27)

$$
+ q_t(\alpha_0)\left(\frac{\partial \dot{k}_t}{\partial \alpha} + \frac{\partial \dot{k}_t}{\partial k_t}\frac{\partial k_t}{\partial \alpha}da\right)
$$

$$
\left. + v_t(\alpha_0)\frac{\partial k_t}{\partial \alpha}da \right\}\exp(-\theta t)dt
$$

*where*

$$
v_t(\alpha_0) = \dot{q}_t(\alpha_0) - \theta q_t(\alpha_0) = -p_t(\alpha_0)\frac{\partial c_t}{\partial k_t} - q_t(\alpha_0)\frac{\partial \dot{k}_t}{\partial k_t},
$$ (28)

*derived from (16), denotes the cost of holding capital.*

With $\alpha_0 = 0.1$, we can calculate the value $dW^*(\alpha, 0)/d\alpha$ in (27) to be about 6.66 for $T = 10$, and about 8.06 for $T = 100$, indicating that a marginal increase in the saving rate from its status quo level 0.1 is socially profitable. The effect of the length of the project period is also positive, that is, the longer the reform prevails, the higher the intertemporal welfare we would have. With $\alpha_0 = 0.3$, we find that $dW^*(\alpha, 0)/d\alpha \simeq -7.21$ for $T = 10$ and $dW^*(\alpha, 0)/d\alpha \simeq -8.06$ for $T = 100$. For $T = 100$, we find that the welfare effect assessed on the basis of the social profit notion is almost identical to the welfare effect found above for a permanent reform $d\alpha$. In theory, the results should be exactly the same as $T \to \infty$ as the different cost–benefit rules are all derived from the same intertemporal welfare function. Even though this social-profit-based rule is correct and flexible (in adapting to projects with alternative lengths), it may entail tedious calculations involving the various prices and both direct and indirect changes in consumption and investment. Fortunately, the social profit expression, as in the integrand in (27), may be readily simplified by purifying all the indirect effects (Li and Löfgren, 2008). Using (16), (19), (20) and (28), we can verify that

$$
v_t(\alpha_0)\frac{\partial k_t}{\partial \alpha}da = -p_t(\alpha_0)\frac{\partial c_t}{\partial k_t}\frac{\partial k_t}{\partial \alpha}da - q_t(\alpha_0)\frac{\partial \dot{k}_t}{\partial k_t}\frac{\partial k_t}{\partial \alpha}da,
$$ (29)

which would net out the indirect effects on NNP in the integrand in (27) involving the first two terms of the second integral. Thus, we have

**Case 5** *The present discounted value of the direct change in NNP resulting from a small project dα over t ∈ [0, T] is given by*

$$dW^*(\alpha, 0) = \int_0^T [p_t(\alpha_0)\tilde{d}c_t + q_t(\alpha_0)\tilde{d}k_t]\exp(-\theta t)\,dt$$

$$= \int_0^T [q_t(\alpha_0) - p_t(\alpha_0)]\mu k_t(\alpha_0)\,d\alpha\exp(-\theta t)\,dt \qquad (30)$$

*where $\tilde{d}c_t = \frac{\partial c_t}{\partial \alpha}d\alpha = -\mu k_t(\alpha_0)\,d\alpha$ and $\tilde{d}k_t = \frac{\partial k_t(k_t, \alpha)}{\partial \alpha}\mu k_t(\alpha_0)\,d\alpha$ denote the direct effects on consumption and investment at time t.*

Since the variation in NNP caused by the direct effects in (30) is equal to the social profit as in (27) at each point in time $t$, the numerical values for $dW^*(\alpha, 0)/d\alpha$ will be exactly the same. So what is the advantage of this cost–benefit rule? Firstly, it 'rediscovered' the welfare significance of (comprehensive) NNP for welfare analysis. NNP is a perfect welfare index when it is measured comprehensively with consumption and investment evaluated at their accounting prices. The present discounted value of direct changes in NNP is thus a correct criterion for evaluating small projects. Secondly, it is much simpler in application as all the indirect/induced effects and the capital costs are canceled out. What a decision maker needs is to look at direct changes in consumption and investment at each point in time without taking into account any feedback effects, and then calculate the net welfare effects with their accounting prices as weights. In other words, one can decompose a whole project into a series of sub-projects $(\tilde{d}c_t, \tilde{d}k_t)$ for each $t \in [0, T]$, evaluate each of them and then aggregate their effects in order to assess the overall welfare change. Finally, for this particular Ramsey-Solow model, this cost–benefit rule has a very intuitive and interesting interpretation. Since $\mu k_t(\alpha_0)\exp(-\theta t) > 0$, the algebraic sign in the second line in (30) would depend on the sign of $q_t(\alpha_0) - p_t(\alpha_0)$, that is, the excess of investment over consumption prices. If the saving rate were optimally chosen to be $\alpha = 0.2$, then $q_t(\alpha_0) - p_t(\alpha_0) = 0$ as required by the optimality condition, so that $dW^*(\alpha, 0)/d\alpha = 0$. For any saving rate $\alpha_0$ below its optimal level, the investment price $q_t(\alpha_0)$ would exceed the consumption price $p_t(\alpha_0)$ such that $q_t(\alpha_0) - p_t(\alpha_0) > 0$ for all $t \in [0, T]$ and $dW^*(\alpha, 0)/d\alpha > 0$. As indicated in Arrow et al. (2003), consumption is excessive in this case, and a small policy reform with a higher saving rate would be welfare improving. On the other hand, when

$\alpha_0 > \alpha* = 0.2$, it can be readily shown that any increase in $\alpha$ would be welfare deteriorating.

## 5   EVALUATING LARGE PROJECTS

A large project involves a discrete change in the policy parameter, which may lead to structural formations. If there are sufficient divisibilities, it should be possible to evaluate a large project on the basis of smaller projects (Starrett, 1988, p.233). Consider a project with a change in the parameter from $a_0$ to $\alpha_1$ for $t \in [0, T]$, which would result in changes in consumption both within the project period and the period beyond. Then, by using $dW = \frac{\partial W}{\partial \alpha} d\alpha$, the generic cost–benefit rule can be stated as:

**Proposition 6** *If a project $\Delta\alpha = \alpha_1 - \alpha_0$ over $t \in [0, T]$ leads to a positive change in the intertemporal welfare at time 0, that is,*

$$\Delta W_0^* = \int_{\alpha_0}^{\alpha_1} dW^*(\alpha, 0) = W^*(\alpha_1, 0) - W^*(\alpha_0, 0) > 0 \qquad (31)$$

*then the project is socially profitable; otherwise not.*

To make this cost–benefit rule operational, Weitzman (2001) takes advantage of the Hamiltonian function as in (6) as a forward-looking welfare measure. For each given $\alpha$, it is true that $H^*(\alpha, 0) = \theta W^*(\alpha, 0)$ with $\theta > 0$. This implies that if $\Delta H_0^* = H^*(\alpha_1, 0) - H^*(\alpha_0, 0) > 0$, then the project $\Delta\alpha$ would be welfare improving. Consider a permanent reform $d\alpha$ with $T \to \infty$. Then, the variation in the Hamiltonian value can be calculated by integrating (6) over $\alpha$ from $\alpha_0$ to $\alpha_1$, which leads to

$$\Delta H^*_{\,0} = \int_{\alpha_0}^{\alpha_1} dH^*(\alpha, 0) = \Delta Y + S = \lambda_0(\alpha_0)(\Delta \overline{Y} + \overline{S}) \qquad (32)$$

where

$$\Delta Y = \Pi_0(\alpha_1)\mathbf{C}_0(\alpha_1) + \Psi_0(\alpha_1)\mathbf{I}_0(\alpha_1) - (\Pi_0(\alpha_0)\mathbf{C}(\alpha_0) + \Psi(\alpha_0)\mathbf{I}(\alpha_0))$$

denotes the utility-metric change in NNP,[6] and

$$S = \int_{\Pi_0(\alpha_1)}^{\Pi_0(\alpha_0)} \mathbf{D}(\mathbf{p}) \, d\mathbf{p}$$

that of the consumer surplus due to price changes from $\Pi_0$ to $\Pi_1$. The insight here is that with the Hamiltonian function as a forward-looking measure of future utilities, the intertemporal welfare change caused by a project can be measured in exactly the same way as the standard textbook static theory of welfare analysis. If the sum of income change and consumer surplus is positive, then the project is welfare improving. The last equality in (21) is the corresponding money-metric version, with $\lambda_0(\alpha_0)$ as the status quo marginal utility of money and

$$\Delta \overline{Y} = \mathbf{P}_0(\alpha_1)\mathbf{C}_0(\alpha_1) + \mathbf{Q}_0(\alpha_1)\mathbf{I}_0(\alpha_1) \\ - (\mathbf{P}(\alpha_0)\mathbf{C}(\alpha_0) + \mathbf{Q}(\alpha_0)\mathbf{I}(\alpha_0)) \tag{33}$$

as the money-metric change in NNP. By defining an ideal price index $\pi(\alpha)$ corresponding to $\lambda_0(\alpha_0)/\lambda_0(\alpha)$, Weitzman (2001) defined the ideal prices by $\mathbf{P}_0(\alpha) = \Pi_0(\alpha)/(\lambda_0(\alpha)\pi(\alpha))$ and $\mathbf{Q}_0(\alpha) = \Psi_0(\alpha)/(\lambda_0(\alpha)\pi(\alpha))$. The corresponding consumer surplus term is

$$\overline{S} = \int_{\mathbf{P}_0(\alpha_1)}^{\mathbf{P}_0(\alpha_0)} \mathbf{D}(\mathbf{p})\, d\mathbf{p}.$$

Thus, for a permanent policy reform $\Delta\alpha$, we have the following discrete cost–benefit rule:

**Proposition 7** *If the change in the Hamiltonian value caused a permanent policy reform $\Delta\alpha$, which is equal to the sum of the change in NNP and consumer surplus as in (32), is positive, then the project is socially profitable; otherwise not.*

Note that this principle is also valid for the instant project with $T \to 0$, as considered above. When the change in $\alpha$ is large enough to affect prices, a consumer surplus term would appear even for the case of an instant project. When the reform period is finite with $0 < T < \infty$, then a discrete cost–benefit rule corresponding to the social profit version in (11) may be more useful, as shown in Li and Löfgren (2010). This amounts to a direct integration of (11) over $\alpha$ from $\alpha_0$ to $\alpha_1$, which leads to

$$\Delta W^* = \int_0^T \int_{\alpha_0}^{\alpha_1} [\mathbf{P}_t^*(\alpha)\, d\mathbf{C}_t(\alpha) + \mathbf{Q}_t^*(\alpha)\, d\mathbf{I}_t(\alpha)$$

$$+ \mathbf{R}_t^*(\alpha)\, d\mathbf{K}_t(\alpha)\lambda_t(\alpha)\exp(-\theta t)]\, d\alpha dt$$

$$= \int_0^T [\Delta Y(t) + S(t) - \kappa(t)] \exp(-\theta t) dt$$

$$= \lambda_0(\alpha_0) \int_0^T [\Delta \overline{Y}(t) + \overline{S}(t) - \overline{\kappa}(t)] \exp\left[-\int_0^t r_s(\alpha_0) ds\right] dt \quad (34)$$

where $\Delta Y(t) + S(t)$ denotes utility-metric income plus the consumer surplus at time $t$, and the extra term

$$\kappa(t) = \theta \int_{\alpha_0}^{\alpha_1} \Psi_t(\alpha) \frac{\partial K_t(\alpha)}{\partial \alpha} d\alpha$$

represents the rental cost of capital reallocation (Li and Löfgren, 2010). The expression $\Delta \overline{Y}(t) + \overline{S}(t) - \overline{\kappa}(t)$ is the corresponding money-metric version. This is now summarized in the following proposition:

**Proposition 8** *If the present discounted value of total changes in the sum of NNP, consumer surplus and the (negative) of capital cost over the project period [0, T] as defined in (34), is positive, then the project is socially profitable; otherwise not.*

By integrating equation (12) over $\alpha$ from $\alpha_0$ to $\alpha_1$, we obtain the following expression for the welfare change:

$$\Delta W^* = \int_0^T \int_{\alpha_0}^{\alpha_1} \{\Pi^*(t) d\widetilde{C}(t) + \Psi^*(t) d\widetilde{I}(t)\} \exp(-\theta t) d\alpha dt$$

$$= \lambda_0 \int_0^T \int_{\alpha_0}^{\alpha_1} \{P^*(t) d\widetilde{C}(t) + Q^*(t) d\widetilde{I}(t)\} \exp\left(-\int_0^t r(\tau) d\tau\right) d\alpha dt$$

$$\equiv \lambda_0 \int_0^T WTP(t) \exp\left(-\int_0^t r(\tau) d\tau\right) dt \quad (35)$$

which implies the following dynamic cost–benefit rule without involving any indirect effects:

**Proposition 9** *If the present value of willingness-to-pay for the discrete change* $\Delta \alpha = \alpha_1 - \alpha_0$, $WTP(t) = \int_{\alpha_0}^{\alpha_1} \{P^*(t) d\widetilde{C}(t) + Q^*(t) d\widetilde{I}(t)\} dt$, *over the project period $t \in [0, T]$ is positive, then the project is socially profitable; otherwise not.*

Note that the willingness-to-pay value can be decomposed into two parts, the usual rectangle part corresponding to the value of direct changes in consumption and investment, and the Dupuit consumer surplus part measuring the overall excess of marginal values over costs. Using the same Ramsey-Solow model as in the previous section, we can show how to evaluate a permanent discrete change in $\alpha$ from 0.1 to 0.2. For simplicity, we still use the utility-metric measure for the illustration, and refer the same case number to the corresponding proposition.

**Case 6** *The change in wealth as in (31) is given by*

$$\Delta W_0^* = -\frac{[(1 - \alpha_1)\mu]^{1-\eta}}{\alpha_1\mu(\eta - 1) + \theta} + \frac{[(1 - \alpha_0)\mu]^{1-\eta}}{\alpha_0\mu(\eta - 1) + \theta}. \tag{36}$$

For a change in $\alpha$ from 0.1 to 0.2, we have $\Delta W_0^* \approx 0.39 > 0$, indicating welfare improvement, whereas a change in $\alpha$ from 0.2 to 0.3 leads to $\Delta W_0^* \approx -0.39 < 0$, a welfare deterioration. As compared to the marginal change earlier with $dW_0^*(\alpha)/d\alpha \approx 8.06$, which implies a hypothetical change $\Delta W_0^* = 8.06 \cdot 0.1 \approx 0.81$ for a 0.1 unit increase, the actual increase is 0.39 is smaller. This is because $W_0^*(\alpha)$ is increasing in $\alpha$ over $\alpha \in [0, \alpha^*]$ but at a decreasing rate. While the effect of the first infinitesimal increase from $\alpha = 0.1$ is the largest, subsequent increases in $\alpha$ smaller and smaller effects. When $\alpha = \alpha^* = 0.2$, which is optimal, we have $dW_0^*(\alpha)/d\alpha = 0$.

**Case 7** *The change in NNP and consumer surplus, $\Delta Y + S$, as in (32) is given by*

$$\Delta H_0^* = p_0(\alpha_1)c_0(\alpha_1) + q_0(\alpha_1)\dot{k}_0(\alpha_1)$$

$$- (p_0(\alpha_0)c_0(\alpha_0) + q_0(\alpha_0)\dot{k}_0(\alpha_0)) + \int_{p_0(\alpha_1)}^{p_0(\alpha_0)} D(p)\,dp \tag{37}$$

*where*

$$D(p) = \left(\frac{p}{\eta - 1}\right)^{-\frac{1}{\eta}}$$

*denotes the demand function based on the status quo situation.*

With the numerical values assumed earlier, we have obtained $\Delta H_0^* \approx 0.06 > 0$, indicating that the increase in the saving rate from $\alpha = 0.1$ to 0.2 is welfare improving. What happens if the saving rate $\alpha$ is increased from

0.2 to 0.3 ? We find that $\Delta H_0^* = -0.06 < 0$, indicating a welfare deterioration. For a change over $[0, T]$ for a finite $T$, say, $T = 10$, we apply the last proposition above as:

**Case 8** *The change in the intertemporal welfare at time* 0 *caused by a discrete policy reform* $\Delta\alpha = 0.1$ *is given by*

$$\Delta W^* = \int_0^{10} [\Delta Y(t) + S(t) - \kappa(t)]\exp(-\theta t)\,dt$$

$$\simeq \begin{cases} 0.34 \text{ for } \alpha_0 = 0.1 \\ -0.34 \text{ for } \alpha_0 = 0.3 \end{cases} \tag{38}$$

*indicating that the increase in saving rate from* 0.1 *to* 0.2 *is welfare improving while the increase in saving rate from* 0.2 *to* 0.3 *is welfare deteriorating.*

Note that the welfare change in absolute size is smaller than that from a permanent change with $\Delta\alpha = 0.1$. In this finite period case, saving is increased only over $[0, 10]$ and then shifts back to its original level, which is why the effect is smaller in size. When $T \to \infty$, the size increases from 0.34 to 0.39, as shown above.

**Case 9** *With* $\lambda_0$ *normalized to unity, we have*

$$\lambda_0 \int_0^T WTP(t)\exp\left(-\int_0^t r(\tau)\,d\tau\right)dt,$$

*which has the same value as in (38).*

As shown in Starrett (1988), the willingness-to-pay at time $t$ can be calculated as an integral under the marginal valuation curve bounded by the initial and final quality levels, which corresponds to the sum of all 'component' projects as each is evaluated conditional on the previous one.

## 6  CONCLUDING REMARKS

In this chapter we have provided an interpretive overview of some recent advances in dynamic cost–benefit analysis. First, we presented a conditionally optimal growth model (Weitzman, 2001; Li and Löfgren, 2008) to serve as a theoretical basis for general dynamic welfare comparisons. Then, we presented five equivalent cost–benefit rules for evaluating small projects using differential techniques. In particular, we have shown that the present value of direct changes in comprehensive NNP evaluated at the efficiency prices of consumption and investment is a correct criterion for cost–benefit analysis of small projects. At each point in time, the variation in comprehensive NNP due to direct perturbations in consumption and investment is exactly equal to the corresponding social profit. As all indirect or induced effects are netted out, this new cost–benefit rule may greatly facilitate practical cost–benefit analysis.

To illustrate these rules, we have also employed the well-known Ramsey-Solow model, which was parameterized by Arrow et al. (2003) for sustainability measurement. We have also extended the analysis to accommodate large projects involving price changes by integrating the small project rules. As expected, the resulting dynamic cost–benefit rules entail a consumer surplus term in a similar way to the standard textbook static analysis results. The novelty here lies in the use of the Hamiltonian function as a forward-looking welfare measure based on ideal accounting prices. It is worth mentioning that all the cost–benefit rules in theory are presented both in utility and money metrics. For simplicity, however, we only use the utility-metric measures for the illustrations. The results are exactly the same when the initial benchmark marginal utility is normalized to unity due to the no-arbitrage condition linking the utility and the money rates of discount.

## ACKNOWLEDGEMENTS

The author would like to thank Thomas Aronsson and Karl-Gustaf Löfgren for valuable comments and suggestions. Financial support from the Swedish Research Council FORMAS is gratefully acknowledged. The usual disclaimer applies.

## NOTES

1.  If the parameters were optimized in an ideal economy, there would be no welfare improving project.
2.  The insight that current wealth equals intertemporal welfare was touched upon by Fisher (1906), since the value of current capital stocks should be equal to the capitalization of the whole stream of future consumption values. We will thus use the terms 'wealth' and 'intertemporal welfare' interchangeably throughout this chapter.
3.  In his original contribution, Weitzman (1976) adopted a linear-in-consumption utility function such that the resulting Hamiltonian can be interpreted both as utility and money NNP. Since Kemp and Long's (1982) generalization to utility forms, the Hamiltonian has tended to become known as utility NNP.

4.  Lind (1982) suggested that all future costs and benefits should be converted to their consumption equivalent and then discounted back to the present, which is consistent with this cost–benefit rule. In practice, due to the diminishing present value of long-run future costs and benefits, based on a positive and constant discount rate, the infinite horizon is replaced by a finite one such as 200 years in Stern et al. (2007).
5.  In other words, a generalized version of Fisher's Separation Theorem holds (see Aronsson and Löfgren, 1999). For cost–benefit rules under externalities, see Johansson and Löfgren (1996), Aronsson et al. (1997), and Aronsson and Löfgren (1998).
6.  Note that this is not utility NNP as defined in (6) as the utility part is linearized here.

# REFERENCES

Aronsson, T. Johansson, P.-O. and Löfgren, K.-G. (1997), *Welfare Measurement, Green NNP and Sustainability: A Growth Theoretical Approach*, Cheltenham: Edward Elgar.

Aronsson, T. and Löfgren, K.-G. (1998), Green Accounting in Imperfect Market Economies, *Environment and Resource Economics* 11(3–4), 273–87.

Aronsson, T. and Löfgren, K.-G. (1999), Welfare Equivalent NNP under Distributional Objectives, *Economic Letters* 63, 239–43.

Aronsson, T., Löfgren, K.-G. and Backlund, K. (2004), *Welfare Measurement in Imperfect Markets*, Cheltenham: Edward Elgar.

Arrow, K., Dasgupta, P. and Mäler, K.-G. (2003), Evaluating Projects and Assessing Sustainable Development in Imperfect Economies, *Environmental and Resource Economics* 26, 647–685.

Asheim, G.B. (2000), Green National Accounting: Why and How? *Environment and Development Economics* 5, 25–48.

Dasgupta, P. and K.-G. Mäler (2000), Net National Product, Wealth and Social Well-Being, *Environment and Development Economics* 5, 69–93.

Dasgupta, A.J. and Pearce D.W. (1972), *Cost–Benefit Analysis: Theory and Practice*, New York: Macmillan.

Dixit, A., Hammond, P. and Hoel, M. (1980), On Hartwick's Rule for Regular Maximin Paths of Capital Accumulation and Resource Depletion, *Review of Economic Studies* 47, 551–556.

Drèze, J. and Stern, N.H. (1987), The Theory of Cost–Benefit Analysis, in Auerbach, A.J. and Felstein, M. (eds), *Handbook of Public Economics* chapter 14, Amsterdam: Elsevier.

Eckstein, O. (1958), *Water Resource Development: The Economics of Project Evaluation*, Cambridge, MA: Harvard University Press.

Fisher, I. (1906), *The Nature of Capital and Income*, New York: MacMillan.

Green Book (1950), *Proposed Practices for Economic Analysis of River Basin Projects*. Washington, DC: U.S. Government.

Johansson, P.-O. and Löfgren, K.-G. (1996), On the Interpretation of Green NNP-Measures as Cost–Benefit Rules, *Environment and Resource Economics* 7, 243–50.

Kemp, M.C. and Long, N.V. (1982), On the Evolution of Social Income in a Dynamic Economy: Variations on a Samuelsonian Theme, in Feiwel, G.R. (ed.), *Samuelson and Neoclassical Economics*, Boston, MA: Kluwer-Nijhoff.

Li, C.Z. and Löfgren, K.-G. (2008), Evaluating Projects in a Dynamic Economy: Some New Envelope Results, *German Economic Review* 9, 1–16.

Li, C.Z. and Löfgren, K.G. (2010), Dynamic cost–benefit analysis of large projects: The role of capital cost, *Economics Letters* (forthcoming).

Lind, R.C. (1982), A Primer on the Major Issues Relating to the Discount Rate for Evaluating National Energy Options', in: Lind, R.C., Arrow, K.L., Corey, G.R. (eds), *Discounting for Time and Risk in Energy Policy*, Baltimore, MO: Johns Hopkins University Press, pp. 21–94.

Little, I.M.D., and Mirrlees, J.A. (1974), *Project Appraisal and Planning for Development Countries: Social Cost–Benefit Analysis*, Paris: OECD.

Maass, A. (1962), *Design of Water Resource Systems*, London, Macmillan.

Samuelson, P.A. (1961), The Evaluation of 'Social Income', Capital Formation, and Wealth, in Lutz, F.A. and Hague, D.C. (eds), *The Theory of Capital*, New York: St. Martins Press, chapter 3, pp. 32–57.

Starrett, D.A. (1988), *Foundations of Public Economics*, Cambridge: Cambridge University Press.

Stern, N. (2007), *The Economics of Climate Change*, The Stern Review, London: Cambridge University Press.

Sugden, R. and Williams, A. (1978), *The Principles of Practical Cost–Benefit Analysis*, Oxford: Oxford University Press.

Weitzman, M.L. (1976), On the Welfare Significance of National Product in a Dynamic Economy, *Quarterly Journal of Economics* 90, 156–162.

Weitzman, M.L. (2001), A Contribution to the Theory of Welfare Accounting, *Scandinavian Journal of Economics* 103, 1–24.

# 8 Some dynamic economic consequences of the climate-sensitivity inference dilemma
*Martin L. Weitzman*

## 1 INTRODUCTION

Equilibrium climate sensitivity is a key parameter that serves as a very useful macro-indicator of the eventual aggregate response of temperature change to the aggregate level of greenhouse gases (GHGs). Decades of scientific research have failed to constrain the upper range of climate sensitivity, which means that alarmingly high distant-future temperature responses are not excluded. This chapter highlights a generic statistical-inference mechanism that makes it difficult to thin down to zero inherently fat-tailed probability estimates of rare extreme outcomes.

Let $\Delta \ln CO_2$ be sustained relative change in concentrations of atmospheric carbon dioxide while $\Delta T$ is equilibrium mean global surface temperature response. Equilibrium climate sensitivity (here denoted $\lambda$) is a benchmark amplifying or scaling multiplier for converting $\Delta \ln CO_2$ into $\Delta T$ by the (reasonably accurate) linear approximation $\Delta T \approx (\lambda / \ln 2) \times \Delta \ln CO_2$. As the Intergovernmental Panel on Climate Change in its IPCC-AR4 (2007) Executive Summary phrases it:

> The equilibrium climate sensitivity is a measure of the climate system response to sustained radiative forcing. It is not a projection but is defined as the global average surface warming following a doubling of carbon dioxide concentrations. It is *likely* to be in the range 2 to 4.5° C with a best estimate of 3° C, and is *very unlikely* to be less than 1.5° C. Values substantially higher than 4.5° C cannot be excluded, but agreement of models with observations is not as good for those values (italics in original).

In this chapter I am mostly concerned with the roughly 15 per cent of those $\lambda$ 'values substantially higher than 4.5° C' which 'cannot be excluded'. A grand total of 22 peer-reviewed studies of climate sensitivity published recently in reputable scientific journals and encompassing a wide variety of methodologies (along with 22 imputed probability density functions (PDFs) of $\lambda$) lie indirectly behind the above-quoted IPCC-AR4 (2007) summary statement; they are of that document in Table 9.3 and Box 10.2 listed. It might be argued that these 22 studies are of uneven reliability and their complicatedly-related PDFs cannot easily be combined, but for the simplistic purposes of this illustrative example I do not perform any kind of formal Bayesian model-averaging or meta-analysis (or even engage in informal cherry picking). Instead I just naively assume that all 22 studies have equal credibility and, for my purposes here, that their PDFs can be simplistically aggregated. The upper 5 per cent probability level averaged over all 22 climate-sensitivity studies cited in IPCC-AR4 (2007) is 7° C, while the median is 6.4° C,[1] which I take as signifying approximately that $P[\lambda > 7° C] \approx 5\%$. Looking at the upper tails of these 22 PDFs, one might roughly presume from a simplistically-aggregated PDF of these 22 studies that $P[\lambda > 10° C] \approx 1\%$. Even if my numbers are somewhat off, it still seems apparent that the upper tails of the PDFs of $\lambda$ appear to be long and fat. A fat-tailed PDF assigns a relatively much higher probability to rare events in the extreme tails than does a thin-tailed PDF.[2] Although both limiting probabilities are infinitesimal, the ratio of a thick-tailed probability divided by a thin-tailed probability approaches infinity in the limit.

A critical question is this. Why, after decades of extensive research, do these upper tails of climate sensitivity PDFs seem so intractably long and fat? The climate science literature appears to have coalesced around an answer along the lines that there might be some physical basis for believing that $1 / \lambda$ is approximately normally distributed, which would make $\lambda$ itself have something like a fat-tailed Cauchy-Lorentz PDF. As a story about feedback processes and measurement errors, some of this logic can make sense and it provides some much-needed insight into the physical nature of an issue that is crucially important for understanding a key driver of global warming. However, as a story about statistical inference, this reasoning is partial and incomplete in the sense that it appears to rely on a very specific data generating process (DGP) that is not fully rigorously specified – nor does this story pinpoint formally what exactly is the relevant problem here of prediction under uncertainty. In this chapter, I suggest that the core logic behind a fat-tailed PDF of climate sensitivity perhaps transcends the underlying physics and may even be more generic than somewhat partial reasoning about the properties of ratios of random variables in a particular DGP. I argue that the relevant posterior-predictive PDF of virtually *any* high-impact low-probability rare event has a deeply built-in tendency to be fat tailed – almost irrespective of the underlying DGP. When these fat tails matter because catastrophic damages have essentially unlimited liability – as with climate change – this aspect is capable of driving the economic analysis.

The essence of the climate sensitivity dilemma highlighted in this chapter is the difficulty of learning extreme-impact tail behavior from finite data alone. Loosely speaking, the driving mechanism is that the operation of taking 'expectations of expectations' or 'probability distributions of probability distributions' spreads apart and fattens the tails of the reduced-form compounded posterior-predictive PDF. It is inherently difficult to determine extreme bad-tail probabilities from finite samples alone because, by definition, we don't get many data-point observations of infrequent events. Therefore, rare disasters located in the stretched-out fattened tails of such posterior-predictive distributions must inherently contain an irreducibly large component of deep structural uncertainty. The underlying sampling-theory principle is that the rarer an event, the more unsure is our estimate of its probability of occurrence – and the larger the sample size required to rule it out for practical purposes. In this spirit (from being constructed out of inductive knowledge), the empirical studies of climate sensitivity are perhaps pre-ordained to find the fat-tailed power-law-like PDFs which they seem, approximately, to find in practice.

Climate sensitivity is not nearly the same thing as temperature change. In previous work,[3] I tried to fudge the distinction by arguing that the shapes of both PDFs are very roughly similar because a doubling of anthropogenically injected $CO_2$-equivalent greenhouse gases (GHGs) relative to pre-industrial-revolution levels is essentially unavoidable within about the next 40–50 years and the GHGs are very likely to remain well above this level for at least the subsequent century or so after first attaining it. But such a discrete two-period formulation suppresses the continuous-time dimension by ignoring the fact that higher $\Delta T$ values are (continuously) correlated with later times of arrival. This chapter addresses more centrally the relationship between dynamic $\Delta T$ trajectories and climate sensitivity. I show that a previous two-period result, that fat-tailed climate sensitivity can have strong economic implications, survives being recast into a more complete dynamic specification, even though (other things being equal) the higher the temperature realization, the later this temperature realization is expected to arrive. When fat climate-sensitivity tails are combined with very uncertain high-temperature damage, this aspect can dominate the discounting aspect in calculations of expected present discounted utility – even at empirically plausible real-world interest rates and even when taking full account of the important continuous correlation that, conditional upon its realization, the higher the temperature, the later is its expected time of arrival.

A central theme of this line of research is that with finite data, it is practically inevitable that rare extreme events will have fat tails. These fat tails, which stubbornly resist the accumulation of finite data, reflect back at us our own prior ignorance concerning how to model or represent or quantify rare extreme events. My message is that we must learn to live with the idea that the answers to cost–benefit analyses of what to do about climate change may very well depend – at least to some degree – upon subjective judgments about how bad it might get, with what probabilities, in the most extreme situations.

## 2   A DYNAMIC AGGREGATIVE MODEL OF GLOBAL WARMING

This section compresses into a single differential equation what is arguably the simplest meaningful dynamic model of the physical process of global warming. Of course this particular one-equation model cannot possibly capture the full complexity of climate change. However, I think the highly aggregated approach taken here is realistic enough to serve as a spring-board for meaningful discussions of some basic climate change issues which, for the purposes of this chapter, are actually clarified when tightly framed in such stark simplicity.

Perhaps the single most useful concept for understanding the process of climate change is that of radiative forcing. GHGs such as $CO_2$ are prime examples of this, but there are many others, such as solar intensity, aerosols and particulates. (The radiative forcing from $CO_2$ happens to be proportional to the logarithm of its atmospheric concentration, but this is not true in general for all forcings.) A key property of radiative forcings is that the various components and subcomponents can be aggregated simply by adding them all up because they combine additively.

Suppose for simplicity that throughout times $t < 0$, the planetary climate system has been in a state of long-run equilibrium at a constant temperature with constant radiative forcing. Imagine that starting at time $t = 0$, and continuing throughout times $t \geq 0$ a sustained perturbation (relative to times $t < 0$) of radiative forcing of constant magnitude $\Delta R_f$ has been additionally imposed. (Whether this constant additional radiative forcing $\Delta R_f$ is itself exogenous or endogenous is irrelevant in this context because only the reduced-form total forcing matters here.) If the earth were a black body planet with no atmosphere and no further feed-backs, the long-run temperature response would be $\Delta T \rightarrow \lambda_0 \Delta R_f$, where $\lambda_0$ is the feedback-free equilibrium-climate-sensitivity constant defined by the fundamental physics of a black-body reference system described by the Stefan-Boltzman law. Even in richer, more realistic situations with feed-backs and complicated dynamics, other things being equal, it is not a bad assumption that at any time $t$ the temperature moves with an instantane-ous velocity approximately proportional to $\lambda_0 \Delta R_f(t) - \Delta T(t)$ – that is, the (linearized) basic equation of temperature motion is

$$\dot{T} = \frac{1}{h}[\lambda_0 \Delta R_f(t) - \Delta T(t)].\tag{1}$$

The positive coefficient $h$ in (1) represents the thermal inertia of the system, in this application primarily standing for the overall planetary capacity of slab-like oceans to take up heat.

The full temperature dynamics of this idealized planetary system can then most simply be described as follows. At time $t \geq 0$, suppose that a system previously in long-run equilibrium is now subjected to an exogenously imposed radiative forcing of $\Delta F(t)$. Let the total change in radiative forcing at time $t \geq 0$ be denoted $\Delta R_f(t)$. If the endogenously induced radiative forcing at time $t \geq 0$ is denoted $\Delta R_i(t)$, then

$$\Delta R_f(t) = \Delta F(t) + \Delta R_i(t).\tag{2}$$

In a simple linear feedback system applied to the problem at hand, the temperature change $\Delta T(t)$ causes a comparatively fast-acting (relative to (1)) endogenous feedback response on induced radiative forcing $\Delta R_i(t)$ according to the formula

$$\Delta R_i(t) = \frac{f}{\lambda_0}\Delta T(t),\tag{3}$$

where the (linear) feedback factor $f$ is a basic parameter of the system. The relevant feedback factors in climate change involve cloud formation, water vapor, albedo, among others. A key property of linear feedback factors is that (as with radiative forcing) the various components and sub-components can be aggregated simply by adding them all up because they combine additively.

Plugging (3) and (2) into (1) yields after simplification the fundamental differential equation

$$\dot{T} = \frac{1}{h}[\lambda_0 \Delta F(t) - (1 - f)\Delta T(t)],\tag{4}$$

whose solution is

$$\Delta T(t) = \frac{\lambda_0}{h}\int_0^t \Delta F(s)\exp\left(-\left(\frac{1-f}{h}\right)(t-s)\right)ds.\tag{5}$$

The oversimplifications of physical reality that have gone into the one-equation temperature change trajectory (5) are too numerous and too tedious to recount here. There is only one major defence of this ultra-macro approach: it seems fair to say that (5) captures the dynamic inter-play of forces along a global-warming path better than any alternative single-differential-equation formula. If we want a sharply focused formu-lation of the big moving picture of a dynamic global-warming trajectory in terms of its primary contributing ingredients, then we are pretty much stuck with (5).

In what follows, it will be analytically convenient to work with the special case where exogenously imposed radiative forcing is constant, so that for all times, $t \geq 0$,

$$\Delta F(t) = \overline{F}, \tag{6}$$

which simplifies (5) into

$$\Delta T(t) = \frac{\lambda_0}{1 - f} \overline{F} \left[ 1 - \exp\left( -\left( \frac{1 - f}{h} \right) t \right) \right]. \tag{7}$$

For notational neatness, assume that all units are expressed in terms of a doubling of $CO_2$. The equilibrium climate sensitivity is then defined as

$$\lambda \equiv \lim_{t \to \infty} \frac{\Delta T(t)}{\overline{F}}, \tag{8}$$

and it is readily apparent from applying (8) to (7) that

$$\lambda = \frac{\lambda_0}{1 - f}, \tag{9}$$

which is one of the most basic relationships of climate change.

Even accepting the enormous oversimplifications of reality that go into an equation like (5) (or (7)), there remain massive uncertainties concern-ing the appropriate values of the structural parameters. The critical feed-back parameter $f$ (and hence, by (9), climate sensitivity $\lambda$) is perhaps the biggest uncertainty in the system. While this chapter concentrates on this particular uncertainty, it should be appreciated that the relevant values of $h$ and of past forcings $\{\Delta F(s)\}$ are also very uncertain. Just glancing at equation (5) is highly suggestive of why it is so difficult in practice to infer $f$ (or $\lambda$) directly from data. The record of past natural forcing experi-ments is extremely noisy and such components as aerosol concentrations are notoriously difficult to identify. Furthermore, it is readily shown that the first-order response of a system like (5) to a change in forcings does not involve long-run parameters like $f$ (or $\lambda$) at all, but more centrally concerns the overall ability of the oceans to take up heat as embodied in the thermal inertia coefficient $h$, which itself is not very well known in this aggregative context. It is statistically very difficult to distinguish between a high-$f$ low-$h$ world and a low-$f$ high-$h$ world. To be able to deduce $f$ (or $\lambda$) at all precisely would require a long and fairly accurate time series of past natural forcings along with a decent knowledge of the relevant thermal inertia – none of which is readily available. A more detailed look at how most scientists frame and view the difficulty of inferring climate sensitivity is examined in the next section.

## 3 WHY IS CLIMATE SENSITIVITY SO UNPREDICTABLE?

The title of this section is taken from the title of an influential recent *Science* article by Roe and Baker (2007), which highlights nicely the core dilemma here. Their explanation overlaps in its logic and spirit with a long series of preceding scientific insights that were similar in tone but were less formally articulated. The starting point for this genre of explanations is the observation that forcings $\Delta F$ and feedback factors $f$ are both linearly additive in individual subcomponents, while neither temperature responses $\Delta T$ nor climate sensitivity $\lambda$ display this linear additivity property.

What bothers scientists most about the climate-sensitivity issue is that, even after some three decades of intensive research, almost no progress has been made on providing a meaningful upper bound for climate sensitivity. I would argue that this concern is somewhat misstated and perhaps even misdirected. It is not the absence of an absolute upper bound on climate sensitivity per se that is disturbing or, for that matter, even mysterious. The absence of an upper bound on $\lambda$ just means that the right tail of the corresponding climate-sensitivity PDF is very long and stretched out because very high values cannot absolutely be ruled out. However, it is not the length of the right tail PDF that is disturbing for policy implications, but rather its thickness. A great many catastrophic possibilities in our world have long tails, but we do not worry about them because we may have some reason to believe that these long tails are thin with probability and their asymptotic PDFs converge rapidly towards zero. The real problem with estimated climate sensitivity PDFs is that the right tail is too 'fat' (or 'thick' or 'heavy') with probability to allow us to feel comfortable with our current state of knowledge. In this sense, the scientific concern about the lack of an absolute upper bound on climate sensitivity is somewhat misconstrued because the real issue is not that the right upper tail is too long (which only means that high values are empirically or theoretically conceivable) but that it is too fat (which means that high values are possible with uncomfortably large probabilities). Although the scientists themselves do not make a distinction between tails that are too long and tails that are too fat, in this section I restate their explanations in terms of the more substantive and more genuinely disturbing issue of why the upper tail of the PDF of climate sensitivity is so fat with probability (as opposed to being so stretched out or long or unbounded).

Inferences about climate sensitivity come from two broad classes or categories of studies. The first group is computer simulations of large-scale climate models with randomized parameters. The second group is noisy observations of past natural experiments via proxies that essentially mimic $\Delta T/\Delta F$. I begin with the first category.

Roe and Baker (2007) come at the climate-sensitivity estimation problem from the perspective of the first category of perturbed-physics simulations of large ensembles of computer models. In computer-simulated numerical modeling of climate, there are hundreds of parameters governing all manner of minute details, such as fall speed of raindrops, how reflectivity changes as snow ages, exchange of turbulent fluxes in the boundary layer, evapotranspiration through plant roots, and so forth. In most cases, these uncertain parameters represent not-directly-observable 'effective' coefficients that are stochastically perturbed in the simulations – and the physical meaning of what they actually represent can be quite unclear. The major feedback parameters that climate scientists typically analyze (water vapor/lapse rate, clouds, surface albedo and so forth) are some very complicated functions of obscure combinations of model parameters. The climate system has complex, non-linear, and even chaotic features.

Despite these non-linear complications and the overall messiness of climate dynamics, Roe and Baker (2007) argue that in practice, feedbacks still combine more-or-less additively. If

$$f = \sum_{j=1}^{m} f_j \tag{10}$$

and if each feedback sub-factor $f_j$ is distributed more-or-less independently of the other feedback sub-factors, then if $m$ is large enough and each $f_j$ is small enough, by the central limit theorem, the overall feedback factor $f$ is distributed approximately normally. The argument closes by noting that climate sensitivity $\lambda$ defined by (9) is then basically distributed as one over a normal PDF, which is essentially a skewed Cauchy-Lorentz-like distribution which has a long upper tail. As I have indicated, I think the real issue here is that this PDF has a fat upper tail (not that it is long). In my version of this story, the upper tail of the Cauchy-Lorentz-like PDF of $\lambda$ is fat because it behaves asymptotically like a power-law distribution $\propto 1/\lambda^2$. (To make the story airtight, one must set aside issues about values of $f$ greater than one, or dividing by zero, or artificial truncations, which, alas, are far from being trivial details because how they are resolved can substantially alter the logic of the argument and its conclusions. Furthermore, the independence assumption is suspicious because of likely negative correlations among the $f_j$, analogous to temperature-constrained $f$ being negatively correlated with $h$ – more on this later.)

Turning to the second category of empirical measurements, a less formal version of what seems generically to be a very similar story to the above Roe-Baker version (of why it is difficult to obtain an upper bound on climate sensitivity) has been present in the scientific literature for some time now. This long-present story concerns noisy observations of past natural experiments by proxies that essentially mimic $\Delta T$ and $\Delta F$, from which $1/\lambda$ is essentially estimated as $\Delta F/\Delta T$. For concreteness, I use the recent formulation in an influential survey article by Allen et al. (2006) entitled *Observational Constraints on Climate Sensitivity*. The mechanism behind this story is analogous to the underlying mechanism of the Roe-Baker story except that here $\Delta F$ plays the role of $f$ and $\Delta T$ plays the role of $\lambda$. Again, the key point of departure is that even though the climate system has complex, non-linear, and even chaotic features, in practice observed changes in radiative forcings still combine more or less additively. If

$$\Delta F = \sum_{j=1}^{m} \Delta F_j \tag{11}$$

and if each radiative sub-forcing $\Delta F_j$ is distributed more-or-less independently of the other radiative sub-forcings, then if $m$ is large enough and each $\Delta F_j$ is small enough, by the central limit theorem, the overall radiative forcing $\Delta F$ is distributed approximately normally.

If one writes

$$\Delta F = \frac{1}{\lambda} \Delta T \tag{12}$$

then, it is further asserted by Allen et al., that the dominant uncertainties in empirical observations are on the left-hand side of equation (12) because empirical uncertainty in measured or inferred $\Delta T$ is typically much smaller than empirical uncertainty in measured or inferred forcings. This line of reasoning – normal measurement errors on noisy observations of $\Delta F$ – strongly suggests estimating the coefficient $1/\lambda$ in (12) by regressing observations of $\Delta F$ as the dependent variable on observations of $\Delta T$

as the independent variable. (There is nothing inherently wrong with this approach so long as one keeps in mind that the causality we actually believe in, which is also what we need for prediction purposes, goes in the reverse direction: $\Delta F \rightarrow \Delta T$.) In the case of regressing $\Delta F$ on $\Delta T$ in (12), if the variance of the error term were known, then under standard Bayesian assumptions, the posterior-predictive distribution of $1/\lambda$ would be normal. Once again, the argument is concluded by noting that climate sensitivity $\lambda$ is then distributed as one over a normal PDF; this, again setting aside issues about negative values or dividing by zero or artificial truncations (that, unfortunately for this argument, are actually substantial), is essentially a skewed Cauchy-Lorentz-like distribution with a long upper tail. And once more the real issue is that this Cauchy-Lorentz-like distribution has a fat upper tail (not that it is long per se), which comes about because this inverted-normal PDF tail behaves asymptotically like a power-law distribution $\propto 1/\lambda^2$.

In the previous paragraph, I have done my best to represent accurately what I think is the prevailing scientific wisdom about why there are observational constraints causing the PDF of climate sensitivity to have a fat upper tail. Alas, I fear this physical reasoning may be somewhat incomplete as stated and perhaps is not even fully rigorous. In what follows, I try to give a more careful rendition of the core inference-prediction problem. Interpreted carefully, the above-stated idea that there are normally-distributed measurement errors on noisy observations of $\Delta F$ translates (12) into a statement about the conditional PDF of $\Delta F$ given $\Delta T$, where both random variables are drawn from some as-yet-unspecified DGP whose joint realizations are bivariate observations of $(\Delta F, \Delta T)$. The formally correct linear-normal translation here is that given any realized value of $\Delta T$, the conditional PDF of $\Delta F$ is

$$\Delta F | \Delta T \sim \mathcal{N}(a + b\Delta T, \nu). \tag{13}$$

However, what we are really interested in for climate-change prediction is not (13), but rather the PDF of $\Delta T | \Delta F$. In other words, what we really want to know is what happens to $\Delta T$ for a given postulated $\Delta F$. It cannot be stressed strongly enough that there is simply no way to infer the PDF of $\Delta T | \Delta F$ from a knowledge of the PDF of $\Delta F | \Delta T$ alone. Essentially, one is required additionally to postulate some knowledge of the bivariate DGP that is jointly generating the observed values of $(\Delta F, \Delta T)$. To illustrate what is involved in this kind of inference-prediction problem as applied to climate change, pretend for the sake of analytical simplicity that the PDF of empirical observations of $(\Delta F, \Delta T)$ is bivariate normal. This is undoubtedly not literally true, but the bivariate normal assumption will serve here to highlight crisply the critical inference-prediction problems involved in explaining why climate sensitivity is so unpredictable – here taken as meaning that the climate sensitivity PDF has a thick upper tail.

Suppose, then, that the complete DGP (data generating process) of what has been measured in past noisy observations is postulated to be bivariate normal in $(\Delta F, \Delta T)$, which (using standard notation) is equivalent to having the key properties:

$$\Delta F \sim \mathcal{N}(\mu_F, \sigma_F^2), \tag{14}$$

$$\Delta T \sim \mathcal{N}(\mu_T, \sigma_T^2), \tag{15}$$

$$\Delta F \mid \Delta T \sim \mathcal{N}\left(\mu_F + \rho \frac{\sigma_F}{\sigma_T}[\Delta T - \mu_T], \sigma_F^2(1 - \rho^2)\right), \tag{16}$$

$$\Delta T \mid \Delta F \sim \mathcal{N}\left(\mu_T + \rho \frac{\sigma_T}{\sigma_F}[\Delta F - \mu_F], \sigma_T^2(1 - \rho^2)\right), \tag{17}$$

$$\rho = \frac{E[(\Delta T - \mu_T)(\Delta F - \mu_F)]}{\sigma_T \sigma_F}. \tag{18}$$

Notice that (16) has the same form as (13), where $a \equiv \mu_F - \rho\sigma_F\mu_T/\sigma_T$, $b \equiv \rho\sigma_F/\sigma_T$, $v \equiv \sigma_F^2(1 - \rho^2)$. However, the incomplete logic involved in trying to infer the tail properties of the PDF of climate sensitivity as anything like the reciprocal of the PDF of $b$ from (13) (which is like trying to infer the tail properties of $\Delta T \mid \Delta F$ from the PDF of $\Delta F \mid \Delta T$ alone) becomes apparent once the entire DGP has been carefully specified – as, for example, in (14)–(18) above.

Once granted that the observed data is being generated by independent draws from the bivariate normal distribution in equations (14)–(18), there is no question but that the critical equation we are interested in for predicting the temperature-change response to a given change in forcing is (17). The bivariate normal system in equations (14)–(18) is telling us the overall DGP for the noisy observations we are measuring in the past data from natural forcing experiments. We are not really interested in this full noise-generating DGP (14)–(18) as an end in itself. For example, we are not really interested in identifying all five parameters in the five-equation system (14)–(18). We are only interested in predicting as accurately as possible what will be the noise-free true future temperature response to a hypothetically known noise-free true change in radiative forcing. Given the model assumptions, this best predictor will come only from regression estimation of (17), irrespective of the rest of the bivariate-normal DGP system (14)–(18).

If we want to conceptualize some 'true' value of climate sensitivity $\lambda$ that is hidden from us by noisy disturbances via errors of measurement or observation (and most scientists seem to prefer to think this way), a natural interpretation of how to estimate $\lambda$ is as follows. Suppose $\lambda$ were known. In the absence of any errors of measurement or observation, the true relationship is that a known 'true' change in constant radiative forcing $\Delta F^*$ would induce (for each parametrically fixed value of $\Delta F^*$) a known 'true' equilibrium temperature response $\Delta T^*$ according to the linear-proportional (but not affine) formula

$$\Delta T^* \,|\, \Delta F^* = \lambda \Delta F^*. \tag{19}$$

The 'true' value of $\lambda$ in equation (19) is the Holy Grail of climate sensitivity we seek, since knowing it would allow us to predict the equilibrium temperature response to various radiative forcings corresponding to various GHG scenarios. The only way that the standard scientific linear description (19) can be made compatible with (17) is by imposing on (17) the a priori known (on the basis of scientific first principles) additional constraint that the affine term is zero:

$$\mu_T - \rho \frac{\sigma_T}{\sigma_F}\mu_F = 0, \tag{20}$$

in which case (17) becomes transformed into

$$\Delta T \,|\, \Delta F \sim \mathcal{N}(\lambda \Delta F, V), \tag{21}$$

where simple algebra then shows that $\lambda = \mu_T/\mu_F$ and $V = \sigma_T^2(1 - \rho^2)$, neither of which is directly observable.

If we are allowed to imagine that the noisy observations come in the form of $n$ independent realizations from the bivariate normal DGP described by equations (14)–(18), then the DGP for observation $i$ ($i = 1, 2, \ldots, n$) of (21) can be written in the familiar linear-normal regression form

$$\Delta T_i = \lambda \Delta F_i + \varepsilon_i, \tag{22}$$

where each 'error term' $\varepsilon_i$ is independent identically distributed $\mathcal{N}(0, V)$. Interestingly, fat tails on the posterior-predictive distribution of $\lambda$ also emerge from this more complete description of the DGP via the following tail-fattening mechanism. Let $\hat{\lambda}$ be the least-squares estimator

$$\hat{\lambda} = \frac{\sum_{i=1}^{n} \Delta T_i \Delta F_i}{\sum_{i=1}^{n} \Delta F_i^2}, \tag{23}$$

where the sample variance is

$$\hat{V} = \frac{1}{n} \sum_{i=1}^{n} (\Delta T_i - \hat{\lambda} \Delta F_i)^2. \tag{24}$$

Under standard Bayesian reference prior assumptions, the posterior-predictive distribution of $\lambda$ is Student-$t$ with $n - 1$ degrees of freedom:

$$\phi(\lambda) \propto \left( 1 + \frac{(\lambda - \hat{\lambda})^2}{\hat{V}} \right)^{-(n+1)/2}. \tag{25}$$

The Student-$t$ PDF (35) is fat-tailed for all $n < \infty$, displaying the asymptotic behavior of a power law in $\lambda$ with exponent $n + 1$. The fatness of the tails is directly proportional to $\hat{V}$ and inversely proportional to $n$, so that the empirical real-world fact that the upper tail of climate sensitivity is actually very fat traces back to a relative scarcity of independent observations ($n$ is small) combined with very noisy observations ($\hat{V}$ is large).

The above reasoning is just one specific example of a generic argument that when you are trying to infer the value of a parameter way outside the range of usual experience or data, you end up with a thick-tailed posterior-predictive distribution. This thick tail reflects back the underlying thickness of the standard non-informative reference family of priors. The posterior-predictive distribution is more thin in proportion to the number of observations, but it is still technically thick for any given $n$. I have already explained this mechanism in some detail in earlier work and don't elaborate further here.[4] What I think all of this shows is that a careful restatement of the Allen et al. (2006) argument still produces fat tails, although by a somewhat different mechanism than the original one they had in mind.

The Roe and Baker tail-fattening mechanism may appear to be along slightly different lines, but I think it is ultimately more similar than different. Something suspicious is happening there when $f \approx 1$ because we don't really believe it is easily physically possible to have $f > 1$ on the grounds that this would result in limitless runaway warming. So probably there is some prior information restricting $f = \Sigma f_j$ from being greater than one. In other words, if a bunch of $f_j$ values are big, then a bunch of other $f_j$ values should be small in order to compensate and keep $f$ from being greater than one. This is somewhat analogous to the argument that observed temperature constrains $f$ and $h$ to be negatively correlated. It means the $f_j$ are not independently distributed and the appeal to the central limit theorem is suspect. But the very complicated macro interactions restricting $f = \Sigma f_j < 1$ are not well modeled by the micro assumption that the $f_j$ are independently distributed. The Roe and Baker story may be a good mechanical description of where the long thick tail is coming from in the simulations that human beings perform on computers, but the physics behind the independence of micro $f_j$ within the simulations is questionable because it is inconsistent with the macro-physics that $f < 1$.

I think that the Roe and Baker tail-fattening mechanism and my tail-fattening mechanism explained above are more similar than different in the following sense. In both situations, we don't know how to represent things far outside the range of average experience. In both cases, the thick tails are coming from prior assumptions built into the modeling process rather than from hard science that justifies these assumptions. In both cases, the fat tails reflect more these prior assumptions than any actual empirical knowledge of overall system behavior in that extreme region where $f$ is close to one and $\lambda$ is very big.

I would emphasize that none of this dependence on subjective prior modeling assumptions makes the problem any less real. To make economic decisions today, we must work with the fat posterior-predictive distributions, which are all coming essentially from lack of prior knowledge about extreme values, reinforced by lack of empirical experience with extreme values. Throughout the rest of the chapter I just assume that the PDF of climate sensitivity $\lambda$ has a thick upper tail – for whatever reason – and examine the consequences for the economics of climate change. Thus, in what follows, the PDF of $\lambda$, which is denoted $\varphi(\lambda)$, is presumed to have an upper tail that declines to zero less rapidly than exponentially (for example, polynomially, as with a power-law PDF).

## 4   ECONOMIC DYNAMICS OF FAT-TAILED TEMPERATURES

From (5) it is immediately apparent that, other things being equal, at any given time, higher values of $f$ (and hence of $\lambda$) imply higher values of $\Delta T$. However, it is also true that higher values of $\lambda$ (or of $f$) make the system take a longer time for $\Delta T$ to reach its long-run equilibrium value. To examine this issue more closely, suppose in what follows that the planet has been subject to a sustained doubling of $CO_2$. With the convention being followed here that all units are expressed in terms of a doubling of

$CO_2$, this means that $\bar{F} = 1$. Substituting $\bar{F} = 1$ and (9) into (7), the time trajectory of temperature change (expressed in terms of $\lambda$) becomes

$$\Delta T_\lambda(t) = \lambda\left[1 - \exp\left(-\frac{\lambda_0 t}{h\lambda}\right)\right]. \tag{26}$$

Equation (26) indicates that $\Delta T \to \lambda$. The question I now examine is length of the time it takes for $\Delta T$ to attain the fraction $\alpha$ of $\lambda$, where $0 < \alpha < 1$. Call this time $t_\alpha(\lambda)$. From (26), $t_\alpha(\lambda)$ must obey the equation

$$\alpha\lambda = \lambda\left[1 - \exp\left(-\frac{\lambda_0 t_\alpha(\lambda)}{h\lambda}\right)\right], \tag{27}$$

which can be rewritten as

$$t_\alpha(\lambda) = \psi(\alpha)\lambda, \tag{28}$$

where

$$\psi(\alpha) = \frac{h}{\lambda_0}(-\ln(1 - \alpha)). \tag{29}$$

From (28), it is apparent that $t_\alpha(\lambda) \propto \lambda$. Thus, for any given $\alpha$, the larger the climate sensitivity $\lambda$, the longer it takes for the system to attain the temperature change $\Delta T = \alpha\lambda$. Nevertheless, if the PDF of $\lambda$ is fat-tailed at the upper end, then eventually there is a positive probability of $\Delta T$ becoming unboundedly high. The formal statement of this possibility is that for any value of $T'$, however large, there exists some time $t'$ such that $t > t'$ implies $P[\Delta T(t) > T'] > 0$. The question I now seek to address is what this possibility of very high temperatures arriving at very distant times does to economic welfare analysis. The answer depends (among many other things) on what is assumed about damage at very high temperatures.

Most existing Integrated Assessment Models (IAMs) treat high-temperature damage by an extremely casual extrapolation of whatever specification is arbitrarily assumed to be the low-temperature 'damage function'. The high-temperature 'damage function' extrapolated from the low-temperature 'damage function' is remarkably sensitive to assumed them because an extraordinarily wide variety of them can be made to fit virtually identically the low-temperature damage that has been assumed by the modeler. In the IAM literature, most damage functions reduce welfare-equivalent consumption by the quadratic-polynomial multiplier $1/[1 + \gamma(\Delta T)^2]$ with $\gamma$ calibrated to some postulated loss for

$\Delta T \approx 2-3°$ C. There was never any more compelling rationale in the first place for this particular loss function than the comfort that economists feel from having worked with it before. In other words, the quadratic-polynomial specification is being used to assess climate-change damages for no better reason than casual familiarity with this particular form from other cost-of-adjustment dynamic economic models, where it had been used primarily for its analytical simplicity.

I would argue strongly on a priori grounds that if, for some unfathomable reason, climate-change economists want dependence of damages to be a function of $(\Delta T)^2$, then a far better choice of functional form at high temperatures for a welfare-equivalent quadratic-based consumption-loss multiplier is the exponential form $\exp(-\gamma(\Delta T)^2)$. Why? Look at the specification choice abstractly. What might be called the 'attenuating pressure' on welfare (denoted $A$) is arriving here as the arbitrarily imposed quadratic form $A(\Delta T) = (\Delta T)^2$, around which some further structure is imposed to convert it into utility units. With isoelastic utility, the exponential specification is equivalent to $dU/U \propto dA$, while for high $A$ the polynomial specification is equivalent to $dU/U \propto dA/A$. For me it is obvious that, between the two, the former is much superior to the latter. Why should the impact of $dA$ on $dU/U$ be artificially and unaccountably diluted through dividing $dA$ by high values of $A$ in the latter case? The same argument applies to any polynomial in $\Delta T$. Of course I cannot prove that my favored choice here is the more reasonable of the two functional forms for high $\Delta T$ (although I truly believe that it is), but no one can disprove it either – and *this* is the point.

The value of $\gamma$ required for calibrating welfare-equivalent consumption at $\Delta T = 3°$ C to be, say, 98 per cent of consumption at $\Delta T = 0°$ C is so miniscule that both the polynomial-quadratic multiplier $1/[1 + \gamma(\Delta T)^2]$ and the exponential-quadratic multiplier $\exp(-\gamma(\Delta T)^2)$ give virtually identical outcomes for relatively small values of $\Delta T \leq 5°$ C, but at ever higher temperatures, they gradually yet ever-increasingly diverge. With a fat-tailed PDF of $\lambda$ and a very long time horizon, there can be a big difference between these two functional forms in the implied willingness to pay (WTP) to avoid or reduce uncertainty in $\Delta T$. I next calculate the WTP to avoid uncertain $\Delta T$ when the consumption-loss welfare-equivalent quadratic-based multiplier is of the exponential form $\exp(-\gamma(\Delta T)^2)$. In what follows I use a utility function of the constant elasticity form

$$U(C) = \frac{C^{1-\eta}}{1 - \eta}, \tag{30}$$

where the coefficient of relative risk aversion is $\eta > 1$ and $C(0)$ is normalized to unity.

Suppose the economy grows at a given rate $g > 0$. The rate of pure time preference is $\delta > 0$. Suppose there is some arbitrarily-imposed time horizon $H$. The random variable of climate sensitivity $\lambda$ has a thick upper tail in its PDF $\varphi(\lambda)$. The base case thought experiment here is a doubling of $CO_2$ beginning at time zero. I now ask: what is the WTP – in terms of a constant fraction of consumption foregone at all times $t$ between 0 and $H$ – to avoid altogether this temperature uncertainty? The answer as a function of the time horizon is denoted here as $WTP(H)$.

Making use of (28), (29) and (30), $WTP(H)$ must satisfy the condition:

$$\frac{\displaystyle\int_0^H ((1 - WTP(H))\exp(gt))^{1-\eta}\exp(-\delta t)\,dt}{1 - \eta}$$

$$= \frac{\displaystyle\int_0^1 \left[\int_0^{H/\psi(\alpha)} (\exp(gt_\alpha(\lambda) - \gamma\alpha^2\lambda^2))^{1-\eta}\exp(-\delta t_\alpha(\lambda))\varphi(\lambda)\,d\lambda\right]d\alpha}{1 - \eta} \quad (31)$$

As $H \to \infty$, it is not difficult to show that with a fat tail in $\varphi(\lambda)$, the integral on the right-hand side of (31) approaches $-\infty$ because the term in $\exp(-\gamma\alpha^2\lambda^2)$ dominates everything else. This fact in turn implies that

$$\lim_{H\to\infty} WTP(H) = 1. \quad (32)$$

When the consumption-reducing welfare-equivalent damage multiplier has the exponential form $\exp(-\gamma(\Delta T)^2)$, then as the horizon $H \to \infty$, the above result (32) implies at the limit that the WTP to avoid (or even reduce) fat-tailed uncertainty in $\Delta T$ approaches 100 per cent of consumption. This does not mean, of course, that we should be spending 100 per cent of consumption to eliminate the climate-change problem. But this example does highlight the remarkable ability of miniscule refinements of the damage function (when combined with fat tails) to dominate climate-change cost–benefit analysis – and the remarkable fragility of policy advice coming out of conventional thin-tailed IAMs with polynomial damage.

I think this example shows that a previous two-period result that fat-tailed climate sensitivity can have strong economic implications survives being recast as a more complete dynamic specification, even though (other things being equal) the higher the temperature realization, the later this temperature realization is expected to arrive. When fat climate-sensitivity tails are combined with very uncertain high-temperature damage, this aspect can dominate the discounting aspect in calculations of expected present discounted utility – even at empirically plausible real-world interest rates and even when taking full account of the important continuous correlation that, conditional upon its realization, the higher the temperature, the later its expected time of arrival.

The model I have used throughout this chapter for the sake of analytical sharpness is so incredibly oversimplified that it can legitimately be criticized on an enormous number of counts as being grossly unrealistic. The temperature dynamics is primitive, climate change involves much more than an instantaneous doubling of atmospheric $CO_2$, the utility function may be wrong (especially for low consumption), results depend on the postulated exponential-quadratic damage function, policy is much richer than a double-or-nothing $CO_2$ decision, there is some possibility of learning and adaptive mitigation (although the inertial commitment of GHGs already in the pipeline is distressingly long), technological change is ignored, and so forth and so on. Nevertheless, I believe that a fair conclusion from this example is that any economic analysis of climate change that does *not* include an explicit treatment of rare climate catastrophes (no matter how far off in the future they may occur) is problematic and its policy conclusions are under a dark cloud until this fat-tailed disaster aspect is modeled explicitly and addressed seriously.

## 5　CONCLUSION

This chapter has two main goals. The first goal is an attempt to place the physical-science measurement-based discussion of why climate sensitivity is so unpredictable into a broader context of statistical inference, prediction and decision making. Here the chapter makes two basic points: (1) it is not the fact that it is difficult to place an upper bound on climate sensitivity that is worrisome, but rather the fact that the upper tail of its PDF is fat with probability; and (2) the fatness of the upper tail of the PDF of climate sensitivity comes primarily from being generically built into any situation where we are trying to estimate the probabilities of rare outlier events from limited data based on incomplete structural knowledge.

The second goal of the chapter is to show that previous findings from a two-period discrete-time formulation survive the introduction of continuous time and more realistic dynamics that take explicit account of the fact that higher temperatures arrive later. The overarching message of the line of research leading to this chapter continues to be that, at least potentially, the influence on cost–benefit economic analysis of fat-tailed structural uncertainty about climate change, coupled with great unsureness about high-temperature damage, can outweigh the influence of discounting or anything else. My message is that we must learn to live with the idea that the answers to cost–benefit analyses of what to do about climate change may very well depend – at least to some degree – upon subjective judgments about how bad it might get, with what probabilities, in the most extreme situations.

## ACKNOWLEDEMENTS

For helpful detailed comments on earlier drafts of this paper, but without implicating them for its remaining defects, I am grateful to Harvey Lam and Richard Tol.

I am also indebted to Gerard Roe for generously helping to guide me through some technical scientific aspects in e-mails, and private conversations, and via his insightful paper Roe (2007). He should not, however, be blamed for my interpretations or the formulation of this chapter.

## NOTES

1. Details of this calculation are available from the author upon request. Eleven of the studies in Table 9.3 overlap with the studies portrayed in Box 10.2. Four of these overlapping studies conflict on the numbers given for the over-5 per cent level. For three of these differences, I chose the Table 9.3 values on the grounds that all of the Box 10.2 values had been modified from the original studies to make them have zero probability mass above 10° C. (The fact that all PDFs in Box 10.2 have been normalized to zero probability above 10° C biases my over-5 per cent averages here towards the low side.) With the fourth conflict (Gregory et al., 2002a), I substituted 8.2° C from Box 10.2 for the $\infty$ in Table 9.3 (which arises only because the method of the study itself does not impose any meaningful upper-bound constraint). The only other modification was to average the three reported volcanic-forcing values of Wigley *et al.* (2005a) in Table 9.3 into one study with the single over-5 per cent value of 6.4° C.
2. As I use the term in this paper, a PDF has a 'fat' (or 'thick' or 'heavy') tail when its moment generating function (MGF) is infinite – that is, the tail probability approaches zero more slowly than exponentially. The standard example of a fat-tailed PDF is a power-law-family distribution, although, for example, a lognormal PDF is also fat-tailed, as is an inverted-normal or inverted-gamma. By this definition, a PDF whose MGF is finite has a 'thin' tail. A normal or a gamma are examples of thin-tailed PDFs, as is *any* PDF having finite supports.
3. Weitzman (2008).
4. See Weitzman (2008), where the fat-tailed properties of this example are extended to a much broader family of distributions than the normal and Student-*t*.

# REFERENCES

Allen, M., N. Andronova, B. Booth, S. Dessai, D. Frame, C. Forest, J. Gregory, G. Hegerl, R. Knutti, C. Piani, D. Sexton and D. Stainforth (2006). 'Observational Constraints on Climate Sensitivity'. Chapter 9 in *Avoiding Dangerous Climate Change*, ed. H.J. Schellnhuber, Cambridge University Press, pp. 281-289.

Allen, Myles R. and David J. Frame (2007). 'Call Off the Quest' *Science* (October 26), 318, pp. 582–583.

Gregory, J.M., R.J. Stouffer, S.C.B. Raper P.A. Stott and N.A. Rayner (2002). 'An Observationally Based Estimate of the Climate Sensitivity'. Journal of Climate, 15, pp. 3117–3121.

IPCC-AR4 (2007). *Climate Change 2007: The Physical Science Basis. Contribution of Working Group I to the Fourth Assessment Report of the Intergovernmental Panel on Climate Change.* Cambridge University Press, 2007 (available online at http://www.ipcc-wg1.unibe.ch/publications/wg1-ar4/wg1-ar4.html, accessed 16 May 2010).

Roe, Gerard H (2007). 'Feedbacks, timescales, and seeing red'. Mimeo, September 2.

Roe, Gerard H. and Marcia B. Baker (2007). 'Why is Climate Sensitivity So Unpredictable?' *Science* (October 26), 318, pp. 629–632.

Weitzman, Martin L (2008). *Climate Change.* Working Paper, February 8 (available online at www.economics.harvard.edu/files/faculty/61_Modeling.pdf, accessed 16 May 2010).

Wigley, T.M.L., C.M Ammann, B.D. Santer and S.C.B. Raper (2005). 'Effects of Climate Sensitivity on the Response to Volcanic Forcing'. Journal of Geophysical Research, 110, D09107, doi: 10.1029/2004JD005557.

# 9 Sustainable consumption programs

*John M. Hartwick*

## 1 INTRODUCTION

We explore the sustainability of an abstract aggregated economy given an apparent threat to its persistence. 'Maintaining capital intact' was a central idea in debates in the 1930s among leading English economists and was in fact formalized in the notion of net national product, a flow of product that could be reproduced next period because the 'erosion' of capital had been addressed with 'replacement' investment. Thus sustainability is about maintaining a flow of a valuable product when its persistence is threatened by 'capital being depleted'. Attention shifted away from the formalities of 'maintaining capital intact' once the central concepts of national accounts were agreed upon, but in 1974, Solow confronted the notion of maintaining intact a stream of actual net product, namely aggregate consumption, when part of the capital base of the economy was being unavoidably depleted, as in using some oil each period for production, a current flow from a finite stock of oil. The bottom line turned out to be: maintain the combined bits of capital in the economy intact as a unit, in a particular sense, and then one can maintain the net product flow (aggregate consumption) non-declining (Hartwick 1977). Solow (1974) becomes the seminal piece in the modern economics literature on the sustainability of net products in an economy.

The issue that the Solow-Hartwick contributions 'solved' was achieving sustainability when one of the capital goods necessary for current production was unavoidably shrinking or being depleted. It is this literature and its 'descendants' which we focus on here. We report on two 'twists': What does sustainability 'look like' when there is population growth and the economy is maintaining per capita consumption non-declining into the indefinite future? The formal analysis of this problem was blocked out by Mitra (1983) and Asheim, Buchholtz, Hartwick, Mitra and Withagen (ABHMW) (2007) have reworked Mitra's discrete-time analysis in a continuous time framework. Cheviakov and Hartwick (2007) have added technical progress and decay in produced capital into the ABHMW framework and we report on new conditions for the sustainability of per capita consumption.

The second 'twist' to the Solow-Hartwick problem in sustainability we report on involves global warming or current oil use causing a current temperature rise via $CO_2$ emissions. Hamilton and Ulph (1995) and Stollery (1998) addressed the formalisms of sustainability with a temperature rise externality, and we report on Stollery's work below (with new contributions from d'Autume and Schubert). Sustainability used to be a term attached to problems in mineral depletion (in maintaining capital intact), but it is now frequently linked to the question of maintaining current economic activity while avoiding adding to global temperature increase. Stollery's work provides us with an oil extraction tax, a Pigouvian tax that internalizes the damage current oil use does to the atmosphere. Somewhat related is the work of Ludwig (1995), and Baranzini and Bourguignon (1995), which deals with a possible boundary-hitting collapse of an economy. We report on this work briefly. D'Autume and Schubert (2008) have taken up the matter of a depletable stock as a consumption amenity (Krautkramer 1985) and we report on their recent results derived under the maximin criterion (unchanging utility here).

Chichilnisky (1996), Li and Löfgren (2000), Alvarez-Cuadrado and Long (2007) and Asheim, Mitra and Tongodden (2006) have dealt with the formal welfare economics of the notion of sustainability and we report on aspects of this work. A part of this literature is the Cairns-Long (2006) work of formalizing maximin as a welfare maximization problem and we report on this also.

## 2    MAXIMIN AND CONTROL THEORY

When Solow (1974) set about exploring paths of constant consumption with production involving exhaustible resources, he side-stepped the issue of how familiar optimal welfare was tied to an outcome that involved constant consumption. The benchmark welfare economics case involves a planner maximizing the discounted future stream of util-valued consumptions. How does a constant consumption program relate to the benchmark case, for example? One step toward clearing this issue up is to formulate a welfare optimizing problem that has constant consumption as its solution. Cairns and Long (2007) take this approach. They introduce a welfare maximizing problem (so-called maximin) which has constant consumption as the optimal outcome. Their step forward is the formulation of a general problem in constant utility as a problem in control theory. In particular, they want the social objective to be maximin and wish to generate the appropriate shadow prices that sustain the optimal program. They focus attention on a 'sustainability constraint' for the social maximin problem and its associated shadow price. They observe that this particular shadow price operates as a meaningful discount factor for a fairly standard dynamic optimization problem related to the maximin problem. There is a nesting here: given the solution to the maximin problem, there exists a sequence of shadow prices that can function as appropriate discount factors for a related and meaningful dynamic optimization problem. They also caution that the shadow prices that sustain a maximin program are inextricably tied to the problem under consideration and as such cannot be used to guide an economy from its current state toward a sustainable (maximin path). In addition, they express great skepticism about the usefulness of trying to generate sustainable programs for an economy via a constrained Benthamite program.

We will set out the Cairns-Long formulation of social maximin and some of their results. There is a vector of stocks, $S \equiv (S_1, S_2, \ldots, S_n)$ and a vector of control variables, $u \equiv (u_1, u_2, \ldots, u_r)$ and $n$ transition equations

$$\dot{S}_i = f_i(S, u, t) \quad i = 1, \ldots, n.$$

For the non-autonomous case, we have $S_{n+1}$ tracking time and satisfying

$$\dot{S}_{n+1}(t) = f_{n+1}(S, u, t) = 1 \quad \text{for all } t. \tag{1}$$

In addition, we have static constraints in

$$g_i(S, u, t) \geqq 0 \quad i = 1, \ldots, l', \tag{2}$$

$$g_i(S, u, t) = 0 \quad i = l' + 1, \ldots, l. \tag{3}$$

A planner strives to maximize the sustained level of felicity, that is, to maximize $\overline{W}$ subject to

$$W(S, u, S_{n+1}) - \overline{W} \geqq 0 \quad \text{for all } s \geqq t.$$

This latter is the 'sustainability constraint'. The Hamiltonian is defined in

$$H(S, u, p, p_{n+1}, S_{n+1}) \equiv \sum_{i=1}^{n} p_i(S_{n+1})f_i(S, u, S_{n+1}) + p_{n+1},$$

where the $p_i$ are shadow prices (co-state variables). There are $l$ multipliers, $\lambda_i$ and another, $w$ in the Lagrangian

$$L(S, u, p, p_{n+1}, S_{n+1}, w) = H(S, u, p, p_{n+1}, S_{n+1})$$

$$+ \sum_{i=1}^{l} \lambda_i(S_{n+1}) g_i(S, u, S_{n+1})$$

$$+ w(S_{n+1})[W(S, u, S_{n+1}) - \overline{W}].$$

This Lagrangian corresponds to the problem of maximizing $\overline{W}$ subject to (1), (2) and (3), where current utility in the economy is $W(S, u, S_{n+1})$. There is a subtle regularity condition for a maximin program to emerge: its crude form is that $w(t)$ must remain positive over time. Key necessary conditions correspond to asset equilibrium conditions (some being general Hotelling rules). In addition we have

$$- \int_0^\infty \frac{\partial L}{\partial \overline{W}} ds = \int_0^\infty w(s) ds = 1,$$

$$\lim_{t \to \infty} H(S, u, p, p_{n+1}, S_{n+1}) = 0$$

and complementary slackness conditions including, $w^*[W - \overline{W}] = 0$, $w \geqq 0$ and $[W - \overline{W}] \geqq 0$.

The results are that for the autonomous case, there is zero net investment at the current shadow prices for a maximin program, and zero net investment implies unchanging utility along a program. For non-autonomous problems, the value of net investment exactly compensates for the value of an exogenous shift at any date. Also, when the value of net investment compensates for 'the value of time', utility is unchanging.

$w(t)$ is the shadow price of the sustainability constraint or 'the shadow value of equity' across generations. It operates as a discount factor for the following control problem:

$$\max \int_0^\infty w(t) W(S, u, t) dt$$

subject to (1), (2) and (3). If we solved the maximin problem and extracted the sequence $\{w(t)\}_0^\infty$, then we could set up a new control problem (above) and solve it to get the same paths for $S(t)$ and $u(t)$. This gives a precise meaning to the idea of $w(t)$ operating as a discount factor. Cairns and Long refer to it as a 'virtual discount factor'. The idea of working with artificial discount factors in maximin problems goes back to Dixit, Hammond, and Hoel (1980), Leonard and Long (1992), and Withagen and Asheim (1998). Cairns and Long (2007) shed much light on this stream of literature.

# 3  SUSTAINABILITY BEYOND MAXIMIN

Maximin is a conservative social welfare criterion. It rules out a small amount of saving in the early periods yielding high levels of consumption in the future. The well-known alternative, discounted utilitarianism, suffers from treating the welfare of distantly future generations with little consideration currently (the problem of the so-called dictatorship of the present in the parlance of Chichilnisky). Chichilnisky (1996), Li and Löfgren (2000), Asheim, Mitra and Tongodden (2006) and Alvarez-Cuadrado and Long (2007) have considered alternative welfare criteria.[1] We take up that of Alvarez-Cuadrado and Long at this point to illustrate the way researchers have been thinking about moving beyond maximin. The Alvarez-Cuadrado and Long (A-C and L) approach has the merit of sharing some of the technical structure of the Cairns-Long analysis of maximin described above. Inspired by Chichilnisky's well-known critique of discounted utilitarianism, A-C and L introduce a welfare criterion that is a weighted sum of the discounted utilitarian criterion and the so-called Rawlsian criterion (dictatorship of the least advantaged). Their criterion then possesses the property of non-dictatorship of the present and non-dictatorship of the least advantaged. This new criterion allows for some saving by the current generation to yield a high level of consumption for future generations and it also protects the current generation from having to do excess saving so that future generations can have a high level of consumption (a possible outcome under discounted utilitarianism).

$x(t)$ is a vector of stocks, $c(t)$ is current consumption and $\rho$ is the constant social discount rate. We ignore the issue of the relative welfare of persons at a point in time and consider that each generation lives for a single period. $\underline{u}$ is a minimum living standard, to be selected by the planner and it is bounded above by $b$, which depends on the initial stocks in the economy. For a given weight $\theta$, $0 < \theta < 1$, the planner maximizes, by choice of path $\{c(t)\}$ and scalar $\underline{u}$

$$\int_0^T (1 - \theta)e^{-\rho t}u(x(t), c(t), t)dt + \theta\underline{u}$$

subject to

$$u(x(t), c(t), t) \geqq \underline{u}, \tag{4}$$

$$h(x(t), c(t), t) \geqq 0, \tag{5}$$

$$g(x(t), c(t), t) = \dot{x}(t), \tag{6}$$

initial stocks

$$x_0 \equiv (x_{10}, x_{20}, \ldots, x_{n0})$$

and terminal stocks, $x_i(T) \geq 0$.

For $\pi(t)$ a vector of co-state variables, we have the Hamiltonian defined in

$$H(t, x(t), c(t), \pi(t)) \equiv (1 - \theta)e^{-\rho t}u(x(t), c(t), t)$$
$$+ \pi(t)g(x(t), c(t), t).$$

For $\lambda(t)$ a vector of Lagrange multipliers, we have our Lagrangian defined by

$$L(t, x(t), c(t), \pi(t), \lambda(t), \omega(t), \underline{u}) = H(.) + \lambda(t)h(x(t), c(t), t)$$
$$+ \omega(t)[u(x(t), c(t), t) - \underline{u}].$$

The planner's optimal path satisfies the necessary conditions:

1. Maximum condition: control variables, $u(t)$ maximize $H(.)$ subject to (4) and (5).
2. Adjoint equations:

$$\dot{\pi}(t) = -\frac{\partial L}{\partial x}$$

3. Transition equations

$$\dot{x}(t) = \frac{\partial L}{\partial \pi}$$

4. The transversality condition with respect to control $u$ is

$$\theta + \int_0^T \frac{\partial L}{\partial \underline{u}} dt \geq 0 \text{ and } = 0 \text{ if } \underline{u} < b,$$

   and that with respect to the final stocks is $\pi(T) \geq 0$, $x(T) \geq 0$, and $\pi(T)x(T) \geq 0$.
5. The Hamiltonian and Lagrangian are continuous functions of time, and

$$\frac{d}{dt}H(.) = \frac{d}{dt}L(.) = \frac{\partial}{\partial t}L(.).$$

   In summary, A-C and L develop a welfare criterion that takes us beyond discounted utilitarianism and beyond maximin. Their criterion can be implemented and yields interesting scenarios for instructive examples. They are also able to link their criterion to the behavior of genuine savings, extending the results of Hamilton and Hartwick (2005) and Hamilton and Withagen (2006).

## 4  MAKING THE FUTURE COUNT

A central test of a welfare criterion is that is does not lead to histories that fail our common sense. For example, discounted utilitarianism can lead to the collapse of consumption when an essential input derives from a finite and depleting stock, say an oil pool. This is the outcome in the so-called Dasgupta-Heal (1974) model. Very small constant social discount rates yield outcomes closer to the benchmark Solow (1974). Asheim, Mitra and Tungodden (2006) (AMT) are motivated by this case to examine the famous axiomatization of constant rate discounting by Koopmans. Since discounting seems to be the problem in Dasgupta-Heal, can Koopmans' axioms be amended to yield more sustainable outcomes in Dasgupta-Heal? AMT explore this matter in depth and offer a revised set of axioms, including the novel 'Hammond equity for the future', which are compatible with no collapse in consumption in the Dasgupta-Heal model. Their set of axioms becomes a substitute set for those of Koopmans, a new set which is compatible with growth in per capita consumption in an economy with an essential exhaustible resource.

Chichilnisky (1996), like AMT, was concerned about the tendency of discounted utilitarianism to place too little consideration on the welfare of distant future generations. She sought out an extended discounted utilitarian social object that ruled out 'dictatorship of the present'. Her new welfare function is a weighted sum of pure discounted utilitarianism and the welfare of the most distant (limiting) generation. Heal (1998; Chapter 6) came up with an illustrative example of the Chichilnisky criterion in action; this has been explored in detail in Figuiere and Tidball (2006). We will illustrate the Chichilnisky welfare function with the Heal example.

There is an exhaustible stock, $S_0$ to be drawn down ($\dot{S}(t) = -c(t)$) with the current drawdown, $c(t)$, yielding utility and the current stock, $S(t)$, also yielding utility in $u(c(t), S(t))$. The drawdown program is to maximize

$$\theta \int_0^\infty u(c(t), S(t))e^{-\delta t}dt + (1 - \theta)\lim_{t \to \infty} u(c(t), S(t))$$

subject to $\dot{S}(t) = -c(t)$ and $S(t) \geqq 0$ for all $t$.

The first line above is the Chichilnisky criterion with $0 < \theta < 1$. Heal observes that what is needed if $S(t)$ is essential to $u(.)$ remaining positive is that some of $S_0$ must be set aside for ever and the problem reduces to the asymptotic depletion of $\varepsilon S_0$, with $(1 - \varepsilon)S_0$ being set aside, unmined, forever. The analysis then reduces to solving for fraction, $\varepsilon$. To implement this solution, Figuiere and Tidball propose using the utility function $\ln c(t) + \pi \ln S(t)$. They observe that the optimal solution involves $c(t)$ proportional to the remaining stock and

$$\varepsilon = \frac{\theta(1 + \pi)}{[1 - (1 - \theta)\beta]\pi + \theta} \text{ for } \beta = \frac{1}{1 + \delta}.$$

This solution has the property that a higher concern for future generations (a lower value for $\theta$) entails a more conservationist policy (smaller $\varepsilon$).

The Chichilnisky welfare function is difficult to work with and the Heal (Figuiere and Tidball) example appears to be the best one available. Figuiere and Tidball illustrate the difficulties of the Chichilnisky approach and propose changes to the criterion in order to make it more widely applicable. The analysis in Li and Löfgren (2000) was also inspired by diffuculties in the application of the Chichilnisky welfare function.

## 5   SUSTAINABLE PER CAPITA CONSUMPTION WITH EXHAUSTIBLE RESOURCES

We now jump forward and accept constant per capita consumption as a good outcome and investigate the details of constant consumption (maximin) programs. Solow (1974) is the benchmark case here and involved no population increase, no decay in produced capital and no technical change. We move forward now with this as our reference case. It was sustained by the investment of exhaustible resource rents in newly produced capital (zero net investment or genuine savings at zero). The way to approach Solow sustainable consumption programs is to start with the accounting relation, $\dot{k} = F(K, R, N) - C - \delta K$, and to divide through by $N$ to get

$$\dot{k} = f(k, r) - c - \delta k - nk,$$

where lower-case letters are the upper-case letters divided by $N$ and $n := \dot{N}/N$. $K$ is the stock of produced capital (machines and buildings and infrastructure), $R$ is the flow of exhaustible resources currently used $(R(t) = -\dot{S}(t)$, where $S(t)$ is the remaining stock), $N$ is population (equal to the labor force), $C$ is aggregate consumption and $\delta$ is an unchanging rate of decay in $K(t)$. Important here of course is $\dot{K}/N = \dot{k} + nk$, from standard differentiation. $F(.)$ was assumed to be constant returns to scale. Hence for our central specialization of $F(.)$: $= K^\alpha R^\beta N^{1-\alpha-\beta}$, we have $f(.)$: $= k^\alpha r^\beta$ with $\alpha$ and $\beta$ positive and $\alpha + \beta < 1$. Oil extraction flow, $R(t)$ derives from stock $S(t)$ as $R(t) = -\dot{S}(t)$ and extraction is assumed to be governed by the asset equilibrium condition (Hotelling rule) $\dot{F}_R/F_R = F_K$, which becomes, in per capita terms $\dot{f}_r/f_r = f_k$.

To check this, we have $Q/N = k^\alpha r^\beta$ and then $f_r = \beta k^\alpha r^{\beta-1}$ and $f_k = \alpha k^{\alpha-1} r^\beta$. The other driver of the model is the savings function, namely invested resource rents or $\dot{k} = RF_R + \gamma Q$, where the latter, $\gamma Q$, are supplementary savings in excess of current resource rents. Supplementary savings are needed for cases in which the population is increasing and/or $K$ capital is decaying. We have no decay in $K$ in what follows immediately (that is, $\delta = 0$).

In per capita terms, the savings rule is $\dot{k} + nk = \beta q + \gamma q$.

Since we are interested in $\dot{c} = 0$ and $c$ is proportional to $q$ for the Cobb-Douglas case, we can begin by focusing on $\dot{q} = 0$. It turns out that the Hotelling rule

$$\frac{\dot{q}}{q} - \frac{\dot{r}}{r} = \frac{\alpha q}{k} \tag{7}$$

and this saving rule

$$\dot{k} = \beta q. \tag{8}$$

yield $\dot{q} = 0$. Given this preliminary result, it follows directly that $k$ must be linear in time, say $k(t) = A + Bt$.

1.  Solow (1974) (zero population growth ($n = 0$ and $\gamma = 0$ and no decay in $K$; think of $N = 1$ for example). In this case $c$ is constant at $(1 - \beta)q$. No supplementary savings is called for, so $\gamma = 0$. In solving the model, we observe that $\dot{k}$ remains constant, or $k(t) = k_0 + \beta \bar{q}t$. Then

$$\frac{\dot{r}}{r} = -\alpha\bar{q}\left[\frac{1}{k_0 + \beta\bar{q}t}\right]$$

and $$r(t) = \zeta[k_0 + \beta\bar{q}t]^{-\alpha/\beta}$$

for $\zeta$ as positive constant. Recall that $r := R/N$ for here $N$ is constant. The other initial conditions are $K(0) = K_0$ and $\int_0^\infty R(t)\,dt = S_0$.

These allow us to solve for $\zeta$ and $R(0)$. Then the value of $c$ emerges in $(1 - \beta)\bar{q}$. Clearly for oil use to be finite, we require that $\int_0^\infty R(t)\,dt$ be finite and this is assured if $\alpha/\beta > 1$, a condition noted by Solow.

2.  We move on to consider the population growth function that is compatible with $\dot{c} = 0$.

    Since $c = k^a r^\beta - \dot{k} - nk$, we get

$$\dot{c} = \dot{q} - \frac{d\dot{k}}{dt} - n\dot{k} - k\dot{n}$$

$$= \left[ -\frac{\dot{k}}{k} - \frac{\dot{n}}{n} \right] nk$$

$$= \left[ \frac{-B}{A + Bt} - \frac{\dot{n}}{n} \right] nk$$

which must equal zero. Hence $\dot{n}/n = -B/(A + Bt)$. Since $n = \dot{N}/N$, we observe that $N(t) = \zeta*[A + Bt]^\rho$ is a satisfactory function for $N(t)$. For $\zeta$ and $\psi$ positive, we have quasi-arithmetic growth in population, in a sense funded by the extra savings, $\gamma Q$.

If we return to the original functions undivided by $N$, (that is, $\dot{k} = (\beta + \gamma)Q$, $\frac{\dot{Q}}{Q} - \frac{\dot{R}}{R} = \frac{\alpha\dot{Q}}{K}$), we obtain quite directly that and so on $\frac{\dot{C}}{C} - \frac{\dot{N}}{N} = 0$ and

$$\frac{\dot{N}(t)}{N(t)} = \frac{\gamma}{\alpha} \left[ \frac{\alpha q}{k} \right]. \tag{9}$$

This is satisfied by

$$N(t) = \zeta*[A + Bt]^{\frac{\gamma}{\alpha B}}.$$

with $[\alpha q/k] = 1/(A + Bk)$, for $A$ and $B$ positive constants. $\zeta$ is a positive constant. It will become clear that $\gamma < \alpha$. Routine deriviation also yields

$$\frac{\dot{K}}{K} = \frac{(\gamma + \beta)}{\alpha} \left[ \frac{\alpha q}{k} \right].$$

Hence we have $K(t) = \Lambda*[A + Bt]^{(\gamma + \beta)/(\alpha B)}$, for $\Lambda$ as positive constant. We also get

$$\frac{\dot{R}}{R} = -\frac{(\alpha - \gamma)}{\alpha} \left[ \frac{\alpha q}{k} \right].$$

Hence we have $R(t) = M^*[A + Bt]^{(\gamma - \alpha)/(\alpha B)}$ for $M$ a positive constant. Recall that we observed $K/N$ was linear in time. Hence the important result: $B = \beta/\alpha$. It follows that $(\gamma - \alpha)/\beta < 1$ is necessary for $\int_0^\infty R(t)dt$ to be finite. This generalizes the condition for the Solow model (which was $\alpha > \beta$).

The above is the core of the model in Asheim et al. (henceforth known as ABHMW, for the initials of the five authors) (2007). The Solow (1974) model is a special case with no extra savings beyond current resource rents and no population growth. Central to the analysis was first obtaining unchanging conditions for output and then proceeding to conditions for unchanging per capita consumption. We make use of this approach now for a more complicated case.

3. We add exogenous technical progress and decay in $K$ to the ABHMW model. Decay in $K$ capital is at a constant rate, $\delta$. Savings is $(\beta + \gamma)Q$ and this covers $\dot{k} + \delta K$. There is exogenous technical progress at rate $\theta$ as in $Q = e^\theta K^\alpha R^\beta N^{1-\alpha-\beta}$. $K$ is produced capital, $R$ is current drawdown from the exhaustible resource stock, $S(t)$ (thus $R(t) = -\dot{S}(t)$), and $N$ is the current population (labor force). In fact, it will be instructive to view technical change as attached to capital as in $Q = [e^{\frac{\theta}{\alpha}}K]^+ R^\beta N^{1-\alpha-\beta}$, since we will see this term $\theta/\alpha$ as central below. The basic account is then $\dot{K} = e^\theta K^\alpha R^\beta N^{1-\alpha-\beta} - C - \delta K$ for $C$ aggregate current consumption and $\delta$ the constant rate of decay in produced capital. In per capita terms, we have $\dot{k} = e^{\theta t}k^\alpha r^\beta - c - k[n + \delta]$ for $n(t): = \dot{N}/N$. We adopt a savings rule, linear in current output (following Asheim et al. 2007):

$$\dot{K} + \delta K = [\beta + \gamma]Q.$$

Dynamic efficiency in extraction satisfies Hotelling rule:

$$\frac{\dot{Q}}{Q} - \frac{\dot{R}}{R} = \frac{\alpha Q}{K}.$$

Consumption is then $[1 - \beta - \gamma]Q$ and thus constant per capita consumption implies

$$\frac{\dot{Q}}{Q} - \frac{\dot{N}}{N} = 0.$$

Since $\frac{\dot{Q}}{Q} = \theta + \alpha\frac{\dot{K}}{K} + \beta\frac{\dot{R}}{R} + (1 - \alpha - \beta)\frac{\dot{N}}{N}$, we can use the above three equations to obtain

$$\frac{\dot{N}}{N} = \frac{\gamma}{\alpha}\left[\frac{\alpha Q}{K}\right] + \left[\frac{\theta}{\alpha} - \delta\right].$$

It follows directly that

$$\frac{\dot{R}}{R} = \left(\frac{\gamma - \alpha}{\alpha}\right)\left[\frac{\alpha Q}{K}\right] + \left[\frac{\theta}{\alpha} - \delta\right]$$

and
$$\frac{\dot{K}}{K} = \left(\frac{\beta + \gamma}{\alpha}\right)\left[\frac{\alpha Q}{K}\right] - \delta.$$

This system of three ordinary differential equations reduces to the system studied in Asheim et al. (2007) when $\theta = \delta = 0$ and $\alpha > \gamma$ and $\gamma > 0$. Solow (1974) had in addition, $\dot{N} = 0$ by assumption. In Solow (1974), $\beta Q$ (resource rents) provided sufficient savings for creating sustainable consumption. In ABHMW with $\dot{N} > 0$, the system needed supplementary savings $\gamma Q$ equal to $nK$ for sustainable per capita consumption. We observe above that our new model requires supplementary savings $\gamma Q$ equal to $nK + [\delta - \frac{\theta}{\alpha}]K$ for sustainable per capita consumption. Since total savings in this new model is $[\beta + \gamma]Q$ and can pay for $\dot{K} + \delta K$, it follows that $\beta Q = \dot{K} - nK + \frac{\theta}{\alpha}K$, which in per capita terms is $\beta q = \dot{k} + \frac{\theta}{\alpha}k$. (The corresponding basic savings in ABHMW is $qy = \dot{k}$.) We make use of this basic savings relation, $\beta q = \dot{k} + \frac{\theta}{\alpha}k$ immediately.

To solve our three equation system, we consider first the 'per capita system' with 'arbitrary' $N(t)$, namely

$$\beta q = \dot{k} + \frac{\theta k}{\alpha}$$

and
$$\frac{\dot{q}}{q} - \frac{\dot{r}}{r} = \frac{\alpha q}{k}.$$

This pair of equations yields the result $\dot{q} = 0$. This step is the same as we pursued in the model above. However now, $k(t)$ is not linear in time because of the new term, $\theta k/\alpha$ We are forced to solve the above pair directly. This pair of equations has the solution

$$k = k(t) = k_0 e^{-\theta t/\alpha} + \frac{\alpha \beta q}{\theta}$$

and
$$r = r(t) = q^{1/\beta}(k(t))^{-\alpha/\beta}e^{-\theta t/\beta}$$

where $k_0 = $ constant and $y = e^{\theta t} k^\alpha(t) r^\beta(t) = k_0^\beta/\theta^\alpha$. That is, $\dot{q} = 0$ for this per capita system. The long-term behavior of this solution is $k \to \frac{\alpha\beta q}{\theta}$, $r \to 0$, and $\frac{\dot{r}}{r} \to -\frac{\theta}{\beta}$.

We now return to our initial three differential equations for this model. Given our solution for $k(t)$, we observe that $\dot{N}/N = \gamma/\alpha[\alpha y/k] - [(\delta\alpha - \theta)/\alpha]$ integrates to

$$N(t) = N_0 e^{[\frac{\theta}{\alpha}\{\frac{s}{\beta}\} - \delta]t}(k(t))^{\frac{\gamma}{\beta}},$$

with $s := \beta + \gamma$, $\frac{\dot{R}}{R} = \frac{-[\alpha - \gamma]}{\alpha}[\frac{\alpha y}{k}] - [\frac{\delta\alpha - \theta}{\alpha}]$ integrates to

$$R(t) = R_0 y^{1/\beta} e^{[\frac{\theta}{\alpha}\{\frac{s - \alpha}{\beta}\} - \delta]t}(k(t))^{-(\alpha - \gamma)/\beta}$$

and $\frac{\dot{K}}{K} = \frac{s}{\alpha}[\frac{\alpha q}{k}] - \delta$ integrates to

$$K(t) = N_0 e^{[\frac{\theta}{\alpha}\{\frac{s}{\beta}\} - \delta]t}(k(t))^{s/\mu}.$$

We asssume that $\alpha > \gamma$. The scenario compatible with a finite initial stock of oil (that is, $\int_0^\infty R(t)\,dt$ is a finite scalar) requires that $\dot{R}$ become negative. $[\frac{\theta}{\alpha}\{\frac{s - \alpha}{\beta}\} - \delta] < 0$ is clearly sufficient since then $R(t)$ tends to zero as $t \to \infty$. This is a condition for the feasibility of the economy persisting over infinite time. We observe that $k$ tends to a constant at the limit, given the above solution for the model. Hence for growth in the economy (that is, for $N(t)$ and $K(t)$ increasing) we require that $[\frac{\theta}{\alpha}\{\frac{s}{\beta}\} - \delta] > 0$. We have then an upper and lower bound on a value of $\delta$ such that the economy is feasible and expanding;[2] namely

$$\frac{\theta}{\alpha}\left\{\frac{s - \alpha}{\beta}\right\} < \delta < \frac{\theta}{\alpha}\left\{\frac{s}{\beta}\right\}.$$

The intuition here is that a sufficiently high value of decay, $\delta$, induces a drag in the economy in order to keep long-run production within the given initial resource stock, but too large a value of $\delta$ rules out output growth compatible with the population growing, as opposed to shrinking.

Note that our approach above, for the case of a Cobb-Douglas production function, was to start with a savings function and a dynamic efficiency function (Hotelling rule) that yielded unchanging per capita output and then to proceed to consider the workings out of the system when unchanging per capita consumption became an added requirement.

A special case of the above model has no technical progress but a positive decay rate $\delta$ for produced capital. One observes that collapse of the economy is inevitable. This collapse case is an extension of this model, namely the ABHMW model with the new possibility of produced capital decaying over time.

# 6    EXTRACTION COSTS IN THE BASIC SOLOW MODEL

Solow and Wan (1975) investigated extraction costs with exhaustible resources. One model they introduced was the basic Solow (1974) model with $Q = F(K, R) - C - aR$ for $a$ constant unit extraction costs. They did not solve this model, nor did Sato and Kim (2002), who also investigated the matter in a different context. We[3] solve this model below. $R$ is current oil use with current stock $S(t)$ and $R(t) = -\dot{S}(t)$. Population is assumed unchanging in this investigation.[4] We work with a Cobb-Douglas production function, $F(K, R): = K^\alpha R^\beta, 0 < \alpha, \beta < 1$.

The Solow-Wan model has the following savings function and Hotelling rule:

$$\frac{d}{dt}K = R(F_R - a),    (10)$$

$$\frac{d}{dt}(F_R - a) = F_K(F_R - a)    (11)$$

Here $a > 0$ is the extraction cost parameter, which makes the problem different from the basic Solow model.

For a Cobb-Douglas production function, the conserved quantity of the Solow-Wan model takes the form

$$c = (1 - \beta)K^\alpha R^\beta = \text{const.}    (12)$$

Therefore we immediately obtain one relation between unknown functions $K(t)$ and $R(t)$:

$$R = R_0 K^{-\frac{\alpha}{\beta}},    (13)$$

where $R_0 = (c/(1 - \beta))^{\frac{1}{\beta}} > 0$ is a constant. To obtain the full solution $(K(t), R(t))$, only one equation remains to be solved. Upon expansion and substitution of (13), the savings equation $\frac{d}{dt}K = (F_R - a)R$, becomes

$$\dot{K} = \beta R_0^\beta - aR_0 K(t)^{-\frac{\alpha}{\beta}}.    (14)$$

Equation (14) is separable and can be completely solved in quadratures. We arrive at the following result:

The exact implicit solution $(K, R) = (K(t), R(t))$ of the Solow-Wan model (10), (11) with extraction cost $a \neq 0$ and with Cobb-Douglas production function $K^{\alpha}R^{\beta}$ is given by

$$\int_{K_0}^{K(t)} \frac{dK_1}{\beta R_0^{\beta} - aR_0 K_1^{-\alpha/\beta}} = t, \tag{15}$$

$$R(t) = R_0(K(t))^{-\frac{\alpha}{\beta}}. \tag{16}$$

In (15) and (16), $K_1$ is an integration variable, and $K_0 > 0$ a constant. The initial conditions for $K(t)$, $R(t)$ at $t = 0$ are respectively

$$K(0) = K_0,$$
$$R(0) = R_0 K_0^{-\frac{\alpha}{\beta}}.$$

Evidently, for $a = 0$, the solution (15), (16) yields the familiar Solow solution.

We turn to different possible scenarios for the Solow-Wan model. We start from the analysis of equation (14). From now on, assume $0 < \beta < \alpha$, as in the Solow model.[5] We will observe that the behavior of the solution to the Solow-Wan model essentially depends on a certain relation between the problem parameters $a$, $\alpha$, $\beta$ and the initial condition $R_0$, $K_0$. Indeed, the following three different cases arise:

1. $K_0 > K_0^*$;
2. $K_0 = K_0^*$;
3. $K_0 < K_0^*$;

where
$$K_0^* = \left(\frac{a}{\beta} R_0^{1-\beta}\right)^{\frac{\beta}{\alpha}}. \tag{17}$$

From the right side of equation (14), since $\alpha/\beta > 1$, it is not hard to see that in the first case, $dK(t)/dt > 0$ at the initial time $t = 0$ and for all times $t$. Similarly, in the second case, $dK(t)/dt > 0$ for all $t$; in the third case, $dK(t)/dt < 0$ for all $t$.

**Case 1.**
In this case, $K_0 > \left(\frac{a}{\beta}R_0^{1-\beta}\right)^{-\frac{\beta}{\alpha}}$, and $\frac{dK(t)}{dt} = 0$ for all times $t$. However, in this case, the limit $a \to 0$ is valid, and the solution $(K, R)$ in this limit tends to

*the solution of the Solow model. Solutions* $(K(t), R(t))$ *corresponding to Case 1 have been generated numerically for* $\alpha = 0.6, \beta = 0.3, R_0 = 1$ *and* $K_0 = 1.826$, *for values* $a = (0, 0.4, 0.9, 0.99, 1)$. *For all of these values of a, we have* $K_0 > K_0^*$ *(Case 1 condition satisfied.) In particular,* $a = 0$ *is a Solow solution.* $a = 1$ *is close to the critical case:* $K_0 > K_0^* \approx 1.8257$.

**Case 2.**
*This case as well as case three, are new compared to the familiar Solow model. In case two, the constant solution is given by*

$$K(0) = K_0^* = \text{const}, \ R(t) = R_0(K_0^*)^{-\frac{\alpha}{\beta}} = \text{const}. \tag{18}$$

*It corresponds to a stagnant economy with no investment, depending totally on mining an available exhaustible resource, and can describe reality only for finite times* $t < T$ *for which resource extraction cost a does not change.*

**Case 3.**
*This case corresponds to a decline of capital due to high oil extraction cost a, resulting in a finite-time collapse of the economy. In case three, the solution (15) can be evaluated using the Lerch special function* $\Phi(z, s, b)$. *Equation (15) then takes the form*

$$R_0^\beta \alpha t = K_0 \Phi\left(\left(\frac{K_0}{K_0^*}\right)^{\frac{\alpha}{\beta}}, 1, -\frac{\beta}{\alpha}\right) - K(t) \Phi\left(\left(\frac{K(t)}{K_0^*}\right)^{\frac{\alpha}{\beta}}, 1, -\frac{\beta}{\alpha}\right), \tag{19}$$

*remaining implicit in* $K(t)$. *The Lerch function is a power series[6] converging for* $|z| < 1$ *(which happens precisely in case three:* $K_0, K(t) < K_0^*$*) and* $b = -\frac{\beta}{\alpha} \neq 0, -1, -2, \ldots$ *(always true for* $0 < \beta < \alpha$*).*

Examples of the solution curves $K(t)$, $R(t)$ for various initial conditions have been generated for $a = 1$ and prescribed parameters $\alpha = 0.6$, $\beta = 0.3$, $R_0 = 1$. For this choice, $K_0^* \approx 1.8257$. We choose several different values of initial capital, falling into cases one, two and three: $K_0 = (3.1, 2, 1.71, K_0^*, 1.8, 1.6)$. Collapse of the economy follows.

## 7   A CONSERVATION LAW APPROACH

Sato and Kim (2002) exploited the idea from classical mechanics that the invariance of the Hamiltonian for a frictionless system is associated with conservation of energy. They took up the Hamiltonian from the analysis of Solow-Wan (1975) and observed that it was equal to zero (see also

Withagen and Asheim, 1998). Solow and Wan had set their analysis up with an economy minimizing the integral of oil use over time subject to it achieving a target level of constant consumption. They investigated what the solution to the Solow-Wan model would be, like if the Hamiltonian were set at a positive constant, $A$ instead of zero. They dealt with the Cobb-Douglas case, $F(K, R): = K^\alpha R^{1-\alpha}$. Ignoring extraction costs,[7] they were dealing with a Hamiltonian

$$H(t) = -R + q_1[K^\alpha R^{1-\alpha} - C] - q_2 R = A.$$

Nesessary conditions for minimizing the integral of oil use include the standard Hotelling rule:

$$F_K = \frac{\dot{F}_R}{F_R}$$

and the new savings rule:

$$\dot{k} = RF_R + \left[\frac{A}{1 + q_2}\right]F_R.$$

$q_2$ is constant in the model. Hence the economy is saving more in the form of a constant, $[\frac{A}{1 + q_2}]$ multiplied by the price of oil. One observes straightaway that $\dot{C} = 0$ is satisfied. Sato and Kim obtain closed form solutions for this pair of equations in $R(t)$ and $K(t)$:

$$K = \frac{(1 - \alpha)^{(2-\alpha)/(1-\alpha)}}{\alpha}\left[\frac{A}{1 + q_2}\right](t + C_0)^{1/(1-\alpha)} + C_1[t + C_0]$$

and $\quad R = (1 - \alpha)^{1/(1-\alpha)}(t + C_0)^{-\alpha/(1-\alpha)}C_1 + \left[\frac{1 - \alpha}{\alpha}\right]\left[\frac{A}{1 + q_2}\right]$

for $C_0$ and $C_1$ constants. One also obtains $q_1 = (t + C_0)^{-\alpha/(1-\alpha)}C_2$.

One observes that for $A = 0$, one retrieves the basic Solow (1974) model. Sato and Kim have arrived at a model with a very particular extra savings formulation. Earlier we observed that 'extra savings' linear in current output could be associated with some population growth, while constant per capita consumption was being maintained. Here the extra savings is allowing the original oil stock to be drawn down more slowly while per capita consumption is being held constant. The consumption level will decline for an increase in $[\frac{A}{1 + q_2}]$. Observe that $R(t)$ contains a constant term. Hence the integral over infinite time will not be finite for the case of $A \neq 0$. Hence the economics of the Sato-Kim model are difficult to interpret, but the analysis represents a step into the realm of conservation law theory.

There is a general doctrine in mathematical physics established by Emmy Noether that corresponding to each invariant (for example, energy), there will be a symmetry in the model (with energy the symmetry is time). This theory has been invoked by Martinet and Rotillon (2007) in a recent analysis of the Solow problem. In Hartwick (2004) I investigated frictionless motion in classical mechanics (for example, a planet moving about the central mass, the sun) as a problem in conservation of capital value (zero net investment per period). Investment is measured in units of energy in our analysis, standard for classical mechanics. I associated 'maintaining the value of capital intact' or 'zero net investment' with frictionless motion in classical mechanics.[8] This investigation was inspired by the 'zero net investment' rule that we associate with the Solow problem.

## 8    THE STOCK WITH INTRINSIC VALUE

Krautkramer (1985) explored oil stock depletion in a problem in which the remaining stock had value, in addition to being a repository of future energy. He made the remaining stock, $S(t)$ an argument in the utility function as in $U(C(t), S(t))$. D'Autume and Schubert (2008) analyze Krautkramer's problem within the confines of maximin, that is, with utility unchanging. The invariant of interest is then $U(.)$ or $\dot{C} + p\dot{S} = 0$ for $p = U_S/U_C$. Production derives from the constant returns to scale function $F(K(t), R(t))$ $(= C(t) + \dot{k}(t))$ with $R = -\dot{S}(t)$. Dynamic efficiency in extraction satisfies

$$\frac{\dot{q}}{q} + \frac{p}{q} = F_K \text{ for } q = F_R.$$

Current exhaustible resource rents are allocated to new capital in $\dot{K} = Rq$. It is routine to show that these last two conditions imply that $\dot{C} = pR$ starting from $C = F(K, R) - \dot{K}$. Hence $U(.)$ is unchanging as time passes. D'Autume and Schubert report the converse result: $\dot{U}(.) = 0$ implies genuine savings equal to zero $(\dot{K} + \dot{S}q = G(t) = 0)$. They make use of the key property of maximin paths, $\dot{G} - GF_K = 0$ (Dixit, Hammond and Hoel, 1980) in their demonstration.

D'Autume and Schubert develop a novel approach to solving maximin problems: they start with a discounted utilitarian welfare function

$$\int_0^\infty e^{-\rho t} \frac{u(C(t), S(t))^{1-1/\sigma}}{1 - 1/\sigma} dt$$

and later let $\sigma \to 0$, which implies a desire for $u(.)$ unchanging. They draw on utility function $u(C, S) = CS^{\varepsilon}$ (a Cobb-Douglas variant) and work with the inverse $C(u, S) = uS^{-\varepsilon}$. The production function they draw on is the Cobb-Douglas, $K^{\alpha}R^{\beta}$. They obtain

$$u^* = (1 - \beta)\left[\frac{\alpha - \beta}{\phi}B\right]^{\beta/(1 - \beta)} \text{ for } \phi = 1 + \frac{(1 - \beta)\varepsilon}{\beta}$$

and $$B = K_0^{\frac{\alpha - \beta}{\beta}}S_0^{\phi} \text{ which also equals } K(t)^{\frac{\alpha - \beta}{\beta}}S(t)^{\phi}.$$

The appendix to this chapter provides details of the d'Autume-Schubert analysis. Clearly for $u$ unchanging, we observe $K$ being substituted for $S$ in the expression for $u^*$ above. When $\varepsilon$ is set at zero, $\phi = 1$ and the solution reverts to that in Solow (1974). It turns out that the procedure that d'Autume and Schubert developed to solve this maximin version of the Krautkramer problem also works for the global warming version of Solow's problem, due to Stollery (1998). We turn to this now.

# 9 CONSTANT UTILITY AND GLOBAL WARMING

Stollery (1998) introduced global warming tied to cumulative oil use. There is a large literature involving oil use in the economy and a negative externality, but recently attention has been focused on oil use, $CO_2$ production and global temperature increase (this last is the negative externality associated with oil use). Stollery was able to link global warming to Solow (1974) in an elegant analysis. In particular, he introduced a Pigouvian tax on oil use that internalized the global warming (temperature increase) externality. We have then the basic Solow (1974) model with two negative temperature-rise effects tied to cumulative extraction, one in the utility function and one in the production function. Given optimized welfare, the full price of oil contains a negative impact term which can be used to define the Pigouvian tax required to sustain optimized welfare; given the constant utility criterion with an unchanging population, Stollery observes that investing oil rents in newly produced capital is sufficient to sustain the optimal path, where rents must be inclusive of the Pigouvian tax. In other words if prices are taken correctly, gross of Pigouvian corrective taxes, then the investment of resource rents in produced capital sustains the constant utility path. The challenge is to define correctly the oil price gross of the appropriate Pigouvian tax. Stollery simplifies matters by assuming that the temperature increase is irreversible. There is no intervention, with its associated cost, that can see a temperature lowered.[9] Thus where the temperature rise is linked to, say, the probability of extinction of the economy (as in Baranzini and Bourguignon (1995) for example; see below), we have a sort of doomsday scenario, with the probability of extinction never declining.

The objective function in Stollery's analysis is the maximization of $U(C(t), T(S_0 - S(t)))$ for $C(t)$ aggregate consumption, $T(.)$ temperature, and $S(t)$ the remaining stock of oil. Utility is assumed to be increasing in $C$ and decreasing in $T$. Population, in the background, is assumed to be unchanging. We leave labor (population) out of the production function. Also an increase in cumulative oil output, $S_0 - S(t)$, over history, implies a higher temperature. On the production side, we have $Q(t) = F(K(t), R(t), T(S_0 - S(t)))$, leading to the account

$$\dot{K}(t) = F(K(t), R(t), T(S_0 - S(t))) - C(t).$$

Temperature also has a negative effect on production in this formulation. The Hotelling rule for this model must incorporate the negative impact of current oil extraction on the temperature variable. This is dealt with by a first-best or Pigouvian tax on current extraction. More on this below. The Hotelling rule for our problem[10] with negative extraction externalities is

$$\frac{\dot{q}}{q} = F_K(t) + \left\{ F_T + \frac{U_T}{U_C} \right\} \frac{T_{S_0 - S(t)}}{q} \quad \text{for } q = F_R.$$

The extra term, $\left\{ F_T + \frac{U_T}{U_C} \right\} \frac{T_{S_0 - S(t)}}{q}$ is a negative rate, a 'tax', which means that a unit extracted receives current price $q$, and when this is invested for a period, it earns only $F_K(t) + \left\{ F_T + \frac{U_T}{U_C} \right\} \frac{T_{S_0 - S(t)}}{q}$. The tax term is negative. It is as if the government has imposed a low ceiling on the rate of return earnable by an extractor. This 'low $r\%$' implies slower extraction in simple, partial equilibrium models, and of course this is the desired impact of a Pigouvian tax in this model.

This Hotelling rule, with tax, and invested resource rents ($\dot{K} = Rq$) yields a constant utility path in this model. To see this, we note first that $d\dot{K}/dt = \dot{R}q + R\dot{q}$ and $\dot{q}$ in turn is defined in the Hotelling rule above. That is,

$$\frac{d\dot{K}}{dt} = \dot{R}q + \left[ qF_K(t) + \left\{ F_T + \frac{U_T}{U_C} \right\} T_{S_0 - S(t)} \right] R(t).$$

We use this in the calculation of $\frac{dU(.)}{dt} = U_C\dot{C} - U_T T_{S_0 - S(t)}\dot{S}$. This should be zero for sustainability of the program. Hence we turn first to evaluate $\dot{C}$ from the accounting relation $C = F(K, R, T) - \dot{k}$. That is, we consider

$$\dot{C} = F_K \dot{K} + qR + F_T \dot{T} - \frac{d\dot{K}}{dt}.$$

We proceed to substitute for $\dot{K} = Rq$, $d\dot{K}/dt$ from above and $\dot{T} = T_{S_0 - S(t)}R$. We obtain

$$\dot{C} = \frac{-U_T T_{S_0 - S(t)} R}{U_C}.$$

This implies that $dU(.)/dt = 0$.

Hence Hotelling's rule, adjusted with a Pigouvian tax on extraction activity and invested resource rents, implies that $dU(.)/dt = 0$. The novelty here is that Pigouvian taxes are needed to sustain the optimum and invested resource rents must be carried out with optimal prices, inclusive of Pigouvian taxes.

The converse to this result is also true and the demonstration is also quite direct. Given $dU(.)/dt = 0$ and Hotelling's rule inclusive of the Pigouvian tax, we obtain $G = 0$, for $G = \dot{K} + S\dot{q}$, $G$ standing for 'genuine savings'.

$dU(.)/dt = 0$ implies that $\dot{C} = -R\frac{U_T}{U_C}T_{S_0 - S(t)}$ and we also have $\dot{G} = \frac{d\dot{K}}{dt} - R\dot{q} - q\dot{R}$, given the definition of $G$. When we taken $\dot{C}$ from the accounting relation, $C = F(K, R, T) - \dot{K}$, and substitute our two relations, $\dot{C}$ and $d\dot{K}/dt$, we obtain

$$\dot{G} - GF_K = F_K(t)qR + \left\{ F_T + \frac{U_T}{U_C} \right\} T_{S_0 - S(t)}R - \dot{q}R.$$

The right-hand side is zero, by our Hotelling rule. Hence $dU(.)/dt = 0$ and Hotelling's rule imply that $\dot{G} - GF_K = 0$. This property, $\dot{G} - GF_K = 0$ has been shown by Dixit, Hammond and Heal (1980) to imply that $G = 0$ for maximin paths. Hence we infer that indeed $G = 0$ for our dynamically efficient, maximin economy, where dynamic efficiency in extraction includes a Pigouvian tax.

Stollery perceived that for the special case of the temperature externality only in the production function, the solution for the Cobb-Douglas case involved $K(t)$ linear in time. He was able to get a complete solution for $Q(t) = K^\alpha R^\beta T^{-\gamma}$ and $T(S(t)) = T_0 e^{-\phi S(t)}$, $\alpha, \beta, \gamma, \phi > 0$ and $\alpha + \beta < 1$. We have then $K(t) = K_0 + \frac{\beta C^*}{1 - \beta}t$ for

$$C^* = (1 - \beta)\left( \frac{\beta(\alpha - \beta)}{\phi\gamma} \right)^{\frac{\beta}{1-\beta}} T_0^{\frac{-\gamma}{1-\beta}} (e^{\phi\frac{\gamma}{\beta}S_0} - 1)^{\frac{\beta}{1-\beta}} K_0^{\frac{\alpha-\beta}{1-\beta}}$$

and

$$S(t) = \frac{\beta}{\phi\gamma} \ln(1 + BK(t)^{\frac{-(\alpha - \beta)}{\beta}})$$

for $B = K_0^{\frac{\alpha-\beta}{\beta}}(e^{\phi\frac{\gamma}{\beta}S_0} - 1)$.

D'Autume, Hartwick and Schubert (2008) were able to characterize the more general case in which temperature enters into the utility function as well as the production function when both functions are both Cobb-Douglas. It turns out that $K(t)$ is linear in time now only at the limit as $S(t)$ approaches zero. That is, one obtains

$$\dot{K} = \beta\frac{C(u, T(S))}{1 - \beta} = \beta\frac{uT(S)^{\varepsilon}}{1 - \beta} = \beta\frac{uT_0^{\varepsilon}e^{\varepsilon(S_0 - S)\phi}}{1 - \beta}$$

and the invariant utility works out to be

$$u^* = (1 - \beta)\left(\frac{\beta(\alpha - \beta)}{(\varepsilon(1 - \beta) + \gamma)\phi}\right)^{\frac{\beta}{1-\beta}}T_0^{-\frac{(\varepsilon(1-\beta)+\gamma)}{1-\beta}}$$

$$(1 - e^{-\frac{\varepsilon(1-\beta)+\gamma}{\beta}S_0})^{\frac{\beta}{1-\beta}}K_0^{\frac{\alpha-\beta}{1-\beta}}$$

for $u = cT(S)^{\varepsilon}\ \varepsilon \geq 0$.

The novelty here is that a Pigouvian tax schedule is needed to sustain the optimum, and invested resource rents must be carried out with optimal prices, inclusive of Pigouvian taxes. This was also recognized by Hamilton and Ulph (1995) in their similar paper on global warming and constant utility paths.

# 10   LUDWIG SUSTAINABLE CONSUMPTION

Ludwig (1995) was concerned about observed collapses, linked to human activity, in certain biological stocks. He asked, in his model, 'is there a prudent level of unchanging harvest, above zero, from an uncertain stock, particularly one exhibiting infrequent unpredictable crashes?' We can relabel his stock as 'the environment', writ large, and his harvest as 'the level of aggregate consumption'. We then have to solve this for maximum sustainable consumption, where sustainability is defined in terms of collapse avoidance. This is also a somewhat pessimistic formulation in which regeneration of the environment is only possible by consumption reduction. The environment has its built-in regenerative capacity and this can be aided by harvest reduction. Of interest here is Ludwig's unapologetic use of simulations to explain where his model takes us. The model is not formulated to yield elegant characterizations of prudent harvesting.

In the familiar certainty case, we have the environment evolving as

$$\dot{X} = rX\left[1 - \frac{X}{M}\right] - C$$

for $X$ the stock, defining the size of the environment, $C$ the consumption or harvest per period, and $r$ a parameter defining the capacity of the environment to grow when $X$ is less than carrying capacity $M$. This formulation of 'the environment' corresponds to a logistic growth curve, with $X$ approaching $M$ at the limit, for the case of $C = 0$. Economists select $C$ to maximize some current function of $C$ (utility of benefits of current $C$) summed with discounting into the distant future (for example, $\int_0^\infty U(C(t))e^{-\rho t}$).

Ludwig is instead interested in an unvarying level of $C$ that implies that the stock $X(t)$ will not hit the extinction threshold in the near future, given exogenous uncertainty about the dynamics of the stock. In his stochastic stock formulation, we have

$$dX = (f(X, r) - C)dt + \sigma dW - \lambda dP$$

where $dW$ is an increment of normalized Brownian motion: $E(dW) = 0$ and $E(dW^2) = dt$. The term $dP$ is an increment of a Poisson process: it occurs with probability $\lambda dt$ in the interval $(t, t + dt)$, and the size of the jump is $\delta$. This formulation implies that $u(x) = 0$ if $x \leq 0$ and $u(\infty) = 1$. Thus we have a small uncertainty in $X$ (Brownian motion) with occasional large crashes, captured in $\lambda dP$. Consumption take, $C$ will be selected in a moment. The probability of avoiding extinction, starting $X$ at $x$ is expressed as $u(x)$, that is

$$u(x) = \Pr[X \text{ hits } \infty \text{ before } 0 | X(0) = x].$$

The dynamics for $X$ imply that $u$ satisfies

$$\frac{\sigma^2 d^2u}{2\ dx^2} + [f(x, r) - C]\frac{du}{dx} + \lambda[u(x - \delta) - u(x)] = 0.$$

Since growth rate $r$ is also uncertain, Ludwig represents information about its value by means of a subjective probability distribution (a Bayesian approach). The probability of extinction is computed by integrating over the distribution of $r$. That is

$$B(x, C) = \int_{-\infty}^{+\infty} (1 - u(x, r, C))p(r)dr$$

where $p(r)$ denotes a Bayesian posterior density. $p(r)$ is selected to be Gaussian; that is,

$$p(r) = \frac{1}{\sqrt{2\pi\gamma^2}}\exp\left(\frac{(r - \hat{r})^2}{2\gamma^2}\right),$$

for $\hat{r}$ the most likely value of $r$. $\gamma$ quantifies the uncertainty about the value of $r$. The value of 'harvest', $C$ is selected to satisfy $B(x, C) = \alpha$ the value of $\alpha$ being a policy choice. Given the policy maker's tolerance for possible extinction (value of $\alpha$), then the appropriate harvest rate gets selected. $C$ becomes the maximum level of consumption that an uncertain environment can yield, contingent on a certain probability of an economic collapse. Ludwig proceeds to calculate $C$ for his model and to compare his computed values with those selected by rules of thumb. He expresses his conclusions in some interesting locutions: 'It is not true that 'what you don't know can't hurt you.' On the contrary, what you don't know is likely to be much more important than what you do know.' And there is 'the general principle that the less information that is available, the more cautious we must be in tampering with our environment'.

## 11   BARANZINI AND BOURGUIGNON

In their 1995 paper, Baranzini and Bourguignon take up the issue of, say, increasing pollution leading to a structural break which results in the extinction of humankind. Their model has an uncomplicated form of stochasticity which can lead to extinction if the pollution flows are not kept low. Society's goal is ever-increasing consumption (sustainable consumption) while not increasing the probability of extinction. The model has the same logic as does Nordhaus's model of global warming (see for example Nordhaus and Boyer, 2000). Here pollution from energy use does not heat the atmosphere explicitly as in the Nordhaus model, but rather directly increases the second-order effect, namely the collapse of the human enterprise on earth. In the Baranzini-Bourguignon model, output is a function of capital, $k$ and energy flow $E$ in

$$\dot{k} = (\mu + E\beta)k - c.$$

The pollution stock $\Lambda$ grows from energy use in $Am$ and in part abates naturally in $\dot{\Lambda} = Am - b\Lambda$. Expected utility an instant at $t$ for society is present value, $u(c)e^{-\delta t}$ weighted by the current probability of survival over the instant, namely $P(t): = e^{-\Lambda}$. Hence the objective is

$$\text{Max}_{\{c,\,A\}} \int_0^\infty u(c)e^{-\{\delta t + \Lambda\}}dt.$$

This problem is solved under the assumption that

$$u(c): = \tfrac{1-\gamma}{\gamma}\left(\tfrac{c-C}{1-\gamma}\right)^\gamma$$

for $C$ a minimum subsistence threshold. Of particular interest is the case $A = 0$ since then $\Lambda$ can never decline. For this possibility to make sense, we have the parameter $\mu > 0$. (The production relationship would be more standard with $\mu = 0$ but then the case of $A = 0$ would not make sense.)

The solution with $A$ held temporarily fixed is

$$c^* = C + (1 - \gamma)\xi_0^{1/(\gamma-1)}e^{\theta t}$$

for $\theta := [(\mu + \beta A) - (\delta + Am)]/(1 - \gamma)$ and $\xi_0$ the initial shadow price of capital. This value works out to be

$$\xi_0^{1/(\gamma-1)} = \frac{\alpha}{(1-\gamma)}\left[k_0 - \frac{C}{(\mu + A\beta)}\right],$$

for

$$\alpha = \tfrac{(\delta - \mu\gamma)}{(1-\gamma)} + A\tfrac{(m-\beta\gamma)}{(1-\gamma)} = (\mu + \beta A) - \theta,$$

which is assumed to be positive. For the case of $A = 0$, one must have $\delta > \mu\gamma$. The present value of expected utility is then

$$W^* = \frac{(1-\gamma)^{(1-\gamma)}}{\gamma}\alpha^{\gamma-1}\left[k_0 - \frac{C}{(\mu + A\beta)}\right]^\gamma.$$

$k_0$, the initial capital, is assumed to be greater than $C/(\mu + A\beta)$. To ensure that $c$ and the probability of survival (non-extinction) never decline, one maximizes $W^*$ by choice of $A$ and solves for the case of $A = 0$. Recall that in this case the pollution stock, $\Lambda$, can only decline. (If $A = 0$, then for production to exist, parameter $\mu$ must be positive, and this strikes us as an odd way to specify the process of production for an economy.) The merit of the Baranzini-Bourguignon analysis is its focus on the issue of whether an optimal growth path can entail a non-declining $c$ as well as a non-declining probability of extinction (economic collapse). It is not clear that their model is well-suited to this line of investigation, but the explicit introduction of uncertainty in potential economic collapse is a valuable contribution to debates about the meaning of long-term sustainability.

## 12   CONCLUDING REMARKS

Sustainability is about keeping an economy from collapsing. The presence of essential inputs to production from finite stocks such as oil pools makes the study of collapse a challenging economic issue. One version of this idea is keeping per capita consumption from ever declining. This view has been our focus here. We first imbedded this idea into welfare economics. One might view the issue here as arriving at some alternative notion to the Benthamite criterion (maximizing the value of discounted streams of util-valued consumption sequences). We then turned to the detailed analysis of economies in which per capita consumption was prevented from declining by the injection of much new durable produced capital. In the simplest case, we have zero net investment or the accumulation of current produced capital in an amount just sufficient to offset the current reduction of say an oil stock. This simple balancing is the benchmark case. We then took up complications arising from population growth and decay in the stock of produced capital.

The case of oil use being linked to a negative externality (global temperature increase) was also reported on in our analysis of constant consumption programs. Here a Pigouvian tax on the use of oil was introduced and we were able to see how the investment of exhaustible resource rents 'went through'. Our final reflection was on different notions of sustainability: when for example an economy is subject to sudden collapse from say overfishing or excessive global warming. We reported on the work of Ludwig and of Baranzini and Bourguignon on this approach. Sustainability is then both a branch of welfare economics as well as a branch of the economics of development over the long run.

## APPENDIX:   SOLVING THE MAXIMIN PROBLEM WITH THE STOCK AMENITY VALUE

The system is

$$\frac{\dot{q}}{q} + \frac{u_S/u_C}{q} = F_K,$$

$$\dot{K} = qR$$

and                                $u = \text{constant}$

for $Y = F(K, R) = K^{\alpha} R^{\beta}$, $\alpha, \beta > 0$ and $\alpha + \beta < 1$. The product account implies that

$$\dot{K} = \beta Y$$

and

$$C = (1 - \beta) Y.$$

We invert the utility function, $u(C, S)$ to $C = C(u, S)$ and our system becomes

$$\dot{K} = \beta Y,$$

$$\dot{S} = - Y^{1/\beta} K^{-\alpha/\beta},$$

and

$$Y = \frac{C(u, S)}{1 - \beta}.$$

Substituting $Y$ in the first two equations yields a system of differential equations in $K$ and $S$. One proceeds to solve by time elimination and variable separation. First we have

$$\frac{dS}{dK} = -\frac{1}{\beta} \left[ \frac{C(u, S)}{1 - \beta} \right]^{1/\beta - 1} K^{-\alpha/\beta},$$

which equals $1/q$. We then separate variables to get

$$-\left[ \frac{C(u, S)}{1 - \beta} \right]^{-\frac{1 - \beta}{\beta}} dS = \frac{1}{\beta} K^{-\alpha/\beta} dK.$$

This integrates to

$$\int_S^{S_0} \left[ \frac{C(u, \psi)}{1 - \beta} \right]^{-\frac{1 - \beta}{\beta}} d\psi = \int_{K_0}^{K} \frac{1}{\beta} \kappa^{-\alpha/\beta} d\kappa. \tag{20}$$

For utility function $CS^{\varepsilon}$ our $C(u, S)$ function is $uS^{-\varepsilon}$ for $\varepsilon > 0$. Now (20) becomes

$$\left( \frac{u}{1 - \beta} \right)^{-\frac{1 - \beta}{\beta}} \frac{S_0^{\phi} - S^{\phi}}{\phi} = \frac{K_0^{1 - \alpha/\beta} - K^{1 - \alpha/\beta}}{\alpha - \beta}. \tag{21}$$

for $\phi = 1 + \frac{1 - \beta}{\beta} \varepsilon$. Produced capital tends to infinity and $S(t)$ tends to zero. If we set $S = 0$ and let $K \to \infty$ in (21) we can obtain the stationary utility level:

$$u^* = (1 - \beta)\left(\frac{\alpha - \beta}{\phi} K_0^{\frac{\alpha-\beta}{\beta}} S_0^\phi\right)^{\frac{\beta}{1-\beta}}.$$

And using (20), we have

$$u^* = (1 - \beta)\left(\frac{\alpha - \beta}{\phi} K^{\frac{\alpha-\beta}{\beta}} S^\phi\right)^{\frac{\beta}{1-\beta}},$$

which allows us to characterize the optimal path by

$$K^{\frac{\alpha-\beta}{\beta}} S^\phi = K_0^{\frac{\alpha-\beta}{\beta}} S_0^\phi = \text{constant}.$$

$K$ is accumulated to compensate for the diminution in $S$ at each instant.

D'Autume and Schubert (2008) use this same approach to solve the Stollery (1998) problem with the temperature externality in both the production and utility functions.

## NOTES

1. Figuiere and Tidball (2006) have worked out a non-renewable resource problem with Chichilnisky's welfare criterion. They also make a careful analysis of the difficulties of doing economics with her criterion.
2. The economy will be feasible and contracting when $\delta > \frac{\theta s}{\alpha \beta}$.
3. Alexei Cheviakov provided much technical assistance with this section.
4. Dasgupta and Heal (1979; p. 305) were aware that Solow (1974) could be amended to allow extra savings so that aggregate consumption could increase for ever, even with the essential resource input to production summing to a finite value.
5. Our analysis remains valid for the case $\alpha + \beta > 1$.
6. $\Phi(z, s, b) = \Sigma_{n=0}^{\infty} \frac{z^n}{(n+b)^s}$.
7. They attempted to solve the model with positive extraction costs but could not make progress.
8. I return to this analysis in a companion piece in a volume on sustainability edited by Lucas Bretschger and Sjak Smulders (2007).
9. The somewhat similar analysis of Hamilton and Ulph (1995) allows for costly intervention to reverse temperature rise. However, they are not able to push their formulation to the detailed solution that Stollery is able to achieve with his.
10. This version of Hotelling's rule could be derived in a variety of optimal growth frameworks. Stollery derived it for a constant utility objective function via a route developed by Leonard and Long (1992, pp. 300–304).

## REFERENCES

Alvarez-Cuadrado, Francisco and Ngo Van Long (2007) 'A Mixed Bentham-Rawls Criterion for Intergenerational Equity: Theory and Implications' typescript.

Asheim, Geir B., Wolfgang Buchholz, John M. Hartwick, Tapan Mitra and Cees Withagen (2007) 'Constant Saving Rates and Quasi-arithmetic Population Growth under Exhaustible

Resource Constraints', *Journal of Environmental Economics and Management*, 53, 2, pp. 213–239.

Asheim, Geir B., Tapan Mitra and Bertil Tungodden (2006) 'Sustainable Recursive Social Welfare Functions', typescript.

Baranzini, Andrea and Francois Bourguignon (1995) 'Is Sustainable Growth Optimal?' *International Tax and Public Finance*, 2, pp. 341–56.

Bretschger, L. and S. Smulders (eds) (2007) *Sustainable Resources Use and Economic Dynamics*, Heidelberg: Springer.

Cairns, Robert and Ngo Van Long (2006) 'Maximin: A Direct Approach to Sustainability', *Environment and Development Economics*, 11, 3, pp. 275–300.

Cheviakov, Alexei F. and John M. Hartwick (2007) 'Constant Consumption with Exhaustible Resources: New Scenarios', paper presented at the *Canadian Economics Association meetings*, Halifax, Nova Scotia, May.

Chichilnisky, Graciella (1996) 'An Axiomatic Approach to Sustainable Development', *Social Choice and Welfare*, 13, 3, pp. 231–257.

Dasgupta, Partha and Geoffrey M. Heal (1979) *Economic Theory and Exhaustible Resources*, New York: Cambridge University Press.

D'Autume, A., J.M. Hartwick and K. Schubert (2008) 'On Stollery's Global Warming Model' typescript.

D'Autume, A. and K. Schubert (2008) 'Hartwick's Rule and Maximin Paths when the Exhaustible Resource has an Amenity Value', *Journal of Environmental Economics and Management*, 56, 3, pp. 260–274.

Dixit, Avinash K., Peter Hammond and Michael Hoel (1980) 'On Hartwick's Rule for Regular Maximin Paths of Capital Accumulation and Resource Depletion', *Review of Economic Studies*, 47, 3, pp. 551–556.

Figuiere, Charles and Mabel Tidball (2006) *Sustainable Exploitation of Natural Resource: a Satisfying Use of Chichilnisky's Criterion* Research Paper, Montpellier, France: UMR LAMETA.

Krautkramer, Jeffrey A. (1985) 'Opimal Growth, Resource Amenities and the Preservation of Natural Environments', *Review of Economic Studies*, 52, pp. 153–170.

Hamilton, Kirk and John Hartwick (2005) 'Investing Exhaustible Resource Rents and the Path of Consumption', *Canadian Journal of Economics*, 38, 2, pp. 615–621.

Hamilton, Kirk and David Ulph (1995) 'The Hartwick Rule in a Greenhouse World', unpublished manuscript, University College, London.

Hamilton, Kirk and Cees Withagen (2006) 'Savings Growth and the Path of Utility' *Canadian Journal of Economics*, 40, 2, pp. 703–713.

Hartwick, John M. (1977) 'Intergenerational Equity and the Investing of Rents from Exhaustible Resources', *American Economic Review*, 66, pp. 253–256.

Hartwick, John M. (2004) 'Sustaining Periodic Motion and Maintaining Capital in Classical Mechanics', *Japan and the World Economy*, 16, 3, pp. 337–358.

Heal, G.M. (1998) 'Interpreting Sustainability', in Heal, G.M. and Vercelli, A. (eds) *Sustainability: Dynamics and University*, Dordrecht: Kluwer.

Leonard, D. and N. V. Long (1992) *Optimal Control Theory and Static Optimization in Economics*, Cambridge: Cambridge University Press.

Li, Chuan-Zhong and Karl-Gustaf Löfgren (2000) 'Renewable Resources and Economic Sustainability: A Dynamic Analysis with Heterogeneous Time Preferences', *Journal of Environmental Economics and Management*, 40, 3, pp. 236–250.

Ludwig, Donald (1995) 'A Theory of Sustainable Harvesting', *SIAM Journal of Applied Mathematics*, 2, April, pp. 564–575.

Martinet, Vincent and Gilles Rotillon (2007) 'Invariance in Growth Theory and Sustainable Development', *Journal of Economic Dynamics and Control*, 31, 8, pp. 2827–2846.

Mitra, T. (1983) 'Limits on Population Growth under Exhaustible Resource Constraints', *International Economic Review*, 24, pp. 155–168.

Nordhaus W.D. and J. Boyer (2000) *Warming the World: Economic Models of Global Warming*. Cambridge MA: MIT Press.

Sato, Ryuzo and Youngduk Kim (2002) 'Hartwick's Rule and Economic Conservation Laws', *Journal of Economic Dynamics and Control*, 26, 3, pp. 437–449.

Solow, Robert M. (1974) 'Integenerational Equity and Exhaustible Resources', *Review of Economics Studies*, Symposium volume, pp. 29–46.

Solow, Robert M. and F.Y. Wan (1975) 'Extraction Costs in the Theory of Exhaustible Resources', *Bell Journal of Economics*, 7, 2, pp. 359–370.

Stollery, Kenneth R. (1998) 'Constant Utility Paths and Irreversible Global Warming', *Canadian Journal of Economics*, 31, 3, pp. 730–742.

Withagen, Cees and Geir B. Asheim (1998) 'Characterizing Sustainability: The Converse of Hartwick's Rule', *Journal of Economic Dynamics and Control*, 23, 1, pp. 159–165.

# 10 The relationship between welfare measures and indicators of sustainable development
*Geir B. Asheim*

## 1 INTRODUCTION

What is the relationship between welfare measures and indicators of sustainable development? This chapter studies the extent to which measures of welfare improvement can also be used as indicators of sustainability. It builds on (and borrows freely from) published papers by myself and co-authors (Asheim, 1994, 2003, 2004, 2007a; Asheim, Buchholz and Withagen, 2003; and Asheim and Weitzman, 2001); most of these papers are included in Asheim (2007b).

The relationship between welfare measures and indicators of sustainable development is particularly interesting in a setting where there is population growth, and thus, in large part of this chapter I will allow for positive population growth.

What constitutes welfare improvement when population is changing? The answer depends on whether a bigger future population for a given flow of per capita consumption leads to higher welfare weights for people living at that time, or alternatively, only per capita consumption matters. When applying, for example, discounted utilitarianism to a situation where population changes exogenously through time, it seems reasonable to represent the instantaneous well-being of each generation by the product of population size and the utility derived from per capita consumption. This is the position of 'total utilitarianism', which has been endorsed by, for example, Meade (1995) and Mirrlees (1967), and which is the basic assumption in Arrow, Dasgupta and Mäler's (2003b) study of savings criteria with a changing population. Within a utilitarian framework, the alternative position of 'average utilitarianism', where the instantaneous well-being of each generation depends only on per capita consumption, has been shown to yield implications that are not ethically defensible.[1]

What does sustainability mean when population is changing? If the economy cares about sustainability (in the sense that current per capita utility should not exceed what is potentially sustainable), then it becomes important to compare the level of individual utility for different generations,

*237*

irrespectively of how population size develops. Therefore, utility derived from per capita consumption seems more relevant in a discussion of sustainability. Hence, with positive population growth, it is possible to have total utility increasing throughout so that welfare improves, while at the same time per capita utility is falling so that development is not sustainable. However, it turns out that the relationship between welfare improvement and sustainability is not straightforward even if population is constant.

Since the major results of this chapter concern the problems of associating measures of welfare improvement with sustainability, it is justified to make rather stringent assumptions concerning the working of the economy, since the problems of such association will be even more serious in an economy with a poorer performance. Hence, in the basic model presented in Section 2, I assume that the economy implements a competitive path. In Section 3, I show the welfare significance of the present value of future consumption changes even in the presence of population growth, while in Section 4, I report on how the present value of future consumption can be measured through national accounting aggregates (both the value of net investments and real net national product (NNP) growth). On this basis, I present in the subsequent four sections a discussion of whether measures of welfare improvement can serve as indicators of sustainability. The main conclusion (first made by Pezzey, 2004) is that welfare improvement is not a sufficient condition for sustainability, but under special conditions it is a necessary one.

## 2   MODEL

Following Arrow, Dasgupta and Mäler (2003b) and Asheim (2004), assume that population $N$ develops exogenously over time. The population trajectory $\{N(t)\}_{t=0}^{\infty}$ is determined by the growth function $\dot{N} = \phi(N)$ and the initial condition $N(0) = N^0$. Two special cases are exponential growth, $\phi(N) = \nu N$, where $\nu$ denotes the constant growth rate, and logistic growth, $\phi(N) = \bar{\nu}N(1 - \frac{N}{N^*})$, where $\bar{\nu}$ denotes the maximum growth rate, and $N^*$ denotes the population size that is asymptotically approached. As mentioned by Arrow, Dasgupta and Mäler (2003b), the latter seems like the more acceptable formulation in a finite world. In general, denote by $\nu(N)$ the rate of growth of population as a function of $N$, where $\nu(N) = \phi(N)/N$.

Let $\mathbf{C}$ represent an $m$-dimensional consumption vector that also includes environmental amenities and other externalities. Let $u$ be a given concave and non-decreasing utility function with continuous partial derivatives that associates the instantaneous well-being for each individual with the utility $u(\mathbf{c})$ that is derived from the per capita vector of consumption flows, $\mathbf{c} := C/N$. Assume an idealized world where $\mathbf{c}$ contains all variable determinants of current instantaneous well-being, implying that an individual's instantaneous well-being is increased by moving from $\mathbf{c}'$ to $\mathbf{c}''$ if and only if $u(\mathbf{c}') < u(\mathbf{c}'')$. At any time, labor supply is assumed to be exogenously given and equal to the population size at that time.

Let $\mathbf{K}$ denote an $n$-dimensional capital vector that includes not only the usual kinds of man-made capital stocks, but also stocks of natural resources, environmental assets, human capital (like education and knowledge capital from R&D-like activities), and other durable productive assets. Moreover, let $\mathbf{I} (= \dot{\mathbf{K}})$ stand for the corresponding $n$-vector of net investments. The net investment flow of a natural capital asset is negative if the overall extraction rate exceeds the replacement rate.

Assume again an idealized world where $\mathbf{K}$ and $N$ contain all variable determinants of current productive capacity, implying that the quadruple $(\mathbf{C}, \mathbf{I}, \mathbf{K}, N)$ is attainable if $(\mathbf{C}, \mathbf{I}, \mathbf{K}, N) \in \mathcal{C}$, where $\mathcal{C}$ is a convex and smooth set, with free disposal of consumption and investment flows. Hence, the set of attainable quadruples does not depend directly on time. However, by letting time be one of the capital components, this formulation encompasses the case where technology changes exogenously through time.[2] We thus make an assumption of 'green' or comprehensive accounting, meaning that current productive capacity depends solely on the vector of capital stocks and the population size.

Society makes decisions according to a resource allocation mechanism that assigns to any vector of capital stocks $\mathbf{K}$ and any population size $N$ a consumption-investment pair $(\mathbf{C}(\mathbf{K}, N), \mathbf{I}(\mathbf{K}, N))$ satisfying that $(\mathbf{C}(\mathbf{K}, N), \mathbf{I}(\mathbf{K}, N), \mathbf{K}, N)$ is attainable.[3] I assume that there exists a unique solution $\{\mathbf{K}^*(t)\}_{t=0}^{\infty}$ to the differential equations $\dot{\mathbf{K}}^*(t) = \mathbf{I}(\mathbf{K}^*(t), N(t))$ that satisfies the initial condition $\mathbf{K}^*(0) = \mathbf{K}^0$, where $\mathbf{K}^0$ is given. Hence, $\{\mathbf{K}^*(t)\}$ is the capital path that the resource allocation mechanism implements. Write $\mathbf{C}^*(t) := \mathbf{C}(\mathbf{K}^*(t), N(t))$ and $\mathbf{I}^*(t) := \mathbf{I}(\mathbf{K}^*(t), N(t))$.

Say that the program $\{\mathbf{C}^*(t), \mathbf{I}^*(t), \mathbf{K}^*(t)\}_{t=0}^{\infty}$ is competitive if, at each $t$,

1. $(\mathbf{C}^*(t), \mathbf{I}^*(t), \mathbf{K}^*(t), N(t))$ is attainable,
2. there exist present value prices of the flows of utility, consumption, labor input and investment, $(\mu(t), \mathbf{p}(t), w(t), \mathbf{q}(t))$, with $\mu(t) > 0$ and $\mathbf{q}(t) \geq 0$, such that

C1 $\mathbf{C}^*(t)$ maximizes $\mu(t)u(C/N(t)) - \mathbf{p}(t)C/N(t)$ over all $\mathbf{C}$,
C2 $(\mathbf{C}^*(t), \mathbf{I}^*(t), \mathbf{K}^*(t), N(t))$ maximizes $\mathbf{p}(t)\mathbf{C} - w(t)N + \mathbf{q}(t)\mathbf{I} + \dot{\mathbf{q}}(t)\mathbf{K}$ over all $(\mathbf{C}, \mathbf{I}, \mathbf{K}, N) \in \mathcal{C}$.

Here C1 corresponds to utility maximization, while C2 corresponds to intertemporal profit maximization.[4] The term 'present value' reflects that discounting is taken care of by the prices. In particular, if relative consumption prices are constant throughout and there is a constant real interest rate $R$, then it holds that $\mathbf{p}(t) = e^{-Rt}\mathbf{p}(0)$. However, I will allow for non-constant relative consumption prices and will return to the question of how to determine real interest rates from $\{\mathbf{p}(t)\}_{t=0}^{\infty}$ in this more general case.

Assume that the implemented program $\{\mathbf{C}^*(t), \mathbf{I}^*(t), \mathbf{K}^*(t)\}_{t=0}^{\infty}$ is competitive with finite utility and consumption values,

$$\int_0^{\infty} \mu(t)N(t)u(\mathbf{C}^*(t)/N(t))dt \text{ and } \int_0^{\infty} \mathbf{p}(t)\mathbf{C}^*(t)dt \text{ exist,}$$

and that it satisfies a capital value transversality condition,

$$\lim_{t\to\infty} \mathbf{q}(t)\mathbf{K}^*(t) = 0. \tag{1}$$

It follows that the implemented program $\{\mathbf{C}^*(t), \mathbf{I}^*(t), \mathbf{K}^*(t)\}_{t=0}^{\infty}$ maximizes

$$\int_0^{\infty} \mu(t)N(t)u(\mathbf{C}/N(t))dt$$

over all programs that are attainable at all times, and satisfies the initial condition. Moreover, writing $\mathbf{c}^*(t) := \mathbf{C}^*(t)/N(t)$, it follows from C1 and C2 that

$$\mathbf{p}(t) = \mu(t)\nabla_c u(\mathbf{c}^*(t)), \tag{2}$$

$$w(t) = \mathbf{p}(t)\frac{\partial\mathbf{C}(\mathbf{K}^*(t), N(t))}{\partial N} + \mathbf{q}(t)\frac{\partial\mathbf{I}(\mathbf{K}^*(t), N(t))}{\partial N}, \tag{3}$$

$$-\dot{\mathbf{q}}(t) = \mathbf{p}(t)\nabla_K\mathbf{C}(\mathbf{K}^*(t), N(t)) + \mathbf{q}(t)\nabla_K\mathbf{I}(\mathbf{K}^*(t), N(t)). \tag{4}$$

## 3    WELFARE SIGNIFICANCE OF THE PRESENT VALUE OF FUTURE CONSUMPTION CHANGES

Write $U(K, N) := Nu(\mathbf{C}(K, N)/N)$ and $U^*(t) := U(\mathbf{K}^*(t), N(t))$ for the flow of total utility. In line with the basic analysis of Arrow, Dasgupta and Mäler (2003b), assume that $U^*(t)$ measures the level of instantaneous social well-being at time $t$.

Assume that, at time $t$, economy's dynamic welfare is given by a Samuelson-Bergson welfare function defined over paths of total utility from time $t$ to infinity, and that this welfare function is time-invariant (that is, does not depend on $t$). Moreover, assume that, for a given initial condition, the optimal path is time-consistent, and that the economy's resource allocation mechanism implements the optimal path. If the welfare indifference surfaces in infinite-dimensional utility space are smooth, then, at time $t$, $\{\mu(s)\}_{s=t}^{\infty}$ are local welfare weights on total utility flows at different times.[5] Following a standard argument in welfare economics, as suggested by Samuelson (1961, p. 52) in the current setting, one can conclude that dynamic welfare is increasing at time $t$ if and only if

$$\int_{t}^{\infty} \mu(s)\, \dot{U}^*(s)\, ds > 0. \tag{5}$$

To show that this welfare analysis includes discounted total utilitarianism, assume for the rest of this paragraph only that the economy through its implemented program maximizes the sum of total utilities discounted at a constant rate $\rho$. Hence, the dynamic welfare of the implemented program at time $t$ is

$$\int_{t}^{\infty} e^{-\rho(s-t)} U^*(s)\, ds.$$

Then the change in dynamic welfare is given by

$$\frac{d}{dt}\left( \int_{t}^{\infty} e^{-\rho(s-t)} U^*(s)\, ds \right) = -U^*(t) + \rho \int_{t}^{\infty} e^{-\rho(s-t)} U^*(s)\, ds$$

$$= e^{\rho t} \int_{t}^{\infty} e^{-\rho s} \dot{U}^*(s)\, ds, \tag{6}$$

where the second equality follows by integrating by parts. Hence, (5) follows by setting

$$\{\mu(t)\}_{t=0}^{\infty} = \{e^{-\rho t}\}_{t=0}^{\infty}.$$

The following result provides a connection between welfare improvement and the present value of future changes in consumption.

**Proposition 1** *Under the assumptions of Section 2,*

$$\int_t^\infty \mu(s)\,\dot{U}^*(s)\,ds = \int_t^\infty \mathbf{p}(s)\,\dot{\mathbf{C}}^*(s)\,ds + \int_t^\infty v(s)\,\phi(N(s))\,ds.$$

*where $v(t) := \mu(t)\,(u(\mathbf{c}^*(t)) - \nabla_c u(\mathbf{c}^*(t))\mathbf{c}^*(t))$ denotes the marginal value of consumption spread, measured in present value terms.*[6]

**Proof.** Since $U^*(t) = N(t)u(\mathbf{C}^*(t)/N(t))$, we obtain

$$\dot{U}^* = \nabla_c u(\mathbf{c}^*)\dot{\mathbf{C}}^* + \phi(N)u(\mathbf{c}^*) - N\nabla_c u(\mathbf{c}^*)\mathbf{c}^*v(N),$$

The result follows from (2) and the definition of $v(t)$, since $v(N)N = \phi(N)$. ∎

**Corollary 1** *The present value of future consumption changes, $\int_t^\infty \mathbf{p}(s)\dot{\mathbf{C}}^*(s)\,ds$, indicates welfare improvement in each of the following two situations:*

1.   *There is a constant population.*
2.   *The utility function u is linearly homogeneous.*

**Proof.** Part (1) follows directly from (5) and Proposition 1. Part (2) follows from (5) and Proposition 1 through the application of Euler's theorem. ∎

These results can be generalized to the case where the economy's resource allocation mechanism does not implement an optimal path. In particular, (6) depends solely on the properties of discounted utilitarianism, and does not rely on the resource allocation mechanism implementing an optimal or even an efficient path. Furthermore, if (2) is used to define consumption shadow prices, then Proposition 1 and Corollary 1 remain true. In the case without population growth, I have, through Asheim (2007a, Proposition 2(b)) generalized the results of this section to the case of any time-invariant Samuelson-Bergson welfare function satisfying a condition of independent future (so that the ranking of two paths that coincide from the current time $t$ to a future time $t'$ is the same at any time between $t$ and $t'$), without making any assumptions about the working of the economy's resource allocation mechanism.

## 4   MEASURING THE PRESENT VALUE OF FUTURE CONSUMPTION CHANGES THROUGH NATIONAL ACCOUNTING AGGREGATES

To tie the current chapter to contributions on the theory of welfare accounting, it is worthwhile recapitulating how the present value of future consumption changes, whose welfare significance was investigated in Section 3, can be measured through national accounting aggregates.

Within the setting of the model in Section 2, there are two ways to measure the present value of future consumption changes, $\int_t^\infty \mathbf{p}(s)\dot{\mathbf{C}}^*(s)\,ds$: through (i) the value of net investments and through (ii) real NNP growth, where each measure has been extended to take care of population growth.

**Proposition 2** *Under the assumptions of Section 2,*

$$\int_t^\infty \mathbf{p}(s)\dot{\mathbf{C}}^*(s)\,ds = \mathbf{q}(t)\mathbf{I}(t) + \int_t^\infty w(s)\phi(N(s))\,ds.$$

**Proof.** By combining (3) and (4), one obtains

$$\mathbf{p}\dot{\mathbf{C}}^* = \mathbf{p}(\nabla_K \mathbf{C} \cdot \mathbf{I}^* + \tfrac{\partial \mathbf{C}}{\partial N} \cdot \phi(N))$$

$$= -(\dot{\mathbf{q}}\mathbf{I}^* + \mathbf{q}\dot{\mathbf{I}}^* + w\phi(N)) = -\tfrac{d}{dt}(\mathbf{q}\mathbf{I}^*) + w\phi(N). \qquad (7)$$

Assuming that $\lim_{t\to\infty} \mathbf{q}(t)\mathbf{I}^*(t) = 0$ holds as an investment value transversality condition, and $\int_t^\infty w(s)\phi(N(s))\,ds$ exists, the result is obtained by integrating (7). ∎

Turn next to the question of how extended real NNP growth can measure the present value of future consumption changes. For this purpose, follow Asheim and Weitzman (2001) and Sefton and Weale (2006) by using a Divisia consumer price index when expressing comprehensive NNP in real prices. The application of a price index $\{\pi(t)\}$ turns the present value prices $\{\mathbf{p}(t), \mathbf{q}(t)\}$ into real prices $\{\mathbf{P}(t), \mathbf{Q}(t)\}$,

$$\mathbf{P}(t) = \mathbf{p}(t)/\pi(t)$$
$$\mathbf{Q}(t) = \mathbf{q}(t)/\pi(t),$$

implying that the real interest rate, $R(t)$, at time $t$ is given by

$$R(t) = -\tfrac{\dot{\pi}(t)}{\pi(t)}.$$

A Divisia consumption price index satisfies

$$\frac{\dot{\pi}(t)}{\pi(t)} = \frac{\dot{\mathbf{p}}(t)\mathbf{C}^*(t)}{\mathbf{p}(t)\mathbf{C}^*(t)},$$

implying that $\dot{\mathbf{P}}\mathbf{C}^* = 0$:

$$\dot{\mathbf{P}}\mathbf{C}^* = \frac{d}{dt}\left(\frac{\mathbf{p}}{\pi}\right)\mathbf{C}^* = \frac{\pi\dot{\mathbf{p}}\mathbf{C}^* - \dot{\pi}\mathbf{p}\mathbf{C}^*}{\pi^2} = 0.$$

Define comprehensive NNP in real Divisia prices, $Y(t)$, as the sum of the real value of consumption and the real value of net investments:

$$Y(t) := \mathbf{P}(t)\mathbf{C}^*(t) + \mathbf{Q}(t)\mathbf{I}^*(t).$$

**Proposition 3** *Under the assumptions of Section 2,*

$$R(t) \cdot \left(\int_t^\infty \tfrac{\mathbf{p}(s)}{\pi(t)}\dot{\mathbf{C}}^*(s)\,ds\right) = \dot{Y}(t) + \frac{d}{dt}\left(\int_t^\infty \tfrac{w(s)}{\pi(t)}\phi(N(s))\,ds\right).$$

**Proof.** Since

$$\frac{d}{dt}(\mathbf{Q}(t)\mathbf{I}^*(t)) = \tfrac{1}{\pi(t)}\frac{d}{dt}(\mathbf{q}(t)\mathbf{I}^*(t)) + R(t)\mathbf{Q}(t)\mathbf{I}^*(t)$$

$$\frac{d}{dt}\left(\int_t^\infty \tfrac{w(s)}{\pi(t)}\phi(N(s))\,ds\right) = -\tfrac{w(t)}{\pi(t)}\phi(N(t)) + R(t)\left(\int_t^\infty \tfrac{w(s)}{\pi(t)}\phi(N(s))\,ds\right),$$

it follows from $\dot{\mathbf{P}}\mathbf{C}^* = 0$ and expression (7) that

$$0 = \tfrac{1}{\pi(t)}(\mathbf{p}(t)\dot{\mathbf{C}}^*(t) + \tfrac{d}{dt}(\mathbf{q}(t)\mathbf{I}^*(t)) - w(t)\phi(N(t)))$$

$$= \frac{d}{dt}(\mathbf{P}(t)\mathbf{C}^*(t)) + \frac{d}{dt}(\mathbf{Q}(t)\mathbf{I}^*(t)) + \frac{d}{dt}\left(\int_t^\infty \tfrac{w(s)}{\pi(t)}\phi(N(s))\,ds\right) \qquad (8)$$

$$- R(t)\left(\mathbf{Q}(t)\mathbf{I}^*(t) + \int_t^\infty \tfrac{w(s)}{\pi(t)}\phi(N(s))\,ds\right).$$

Hence, the result is obtained by using Proposition 2 and the definitions above. ∎

# 5   SUSTAINED DEVELOPMENT IMPLIES WELFARE IMPROVEMENT

Proposition 1 shows that the present value of future consumption changes is an indicator of welfare improvement, also under exogenous population growth, while Propositions 2 and 3 show how the present value of future consumption changes can be measured by means of national accounting aggregates. The remaining four sections of this chapter consider the relationship between the present value of future consumption changes, and thus the national accounting aggregates of Propositions 2 and 3, on the one hand, and the sustainability of the path, on the other hand.

To concentrate attention on intergenerational issues, abstract throughout from intratemporal distribution by assuming that all individuals living at time $t$ obtain the average utility level, $u(\mathbf{c}^*(t))$, where $\mathbf{c}^*(t) = \mathbf{C}^*(t)/N(t)$ is the per capita consumption along the implemented path. Following Pezzey (1997), one can distinguish between sustainable and sustained development. A path constitutes sustainable development if, at each time $t$, the per capita utility level at time $t$ can potentially be shared by all individuals of future generations. A path constitutes sustained development if, at each time, $u(\mathbf{c}^*(t))$ is non-decreasing. Any sustained development is also sustainable. On the other hand, the converse does not hold, since a development can be sustainable even if a generation makes a sacrifice for the benefit of successors that lowers its own per capita utility below those of its predecessors.

If population growth is non-negative and development is sustained, then it is a straightforward conclusion that that the present value of future consumption changes is non-negative and that welfare improves.

**Proposition 4** *If $v(N(s)) \geq 0$ and $du(\mathbf{c}^*(s))/dt \geq 0$ for all $s > t$, then*

$$\int_t^\infty \mathbf{p}(s)\dot{\mathbf{C}}^*(s)\,ds \geq 0.$$

*If, in addition, $u(\mathbf{c}^*(t)) \geq 0,$[7] then*

$$\int_t^\infty \mu(s)\dot{U}^*(s)\,ds \geq 0.$$

**Proof.** Since $\mathbf{c}^* = \mathbf{C}^*/N$, the following holds at each $s > t$:

$$du(\mathbf{c}^*)/dt = \nabla_c u(\mathbf{c}^*)(\dot{\mathbf{C}}^*/N - \mathbf{c}^*v(N)).$$

By (2) and the premises of the proposition, $\mathbf{p}(s)\dot{\mathbf{C}}^*(s) \geq 0$ at each $s > t$, thereby establishing the first part of the proposition. Since $U^* = Nu(\mathbf{c}^*)$, we have

$$\dot{U}^* = Ndu(\mathbf{c}^*)/dt + v(N)Nu(\mathbf{c}^*),$$

thereby establishing the second part. ■

It is an equally obvious result that welfare improvement, measured by a positive present value of future consumption changes, or a positive present value of future changes in total utility, cannot serve as an indicator of sustainability if there is positive population growth. The reason is that declining per capita utility throughout (that is, $du(\mathbf{c}^*(s))/dt < 0$ for all $s > t$) is consistent with a positive present value of future consumption changes and a positive present value of future changes in total utility if population growth is sufficiently large.

Therefore, an investigation of converse versions of Proposition 4 is of interest only in the case of constant population. In this case, it follows from Propositions 1 and 2 that both the present value of future consumption changes, $\int_t^\infty \mathbf{p}(s)\dot{\mathbf{C}}^*(s)ds$, and the value of net investments, $\mathbf{q}(t)\mathbf{I}^*(t)$, are exact indicators of welfare improvement independently of the properties of the function $u$ (see note 6). The next section reports on a negative result: that a positive value of net investments at time $t$ does not imply that development at time $t$ is sustainable.

The subsequent Section 7 presents an investigation of the question whether sustainable development, rather than the stronger premise of sustained development used in Proposition 4, is sufficient for non-negative values of net investments, when there is no population growth that facilitates an expansion of the economy. It follows from the analysis of Pezzey (2004) that it is indeed the case that development is sustainable only if the value of net investments is non-negative, in the special case where the economy implements a discounted utilitarian optimum. However this result does not hold in general.

In both the next two sections I adopt the rather stringent assumptions on the working of the economy imposed in Section 2 and follow the analysis presented in Asheim, Buchholz and Withagen (2003). The population is assumed to be constant and normalized to 1, implying that $\mathbf{c} = \mathbf{C}$. As the results on the relationship between sustainability and the value of net investments are negative, such stringent assumptions make the results stronger. In the concluding remark, I discuss the reliability of welfare improvement, as measured by the value of net investments, as an indicator of sustainable development in an economy that works less perfectly.

# 6   DOES A NON-NEGATIVE VALUE OF NET INVESTMENTS IMPLY SUSTAINABLE DEVELOPMENT?

Consider the following claim: if the value of net investments $\mathbf{q}(t)\mathbf{I}^*(t)$ is non-negative for $t \in (0,T)$, then, for any $t \in (0, T)$, $u(\mathbf{c}^*(t))$ can be sustained forever given $\mathbf{K}^*(t)$. This claim is not true in the Dasgupta-Heal-Solow model (see, for example, Dasgupta and Heal, 1974, and

Solow, 1974). In this model, there are two capital stocks: man-made capital, denoted by $K_M$, and a non-renewable natural resource, the stock of which is denoted by $K_N$. So, $\mathbf{K} = (K_M, K_N)$. The initial stocks are given by $\mathbf{K}^0 = (K_M^0, K_N^0)$. The technology is described by a Cobb-Douglas production function $F(K_M, -I_N) = K_M^a(-I_N)^b$ depending on two inputs, man-made capital $K_M$ and the raw material $-I_N$ that can be extracted without cost from the non-renewable resource. The output from the production process is used for consumption and for investments in man-made capital $I_M$. Hence, $(c(t), \mathbf{I}(t), \mathbf{K}(t), 1)$ is attainable at time $t$ if and only if $c(t) + I_M(t) \le K_M(t)^a(-I_N(t))^b$ where $a > 0, b > 0$ and $a + b \le 1$, and $c(t) \ge 0$, $K_M(t) \ge 0$, $K_N(t) \ge 0$ and $-I_N(t) \ge 0$. With $r(t) := -I_N(t)$ denoting the flow of raw material, these assumptions entail

$$\int_0^\infty r(t)\,dt \le K_N^0 \quad \text{and} \quad r(t) \ge 0 \text{ for all } t \ge 0.$$

Writing $i(t) := I_M(t)$, the competitiveness condition C2 requires that

$$c^*(t) + i^*(t) = K_M^*(t)^a r^*(t)^b \tag{9}$$

$$p(t) = q_M(t) \tag{10}$$

$$q_M(t) \cdot b \cdot K_M^*(t)^a r^*(t)^{b-1} = 1 \tag{11}$$

$$q_M(t) \cdot a \cdot K_M^*(t)^{a-1} r^*(t)^b = -\dot{q}_M(t), \tag{12}$$

where (11) follows from $q_M(t) \cdot b \cdot K_M^*(t)^a r^*(t)^{b-1} = q_N(t)$ and $0 = \dot{q}_N(t)$ by choosing extracted raw material as numeraire: $q_N(t) \equiv 1$. Note that (11) and (12) entail that the growth rate of the marginal product of raw material equals the marginal product of man-made capital; thus, the Hotelling rule is satisfied.

Assume that $a > b > 0$. Then there is a strictly positive maximum constant rate of consumption $\bar{c}$ that can be sustained forever given $\mathbf{K}^0$ (see, for example, Dasgupta and Heal, 1974, p. 203). It is well known that this constant consumption level can be implemented along a competitive path where net investment in man-made capital is at a constant level $\bar{i} = b\bar{c}/(1 - b)$. To give a counterexample to the claim above, fix a consumption level $c^* > \bar{c}$. Set $i^* = bc^*/(1 - b)$ and define $T$ by

$$\int_0^T (i^*/b)^{\frac{1}{b}}(K_M^0 + i^*t)^{-\frac{a}{b}}\,dt = K_N^0. \tag{13}$$

For $t \in (0, T)$, consider the path described by $\mathbf{K}^*(0) = \mathbf{K}^0$ and

$$c^*(t) = c^*$$
$$i^*(t) = i^*$$
$$r^*(t) = (i^*/b)^{\frac{1}{b}}(K_M^0 + i^*t)^{-\frac{a}{b}},$$

which by (13) implies that the resource stock is exhausted at time $T$. This feasible path is competitive during $(0, T)$ at prices $p(t) = q_M(t) = r^*(t)/i^*$ and $q_N(t) = 1$, implying that the value of net investments $q_M(t)i^* - q_N(t)r^*(t)$ is zero. Hence, even though the competitiveness condition C2 is satisfied (while C1 does not apply) and the value of net investments is non-negative during the interval $(0, T)$, the constant rate of consumption during this interval is not sustainable forever.

The path described above for the Dasgupta-Heal-Solow model is in fact not efficient, since the capital value transversality condition (1) is not satisfied: at time $T$ a certain stock of man-made capital, $K_M^*(T) = K_M^0 + i^*T$, has been accumulated. at the same time the flow of extracted raw material falls abruptly to zero due the exhaustion of the resource. With a Cobb-Douglas production function, the marginal productivity of $r$ is a strictly decreasing function of the flow of raw material for a given positive stock of man-made capital. This implies that profitable arbitrage opportunities can be exploited by shifting resource extraction from just before $T$ to just after $T$, implying that the Hotelling rule is not satisfied at that time.

As the path in this counterexample is inefficient, it might be possible that the value of net investments does not indicate sustainability in the example due to this lack of efficiency. However, this is not true either. The claim above does not become valid even if we consider paths for which competitiveness holds throughout and the capital value transversality condition is satisfied.

Again, counterexamples can be provided in the framework of the Dasgupta-Heal-Solow model. Asheim (1994) and Pezzy (1994) independently gave a counterexample by considering paths where the sum of utilities discounted at a constant utility discount rate is maximized. If, for some discount rate, the initial consumption level along such a discounted utilitarian optimum exactly equals the maximum sustainable consumption level given $K_M^0$ and $K_N^0$, then there exists an initial interval during which the value of net investments is strictly positive, while consumption is unsustainable given the current capital stocks $K_M^*(t)$ and $K_N^*(t)$. It is not quite obvious, however, that the premise of this statement can be fulfilled, that is, that there exists some discount rate such that initial consumption along the optimal path is barely sustainable. This was subsequently established for the Cobb-Douglas case by Pezzy and Withagen (1998). The fact that

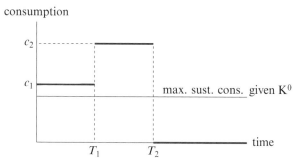

*Figure 10.1 Non-negative value of net investments does not imply sustainability*

their proof is quite intricate indicates, however, that this is not a trivial exercise.

Consequently, another type of counterexample is provided here. This example is also within the Dasgupta-Heal-Solow model and resembles the one given above. In particular, a path identical to that described in the first counterexample during an initial phase can always be extended to an efficient path. Moreover, this second counterexample can be used to show that there exist regular paths with non-negative value of net investments during an initial phase even if $a \leq b$, entailing that a positive and constant rate of consumption cannot be sustained indefinitely.

The example, illustrated in Figure 10.1, consists of three separate phases with constant consumption, constructed so that there are no profitable arbitrage opportunities at any time, not even at the two points, $T_1$ and $T_2$, where consumption is not continuous. Both capital stocks are exhausted at $T_2$, implying that consumption equals zero for $(T_2, \infty)$.

In the construction of the example, $K_M^0$ is given, while $K_N^0$ is treated as a parameter. Fix some consumption level $c_1 > 0$ and some terminal time $T_1$ of the first phase of the path. In the interval $(0, T_1)$ the path is – as in the first example – described by $\mathbf{K}^*(0) = \mathbf{K}^0$ and

$$c^*(t) = c_1$$

$$i^*(t) = i_1$$

$$r^*(t) = (i_1/b)^{\frac{1}{b}}(K_M^0 + i_1 t)^{-\frac{a}{b}},$$

where $i_1 = bc_1/(1 - b)$, but with the difference that the resource stock will not be exhausted at time $T_1$. As in the first example, the value of net investments equals zero during this phase.

The second phase starts at time $T_1$. Consumption jumps upward discontinuously to $c_2 > c_1$, but we ensure that the flow of raw material is continuous to remove profitable arbitrage opportunities. Consumption is constant at the new and higher level $c_2$, and, by the generalized Hartwick rule first established by Dixit, Hammond and Hoel (1980), the value of net investments measured in present value prices must be constant. That is, there exists $v_2 < 0$ such that, for all $t \in (T_1, T_2)$, $q_M(t)i*(t) = r*(t) + v_2$. By (9) and (11), this equality may (for any $c$ and $v$) be written as

$$K_M(t)^a r(t)^b - c = b \cdot K_M(t)^a r(t)^{b-1}(r(t) + v). \tag{14}$$

As $K_M^a r^b - b \cdot K_M^a r^{b-1} r = (1 - b) \cdot K_M^a r^b$, this implies

$$c = (1 - b) \cdot K_M(t)^a r(t)^b \left( 1 - \frac{b}{1 - b} \cdot \frac{v}{r(t)} \right). \tag{15}$$

Since both $K_M^*(t)$ and $r*(t)$ are continuous at time $T_1$, we can now use (15) to determine $v_2$ as follows:

$$c_2 = (1 - b) \cdot K_M^*(T_1)^a r*(T_1)^b \left( 1 - \frac{b}{1 - b} \cdot \frac{v_2}{r*(T_1)} \right). \tag{16}$$

By choosing $c_2 > K_M^*(T_1)^a r*(T_1)^b$ ($>c_1$) and fixing $v_2$ according to (16), $q_M(t)i*(t) = r*(t) + v_2$ combined with (9) determines a competitive path along which investment in man-made capital becomes increasingly negative. Determine $T_2$ as the time at which the stock of man-made capital reaches 0, and determine $K_N^0$ such that the resource stock is exhausted simultaneously. With both stocks exhausted, consumption equals 0 during the third phase $(T_2, \infty)$.

The Hotelling rule holds for $(0, T_1)$ and $(T_1, T_2)$, and by the construction of $v_2$, a jump in the marginal productivity of the natural resource at $T_1$ is avoided such that the Hotelling rule obtains even at $T_1$. Thus, the path is competitive throughout. By letting $u(c) = c$ and, for all $t \in (0, T_2)$, $\mu(t) = p(t)$, it follows that the path satisfies all assumptions of Section 2.

Note that the above construction is independent of whether $a > b$. If $a \le b$, so that no positive and constant rate of consumption can be sustained indefinitely, we have thus shown that having a non-negative value of net investments during an initial phase of a regular path is compatible with consumption exceeding the sustainable level.

However, even if $a > b$, so that the production function allows for a positive level of sustainable consumption, a counterexample can be obtained. For this purpose, increase $c_2$ beyond all bounds so that $v_2$

becomes more negative. Then $T_2$ decreases and converges to $T_1$, and the aggregate input of raw material in the interval $(T_1, T_2)$ – being bounded above by $r(T_1) \cdot (T_2 - T_1)$ since $r(t)$ is decreasing – converges to 0. This in turn means that, for large enough $c_2$, $c_1$ cannot be sustained forever given the choice of $K_N^0$ needed to achieve exhaustion of the resource at time $T_2$.

## 7 DOES SUSTAINABLE DEVELOPMENT IMPLY A NON-NEGATIVE VALUE OF NET INVESTMENTS?

The counterexample of Figure 10.1 shows that a non-negative value of net investments on an open interval is not a sufficient condition for consumption to be sustainable. Consider in this section whether this is a necessary condition: does a negative value of net investments during a time interval imply that consumption exceeds the sustainable level? The following result, due to Pezzy (2004), shows that such a converse implication holds under discounted utilitarianism.

**Proposition 5** *Let $T > 0$ be given. Consider a path $\{\mathbf{c}^*(t), \mathbf{I}^*(t), \mathbf{K}^*(t)\}_{t=0}^{\infty}$ satisfying the assumptions of Section 2 in a constant-population economy, with $\{\mu(t)\}_{t=0}^{\infty} = \{e^{-\rho t}\}_{t=0}^{\infty}$. If the value of net investments $\mathbf{q}(t)\mathbf{I}^*(t)$ is negative for $t \in (0, T)$, then, for any $t \in (0, T)$, $u(\mathbf{c}^*(t))$ cannot be sustained forever given $\mathbf{K}^*(t)$.*

**Proof.** It follows from (2) and (7) that $\mu(t)du(\mathbf{c}^*(t))/dt + d(\mathbf{q}(t)\mathbf{I}^*(t))/dt = 0$, implying $d(\mu(t)u(\mathbf{c}^*(t)))/dt + d(\mathbf{q}(t)\mathbf{I}^*(t))/dt = \dot{\mu}(t)u(\mathbf{c}^*(t))$. By combining this with $\mu(t) = e^{-\rho t}$ and $\lim_{t \to \infty} \mathbf{q}(t)\mathbf{I}^*(t) = 0$, so that $\int_t^{\infty} \mu(s)ds = \mu(t)/\rho$ and

$$\mu(t)u(\mathbf{c}^*(t)) + \mathbf{q}(t)\mathbf{I}^*(t) = -\int_t^{\infty} \dot{\mu}(s)u(\mathbf{c}^*(s))ds$$

$$= \rho \int_t^{\infty} \mu(s)u(\mathbf{c}^*(s))ds,$$

Weitzman's (1976) main result can be established:

$$\int_t^{\infty} \mu(s)\left(u(\mathbf{c}^*(t)) + \frac{\mathbf{q}(t)}{\mu(t)}\mathbf{I}^*(t)\right)ds = \int_t^{\infty} \mu(s)u(\mathbf{c}^*(s))ds. \qquad (17)$$

Since the path satisfies the condition of Section 2, it maximizes $\int_t^{\infty} \mu(s)u(\mathbf{c}(s))ds$ over all feasible paths. This, combined with (17), implies

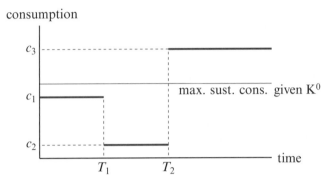

*Figure 10.2    Sustainability does not imply a non-negative value of net investments*

that the maximum sustainable utility level given $\mathbf{K}^*(t)$ cannot exceed $u(\mathbf{c}^*(t)) + \mathbf{q}(t)\mathbf{I}^*(t)/\mu(t)$. Suppose $\mathbf{q}(t)\mathbf{I}^*(t) < 0$ for $t \in (0,T)$. Then $u(\mathbf{c}^*(t)) > u(\mathbf{c}^*(t)) + \mathbf{q}(t)\mathbf{I}^*(t)/\mu(t)$. Hence, $u(\mathbf{c}^*(t))$ exceeds the maximum sustainable utility level and cannot be sustained forever given $\mathbf{K}^*(t)$. ∎

It is not, however, a general result that sustainability implies a non-negative value of net investments. This will be established next by showing that the following claim is not true, even under the conditions of Section 2: if the value of net investments $\mathbf{q}(t)\mathbf{I}^*(t)$ is negative for $t \in (0, T)$, then, for any $t \in (0, T)$, $u(\mathbf{c}^*(t))$ cannot be sustained forever given $\mathbf{K}^*(t)$.

Also in this case, a counterexample will be provided in the framework of the Dasgupta-Heal-Solow model. Assume that $a > b$ so that the production function allows for a positive level of sustainable consumption. Again, the example (which is illustrated in Figure 10.2) consists of three separate phases with constant consumption, constructed so that there are no profitable arbitrage opportunities at any time, not even at the two points, $T_1$ and $T_2$, where consumption is not continuous.

As before, $K_M^0$ is given, while $K_N^0$ is treated as a parameter. Fix some consumption level $c_1 > 0$ and some terminal time $T_1$ of the first phase of the path. Construct a path that has constant consumption $c_1$ and obeys the generalized Hartwick rule by having a negative and constant value of net investment, that is, $q_M(t)i^*(t) = r^*(t) + v_1$ with $v_1 < 0$ in the interval $(0, T_1)$, where $T_1$ is small enough to ensure that $K_M^*(T_1) > 0$. Let the path have, as its second phase, constant consumption $c_2 > 0$ and obey the generalized Hartwick rule with $v_2 > 0$ in the interval $(T_1, T_2)$. To satisfy the Hotelling rule at time $T_1$, $c_2$ and $v_2$ must fulfill (16); hence, by choosing $c_2 < (1 - b) \cdot K_M^*(T_1)^a r^*(T_1)^b$, it follows that $v_2 > 0$. Let $K_M^*(T_2)$ and $r^*(T_2)$ be the stock of man-made capital and the flow of raw material, respectively, at time $T_2$. At this point, the path switches over to the third phase with zero value of net investments, where the constant level of consumption is determined by $c_3 = (1 - b) K_M^*(T_2)^a r^*(T_2)^b$.

Since $a > b$, the production function allows for a positive level of sustainable consumption, and there exists an appropriate choice of $K_N^0$ that ensures resource exhaustion as $t \to \infty$ so that the capital value transversality condition (1) is satisfied. This initial resource stock depends on $T_1$ and $T_2$, but it is finite in any case. Keep $T_1$ fixed and increase $T_2$. As $T_2$ goes to infinity, then the stock $K_N^0$ needed will also tend to infinity.[8] The same holds true for the maximum sustainable consumption level $c^*$ that is feasible given $K_M^0$ and the initial resource stock $K_N^0$ determined in this way. Hence, by shifting $T_2$ far enough into the future, it follows that $c_1 < c^*$. Thus, a regular path can be constructed which has a first phase with a negative value of net investments even though the rate of consumption during this phase is sustainable given the initial stocks.

Both our counterexamples are consistent with the result of Proposition 2 (in the case with no population growth) that the value of net investments measures the present value of all future changes in utility. It follows directly from that result that if along an efficient path utility is monotonically decreasing/increasing indefinitely, then the value of net investments will be negative/positive, while utility will exceed/fall short of the sustainable level. The value of net investments thus indicates sustainability correctly along such monotone utility paths. Hence, the counterexamples of Figures 10.1 and 10.2 are minimal by having consumption (and thus utility) constant except at two points in time.

It is worth emphasizing the point made in Asheim (1994) and elsewhere that the relative equilibrium prices of different capital stocks today depend on the properties of the whole future path. The counterexamples of Figures 10.1 and 10.2 show how the relative price of natural capital depends positively on the consumption level of the generations in the distant future. Thus, the future development – in particular, the distribution of consumption between the intermediate and the distant future – affects the value of net investments today and, thereby, the usefulness of this measure as an indicator of sustainability today.

# 8   CONCLUDING REMARK

As shown in Sections 3 and 4, the value of net investments measures welfare improvement in an economy with no population growth, given that the assumptions of Section 2 are satisfied and the economy's dynamic welfare is given by a time-invariant Samuelson-Bergson welfare function that leads to a time-consistent optimal path. In Sections 6 and 7, we have shown that the value of net investments cannot serve as a reliable indicator of sustainability, even in a constant-population economy that satisfies the assumptions of Section 2.

It is worth noticing that the reliability of the value of net investments as an indicator of sustainability is further undermined if the resource allocation mechanism implements neither an optimal nor an efficient path. Consider, for example, an economy where traditional growth is promoted through high investment in reproducible capital goods, but where incorrect (or lack of) pricing of natural capital leads to depletion of natural and environmental resources that is excessive both from the perspective of short-run efficiency and long-run sustainability. Then utility growth in the short to intermediate run will, if the utility discount rate $\rho$ is large enough, lead to current growth in discounted utilitarian dynamic welfare. Hence, both the value of net investments and real NNP growth will be positive.[9] At the same time, the resource depletion may seriously undermine the long-run livelihood of future generations, so that current utility far exceeds the level that can be sustained forever.

## NOTES

1. See Dasgupta (2001b, Section 6.4) for a discussion of the deficiency of 'average utilitarianism'.
2. This leads to the problem of measuring the 'value of passage of time' using forward-looking terms. Methods for such measurement have been suggested by, for example, Aronsson et al. (1997), Kemp and Long (1982), Pezzey (2004), Seffon and Weale (1996), and Vellinga and Withagen (1996).
3. This is inspired by Dasgupta and Mäler (2000), Dasgupta (2001a, p. C20) and Arrow, Dasgupta and Mäler (2003a).
4. To see that $\mathbf{p}(t)\mathbf{C} - w(t)N + \mathbf{q}(t)\mathbf{I} + \dot{\mathbf{q}}(t)\mathbf{K}$ is instantaneous profit, note that $\mathbf{p}(t)\mathbf{C} + \mathbf{q}(t)\mathbf{I}$ is the value of production, $w(t)N$ is the cost of labor and $-\mathbf{q}(t)\mathbf{K}$ is the cost of holding capital.
5. By identifying the level of instantaneous social well-being at time $t$ with $U^*(t)$, we assume that there are stable welfare indifference surfaces in infinite-dimensional space when the well-being of each generation is measured by total utility, irrespectively of how consumption flows and population size develop. Discounted total utilitarianism leads to linear indifference surfaces in this space.
6. That $v(t)$ is positive means that instantaneous well-being is increased if an additional individual is brought into the economy even when the total consumption flows are kept fixed and must be spread over an additional person. See Asheim (2004, Sect. 4) for a discussion of the term $v(t)$.
7. That $u(\mathbf{c}^*(t))$ is positive means that instantaneous well-being is increased if an additional individual is brought into the economy and offered the existing per capita consumption flows.

8. It follows from (1.5) and $c_2 > 0$ that $r*(t) > bv_2/(1 - b)$ ( $> 0$ ) for all $t \in (T_1, T_2)$.
9. It follows from Asheim (2007a, Propositions 1(b) and 2(b)) that the value of net investments and real NNP growth measure welfare improvement even if the resource allocation mechanism is imperfect, provided that appropriate shadow prices are applied.

# REFERENCES

Aronsson, T., Johansson, P.-O., and Löfgren, K.-G. (1997), *Welfare Measurement, Sustainability and Green National Accounting*. Edward Elgar, Cheltenham.

Arrow, K., Dasgupta, P.S. and Mäler, K.-G. (2003a), Evaluating projects and assessing sustainable development in imperfect economies. *Environmental and Resource Economics* **26**, 647–685.

Arrow, K.J., Dasgupta, P.S. and Mäler, K.-G. (2003b), The genuine savings criterion and the value of population. *Economic Theory* **21**, 217–225.

Asheim, G.B. (1994), Net National Product as an Indicator of Sustainability. *Scandinavian Journal of Economics* **96**, 257–265.

Asheim, G.B. (2003), Green national accounting for welfare and sustainability: A taxonomy of assumptions and results, *Scottish Journal of Political Economy* **50**, 113–130.

Asheim, G.B. (2004), Green national accounting with a changing population. *Economic Theory* **23**, 601–619.

Asheim, G.B. (2007a), Can NNP be use for welfare comparisons? *Environment and Development Economics* **12**, 11–31.

Asheim, G.B. (2007b), *Justifying, Characterizing and Indicating Sustainability*. Springer, Dordrecht.

Asheim, G.B., Buchholz, W. and Withagen, C. (2003), The Hartwick Rule: Myths and Facts, *Evironmental and Resource Economics* **25**, 129–150.

Asheim, G.B. and Weitzman, M.L. (2001), Does NNP growth indicate welfare improvement? *Economics Letters* **73**, 233–239.

Dasgupta, P.S. (2001a), Valuing objects and evaluating policies in imperfect economies, *Economic Journal* **111**, C1–C29.

Dasgupta, P.S. (2001b), *Human Well-Being and the Natural Environment*. Oxford University Press, Oxford.

Dasgupta, P.S. and Heal, G.M. (1974), The optimal depletion of exhaustible resources, *Review of Economic Studies* (Symposium), 3–28.

Dasgupta, P.S. and Mäler, K.-G. (2000), Net national product, wealth, and social well-being, *Environment and Development Economics* **5**, 69–93.

Dixit, A., Hammond, P. and Hoel, M. (1980), On Hartwick's rule for regular maximin paths of capital accumulation and resource depletion, *Review of Economic Studies* **47**, 551–556.

Kemp, M.C. and Long, N.V. (1982), On the evaluation of social income in a dynamic economy: Variations on a Samuelsonian theme, in G.R. Feiwel (ed.), *Samuelson and Neoclassical Economics*, Kluwer Academic Press, Dordrecht, 185–189.

Meade, J.E. (1955), *Trade and Welfare*. Oxford University Press, Oxford.

Mirrlees, J.A. (1967), Optimal growth when the technology is changing. *Review of Economic Studies* (Symposium Issue) **34**, 95–124.

Pezzey, J.C.V. (1994), *Theoretical Essays on Sustainability and Environmental Policy*. PhD Thesis, University of Bristol.

Pezzey, J.C.V. (1997), Sustainability constraints versus 'optimality' versus intertemporal concern, and axioms versus data, *Land Economics* **73**, 448–466.

Pezzey, J.C.V. (2004), One-sided unsustainability tests with amenities and shifts in technology, trade and population, *Journal of Environmental Economics and Management* **48**, 613–631.

Pezzey, J.C.V. and Withagen, C.A. (1998). The rise, fall and sustainability of capital-resource economies, *Scandinavian Journal of Economics* **100**, 513–527.

Samuelson, P. (1961), The evaluation of 'social income': Capital formation and wealth, in
    F.A. Lutz and D.C. Hague (eds), *The Theory of Capital*, St. Martin's Press, New York,
    32–57.
Sefton, J.A. and Weale, M.R. (1996), The net national product and exhaustible resources:
    The effects of foreign trade, *Journal of Public Economics* **61**, 21–47.
Sefton, J.A. and Weale, M.R. (2006), The concept of income in a general equilibrium, *Review
    of Economic Studies* **73**, 219–249.
Solow, R.M. (1974), Intergenerational equity and exhaustible resources, *Review of Economic
    Studies* (Symposium), 29–45.
Vellinga, N. and Withagen, C. (1996), On the concept of green national income, *Oxford
    Economic Papers* **48**, 499–514.
Weitzman, M.L. (1976), On the welfare significance of national product in a dynamic
    economy, *Quarterly Journal of Economics* **90**, 156–162.

# 11 Genuine saving, social welfare and rules for sustainability
*Kirk Hamilton*

## 1 INTRODUCTION

Environmental accounting has its roots in concerns that the national accounts are neither accounting for the depreciation of environmental capital (when a mineral is extracted for example) nor measuring the damage from pollution of the environment which is a by-product of the generation of GDP. These concerns appear in a variety of guises in the symposium volume on environmental accounting edited by Ahmad *et al.* (1989), as well as in empirical work such as the Repetto *et al.* (1989) study of Indonesia. While these early studies focused on adjusted measures of income, Pearce and Atkinson (1993) were the first to explicitly link the changes in wealth associated with depletion and damage to the environment to an evolving theory of sustainable development.

The links between sustainable development and the depletion of natural resources were laid down in earlier theoretical work in the 1970s. As a result of the concerns raised by the first oil crisis, a 1974 symposium volume of the *Review of Economic Studies* drew together papers by leading economists on the question of the sustainability of economies that are dependent on exhaustible resources. In a key contribution, Solow (1974) showed that constant consumption is feasible over an infinite time horizon in an economy with an exhaustible resource if the production function is Cobb-Douglas (so that the elasticity of substitution between natural resources and other factors is unity), the elasticity of output with respect to produced capital is greater than the elasticity with respect to the resource, and resource pricing is dynamically efficient. This economy is sustainable by Pezzey's (1989) definition, in that the path for consumption is everywhere non-declining.

Hartwick's (1977) insight, that underlying the Solow result is a simple rule ('invest resource rents'), laid the foundation for the theory of sustainable development. This 'Hartwick rule' also suggested how environmental accounting, in this instance accounting for exhaustible resources, could underpin policy rules for achieving sustainable development. While the environmental accounting literature subsequently returned to the focus on measuring income (see, for instance, Hartwick, 1990, and Mäler, 1991), Hartwick's rule remained a fundamental result concerning the sustainability of development.

From the perspective of the literature on sustainable development in 2008, it is clear that the Hartwick rule implies maintaining a net (or 'genuine') level of saving that is precisely 0 at each point in time. Subsequent papers in the Hartwick rule literature, particularly Dixit *et al.* (1980), showed that this result generalizes to multiple assets, and not just stocks of exhaustible resources.

This chapter is not solely about environmental accounting, therefore. It is about asset accounting in general, and the linkage between asset accounts, social welfare and sustainable development. But as the empirical portion of the chapter will show, depletion of natural assets is a significant source of potential unsustainability in many developing countries today. For these countries, environmental accounting is very much a live issue.

The plan of the chapter is as follows. The next section will lay out the basic theory of asset accounting, social welfare and sustainability. This is followed by a presentation of a general rule for sustainable development, along with special cases of this rule. The question of measuring changes in social welfare in optimal and competitive economies is examined. Next is the presentation of empirical results on 'adjusted net saving' published by the World Bank. The following section presents the results of econometric tests of these saving measures – is adjusted net saving as published actually correlated with future changes in social welfare as theory predicts? The chapter ends with consideration of some empirical and conceptual issues. Finally the Appendix provides a compact derivation of the main theoretical results, using the example of a Dasgupta-Heal extractive economy.

## 2   SOCIAL WELFARE

When economists speak of 'social welfare', they are explicitly including an intertemporal dimension. The issue, of course, is that measuring current well-being does not tell you whether this well-being can be sustained in the future.

The fact that income or consumption does not have a direct welfare interpretation was highlighted in a seminal paper by Samuelson (1961), who argued that the choice of a welfare measure has to be made 'in the space of all present and future consumption . . . the only valid approximation to a measure of welfare comes from computing *wealth-like* magnitudes not income magnitudes' (Samuelson, 1961, pp 50–57; italics in original). Irving Fisher (1906) provided the original insight that the most complete measure of current wealth should be the present value of future consumption.

In a recent paper, Hamilton and Hartwick (2005) make these notions concrete in a competitive economy with a constant returns to scale production technology.[1] Total wealth $W$ is defined as the sum of asset values,

$$W = \sum_{i=1}^{N} p_i K_i \qquad (1)$$

Here the $K_i$ are the stocks of assets in the economy, and the $p_i$ are their shadow prices. To measure sustainability, it is important that the wealth measure spans as wide a range of assets as possible, including assets with negative shadow prices such as pollution stocks. Hamilton and Hartwick show that for interest rate $r$ and consumption $C$,

$$W = \sum_{i=1}^{N} p_i K_i = \int_{t}^{\infty} C(s) \cdot e^{-\int_{t}^{s} r(\tau)d\tau} ds. \qquad (2)$$

This is just Irving Fisher made explicit: total wealth is equal to the present value of future consumption, which in turn corresponds to Samuelson's notion of total wealth as a measure of social welfare.[2] Hamilton and Withagen (2007) show that this result holds for multiple consumption goods.

## 2.1 Saving and Social Welfare

If wealth measures social welfare, then changes in wealth should tell us about changes in social welfare and – as will be made explicit below – sustainability. Hamilton and Clemens (1999) ground the insights of Pearce and Atkinson (1993) in the theory of optimal growth. They show that genuine saving $G$, defined as the change in real asset values,

$$G = \sum_{i=1}^{N} p_i \dot{K}_i, \qquad (3)$$

is equal to the change in social welfare in an optimal economy. That is, for utility $U$, social welfare $V$ (here measured in utility units), marginal utility of consumption $U_C$, and constant pure rate of time preference $\rho$, the following expressions hold:

$$V = \int_{t}^{\infty} U(C,\ldots) \cdot e^{-\rho(s-t)}ds \qquad (4)$$

and

$$G = \frac{\dot{V}}{U_C}. \qquad (5)$$

Social welfare is equal to the present value of utility, and genuine saving is equal to the instantaneous change in social welfare measured in dollars.[3] The utility function can include consumption $C$ and any other set of goods and bads to which people attribute value.

While Hamilton and Clemens (1999) analyze optimal economies, Dasgupta and Mäler (2000) consider non-optimal economies which are driven by an allocation mechanism which determines the path of all future stocks and flows in the economy. For shadow (or 'accounting') prices defined as the contribution to social welfare made by each asset at the margin, Dasgupta and Mäler show that the equivalent to expression (5) will hold – genuine saving in the non-optimal economy is proportional to the change in social welfare.

## 3   RULES FOR SUSTAINABLE DEVELOPMENT

Given the link between genuine saving, changes in social welfare and unsustainable development, the obvious next question is how saving features in policy rules for achieving sustainable development. The Hartwick rule, where genuine saving is set equal to 0 at each point in time, provides one example. This section looks at generalizing the Hartwick rule.

One alternative to presuming either optimality or a full allocation mechanism in an economy is to assume that the economy is competitive – roughly speaking, this implies that producers maximize profits over time, while households maximize their utility. This is the key assumption in Hamilton and Withagen (2007), who derive the following expression in competitive economies:

$$\dot{U} = U_C G(r - \dot{G}/G) \qquad (6)$$

This relates the change in utility to the difference between the interest rate and the growth rate of genuine saving, which provides the basis for the following rules.

## 3.1 General Rule for Sustainability

In a competitive economy, a policy that ensures that $G > 0$ and $\dot{G}/G < r$ at each time will ensure that the economy is sustainable.

## 3.2 Special Cases of the General Rule for Sustainability

The following special cases of the rule for sustainability have been shown to hold and be feasible in a Dasgupta-Heal[4] economy:

- *The Hartwick rule.* As noted in the introduction, perhaps the most famous rule for sustainability is that of Hartwick (1977), who shows that if genuine saving is equal to 0 at each point in the future, then utility will be constant. This, it can be seen, is a special case of the general rule for sustainability specified by Hamilton and Withagen (and foreshadowed in Hamilton and Hartwick 2005). Hartwick (1977) shows that the zero genuine saving rule is feasible if (i) the Hotelling rule holds, and (ii) the production technology is Cobb-Douglas with $\beta < \alpha$, where $\alpha$ and $\beta$ are the elasticities of output with respect to produced capital and natural resources respectively.
- *Constant genuine saving rate.* Hamilton and Withagen (2007) show that if $F$ is production, $R$ is resource extraction and $p$ its shadow price, then

$$G = \dot{K} - pR = \gamma F \text{ for constant } \gamma \text{ satisfying } 0 < \gamma < \alpha - \beta \quad (7)$$

  is a feasible policy rule for sustainability, yielding unbounded consumption in the competitive Dasgupta-Heal economy.[5]
- *Constant level of genuine saving.* Hamilton et al. (2006) show that if genuine saving is held fixed at some constant level $\bar{G}$ satisfying $0 < \bar{G} < \alpha F(K_0, R(0))$ then consumption is again unbounded in the competitive Dasgupta-Heal economy.

The Hartwick rule is an important result in the theory of sustainability, because it shows that a simple policy rule can yield a sustainable path in the face of severe constraints: fixed technology and an exhaustible resource that is an essential input to production. It turns out to be a special case of a more general rule which yields the potential for increasing (and unbounded) consumption.

## 4   SOCIAL WELFARE AND SUSTAINABILITY

The next question explored in the literature concerns the relationship between saving, sustainability and social welfare in optimal and competitive economies. The exact relationship turns out to hinge upon whether the instantaneous utility discount rate (or pure rate of time preference) is constant or time-varying.

For an optimal economy with utility discount factor $1 \geq v(t) > 0$, $\dot{v} < 0$, Aronsson *et al.* (1997) and Hamilton (1997) show that the analogue to expression (5) is,[6]

$$G = \frac{1}{U_C} \int_t^\infty \dot{U} \frac{v(s)}{v(t)} ds. \tag{8}$$

It follows that if $G < 0$ at one point, then it must be the case that $\dot{U} < 0$ over some future interval, which in turn implies that the economy is on an unsustainable path.

However, in general it is the case that,

$$\int_t^\infty \dot{U} \frac{v(s)}{v(t)} ds \neq \frac{d}{dt} \int_t^\infty U \frac{v(s)}{v(t)} ds \, (= \dot{V})$$

and so the sign of $G$ does not indicate whether social welfare is rising or falling.

If there is a constant pure rate of time preference $\rho$, so that $v(t) = e^{-\rho t}$, it follows that,

$$\dot{V} = \int_t^\infty \dot{U} \cdot e^{-\rho(s-t)} ds. \tag{9}$$

For an optimal economy with constant pure rate of time preference, therefore, $G < 0$ implies that social welfare is falling and that the economy is on an unsustainable path (Pezzey (2004) refers to $G$ as a one-sided sustainability indicator).

Since expressions (6) and (9) hold in a competitive economy with constant pure rate of time preference, it follows that if the general rule for sustainability ($G > 0$ and $\dot{G}/G < r$) applies at each point of an unbounded interval $[t, \infty)$, then both utility and social welfare are rising at each point in time (this result is derived in Hamilton and Withagen 2007).

For the optimal economy, a point estimate of genuine saving $G$ indicates whether the development path is an unsustainable one; if the pure rate of time preference is constant, then $G$ measures the (dollar-valued) instantaneous change in social welfare. In contrast, if the general rule for sustainability is applied over an unbounded interval in a competitive economy, then the path is sustainable and social welfare is rising everywhere along the path. In the competitive economy, genuine saving becomes a policy variable for achieving sustainability and increasing social welfare when the pure rate of time preference is constant.

### 4.1 A Footnote on Flows versus Stocks

The foregoing results on genuine saving and sustainability all hinge directly on the value of $G$, which, as expression (3) illustrates, is a measure of the real change in the value of stocks. As Atkinson and Hamilton (2007) show, however, there is a relationship between pure flows and social welfare. Their example is noise pollution, which is assumed to negatively affect utility in an optimal Dasgupta-Heal economy.

For noise level $e$, total utility is given by $U(C,e)$, $U_e < 0$. For resource stock $S$, genuine saving is measured as $G = \dot{k} + p\dot{S}$, where $p$ is the shadow price of resources in the ground. Defining the marginal damage from noise as $b \equiv -U_e/U_C$, using expressions (5) and (6) it is possible to show that,

$$\frac{1}{r}(\dot{C} - b\dot{e} + \dot{G}) = \frac{1}{U_C}\frac{d}{dt}\int_t^\infty U(C,e) \cdot e^{-\rho(s-t)}ds = \frac{\dot{V}}{U_C}. \qquad (10)$$

The term $\dot{C} - b\dot{e} + \dot{G}$ can be interpreted as the sum of the change in the real value of consumption (measured broadly to include noise pollution) and the change in the total value of genuine saving. The sign of this term indicates whether social welfare is rising or falling, while this term divided by the interest rate measures the dollar-valued change in social welfare (see Asheim and Weitzman 2001).

## 5  SUMMING UP THE THEORY

The theoretical work on wealth, social welfare and sustainability carried out over more than three decades[7] has laid a firm foundation for both the practice and the measurement of sustainable development. The main results summarized in the chapter include the following:

- For competitive economies with constant returns to scale, total wealth (the sum of the value of individual assets, suitably shadow priced) is equal to the present value of a generalized measure of future consumption.

- The change in real wealth – genuine saving – measures the change in social welfare in optimal economies with a constant pure rate of time preference. For suitable definitions of prices, and/or inclusion of the present value of the welfare impacts of externalities in genuine saving, this result holds true for non-optimal economies as well.
- Point measures of negative genuine saving imply that utility must fall over some future interval on the optimal path – that is, that the economy is not sustainable by standard definitions.
- For competitive economies, there is a general rule for sustainability: maintaining positive genuine saving and ensuring that it grows at a rate less than the interest rate will ensure continuously rising utility.
- Special cases of the general rule for sustainability include the Hartwick rule (maintaining zero genuine saving), maintaining constant positive levels of genuine saving, and maintaining constant positive genuine saving rates.
- While point estimates of genuine saving indicate whether social welfare is rising or falling in optimal economies with a constant pure rate of time preference, in competitive economies[8] it is only by following the general rule for sustainability over unbounded intervals that increasing social welfare can be assured.

## 6   EMPIRICAL EXPERIENCE

As noted in the introduction, there has been more than twenty years of empirical efforts to adjust national accounts to include the effects of depleting and damaging the environment. This section of the chapter takes a selective look at recent empirical work, focusing on the measurement efforts at the World Bank, where there has been an ongoing attempt to ensure that theory and practice are in alignment.

The World Bank has been publishing genuine saving (formally termed 'adjusted net saving') in the *World Development Indicators* since 1999 and has constructed a time series of saving estimates, including depletion of natural resources, dating back to 1970. This time series lends itself to simulations and hypothesis testing concerning saving and sustainability.

Hamilton *et al.* (2006) use this time series to develop a 'Hartwick rule counterfactual' – how rich would resource-dependent countries be if they had invested the rents on exhaustible natural resources in produced capital over 1970–2000? Figure 11.1 shows the results of calculating the counterfactual produced capital stock (using a perpetual inventory model) under two assumptions: zero genuine saving (the standard Hartwick rule), and

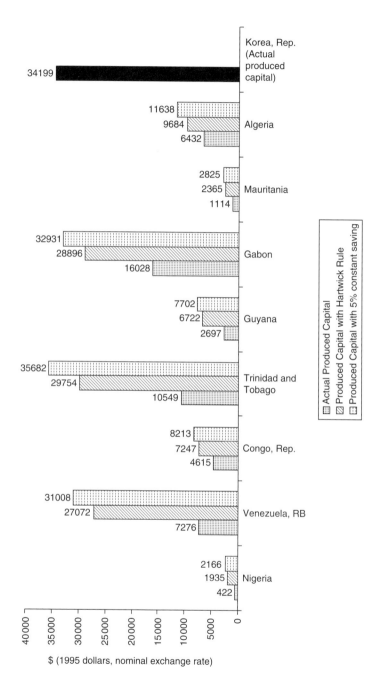

*Source:* Hamilton *et al.* (2006).

*Figure 11.1  Actual and counterfactual produced assets per capita, 2000*

constant positive genuine saving (equal to 5 per cent of midpoint GDP). Year 2000 produced capital per person in South Korea is also shown as a benchmark.

For many of the most resource-dependent countries featured in Figure 11.1, the results are striking. Venezuela and Trinidad and Tobago would be 3–4 times as rich, and Gabon twice as rich, if they had in fact invested their resource rents. Nigeria would not be hugely wealthy, but its wealth would have increased five-fold. Moreover, these simulations are purely mechanical, ignoring the likely positive growth effects associated with shifting an economy away from high dependence on resource extraction.

Table 11.1 shows the decomposition of genuine saving by region and by country characteristic (fragile states, emerging market states, other developing countries, and high income countries[9]) in 2005. The World Bank figures for genuine saving treat education expenditures as investment in human capital (contrary to standard national accounting practice) and deduct damages from $CO_2$ emissions based on an assumed property right: that countries have the right not to be polluted by their neighbors.

The figures in Table 11.1 show distinctive patterns. Aggregate world genuine saving is moderately positive, as is also the case for high-income countries. Saving is robust in East Asia and the Pacific and South Asia, while it is moderately negative in Eastern Europe and Central Asia, the Middle East and North Africa, and Sub-Saharan Africa. Genuine saving is sharply negative in oil-producing countries and fragile states.

Figure 11.2 shows recent trends in genuine saving by country classes with similar characteristics. While high-income and emerging market economies maintained stable and fairly robust levels of saving over 1990–2005, fragile states experienced erratic and generally sharply negative savings. Genuine saving in other developing countries was on a downward trend from moderately positive to moderately negative levels over this 15 year period.

The empirical measures of genuine saving published by the World Bank show that negative saving, and therefore potentially unsustainable development, is more than a theoretical possibility. In any given year, 20–30 countries have negative savings.

## 7    TESTING GENUINE SAVING

The theory relating genuine saving to changes in social welfare is clear, and empirical measures of genuine saving have been published for over 150 countries covering more than 30 years. As an empirical matter, the obvious next question is whether there is evidence that saving is actually

*Table 11.1  Genuine saving, 2005 (percent of GNI)*

| | Gross national saving | Human capital | Consumption of fixed capital | Natural resource depletion | PM10 | CO2 | Genuine saving |
|---|---|---|---|---|---|---|---|
| East Asia & Pacific | 44.4 | 2.2 | 10.3 | 7.8 | 1.2 | 1.2 | 26.1 |
| E. Europe & Central Asia | 23.9 | 4.1 | 10.4 | 17.5 | 0.6 | 1.2 | -1.7 |
| Latin America & Caribbean | 21.0 | 4.3 | 12.0 | 8.6 | 0.4 | 0.4 | 3.9 |
| Middle East & North Africa | 33.7 | 4.5 | 10.9 | 32.2 | 0.6 | 1.2 | -6.7 |
| South Asia | 29.4 | 3.5 | 9.1 | 5.5 | 0.8 | 1.2 | 16.5 |
| Sub-Saharan Africa | 17.3 | 3.8 | 10.7 | 16.1 | 0.4 | 0.7 | -6.8 |
| Emerging market | 30.6 | 3.5 | 10.7 | 9.9 | 0.8 | 1.0 | 11.7 |
| Other developing countries | 30.0 | 3.7 | 10.2 | 27.0 | 0.6 | 0.9 | -5.0 |
| Fragile states | 19.9 | 3.4 | 10.0 | 33.4 | 0.9 | 1.1 | -22.2 |
| High income | 18.6 | 4.6 | 13.1 | 1.4 | 0.3 | 0.3 | 8.2 |
| **World** | **22.1** | **4.3** | **12.3** | **4.9** | **0.4** | **0.5** | **8.1** |
| High oil producers | 34.6 | 3.6 | 9.1 | 41.7 | 0.5 | 1.5 | -14.4 |

*Source:* World Bank (2007).

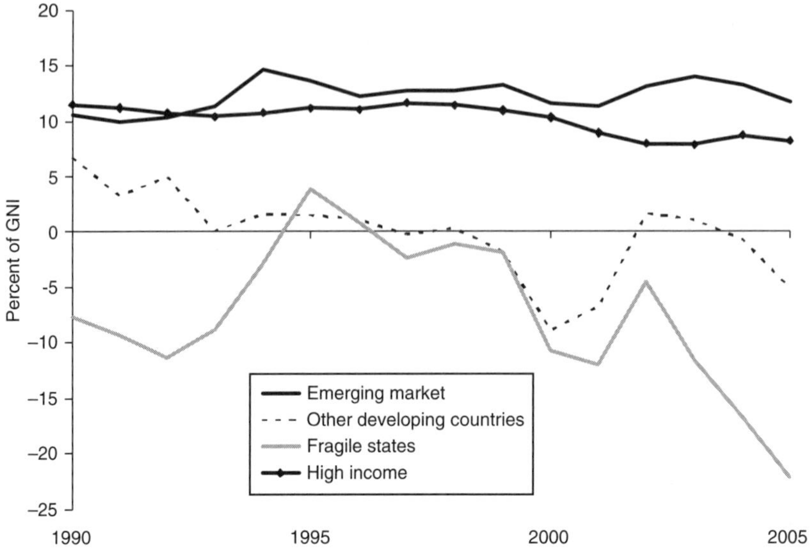

*Source:* World Bank (2007).

*Figure 11.2    Trends in genuine saving, 1990–2005*

correlated with changes in social welfare, a proposition that can be tested using the time series data.

Ferreira and Vincent (2005) use the World Bank historical data on consumption and genuine saving to test a basic proposition linking current saving to future welfare. They start with a result from Weitzman (1976), [10] for constant consumption rate of interest $r$:

$$G = r \int_t^\infty C(s)\, e^{-r(s-t)} ds - C. \tag{11}$$

Genuine saving is equal to the difference between a particular weighted average of future consumption and current consumption. This relationship is tested econometrically using per capita data from 1970 to 2000. Ferreira and Vincent find that the relationship holds best for non-OECD countries, and that there is a better fit as more stringent measures of saving are tested, that is, when going from gross saving to net saving to genuine saving (but excluding the adjustment for investment in human capital, which performs very badly).

Ferreira *et al.* (2008) develop a much less restrictive model linking saving per capita to changes in per capita social welfare. For a competitive economy, they define genuine saving per capita $g$ as,

$$g = \frac{\dot{K}}{N} - F_R q - \gamma w.$$

Here $N$ is total population, $q$ is resource extraction per capita, $F_R$ is the shadow price of the resource, $\gamma$ is the population growth rate and $w$ is total wealth per capita. The last term is therefore Malthusian in its effect, representing the wealth-diluting effect of population growth. If $\gamma$ varies over time, then the analogue to expression (5) for this economy is,

$$\int_t^\infty \dot{c} \cdot e^{-\int_t^s r(\tau) - \gamma(\tau)d\tau} ds = g(t) - \int_t^\infty \dot{\gamma} \cdot w \cdot e^{-\int_t^s r(\tau) - \gamma(\tau)d\tau} ds. \tag{12}$$

The left-hand side of expression (12) is the dollar-valued measure of the change in social welfare in per capita terms (note that the discount rate is equal to the interest rate minus the population growth rate). The right-hand side is the most general measure of genuine saving per capita, accounting for the effects of the exogenously changing population growth rate.

This relationship between genuine saving and social welfare is tested econometrically for a panel of developing countries over the period 1970–1982, employing increasingly complete measures of genuine saving, as in Ferreira and Vincent (2005).[11] Ferreira *et al.* find that saving per capita is correlated with the change in social welfare per capita *only* when the measure of net saving is adjusted to reflect the depletion of natural resources. Environmental accounting turns out to be fundamental to the usefulness of genuine saving as an indicator of changes in social welfare.

Genuine saving may be unique among the set of potential indicators of sustainable development,[12] in that it has passed this key empirical test: historical data support the proposition that genuine saving is robustly correlated with changes in social welfare.

# 8   SAVING AND SUSTAINABILITY: EMPIRICAL AND CONCEPTUAL ISSUES

Although Ferreira *et al.* (2008) find a strong relationship between net saving and changes in social welfare, they suggest that measurement error probably explains the lack of significant improvement in the relationship

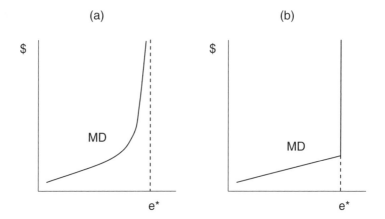

*Figure 11.3    Thresholds with alternative marginal damage curves for pollution emissions*

when the wealth-diluting effects of population growth are taken into account. While at the conceptual level the literature has made considerable progress on accounting for exhaustible resources, living resources, pollution, technological change and exogenous resource price changes (see Hamilton and Atkinson 2006 for a recent exposition of some of these issues), there remain significant empirical challenges. Real-world data are often incomplete and imperfectly measured. Key data, such as marginal extraction or harvest costs, are generally not available for most natural resources.

Limited substitution possibilities between different types of assets also present a challenge to the measurement of sustainable development. While empirical estimates of genuine saving may be non-negative in a given situation, if the elasticity of substitution between natural and produced assets is less than 1, then the underlying theory suggests that the economy will not be sustainable – Dasgupta and Heal (1979) and Hamilton (1995) show that the Hartwick rule path is not feasible for a CES production function with an exhaustible resource as an essential input and an elasticity of substitution less than unity.

Threshold effects are another challenging issue for the measurement of sustainability. An example of a threshold would be a point where the emissions or the accumulated stock of a pollutant force a natural system to change state suddenly – for instance, if greenhouse gases accumulate to the point where there is a runaway greenhouse effect, yielding potentially unbounded marginal damages.

Figure 11.3 depicts a situation where marginal damages are unbounded when a threshold level of emissions e* is reached. Whether genuine saving (defined to include the damage to economic assets associated with exposure to pollution emissions) can serve as a useful indicator of sustainability in the presence of this threshold depends critically on whether the marginal damage curve is smooth as the threshold is approached. If the marginal damage curve is unbounded but smooth, as seen in Figure 11.3(a), then genuine saving will turn negative before the threshold is reached – at this point, policy could be altered in order to keep the economy operating below the threshold. If, however, the marginal damage curve is not smooth at the threshold level, as in Figure 11.3(b), then genuine saving has limited ability to measure sustainability – the economy could be approaching the threshold level e* with positive saving, owing to the relatively flat marginal damage curve, but then suddenly face catastrophe when the threshold is reached.

An additional limitation of genuine saving as a sustainability indicator is that, as a practical matter, it can never truly be comprehensive in its coverage of assets. This is important because the underlying theory implicitly assumes that the asset accounting is complete, in the sense that all assets appearing as inputs into the production or utility functions are accounted for in the model. In the face of incomplete empirical measures, genuine saving figures therefore represent hurdle values for sustainability – for example, if genuine saving is measured to be +10 per cent of GNI in a given country, then the depreciation of any 'missing' assets must equal at least −10 per cent of GNI before it could be concluded that the country is on an unsustainable path.

Constructing complete asset accounts for an economy would be a non-trivial exercise. Table 11.2 shows the decomposition of wealth for selected South Asian countries, drawn from World Bank (2006). Figures on produced assets are calculated using investment data and a perpetual inventory model. For natural resources (the next five columns), unit rental values are estimated and combined with data on physical extent in order to arrive at asset values. Total wealth (the final column) is estimated using data on consumption and equation (2), which equates total wealth to the present value of future consumption.[13] 'Intangible' wealth is calculated as the difference between total wealth and the specific asset values reported in the first six columns of the table.

What is striking in Table 11.2 is the very large share (51.7 per cent–76.1 per cent) of intangible wealth in the total. Since this is measured as a residual, it is in some sense a measure of our ignorance. World Bank (2006) decomposes this wealth residual econometrically using cross-sectional data, and concludes that roughly half of the residual consists of human capital, while the other half is the value of institutional quality.

*Table 11.2   Decomposition of wealth per capita in South Asia, 2000 ($/capita and %)*

| | Produced | Subsoil | Forests | Cropland | Pasture | PA | Intangible | Total |
|---|---|---|---|---|---|---|---|---|
| Bangladesh | 817 | 83 | 7 | 810 | 52 | 9 | 4221 | 6000 |
| | 13.6% | 1.4% | 0.1% | 13.5% | 0.9% | 0.2% | 70.4% | |
| India | 1154 | 201 | 74 | 1340 | 192 | 122 | 3738 | 6820 |
| | 16.9% | 2.9% | 1.1% | 19.7% | 2.8% | 1.8% | 54.8% | |
| Nepal | 609 | 0 | 271 | 767 | 111 | 81 | 1964 | 3802 |
| | 16.0% | 0.0% | 7.1% | 20.2% | 2.9% | 2.1% | 51.7% | |
| Pakistan | 975 | 265 | 11 | 549 | 448 | 94 | 5529 | 7871 |
| | 12.4% | 3.4% | 0.1% | 7.0% | 5.7% | 1.2% | 70.2% | |
| Sri Lanka | 2710 | 0 | 82 | 485 | 84 | 166 | 11204 | 14731 |
| | 18.4% | 0.0% | 0.6% | 3.3% | 0.6% | 1.1% | 76.1% | |

*Note:*   PA: Protected Area. Numbers may not add up precisely due to rounding.

*Source:*   World Bank (2006) (selected countries).

While good microdata on educational attainment and employment earnings could underpin a fairly robust estimate of human capital in a given country, similarly robust ways to measure social or institutional capital appear to be out of reach at the moment.

# 9   CONCLUSIONS

This chapter has implicitly argued that the primary reason for constructing environmental accounts is to measure the contribution that changes in environmental assets make to changes in social welfare. If properly shadow priced, environmental asset accounts can clearly play this role.

For a complete measure of the change in social welfare, however, environmental accounts must form part of a comprehensive set of asset accounts. From this perspective, environmental assets have no special standing. But they do have many unique properties which lend considerable interest to their accounting. They yield rents, which can influence the behavior of economic actors. Some are finite and exhaustible. Others yield important external benefits, complicating the accounting. Still others are highly persistent global pollutants, which gives rise to enormous policy dilemmas, as the current discussion of international climate policy indicates. Moreover, the empirical work of Ferreira *et al.* (2008) shows that it is only when net saving is adjusted to reflect depletion of natural resources that a link between saving and social welfare in developing countries can be discerned.

From a development perspective, the other key feature of natural assets is that they often account for a very large share of national wealth – larger than produced capital in most low-income countries, as Table 11.2 suggests. Depletion of natural resources is 27 per cent of GNI in low-income countries, as Table 11.1 shows for 2005. As a result, development challenges are often closely linked to natural resource management challenges.

One central message of this chapter concerns the important role that genuine saving can play for countries aiming to accelerate development. It is simultaneously an indicator of the change in social welfare, an indicator of unsustainable development (when it is negative), and a key policy variable for countries aiming for sustainable development. Policies that affect the level of genuine saving, including monetary, fiscal, human resource, natural resource and environmental policies, can all potentially play a role in determining whether social welfare is rising or falling in an individual country.

The other central message of the chapter is that there is a general rule for sustainable development: ensure that genuine saving is positive and growing at a rate less than the interest rate at each point in time. If the elasticity of substitution between natural and other assets is equal to 1, simple variants of this rule can yield rising and unbounded consumption even in the face of fixed technology and finite resources.

Given the central role that genuine saving plays in the theory of social welfare and sustainable development, the empirical tests reported in the chapter reinforce the importance of this measure as a potential guide to policy. Policy makers can take actions to boost genuine saving and have confidence that there is evidence that saving today really does translate into increases in social welfare.

## APPENDIX:   KEY RESULTS ON WEALTH, SOCIAL WELFARE AND SUSTAINABILITY

The linkages between genuine saving, social welfare and sustainable development are simple to derive for the Dasgupta-Heal economy. Here capital $K$ and flow of natural resources $R$ are essential inputs to the production of a composite good, and output is divided between consumption and investment, $F(K, R) = C + \dot{K}$. The finite stock of natural resource $S$ is depleted by the amount $R$ at each point in time, $\dot{S} = -R$. Utility is given by $U(C)$ and is discounted by the declining function $1 \geq v(t) > 0$, $\dot{v} < 0$.

For a competitive economy, the interest rate is $F_K$, the shadow price in dollars of the resource is $F_R$, and this price follows a dynamically efficient path (the Hotelling rule), $\dot{F}_R/F_R = F_K$. Total wealth $W$ and the change in wealth are measured as,

$$W = K + F_R S \quad \text{and} \quad \dot{W} = \dot{K} + \dot{F}_R S + F_R \dot{S} = \dot{K} + F_K F_R S + F_R \dot{S}.$$

If production is characterized by constant returns to scale in the competitive economy, then consumption is given by

$$C = F - \dot{K} = F_K K + F_R R - \dot{K} = F_K K - F_R \dot{S} - \dot{K}.$$

Combining these expressions for consumption and change in wealth gives

$$C + \dot{W} = F_K W.$$

Taking a particular integral of this expression yields the basic wealth accounting relationship,

$$W = K + F_R S = \int_t^\infty C(s) \cdot e^{-\int_t^s F_K(\tau)d\tau} ds.$$

Now define genuine saving $G$ in this economy to be the change in real wealth,

$$G \equiv \dot{K} + F_R \dot{S} = \dot{K} - F_R R.$$

For this economy, it is straightforward to derive the link between savings growth and the path for utility,

$$
\begin{aligned}
\dot{U} &= U_C \dot{C} \\
&= U_C(F_K \dot{K} + F_R \dot{R} - \ddot{K}) \\
&= U_C(F_K \dot{K} - \dot{F}_R R + \dot{F}_R R + F_R \dot{R} - \ddot{K}) \\
&= U_C(F_K \dot{K} - F_K F_R R + F_R \dot{R} + \dot{F}_R R - \ddot{K}) \\
&= U_C(F_K G - \dot{G}).
\end{aligned}
\tag{A1}
$$

This is the basis for the generalized rule for sustainability: if genuine saving is positive and growing at a rate less than the rate of interest $F_K$ everywhere along a path, then utility is everywhere rising along this path.

Next we turn to the optimal economy, where social welfare $V$ is maximized over an infinite horizon, subject to the basic accounting identities of the Dasgupta-Heal economy:

$$\max V = \int_t^\infty \frac{v(s)}{v(t)} U(C(s))\,ds.$$

For shadow prices $\gamma_1$ and $\gamma_2$ the present value Hamiltonian $H$ is given by,

$$H = v(U + \gamma_1 \dot{K} + \gamma_2 \dot{S}) = v(U + U_C(\dot{K} + F_R \dot{S}))$$

$$= v(U + U_C(F - C + F_R \dot{S})).$$

From the first-order conditions for this problem, it is easily verified that the present value shadow price in utils for produced capital is $\gamma_1 = v U_C$, while the present value shadow price in utils for the resource is $\gamma_2 = v U_C F_R$.

The dynamic first-order condition for produced capital yields the Ramsey rule,

$$\tfrac{d}{dt}(v U_C) = -\frac{\partial H}{\partial K} = -v U_C F_K, \text{ or } \frac{\tfrac{d}{dt}(v U_C)}{v U_C} = -F_K.$$

For time $s > t$, the latter expression can be rewritten as

$$U_C(s) = \frac{v(t)}{v(s)} U_C(t) \cdot e^{-\int_t^s F_K(\tau)d\tau}.
\tag{A2}$$

In the optimal economy, expression (A1), linking growth in utility to the rate of growth of genuine saving, will also hold. We can therefore take a particular integral of expression (A1) to yield

$$G = \int_t^\infty \frac{\dot{U}(C(s))}{U_C(s)} e^{-\int_t^s F_K(\tau)d\tau} ds$$

or, applying expression (A2),

$$G = \frac{1}{U_C} \int_t^\infty \frac{v(s)}{v(t)} \dot{U}(C(s)) ds.$$

The latter expression links genuine saving to the Pezzey (1989) definition of sustainability: if genuine saving is negative at any one point in time, then utility must be falling over some interval of time in the future. A point measure of negative genuine saving is an indicator of unsustainability in the optimal economy.

If the pure rate of time preference is a constant $\rho$, then $v(t) = e^{-\rho t}$, and it follows that

$$G = \frac{1}{U_C} \int_t^\infty \dot{U}(C(s)) \cdot e^{-\rho(s-t)} ds = \frac{1}{U_C} \cdot \frac{d}{dt}\left( \int_t^\infty U(C(s)) \cdot e^{-\rho(s-t)} ds \right) = \frac{1}{U_C} \dot{V}.$$

This is the basic result from Hamilton and Clemens (1999): genuine saving is equal to the dollar-valued instantaneous change in social welfare in an optimal economy with fixed pure rate of time preference.

On any path with constant pure rate of time preference, we have $\dot{V} = \int_t^\infty \dot{U}(C(s)) \cdot e^{-\rho(s-t)} ds$. It therefore follows from expression (A1) that if genuine saving is positive and growing at a rate less than the interest rate over an unbounded interval $(t, \infty)$ in the competitive economy with constant pure rate of time preference, then social welfare is everywhere increasing over this interval.

## NOTES

1. See Dixit, Hammond and Höel (1980) for details on a competitive economy. A key consequence of assuming a competitive economy is that shadow prices should be dynamically efficient, for example, the Hotelling rule for the scarcity rents on exhaustible resources. While Hamilton and Hartwick (2005) actually establish their result in an optimal economy, it holds in a competitive economy as well.
2. This result, and the main theoretical results which follow, are derived in the Appendix to this chapter for a Dasgupta-Heal economy.

3. This result is foreshadowed in Aronsson *et al.* (1997, expression 6.18), who show that net saving measured in utils is equal to the present value of changes in utility for a general (possibly time-varying) pure rate of time preference.
4. Dasgupta and Heal (1979) analyze an economy characterized by fixed technology and a finite exhaustible resource which is essential for production. Production depends only on inputs of produced capital and resources extracted, and results in a composite good which can be invested or consumed. Some results based on this model rely on production being Cobb-Douglas with constant returns to scale.
5. Asheim and Buchholz (2004) derive a similar result for a constant gross saving rate rule.
6. Based on Aronsson and Löfgren (1995, 1996), it is possible to show that if a non-optimal economy has an externality which is not internalized, then genuine saving has to be augmented by a term reflecting the present value of the future welfare impacts of this externality in order to preserve the equality between genuine saving and changes in social welfare. This is akin to the treatment of exogenous technological or price change in optimal economies. Aronsson and Löfgren (1999) examine an 'approximately Pigouvian' internalization of this externality using current willingness to pay data.
7. The seminal piece on the theory of national accounting is Weitzman (1976).
8. Also with constant pure rates of time preference.
9. Fragile states are characterized by very weak institutions, while emerging market states consist of middle-income countries ($876–$10,725 GNI per capita) plus India.
10. Weitzman (1976) assumes a constant consumption rate of interest in a competitive dynamic economy. Aronsson *et al.* (1997 Ch. 3) show that there is a corresponding expression in utility units when there is a constant pure rate of time preference.
11. Since it is undesirable to have a term involving future values of key variables as the basis of the empirical test of genuine saving in Ferreira *et al.* (2008), the authors' most stringent test shifts the term in $\dot{\gamma} \cdot w$ to the left-hand side of expression (12). Strictly speaking, it is therefore a test of whether $g$ is correlated with the change in social welfare plus the present value of the wealth-diluting effects of time-varying population growth rates. The econometric results are not materially different from the case where population growth rates are constant ($\dot{\gamma} = 0$).
12. For a discussion of alternative indicators of sustainable development, see OECD (2000).
13. See World Bank (2006), Appendix 1 for the specifics of constructing the accounts.

# REFERENCES

Ahmad, Y., S. El Serafy and E. Lutz, eds, 1989. *Environmental Accounting for Sustainable Development*, Washington DC: The World Bank.

Aronsson, T., P.-O. Johansson and K.-G. Löfgren, 1997. *Welfare Measurement, Sustainabiliy and Green National Accounting: A growth theoretical approach.* Cheltenham: Edward Elgar.

Aronsson, T. and K.-G. Löfgren, 1995. National Product Related Welfare Measures in the Presence of Technological Change: Externalities and Uncertainty. *Environmental and Resource Economics* 5: 321–332.

Aronsson, T. and K.-G. Löfgren, 1996. Social Accounting and Welfare Measurement in a Growth Model with Human Capital. *Scandinavian Journal of Economics* 98(2): 185–201.

Aronsson, T. and K.-G. Löfgren, 1999. Pollution Tax Design and 'Green' National Accounting. *European Economic Review* 43: 1457–1474.

Asheim, G. and W. Buchholz, 2004. A General Approach to Welfare Measurement Through National Income Accounting. *Scandinavian Journal of Economics* 106, 361–384.

Asheim, G.B., and M.L. Weitzman, 2001. Does NNP Growth Indicate Welfare Improvement? *Economics Letters* 73:2: 233–239.

Atkinson, G. and K. Hamilton, 2007. Progress Along the Path: Evolving issues in the measurement of sustainable development. *Environment and Resource Economics* 37: 43–61.
Dasgupta, P. and G. Heal, 1979. *Economic Theory and Exhaustible Resources*, Cambridge: Cambridge University Press.
Dasgupta, P. and K.-G. Mäler, 2000. Net National Product, Wealth, and Social Well-Being. *Environment and Development Economics* 5(1–2): 69–93.
Dixit, A., Hammond, P. and Hoel, M., 1980, On Hartwick's Rule for Regular Maximin Paths of Capital Accumulation and Resource Depletion. *Review of Economic Studies* XLVII, 551–556.
Ferreira, S., K. Hamilton and J. Vincent, 2008. Comprehensive Wealth and Future Consumption: Accounting for population growth. *World Bank Economic Review* 22(2): 233–248.
Ferreira, S., and J. Vincent. 2005. Genuine Savings: Leading Indicator of Sustainable Development? *Economic Development and Cultural Change* 53:3, 737–754.
Fisher, I., 1906. *The Nature of Capital and Income*, New York: Macmillan.
Hamilton, K., 1995. Sustainable Development, the Hartwick Rule and Optimal Growth. *Environmental and Resource Economics* 5(4): 393–411.
Hamilton, K., 1997. Defining Income and Assessing Sustainability. Environment Department, The World Bank (mimeo).
Hamilton, K. and G. Atkinson, 2006. *Wealth, Welfare and Sustainability: Advances in measuring sustainable development.* Cheltenham: Edward Elgar.
Hamilton, K. and M. Clemens, 1999. Genuine Savings Rates in Developing Countries. *The World Bank Economic Review*, 13(2): 333–356.
Hamilton, K. and J.M. Hartwick, 2005. Investing Exhaustible Resource Rents and the Path of Consumption. *Canadian Journal of Economics* 38(2): 615–621.
Hamilton, K., G. Ruta and L. Tajibaeva, 2006. Capital Accumulation and Resource Depletion: A Hartwick Rule Counterfactual. *Environmental and Resource Economics* 34: 517–533.
Hamilton, K. and C. Withagen, 2007. Savings Growth and the Path of Utility. *Canadian Journal of Economics* 40(2): 703–713.
Hartwick, J.M., 1977. Intergenerational Equity and the Investing of Rents from Exhaustible Resources. *American Economic Review* 67(5): 972–974.
Hartwick, J.M., 1990. Natural Resources, National Accounting and Economic Depreciation. *Journal of Public Economics* 43: 291–304.
Mäler, K.-G., 1991. National Accounts and Environmental Resources. *Environmental and Resource Economics* 1: 1–15.
OECD, 2000. *Frameworks to Measure Sustainable Development.* Paris: OECD.
Pearce, D.W. and G. Atkinson, 1993. Capital Theory and the Measurement of Sustainable Development: An indicator of weak sustainability. *Ecological Economics* 8: 103–108.
Pezzey, J. 1989. *Economic Analysis of Sustainable Growth and Sustainable Development*, Environment Department Working Paper No. 15. Washington, DC: The World Bank.
Pezzey, J., 2004. One-sided Sustainability Tests with Amenities, and Changes in Technology, Trade and Population. *Journal of Environmental Economics and Management* 48(1): 613–631.
Repetto, R., W. Magrath, M. Wells, C. Beer and F. Rossini, 1989. *Wasting Assets: Natural resources in the national accounts.* Washington, DC: World Resources Institute.
Samuelson, P., 1961. The Evaluation of 'Social Income'. Capital formation and wealth, in F. A. Lutz and D. C. Hague (eds), *The Theory of Capital*, New York: St. Martin's Press.
Solow, R.M., 1974. Intergenerational Equity and Exhaustible Resources. *Review of Economic Studies* 41, Symposium on the Economics of Exhaustible Resources, pp. 29–45.
Weitzman, M., 1976. On the Welfare Significance of National Product in a Dynamic Economy. *Quarterly Journal of Economics* 90(1): 156–162
World Bank, 2006. *Where is the Wealth of Nations? Measuring capital for the 21st century.* Washington, DC: The World Bank.
World Bank, 2007. *World Development Indicators.* Washington, DC: The World Bank.

# Index